PostgreSQL 9.4 Vol1: The SQL Language

A catalogue record for this book is available from the Hong Kong Public Libraries.

Published in Hong Kong by Samurai Media Limited.

Email: info@samuraimedia.org

ISBN 978-988-8381-31-9

Table of Contents

Preface

This book is the official documentation of PostgreSQL. It has been written by the PostgreSQL developers and other volunteers in parallel to the development of the PostgreSQL software. It describes all the functionality that the current version of PostgreSQL officially supports.

To make the large amount of information about PostgreSQL manageable, this book has been organized in several parts. Each part is targeted at a different class of users, or at users in different stages of their PostgreSQL experience:

- Part I is an informal introduction for new users.

- Part II documents the SQL query language environment, including data types and functions, as well as user-level performance tuning. Every PostgreSQL user should read this.

- Part III describes the installation and administration of the server. Everyone who runs a PostgreSQL server, be it for private use or for others, should read this part.

- Part IV describes the programming interfaces for PostgreSQL client programs.

- Part V contains information for advanced users about the extensibility capabilities of the server. Topics include user-defined data types and functions.

- Part VI contains reference information about SQL commands, client and server programs. This part supports the other parts with structured information sorted by command or program.

- Part VII contains assorted information that might be of use to PostgreSQL developers.

1. What is PostgreSQL?

PostgreSQL is an object-relational database management system (ORDBMS) based on POSTGRES, Version 4.2[1], developed at the University of California at Berkeley Computer Science Department. POSTGRES pioneered many concepts that only became available in some commercial database systems much later.

PostgreSQL is an open-source descendant of this original Berkeley code. It supports a large part of the SQL standard and offers many modern features:

- complex queries
- foreign keys
- triggers
- updatable views
- transactional integrity
- multiversion concurrency control

Also, PostgreSQL can be extended by the user in many ways, for example by adding new

- data types

---

1.   http://db.cs.berkeley.edu/postgres.html

- functions
- operators
- aggregate functions
- index methods
- procedural languages

And because of the liberal license, PostgreSQL can be used, modified, and distributed by anyone free of charge for any purpose, be it private, commercial, or academic.

2. A Brief History of PostgreSQL

The object-relational database management system now known as PostgreSQL is derived from the POSTGRES package written at the University of California at Berkeley. With over two decades of development behind it, PostgreSQL is now the most advanced open-source database available anywhere.

2.1. The Berkeley POSTGRES Project

The POSTGRES project, led by Professor Michael Stonebraker, was sponsored by the Defense Advanced Research Projects Agency (DARPA), the Army Research Office (ARO), the National Science Foundation (NSF), and ESL, Inc. The implementation of POSTGRES began in 1986. The initial concepts for the system were presented in *The design of POSTGRES* , and the definition of the initial data model appeared in *The POSTGRES data model* . The design of the rule system at that time was described in *The design of the POSTGRES rules system*. The rationale and architecture of the storage manager were detailed in *The design of the POSTGRES storage system* .

POSTGRES has undergone several major releases since then. The first "demoware" system became operational in 1987 and was shown at the 1988 ACM-SIGMOD Conference. Version 1, described in *The implementation of POSTGRES* , was released to a few external users in June 1989. In response to a critique of the first rule system (*A commentary on the POSTGRES rules system*), the rule system was redesigned (*On Rules, Procedures, Caching and Views in Database Systems*), and Version 2 was released in June 1990 with the new rule system. Version 3 appeared in 1991 and added support for multiple storage managers, an improved query executor, and a rewritten rule system. For the most part, subsequent releases until Postgres95 (see below) focused on portability and reliability.

POSTGRES has been used to implement many different research and production applications. These include: a financial data analysis system, a jet engine performance monitoring package, an asteroid tracking database, a medical information database, and several geographic information systems. POSTGRES has also been used as an educational tool at several universities. Finally, Illustra Information Technologies (later merged into Informix[2], which is now owned by IBM[3]) picked up the code and commercialized it. In late 1992, POSTGRES became the primary data manager for the Sequoia 2000 scientific computing project[4].

The size of the external user community nearly doubled during 1993. It became increasingly obvious that maintenance of the prototype code and support was taking up large amounts of time that should have been

---

2. http://www.informix.com/
3. http://www.ibm.com/
4. http://meteora.ucsd.edu/s2k/s2k_home.html

devoted to database research. In an effort to reduce this support burden, the Berkeley POSTGRES project officially ended with Version 4.2.

2.2. Postgres95

In 1994, Andrew Yu and Jolly Chen added an SQL language interpreter to POSTGRES. Under a new name, Postgres95 was subsequently released to the web to find its own way in the world as an open-source descendant of the original POSTGRES Berkeley code.

Postgres95 code was completely ANSI C and trimmed in size by 25%. Many internal changes improved performance and maintainability. Postgres95 release 1.0.x ran about 30-50% faster on the Wisconsin Benchmark compared to POSTGRES, Version 4.2. Apart from bug fixes, the following were the major enhancements:

- The query language PostQUEL was replaced with SQL (implemented in the server). (Interface library libpq was named after PostQUEL.) Subqueries were not supported until PostgreSQL (see below), but they could be imitated in Postgres95 with user-defined SQL functions. Aggregate functions were re-implemented. Support for the GROUP BY query clause was also added.

- A new program (psql) was provided for interactive SQL queries, which used GNU Readline. This largely superseded the old monitor program.

- A new front-end library, libpgtcl, supported Tcl-based clients. A sample shell, pgtclsh, provided new Tcl commands to interface Tcl programs with the Postgres95 server.

- The large-object interface was overhauled. The inversion large objects were the only mechanism for storing large objects. (The inversion file system was removed.)

- The instance-level rule system was removed. Rules were still available as rewrite rules.

- A short tutorial introducing regular SQL features as well as those of Postgres95 was distributed with the source code

- GNU make (instead of BSD make) was used for the build. Also, Postgres95 could be compiled with an unpatched GCC (data alignment of doubles was fixed).

2.3. PostgreSQL

By 1996, it became clear that the name "Postgres95" would not stand the test of time. We chose a new name, PostgreSQL, to reflect the relationship between the original POSTGRES and the more recent versions with SQL capability. At the same time, we set the version numbering to start at 6.0, putting the numbers back into the sequence originally begun by the Berkeley POSTGRES project.

Many people continue to refer to PostgreSQL as "Postgres" (now rarely in all capital letters) because of tradition or because it is easier to pronounce. This usage is widely accepted as a nickname or alias.

The emphasis during development of Postgres95 was on identifying and understanding existing problems in the server code. With PostgreSQL, the emphasis has shifted to augmenting features and capabilities, although work continues in all areas.

Details about what has happened in PostgreSQL since then can be found in Appendix E.

3. Conventions

The following conventions are used in the synopsis of a command: brackets ([and]) indicate optional parts. (In the synopsis of a Tcl command, question marks (?) are used instead, as is usual in Tcl.) Braces ({ and }) and vertical lines (|) indicate that you must choose one alternative. Dots (. . .) mean that the preceding element can be repeated.

Where it enhances the clarity, SQL commands are preceded by the prompt =>, and shell commands are preceded by the prompt $. Normally, prompts are not shown, though.

An *administrator* is generally a person who is in charge of installing and running the server. A *user* could be anyone who is using, or wants to use, any part of the PostgreSQL system. These terms should not be interpreted too narrowly; this book does not have fixed presumptions about system administration procedures.

4. Further Information

Besides the documentation, that is, this book, there are other resources about PostgreSQL:

Wiki

The PostgreSQL wiki[5] contains the project's FAQ[6] (Frequently Asked Questions) list, TODO[7] list, and detailed information about many more topics.

Web Site

The PostgreSQL web site[8] carries details on the latest release and other information to make your work or play with PostgreSQL more productive.

Mailing Lists

The mailing lists are a good place to have your questions answered, to share experiences with other users, and to contact the developers. Consult the PostgreSQL web site for details.

Yourself!

PostgreSQL is an open-source project. As such, it depends on the user community for ongoing support. As you begin to use PostgreSQL, you will rely on others for help, either through the documentation or through the mailing lists. Consider contributing your knowledge back. Read the mailing lists and answer questions. If you learn something which is not in the documentation, write it up and contribute it. If you add features to the code, contribute them.

---

5. http://wiki.postgresql.org
6. http://wiki.postgresql.org/wiki/Frequently_Asked_Questions
7. http://wiki.postgresql.org/wiki/Todo
8. http://www.postgresql.org

5. Bug Reporting Guidelines

When you find a bug in PostgreSQL we want to hear about it. Your bug reports play an important part in making PostgreSQL more reliable because even the utmost care cannot guarantee that every part of PostgreSQL will work on every platform under every circumstance.

The following suggestions are intended to assist you in forming bug reports that can be handled in an effective fashion. No one is required to follow them but doing so tends to be to everyone's advantage.

We cannot promise to fix every bug right away. If the bug is obvious, critical, or affects a lot of users, chances are good that someone will look into it. It could also happen that we tell you to update to a newer version to see if the bug happens there. Or we might decide that the bug cannot be fixed before some major rewrite we might be planning is done. Or perhaps it is simply too hard and there are more important things on the agenda. If you need help immediately, consider obtaining a commercial support contract.

5.1. Identifying Bugs

Before you report a bug, please read and re-read the documentation to verify that you can really do whatever it is you are trying. If it is not clear from the documentation whether you can do something or not, please report that too; it is a bug in the documentation. If it turns out that a program does something different from what the documentation says, that is a bug. That might include, but is not limited to, the following circumstances:

- A program terminates with a fatal signal or an operating system error message that would point to a problem in the program. (A counterexample might be a "disk full" message, since you have to fix that yourself.)

- A program produces the wrong output for any given input.

- A program refuses to accept valid input (as defined in the documentation).

- A program accepts invalid input without a notice or error message. But keep in mind that your idea of invalid input might be our idea of an extension or compatibility with traditional practice.

- PostgreSQL fails to compile, build, or install according to the instructions on supported platforms.

Here "program" refers to any executable, not only the backend process.

Being slow or resource-hogging is not necessarily a bug. Read the documentation or ask on one of the mailing lists for help in tuning your applications. Failing to comply to the SQL standard is not necessarily a bug either, unless compliance for the specific feature is explicitly claimed.

Before you continue, check on the TODO list and in the FAQ to see if your bug is already known. If you cannot decode the information on the TODO list, report your problem. The least we can do is make the TODO list clearer.

5.2. What to Report

The most important thing to remember about bug reporting is to state all the facts and only facts. Do not speculate what you think went wrong, what "it seemed to do", or which part of the program has a fault. If you are not familiar with the implementation you would probably guess wrong and not help us a bit.

And even if you are, educated explanations are a great supplement to but no substitute for facts. If we are going to fix the bug we still have to see it happen for ourselves first. Reporting the bare facts is relatively straightforward (you can probably copy and paste them from the screen) but all too often important details are left out because someone thought it does not matter or the report would be understood anyway.

The following items should be contained in every bug report:

- The exact sequence of steps *from program start-up* necessary to reproduce the problem. This should be self-contained; it is not enough to send in a bare SELECT statement without the preceding CREATE TABLE and INSERT statements, if the output should depend on the data in the tables. We do not have the time to reverse-engineer your database schema, and if we are supposed to make up our own data we would probably miss the problem.

  The best format for a test case for SQL-related problems is a file that can be run through the psql frontend that shows the problem. (Be sure to not have anything in your ~/.psqlrc start-up file.) An easy way to create this file is to use pg_dump to dump out the table declarations and data needed to set the scene, then add the problem query. You are encouraged to minimize the size of your example, but this is not absolutely necessary. If the bug is reproducible, we will find it either way.

  If your application uses some other client interface, such as PHP, then please try to isolate the offending queries. We will probably not set up a web server to reproduce your problem. In any case remember to provide the exact input files; do not guess that the problem happens for "large files" or "midsize databases", etc. since this information is too inexact to be of use.

- The output you got. Please do not say that it "didn't work" or "crashed". If there is an error message, show it, even if you do not understand it. If the program terminates with an operating system error, say which. If nothing at all happens, say so. Even if the result of your test case is a program crash or otherwise obvious it might not happen on our platform. The easiest thing is to copy the output from the terminal, if possible.

  Note: If you are reporting an error message, please obtain the most verbose form of the message. In psql, say \set VERBOSITY verbose beforehand. If you are extracting the message from the server log, set the run-time parameter log_error_verbosity to verbose so that all details are logged.

  Note: In case of fatal errors, the error message reported by the client might not contain all the information available. Please also look at the log output of the database server. If you do not keep your server's log output, this would be a good time to start doing so.

- The output you expected is very important to state. If you just write "This command gives me that output." or "This is not what I expected.", we might run it ourselves, scan the output, and think it looks OK and is exactly what we expected. We should not have to spend the time to decode the exact semantics behind your commands. Especially refrain from merely saying that "This is not what SQL says/Oracle does." Digging out the correct behavior from SQL is not a fun undertaking, nor do we all know how all the other relational databases out there behave. (If your problem is a program crash, you can obviously omit this item.)

- Any command line options and other start-up options, including any relevant environment variables or configuration files that you changed from the default. Again, please provide exact information. If you are using a prepackaged distribution that starts the database server at boot time, you should try to find out how that is done.

- Anything you did at all differently from the installation instructions.

- The PostgreSQL version. You can run the command SELECT version(); to find out the version of the server you are connected to. Most executable programs also support a --version option; at least postgres --version and psql --version should work. If the function or the options do not exist then your version is more than old enough to warrant an upgrade. If you run a prepackaged version, such as RPMs, say so, including any subversion the package might have. If you are talking about a Git snapshot, mention that, including the commit hash.

  If your version is older than 9.4.4 we will almost certainly tell you to upgrade. There are many bug fixes and improvements in each new release, so it is quite possible that a bug you have encountered in an older release of PostgreSQL has already been fixed. We can only provide limited support for sites using older releases of PostgreSQL; if you require more than we can provide, consider acquiring a commercial support contract.

- Platform information. This includes the kernel name and version, C library, processor, memory information, and so on. In most cases it is sufficient to report the vendor and version, but do not assume everyone knows what exactly "Debian" contains or that everyone runs on i386s. If you have installation problems then information about the toolchain on your machine (compiler, make, and so on) is also necessary.

Do not be afraid if your bug report becomes rather lengthy. That is a fact of life. It is better to report everything the first time than us having to squeeze the facts out of you. On the other hand, if your input files are huge, it is fair to ask first whether somebody is interested in looking into it. Here is an article[9] that outlines some more tips on reporting bugs.

Do not spend all your time to figure out which changes in the input make the problem go away. This will probably not help solving it. If it turns out that the bug cannot be fixed right away, you will still have time to find and share your work-around. Also, once again, do not waste your time guessing why the bug exists. We will find that out soon enough.

When writing a bug report, please avoid confusing terminology. The software package in total is called "PostgreSQL", sometimes "Postgres" for short. If you are specifically talking about the backend process, mention that, do not just say "PostgreSQL crashes". A crash of a single backend process is quite different from crash of the parent "postgres" process; please don't say "the server crashed" when you mean a single backend process went down, nor vice versa. Also, client programs such as the interactive frontend "psql" are completely separate from the backend. Please try to be specific about whether the problem is on the client or server side.

5.3. Where to Report Bugs

In general, send bug reports to the bug report mailing list at <pgsql-bugs@postgresql.org>. You are requested to use a descriptive subject for your email message, perhaps parts of the error message.

---

9.   http://www.chiark.greenend.org.uk/~sgtatham/bugs.html

Another method is to fill in the bug report web-form available at the project's web site[10]. Entering a bug report this way causes it to be mailed to the <pgsql-bugs@postgresql.org> mailing list.

If your bug report has security implications and you'd prefer that it not become immediately visible in public archives, don't send it to pgsql-bugs. Security issues can be reported privately to <security@postgresql.org>.

Do not send bug reports to any of the user mailing lists, such as <pgsql-sql@postgresql.org> or <pgsql-general@postgresql.org>. These mailing lists are for answering user questions, and their subscribers normally do not wish to receive bug reports. More importantly, they are unlikely to fix them.

Also, please do *not* send reports to the developers' mailing list <pgsql-hackers@postgresql.org>. This list is for discussing the development of PostgreSQL, and it would be nice if we could keep the bug reports separate. We might choose to take up a discussion about your bug report on pgsql-hackers, if the problem needs more review.

If you have a problem with the documentation, the best place to report it is the documentation mailing list <pgsql-docs@postgresql.org>. Please be specific about what part of the documentation you are unhappy with.

If your bug is a portability problem on a non-supported platform, send mail to <pgsql-hackers@postgresql.org>, so we (and you) can work on porting PostgreSQL to your platform.

> **Note:** Due to the unfortunate amount of spam going around, all of the above email addresses are closed mailing lists. That is, you need to be subscribed to a list to be allowed to post on it. (You need not be subscribed to use the bug-report web form, however.) If you would like to send mail but do not want to receive list traffic, you can subscribe and set your subscription option to nomail. For more information send mail to <majordomo@postgresql.org> with the single word help in the body of the message.

---

10. http://www.postgresql.org/

I. Tutorial

Welcome to the PostgreSQL Tutorial. The following few chapters are intended to give a simple introduction to PostgreSQL, relational database concepts, and the SQL language to those who are new to any one of these aspects. We only assume some general knowledge about how to use computers. No particular Unix or programming experience is required. This part is mainly intended to give you some hands-on experience with important aspects of the PostgreSQL system. It makes no attempt to be a complete or thorough treatment of the topics it covers.

After you have worked through this tutorial you might want to move on to reading Part II to gain a more formal knowledge of the SQL language, or Part IV for information about developing applications for PostgreSQL. Those who set up and manage their own server should also read Part III.

Chapter 1. Getting Started

1.1. Installation

Before you can use PostgreSQL you need to install it, of course. It is possible that PostgreSQL is already installed at your site, either because it was included in your operating system distribution or because the system administrator already installed it. If that is the case, you should obtain information from the operating system documentation or your system administrator about how to access PostgreSQL.

If you are not sure whether PostgreSQL is already available or whether you can use it for your experimentation then you can install it yourself. Doing so is not hard and it can be a good exercise. PostgreSQL can be installed by any unprivileged user; no superuser (root) access is required.

If you are installing PostgreSQL yourself, then refer to Chapter 15 for instructions on installation, and return to this guide when the installation is complete. Be sure to follow closely the section about setting up the appropriate environment variables.

If your site administrator has not set things up in the default way, you might have some more work to do. For example, if the database server machine is a remote machine, you will need to set the PGHOST environment variable to the name of the database server machine. The environment variable PGPORT might also have to be set. The bottom line is this: if you try to start an application program and it complains that it cannot connect to the database, you should consult your site administrator or, if that is you, the documentation to make sure that your environment is properly set up. If you did not understand the preceding paragraph then read the next section.

1.2. Architectural Fundamentals

Before we proceed, you should understand the basic PostgreSQL system architecture. Understanding how the parts of PostgreSQL interact will make this chapter somewhat clearer.

In database jargon, PostgreSQL uses a client/server model. A PostgreSQL session consists of the following cooperating processes (programs):

- A server process, which manages the database files, accepts connections to the database from client applications, and performs database actions on behalf of the clients. The database server program is called `postgres`.

- The user's client (frontend) application that wants to perform database operations. Client applications can be very diverse in nature: a client could be a text-oriented tool, a graphical application, a web server that accesses the database to display web pages, or a specialized database maintenance tool. Some client applications are supplied with the PostgreSQL distribution; most are developed by users.

As is typical of client/server applications, the client and the server can be on different hosts. In that case they communicate over a TCP/IP network connection. You should keep this in mind, because the files that can be accessed on a client machine might not be accessible (or might only be accessible using a different file name) on the database server machine.

The PostgreSQL server can handle multiple concurrent connections from clients. To achieve this it starts ("forks") a new process for each connection. From that point on, the client and the new server process communicate without intervention by the original `postgres` process. Thus, the master server process is always running, waiting for client connections, whereas client and associated server processes come and go. (All of this is of course invisible to the user. We only mention it here for completeness.)

1.3. Creating a Database

The first test to see whether you can access the database server is to try to create a database. A running PostgreSQL server can manage many databases. Typically, a separate database is used for each project or for each user.

Possibly, your site administrator has already created a database for your use. He should have told you what the name of your database is. In that case you can omit this step and skip ahead to the next section.

To create a new database, in this example named `mydb`, you use the following command:

```
$ createdb mydb
```

If this produces no response then this step was successful and you can skip over the remainder of this section.

If you see a message similar to:

```
createdb: command not found
```

then PostgreSQL was not installed properly. Either it was not installed at all or your shell's search path was not set to include it. Try calling the command with an absolute path instead:

```
$ /usr/local/pgsql/bin/createdb mydb
```

The path at your site might be different. Contact your site administrator or check the installation instructions to correct the situation.

Another response could be this:

```
createdb: could not connect to database postgres: could not connect to server:
        Is the server running locally and accepting
        connections on Unix domain socket "/tmp/.s.PGSQL.5432"?
```

This means that the server was not started, or it was not started where `createdb` expected it. Again, check the installation instructions or consult the administrator.

Another response could be this:

```
createdb: could not connect to database postgres: FATAL:  role "joe" does not e
```

where your own login name is mentioned. This will happen if the administrator has not created a PostgreSQL user account for you. (PostgreSQL user accounts are distinct from operating system user accounts.) If you are the administrator, see Chapter 20 for help creating accounts. You will need to become the operating system user under which PostgreSQL was installed (usually `postgres`) to create the first user account. It could also be that you were assigned a PostgreSQL user name that is different from your operating system user name; in that case you need to use the -U switch or set the PGUSER environment variable to specify your PostgreSQL user name.

If you have a user account but it does not have the privileges required to create a database, you will see the following:

```
createdb: database creation failed: ERROR:  permission denied to create databas
```

Not every user has authorization to create new databases. If PostgreSQL refuses to create databases for you then the site administrator needs to grant you permission to create databases. Consult your site administrator if this occurs. If you installed PostgreSQL yourself then you should log in for the purposes of this tutorial under the user account that you started the server as. [1]

You can also create databases with other names. PostgreSQL allows you to create any number of databases at a given site. Database names must have an alphabetic first character and are limited to 63 bytes in length. A convenient choice is to create a database with the same name as your current user name. Many tools assume that database name as the default, so it can save you some typing. To create that database, simply type:

```
$ createdb
```

If you do not want to use your database anymore you can remove it. For example, if you are the owner (creator) of the database mydb, you can destroy it using the following command:

```
$ dropdb mydb
```

(For this command, the database name does not default to the user account name. You always need to specify it.) This action physically removes all files associated with the database and cannot be undone, so this should only be done with a great deal of forethought.

More about createdb and dropdb can be found in createdb and dropdb respectively.

1.4. Accessing a Database

Once you have created a database, you can access it by:

- Running the PostgreSQL interactive terminal program, called *psql*, which allows you to interactively enter, edit, and execute SQL commands.
- Using an existing graphical frontend tool like pgAdmin or an office suite with ODBC or JDBC support to create and manipulate a database. These possibilities are not covered in this tutorial.
- Writing a custom application, using one of the several available language bindings. These possibilities are discussed further in Part IV.

1.　As an explanation for why this works: PostgreSQL user names are separate from operating system user accounts. When you connect to a database, you can choose what PostgreSQL user name to connect as; if you don't, it will default to the same name as your current operating system account. As it happens, there will always be a PostgreSQL user account that has the same name as the operating system user that started the server, and it also happens that that user always has permission to create databases. Instead of logging in as that user you can also specify the -U option everywhere to select a PostgreSQL user name to connect as.

You probably want to start up psql to try the examples in this tutorial. It can be activated for the mydb database by typing the command:

```
$ psql mydb
```

If you do not supply the database name then it will default to your user account name. You already discovered this scheme in the previous section using createdb.

In psql, you will be greeted with the following message:

```
psql (9.4.4)
Type "help" for help.

mydb=>
```

The last line could also be:

```
mydb=#
```

That would mean you are a database superuser, which is most likely the case if you installed PostgreSQL yourself. Being a superuser means that you are not subject to access controls. For the purposes of this tutorial that is not important.

If you encounter problems starting psql then go back to the previous section. The diagnostics of createdb and psql are similar, and if the former worked the latter should work as well.

The last line printed out by psql is the prompt, and it indicates that psql is listening to you and that you can type SQL queries into a work space maintained by psql. Try out these commands:

```
mydb=> SELECT version();
                             version
--------------------------------------------------------------------
 PostgreSQL 9.4.4 on i586-pc-linux-gnu, compiled by GCC 2.96, 32-bit
(1 row)

mydb=> SELECT current_date;
    date
------------
 2002-08-31
(1 row)

mydb=> SELECT 2 + 2;
 ?column?
----------
        4
(1 row)
```

The psql program has a number of internal commands that are not SQL commands. They begin with the backslash character, "\". For example, you can get help on the syntax of various PostgreSQL SQL commands by typing:

```
mydb=> \h
```

To get out of `psql`, type:

```
mydb=> \q
```

and `psql` will quit and return you to your command shell. (For more internal commands, type `\?` at the `psql` prompt.) The full capabilities of `psql` are documented in psql. In this tutorial we will not use these features explicitly, but you can use them yourself when it is helpful.

Chapter 2. The SQL Language

2.1. Introduction

This chapter provides an overview of how to use SQL to perform simple operations. This tutorial is only intended to give you an introduction and is in no way a complete tutorial on SQL. Numerous books have been written on SQL, including *Understanding the New SQL* and *A Guide to the SQL Standard*. You should be aware that some PostgreSQL language features are extensions to the standard.

In the examples that follow, we assume that you have created a database named mydb, as described in the previous chapter, and have been able to start psql.

Examples in this manual can also be found in the PostgreSQL source distribution in the directory src/tutorial/. (Binary distributions of PostgreSQL might not compile these files.) To use those files, first change to that directory and run make:

```
$ cd ..../src/tutorial
$ make
```

This creates the scripts and compiles the C files containing user-defined functions and types. Then, to start the tutorial, do the following:

```
$ cd ..../tutorial
$ psql -s mydb
...

mydb=> \i basics.sql
```

The \i command reads in commands from the specified file. psql's -s option puts you in single step mode which pauses before sending each statement to the server. The commands used in this section are in the file basics.sql.

2.2. Concepts

PostgreSQL is a *relational database management system* (RDBMS). That means it is a system for managing data stored in *relations*. Relation is essentially a mathematical term for *table*. The notion of storing data in tables is so commonplace today that it might seem inherently obvious, but there are a number of other ways of organizing databases. Files and directories on Unix-like operating systems form an example of a hierarchical database. A more modern development is the object-oriented database.

Each table is a named collection of *rows*. Each row of a given table has the same set of named *columns*, and each column is of a specific data type. Whereas columns have a fixed order in each row, it is important to remember that SQL does not guarantee the order of the rows within the table in any way (although they can be explicitly sorted for display).

Tables are grouped into databases, and a collection of databases managed by a single PostgreSQL server instance constitutes a database *cluster*.

2.3. Creating a New Table

You can create a new table by specifying the table name, along with all column names and their types:

```
CREATE TABLE weather (
    city            varchar(80),
    temp_lo         int,        -- low temperature
    temp_hi         int,        -- high temperature
    prcp            real,       -- precipitation
    date            date
);
```

You can enter this into `psql` with the line breaks. `psql` will recognize that the command is not terminated until the semicolon.

White space (i.e., spaces, tabs, and newlines) can be used freely in SQL commands. That means you can type the command aligned differently than above, or even all on one line. Two dashes ("--") introduce comments. Whatever follows them is ignored up to the end of the line. SQL is case insensitive about key words and identifiers, except when identifiers are double-quoted to preserve the case (not done above).

`varchar(80)` specifies a data type that can store arbitrary character strings up to 80 characters in length. `int` is the normal integer type. `real` is a type for storing single precision floating-point numbers. `date` should be self-explanatory. (Yes, the column of type `date` is also named `date`. This might be convenient or confusing — you choose.)

PostgreSQL supports the standard SQL types `int`, `smallint`, `real`, `double precision`, `char(N)`, `varchar(N)`, `date`, `time`, `timestamp`, and `interval`, as well as other types of general utility and a rich set of geometric types. PostgreSQL can be customized with an arbitrary number of user-defined data types. Consequently, type names are not key words in the syntax, except where required to support special cases in the SQL standard.

The second example will store cities and their associated geographical location:

```
CREATE TABLE cities (
    name            varchar(80),
    location        point
);
```

The `point` type is an example of a PostgreSQL-specific data type.

Finally, it should be mentioned that if you don't need a table any longer or want to recreate it differently you can remove it using the following command:

```
DROP TABLE tablename;
```

2.4. Populating a Table With Rows

The `INSERT` statement is used to populate a table with rows:

```
INSERT INTO weather VALUES ('San Francisco', 46, 50, 0.25, '1994-11-27');
```

Note that all data types use rather obvious input formats. Constants that are not simple numeric values usually must be surrounded by single quotes ('), as in the example. The date type is actually quite flexible in what it accepts, but for this tutorial we will stick to the unambiguous format shown here.

The point type requires a coordinate pair as input, as shown here:

```
INSERT INTO cities VALUES ('San Francisco', '(-194.0, 53.0)');
```

The syntax used so far requires you to remember the order of the columns. An alternative syntax allows you to list the columns explicitly:

```
INSERT INTO weather (city, temp_lo, temp_hi, prcp, date)
    VALUES ('San Francisco', 43, 57, 0.0, '1994-11-29');
```

You can list the columns in a different order if you wish or even omit some columns, e.g., if the precipitation is unknown:

```
INSERT INTO weather (date, city, temp_hi, temp_lo)
    VALUES ('1994-11-29', 'Hayward', 54, 37);
```

Many developers consider explicitly listing the columns better style than relying on the order implicitly.

Please enter all the commands shown above so you have some data to work with in the following sections.

You could also have used COPY to load large amounts of data from flat-text files. This is usually faster because the COPY command is optimized for this application while allowing less flexibility than INSERT. An example would be:

```
COPY weather FROM '/home/user/weather.txt';
```

where the file name for the source file must be available on the machine running the backend process, not the client, since the backend process reads the file directly. You can read more about the COPY command in COPY.

2.5. Querying a Table

To retrieve data from a table, the table is *queried*. An SQL SELECT statement is used to do this. The statement is divided into a select list (the part that lists the columns to be returned), a table list (the part that lists the tables from which to retrieve the data), and an optional qualification (the part that specifies any restrictions). For example, to retrieve all the rows of table weather, type:

```
SELECT * FROM weather;
```

Here * is a shorthand for "all columns". [1] So the same result would be had with:

```
SELECT city, temp_lo, temp_hi, prcp, date FROM weather;
```

The output should be:

---

1. While SELECT * is useful for off-the-cuff queries, it is widely considered bad style in production code, since adding a column to the table would change the results.

```
    city       | temp_lo | temp_hi | prcp |    date
---------------+---------+---------+------+------------
 San Francisco |      46 |      50 | 0.25 | 1994-11-27
 San Francisco |      43 |      57 |    0 | 1994-11-29
 Hayward       |      37 |      54 |      | 1994-11-29
(3 rows)
```

You can write expressions, not just simple column references, in the select list. For example, you can do:

```
SELECT city, (temp_hi+temp_lo)/2 AS temp_avg, date FROM weather;
```

This should give:

```
    city       | temp_avg |    date
---------------+----------+------------
 San Francisco |       48 | 1994-11-27
 San Francisco |       50 | 1994-11-29
 Hayward       |       45 | 1994-11-29
(3 rows)
```

Notice how the AS clause is used to relabel the output column. (The AS clause is optional.)

A query can be "qualified" by adding a WHERE clause that specifies which rows are wanted. The WHERE clause contains a Boolean (truth value) expression, and only rows for which the Boolean expression is true are returned. The usual Boolean operators (AND, OR, and NOT) are allowed in the qualification. For example, the following retrieves the weather of San Francisco on rainy days:

```
SELECT * FROM weather
    WHERE city = 'San Francisco' AND prcp > 0.0;
```

Result:

```
    city       | temp_lo | temp_hi | prcp |    date
---------------+---------+---------+------+------------
 San Francisco |      46 |      50 | 0.25 | 1994-11-27
(1 row)
```

You can request that the results of a query be returned in sorted order:

```
SELECT * FROM weather
    ORDER BY city;
```

```
    city       | temp_lo | temp_hi | prcp |    date
---------------+---------+---------+------+------------
 Hayward       |      37 |      54 |      | 1994-11-29
 San Francisco |      43 |      57 |    0 | 1994-11-29
 San Francisco |      46 |      50 | 0.25 | 1994-11-27
```

In this example, the sort order isn't fully specified, and so you might get the San Francisco rows in either order. But you'd always get the results shown above if you do:

```
SELECT * FROM weather
    ORDER BY city, temp_lo;
```

You can request that duplicate rows be removed from the result of a query:

```
SELECT DISTINCT city
    FROM weather;

     city
---------------
 Hayward
 San Francisco
(2 rows)
```

Here again, the result row ordering might vary. You can ensure consistent results by using DISTINCT and ORDER BY together: [2]

```
SELECT DISTINCT city
    FROM weather
    ORDER BY city;
```

2.6. Joins Between Tables

Thus far, our queries have only accessed one table at a time. Queries can access multiple tables at once, or access the same table in such a way that multiple rows of the table are being processed at the same time. A query that accesses multiple rows of the same or different tables at one time is called a *join* query. As an example, say you wish to list all the weather records together with the location of the associated city. To do that, we need to compare the city column of each row of the weather table with the name column of all rows in the cities table, and select the pairs of rows where these values match.

> **Note:** This is only a conceptual model. The join is usually performed in a more efficient manner than actually comparing each possible pair of rows, but this is invisible to the user.

This would be accomplished by the following query:

```
SELECT *
    FROM weather, cities
    WHERE city = name;

     city      | temp_lo | temp_hi | prcp |    date    |    name       | locati
---------------+---------+---------+------+------------+---------------+-------
 San Francisco |      46 |      50 | 0.25 | 1994-11-27 | San Francisco | (-194,
 San Francisco |      43 |      57 |    0 | 1994-11-29 | San Francisco | (-194,
(2 rows)
```

---

2.   In some database systems, including older versions of PostgreSQL, the implementation of DISTINCT automatically orders the rows and so ORDER BY is unnecessary. But this is not required by the SQL standard, and current PostgreSQL does not guarantee that DISTINCT causes the rows to be ordered.

Observe two things about the result set:

- There is no result row for the city of Hayward. This is because there is no matching entry in the `cities` table for Hayward, so the join ignores the unmatched rows in the `weather` table. We will see shortly how this can be fixed.

- There are two columns containing the city name. This is correct because the lists of columns from the `weather` and `cities` tables are concatenated. In practice this is undesirable, though, so you will probably want to list the output columns explicitly rather than using `*`:

```
SELECT city, temp_lo, temp_hi, prcp, date, location
    FROM weather, cities
    WHERE city = name;
```

Exercise: Attempt to determine the semantics of this query when the WHERE clause is omitted.

Since the columns all had different names, the parser automatically found which table they belong to. If there were duplicate column names in the two tables you'd need to *qualify* the column names to show which one you meant, as in:

```
SELECT weather.city, weather.temp_lo, weather.temp_hi,
       weather.prcp, weather.date, cities.location
    FROM weather, cities
    WHERE cities.name = weather.city;
```

It is widely considered good style to qualify all column names in a join query, so that the query won't fail if a duplicate column name is later added to one of the tables.

Join queries of the kind seen thus far can also be written in this alternative form:

```
SELECT *
    FROM weather INNER JOIN cities ON (weather.city = cities.name);
```

This syntax is not as commonly used as the one above, but we show it here to help you understand the following topics.

Now we will figure out how we can get the Hayward records back in. What we want the query to do is to scan the `weather` table and for each row to find the matching `cities` row(s). If no matching row is found we want some "empty values" to be substituted for the `cities` table's columns. This kind of query is called an *outer join*. (The joins we have seen so far are inner joins.) The command looks like this:

```
SELECT *
    FROM weather LEFT OUTER JOIN cities ON (weather.city = cities.name);
```

city	temp_lo	temp_hi	prcp	date	name	locati
Hayward	37	54		1994-11-29		
San Francisco	46	50	0.25	1994-11-27	San Francisco	(-194,
San Francisco	43	57	0	1994-11-29	San Francisco	(-194,

(3 rows)

This query is called a *left outer join* because the table mentioned on the left of the join operator will have each of its rows in the output at least once, whereas the table on the right will only have those rows output that match some row of the left table. When outputting a left-table row for which there is no right-table match, empty (null) values are substituted for the right-table columns.

Exercise: There are also right outer joins and full outer joins. Try to find out what those do.

We can also join a table against itself. This is called a *self join*. As an example, suppose we wish to find all the weather records that are in the temperature range of other weather records. So we need to compare the temp_lo and temp_hi columns of each weather row to the temp_lo and temp_hi columns of all other weather rows. We can do this with the following query:

```
SELECT W1.city, W1.temp_lo AS low, W1.temp_hi AS high,
    W2.city, W2.temp_lo AS low, W2.temp_hi AS high
    FROM weather W1, weather W2
    WHERE W1.temp_lo < W2.temp_lo
    AND W1.temp_hi > W2.temp_hi;
```

```
     city       | low | high |     city       | low | high
---------------+-----+------+---------------+-----+------
 San Francisco |  43 |   57 | San Francisco |  46 |   50
 Hayward       |  37 |   54 | San Francisco |  46 |   50
(2 rows)
```

Here we have relabeled the weather table as W1 and W2 to be able to distinguish the left and right side of the join. You can also use these kinds of aliases in other queries to save some typing, e.g.:

```
SELECT *
    FROM weather w, cities c
    WHERE w.city = c.name;
```

You will encounter this style of abbreviating quite frequently.

2.7. Aggregate Functions

Like most other relational database products, PostgreSQL supports *aggregate functions*. An aggregate function computes a single result from multiple input rows. For example, there are aggregates to compute the count, sum, avg (average), max (maximum) and min (minimum) over a set of rows.

As an example, we can find the highest low-temperature reading anywhere with:

```
SELECT max(temp_lo) FROM weather;
```

```
 max
-----
  46
(1 row)
```

If we wanted to know what city (or cities) that reading occurred in, we might try:

```
SELECT city FROM weather WHERE temp_lo = max(temp_lo);        WRONG
```

but this will not work since the aggregate `max` cannot be used in the `WHERE` clause. (This restriction exists because the `WHERE` clause determines which rows will be included in the aggregate calculation; so obviously it has to be evaluated before aggregate functions are computed.) However, as is often the case the query can be restated to accomplish the desired result, here by using a *subquery*:

```
SELECT city FROM weather
    WHERE temp_lo = (SELECT max(temp_lo) FROM weather);

     city
---------------
 San Francisco
(1 row)
```

This is OK because the subquery is an independent computation that computes its own aggregate separately from what is happening in the outer query.

Aggregates are also very useful in combination with `GROUP BY` clauses. For example, we can get the maximum low temperature observed in each city with:

```
SELECT city, max(temp_lo)
    FROM weather
    GROUP BY city;

     city      | max
---------------+-----
 Hayward       |  37
 San Francisco |  46
(2 rows)
```

which gives us one output row per city. Each aggregate result is computed over the table rows matching that city. We can filter these grouped rows using `HAVING`:

```
SELECT city, max(temp_lo)
    FROM weather
    GROUP BY city
    HAVING max(temp_lo) < 40;

  city   | max
---------+-----
 Hayward |  37
(1 row)
```

which gives us the same results for only the cities that have all `temp_lo` values below 40. Finally, if we only care about cities whose names begin with "s", we might do:

```
SELECT city, max(temp_lo)
    FROM weather
    WHERE city LIKE 'S%'❶
    GROUP BY city
    HAVING max(temp_lo) < 40;
```

❶ The LIKE operator does pattern matching and is explained in Section 9.7.

It is important to understand the interaction between aggregates and SQL's WHERE and HAVING clauses. The fundamental difference between WHERE and HAVING is this: WHERE selects input rows before groups and aggregates are computed (thus, it controls which rows go into the aggregate computation), whereas HAVING selects group rows after groups and aggregates are computed. Thus, the WHERE clause must not contain aggregate functions; it makes no sense to try to use an aggregate to determine which rows will be inputs to the aggregates. On the other hand, the HAVING clause always contains aggregate functions. (Strictly speaking, you are allowed to write a HAVING clause that doesn't use aggregates, but it's seldom useful. The same condition could be used more efficiently at the WHERE stage.)

In the previous example, we can apply the city name restriction in WHERE, since it needs no aggregate. This is more efficient than adding the restriction to HAVING, because we avoid doing the grouping and aggregate calculations for all rows that fail the WHERE check.

2.8. Updates

You can update existing rows using the UPDATE command. Suppose you discover the temperature readings are all off by 2 degrees after November 28. You can correct the data as follows:

```
UPDATE weather
    SET temp_hi = temp_hi - 2,  temp_lo = temp_lo - 2
    WHERE date > '1994-11-28';
```

Look at the new state of the data:

```
SELECT * FROM weather;
```

city	temp_lo	temp_hi	prcp	date
San Francisco	46	50	0.25	1994-11-27
San Francisco	41	55	0	1994-11-29
Hayward	35	52		1994-11-29
(3 rows)

2.9. Deletions

Rows can be removed from a table using the DELETE command. Suppose you are no longer interested in the weather of Hayward. Then you can do the following to delete those rows from the table:

```
DELETE FROM weather WHERE city = 'Hayward';
```

All weather records belonging to Hayward are removed.

```
SELECT * FROM weather;

      city       | temp_lo | temp_hi | prcp |    date
---------------+---------+---------+------+------------
 San Francisco |      46 |      50 | 0.25 | 1994-11-27
 San Francisco |      41 |      55 |    0 | 1994-11-29
(2 rows)
```

One should be wary of statements of the form

```
DELETE FROM tablename;
```

Without a qualification, DELETE will remove *all* rows from the given table, leaving it empty. The system will not request confirmation before doing this!

Chapter 3. Advanced Features

3.1. Introduction

In the previous chapter we have covered the basics of using SQL to store and access your data in PostgreSQL. We will now discuss some more advanced features of SQL that simplify management and prevent loss or corruption of your data. Finally, we will look at some PostgreSQL extensions.

This chapter will on occasion refer to examples found in Chapter 2 to change or improve them, so it will be useful to have read that chapter. Some examples from this chapter can also be found in advanced.sql in the tutorial directory. This file also contains some sample data to load, which is not repeated here. (Refer to Section 2.1 for how to use the file.)

3.2. Views

Refer back to the queries in Section 2.6. Suppose the combined listing of weather records and city location is of particular interest to your application, but you do not want to type the query each time you need it. You can create a *view* over the query, which gives a name to the query that you can refer to like an ordinary table:

```
CREATE VIEW myview AS
    SELECT city, temp_lo, temp_hi, prcp, date, location
        FROM weather, cities
        WHERE city = name;

SELECT * FROM myview;
```

Making liberal use of views is a key aspect of good SQL database design. Views allow you to encapsulate the details of the structure of your tables, which might change as your application evolves, behind consistent interfaces.

Views can be used in almost any place a real table can be used. Building views upon other views is not uncommon.

3.3. Foreign Keys

Recall the weather and cities tables from Chapter 2. Consider the following problem: You want to make sure that no one can insert rows in the weather table that do not have a matching entry in the cities table. This is called maintaining the *referential integrity* of your data. In simplistic database systems this would be implemented (if at all) by first looking at the cities table to check if a matching record exists, and then inserting or rejecting the new weather records. This approach has a number of problems and is very inconvenient, so PostgreSQL can do this for you.

The new declaration of the tables would look like this:

```
CREATE TABLE cities (
        city        varchar(80) primary key,
        location    point
);
```

```
CREATE TABLE weather (
        city        varchar(80) references cities(city),
        temp_lo     int,
        temp_hi     int,
        prcp        real,
        date        date
);
```

Now try inserting an invalid record:

```
INSERT INTO weather VALUES ('Berkeley', 45, 53, 0.0, '1994-11-28');
```

```
ERROR:  insert or update on table "weather" violates foreign key constraint "we
DETAIL:  Key (city)=(Berkeley) is not present in table "cities".
```

The behavior of foreign keys can be finely tuned to your application. We will not go beyond this simple example in this tutorial, but just refer you to Chapter 5 for more information. Making correct use of foreign keys will definitely improve the quality of your database applications, so you are strongly encouraged to learn about them.

3.4. Transactions

Transactions are a fundamental concept of all database systems. The essential point of a transaction is that it bundles multiple steps into a single, all-or-nothing operation. The intermediate states between the steps are not visible to other concurrent transactions, and if some failure occurs that prevents the transaction from completing, then none of the steps affect the database at all.

For example, consider a bank database that contains balances for various customer accounts, as well as total deposit balances for branches. Suppose that we want to record a payment of $100.00 from Alice's account to Bob's account. Simplifying outrageously, the SQL commands for this might look like:

```
UPDATE accounts SET balance = balance - 100.00
    WHERE name = 'Alice';
UPDATE branches SET balance = balance - 100.00
    WHERE name = (SELECT branch_name FROM accounts WHERE name = 'Alice');
UPDATE accounts SET balance = balance + 100.00
    WHERE name = 'Bob';
UPDATE branches SET balance = balance + 100.00
    WHERE name = (SELECT branch_name FROM accounts WHERE name = 'Bob');
```

The details of these commands are not important here; the important point is that there are several separate updates involved to accomplish this rather simple operation. Our bank's officers will want to be assured that either all these updates happen, or none of them happen. It would certainly not do for a system failure to result in Bob receiving $100.00 that was not debited from Alice. Nor would Alice long remain a happy customer if she was debited without Bob being credited. We need a guarantee that if something goes wrong partway through the operation, none of the steps executed so far will take effect. Grouping the updates into a *transaction* gives us this guarantee. A transaction is said to be *atomic*: from the point of view of other transactions, it either happens completely or not at all.

We also want a guarantee that once a transaction is completed and acknowledged by the database system, it has indeed been permanently recorded and won't be lost even if a crash ensues shortly thereafter. For example, if we are recording a cash withdrawal by Bob, we do not want any chance that the debit to his account will disappear in a crash just after he walks out the bank door. A transactional database guarantees that all the updates made by a transaction are logged in permanent storage (i.e., on disk) before the transaction is reported complete.

Another important property of transactional databases is closely related to the notion of atomic updates: when multiple transactions are running concurrently, each one should not be able to see the incomplete changes made by others. For example, if one transaction is busy totalling all the branch balances, it would not do for it to include the debit from Alice's branch but not the credit to Bob's branch, nor vice versa. So transactions must be all-or-nothing not only in terms of their permanent effect on the database, but also in terms of their visibility as they happen. The updates made so far by an open transaction are invisible to other transactions until the transaction completes, whereupon all the updates become visible simultaneously.

In PostgreSQL, a transaction is set up by surrounding the SQL commands of the transaction with BEGIN and COMMIT commands. So our banking transaction would actually look like:

```
BEGIN;
UPDATE accounts SET balance = balance - 100.00
    WHERE name = 'Alice';
-- etc etc
COMMIT;
```

If, partway through the transaction, we decide we do not want to commit (perhaps we just noticed that Alice's balance went negative), we can issue the command ROLLBACK instead of COMMIT, and all our updates so far will be canceled.

PostgreSQL actually treats every SQL statement as being executed within a transaction. If you do not issue a BEGIN command, then each individual statement has an implicit BEGIN and (if successful) COMMIT wrapped around it. A group of statements surrounded by BEGIN and COMMIT is sometimes called a *transaction block*.

> **Note:** Some client libraries issue BEGIN and COMMIT commands automatically, so that you might get the effect of transaction blocks without asking. Check the documentation for the interface you are using.

It's possible to control the statements in a transaction in a more granular fashion through the use of *savepoints*. Savepoints allow you to selectively discard parts of the transaction, while committing the rest. After defining a savepoint with SAVEPOINT, you can if needed roll back to the savepoint with ROLLBACK TO. All the transaction's database changes between defining the savepoint and rolling back to it are discarded, but changes earlier than the savepoint are kept.

After rolling back to a savepoint, it continues to be defined, so you can roll back to it several times. Conversely, if you are sure you won't need to roll back to a particular savepoint again, it can be released, so the system can free some resources. Keep in mind that either releasing or rolling back to a savepoint will automatically release all savepoints that were defined after it.

All this is happening within the transaction block, so none of it is visible to other database sessions. When and if you commit the transaction block, the committed actions become visible as a unit to other sessions, while the rolled-back actions never become visible at all.

Remembering the bank database, suppose we debit $100.00 from Alice's account, and credit Bob's account, only to find later that we should have credited Wally's account. We could do it using savepoints like this:

```
BEGIN;
UPDATE accounts SET balance = balance - 100.00
    WHERE name = 'Alice';
SAVEPOINT my_savepoint;
UPDATE accounts SET balance = balance + 100.00
    WHERE name = 'Bob';
-- oops ... forget that and use Wally's account
ROLLBACK TO my_savepoint;
UPDATE accounts SET balance = balance + 100.00
    WHERE name = 'Wally';
COMMIT;
```

This example is, of course, oversimplified, but there's a lot of control possible in a transaction block through the use of savepoints. Moreover, ROLLBACK TO is the only way to regain control of a transaction block that was put in aborted state by the system due to an error, short of rolling it back completely and starting again.

3.5. Window Functions

A *window function* performs a calculation across a set of table rows that are somehow related to the current row. This is comparable to the type of calculation that can be done with an aggregate function. But unlike regular aggregate functions, use of a window function does not cause rows to become grouped into a single output row — the rows retain their separate identities. Behind the scenes, the window function is able to access more than just the current row of the query result.

Here is an example that shows how to compare each employee's salary with the average salary in his or her department:

```
SELECT depname, empno, salary, avg(salary) OVER (PARTITION BY depname) FROM emp

 depname  | empno | salary |         avg
----------+-------+--------+----------------------
 develop  |    11 |   5200 | 5020.0000000000000000
 develop  |     7 |   4200 | 5020.0000000000000000
 develop  |     9 |   4500 | 5020.0000000000000000
 develop  |     8 |   6000 | 5020.0000000000000000
```

```
develop    |   10 |   5200 | 5020.000000000000000
personnel  |    5 |   3500 | 3700.000000000000000
personnel  |    2 |   3900 | 3700.000000000000000
sales      |    3 |   4800 | 4866.666666666666667
sales      |    1 |   5000 | 4866.666666666666667
sales      |    4 |   4800 | 4866.666666666666667
(10 rows)
```

The first three output columns come directly from the table `empsalary`, and there is one output row for each row in the table. The fourth column represents an average taken across all the table rows that have the same `depname` value as the current row. (This actually is the same function as the regular `avg` aggregate function, but the `OVER` clause causes it to be treated as a window function and computed across an appropriate set of rows.)

A window function call always contains an `OVER` clause directly following the window function's name and argument(s). This is what syntactically distinguishes it from a regular function or aggregate function. The `OVER` clause determines exactly how the rows of the query are split up for processing by the window function. The `PARTITION BY` list within `OVER` specifies dividing the rows into groups, or partitions, that share the same values of the `PARTITION BY` expression(s). For each row, the window function is computed across the rows that fall into the same partition as the current row.

You can also control the order in which rows are processed by window functions using `ORDER BY` within `OVER`. (The window `ORDER BY` does not even have to match the order in which the rows are output.) Here is an example:

```
SELECT depname, empno, salary,
       rank() OVER (PARTITION BY depname ORDER BY salary DESC)
FROM empsalary;
```

```
 depname   | empno | salary | rank
-----------+-------+--------+------
 develop   |     8 |   6000 |    1
 develop   |    10 |   5200 |    2
 develop   |    11 |   5200 |    2
 develop   |     9 |   4500 |    4
 develop   |     7 |   4200 |    5
 personnel |     2 |   3900 |    1
 personnel |     5 |   3500 |    2
 sales     |     1 |   5000 |    1
 sales     |     4 |   4800 |    2
 sales     |     3 |   4800 |    2
(10 rows)
```

As shown here, the `rank` function produces a numerical rank within the current row's partition for each distinct `ORDER BY` value, in the order defined by the `ORDER BY` clause. `rank` needs no explicit parameter, because its behavior is entirely determined by the `OVER` clause.

The rows considered by a window function are those of the "virtual table" produced by the query's `FROM` clause as filtered by its `WHERE`, `GROUP BY`, and `HAVING` clauses if any. For example, a row removed because it does not meet the `WHERE` condition is not seen by any window function. A query can contain multiple window functions that slice up the data in different ways by means of different `OVER` clauses, but they all act on the same collection of rows defined by this virtual table.

We already saw that ORDER BY can be omitted if the ordering of rows is not important. It is also possible to omit PARTITION BY, in which case there is just one partition containing all the rows.

There is another important concept associated with window functions: for each row, there is a set of rows within its partition called its *window frame*. Many (but not all) window functions act only on the rows of the window frame, rather than of the whole partition. By default, if ORDER BY is supplied then the frame consists of all rows from the start of the partition up through the current row, plus any following rows that are equal to the current row according to the ORDER BY clause. When ORDER BY is omitted the default frame consists of all rows in the partition. [1] Here is an example using sum:

```
SELECT salary, sum(salary) OVER () FROM empsalary;

 salary |  sum
--------+-------
   5200 | 47100
   5000 | 47100
   3500 | 47100
   4800 | 47100
   3900 | 47100
   4200 | 47100
   4500 | 47100
   4800 | 47100
   6000 | 47100
   5200 | 47100
(10 rows)
```

Above, since there is no ORDER BY in the OVER clause, the window frame is the same as the partition, which for lack of PARTITION BY is the whole table; in other words each sum is taken over the whole table and so we get the same result for each output row. But if we add an ORDER BY clause, we get very different results:

```
SELECT salary, sum(salary) OVER (ORDER BY salary) FROM empsalary;

 salary |  sum
--------+-------
   3500 |  3500
   3900 |  7400
   4200 | 11600
   4500 | 16100
   4800 | 25700
   4800 | 25700
   5000 | 30700
   5200 | 41100
   5200 | 41100
   6000 | 47100
(10 rows)
```

Here the sum is taken from the first (lowest) salary up through the current one, including any duplicates of the current one (notice the results for the duplicated salaries).

Window functions are permitted only in the SELECT list and the ORDER BY clause of the query. They are forbidden elsewhere, such as in GROUP BY, HAVING and WHERE clauses. This is because they logically

---

1. There are options to define the window frame in other ways, but this tutorial does not cover them. See Section 4.2.8 for details.

execute after the processing of those clauses. Also, window functions execute after regular aggregate functions. This means it is valid to include an aggregate function call in the arguments of a window function, but not vice versa.

If there is a need to filter or group rows after the window calculations are performed, you can use a sub-select. For example:

```
SELECT depname, empno, salary, enroll_date
FROM
  (SELECT depname, empno, salary, enroll_date,
          rank() OVER (PARTITION BY depname ORDER BY salary DESC, empno) AS pos
    FROM empsalary
  ) AS ss
WHERE pos < 3;
```

The above query only shows the rows from the inner query having `rank` less than 3.

When a query involves multiple window functions, it is possible to write out each one with a separate `OVER` clause, but this is duplicative and error-prone if the same windowing behavior is wanted for several functions. Instead, each windowing behavior can be named in a `WINDOW` clause and then referenced in `OVER`. For example:

```
SELECT sum(salary) OVER w, avg(salary) OVER w
  FROM empsalary
  WINDOW w AS (PARTITION BY depname ORDER BY salary DESC);
```

More details about window functions can be found in Section 4.2.8, Section 9.21, Section 7.2.4, and the SELECT reference page.

3.6. Inheritance

Inheritance is a concept from object-oriented databases. It opens up interesting new possibilities of database design.

Let's create two tables: A table `cities` and a table `capitals`. Naturally, capitals are also cities, so you want some way to show the capitals implicitly when you list all cities. If you're really clever you might invent some scheme like this:

```
CREATE TABLE capitals (
  name       text,
  population real,
  altitude   int,    -- (in ft)
  state      char(2)
);

CREATE TABLE non_capitals (
  name       text,
  population real,
  altitude   int    -- (in ft)
);
```

```
CREATE VIEW cities AS
  SELECT name, population, altitude FROM capitals
    UNION
  SELECT name, population, altitude FROM non_capitals;
```

This works OK as far as querying goes, but it gets ugly when you need to update several rows, for one thing.

A better solution is this:

```
CREATE TABLE cities (
  name        text,
  population  real,
  altitude    int     -- (in ft)
);

CREATE TABLE capitals (
  state       char(2)
) INHERITS (cities);
```

In this case, a row of `capitals` *inherits* all columns (`name`, `population`, and `altitude`) from its *parent*, `cities`. The type of the column `name` is `text`, a native PostgreSQL type for variable length character strings. State capitals have an extra column, `state`, that shows their state. In PostgreSQL, a table can inherit from zero or more other tables.

For example, the following query finds the names of all cities, including state capitals, that are located at an altitude over 500 feet:

```
SELECT name, altitude
  FROM cities
  WHERE altitude > 500;
```

which returns:

```
   name     | altitude
-----------+----------
 Las Vegas |     2174
 Mariposa  |     1953
 Madison   |      845
(3 rows)
```

On the other hand, the following query finds all the cities that are not state capitals and are situated at an altitude over 500 feet:

```
SELECT name, altitude
    FROM ONLY cities
    WHERE altitude > 500;

   name     | altitude
-----------+----------
```

```
Las Vegas |     2174
Mariposa  |     1953
(2 rows)
```

Here the ONLY before cities indicates that the query should be run over only the cities table, and not tables below cities in the inheritance hierarchy. Many of the commands that we have already discussed — SELECT, UPDATE, and DELETE — support this ONLY notation.

> **Note:** Although inheritance is frequently useful, it has not been integrated with unique constraints or foreign keys, which limits its usefulness. See Section 5.8 for more detail.

3.7. Conclusion

PostgreSQL has many features not touched upon in this tutorial introduction, which has been oriented toward newer users of SQL. These features are discussed in more detail in the remainder of this book.

If you feel you need more introductory material, please visit the PostgreSQL web site[2] for links to more resources.

---

2.   http://www.postgresql.org

II. The SQL Language

This part describes the use of the SQL language in PostgreSQL. We start with describing the general syntax of SQL, then explain how to create the structures to hold data, how to populate the database, and how to query it. The middle part lists the available data types and functions for use in SQL commands. The rest treats several aspects that are important for tuning a database for optimal performance.

The information in this part is arranged so that a novice user can follow it start to end to gain a full understanding of the topics without having to refer forward too many times. The chapters are intended to be self-contained, so that advanced users can read the chapters individually as they choose. The information in this part is presented in a narrative fashion in topical units. Readers looking for a complete description of a particular command should see Part VI.

Readers of this part should know how to connect to a PostgreSQL database and issue SQL commands. Readers that are unfamiliar with these issues are encouraged to read Part I first. SQL commands are typically entered using the PostgreSQL interactive terminal psql, but other programs that have similar functionality can be used as well.

Chapter 4. SQL Syntax

This chapter describes the syntax of SQL. It forms the foundation for understanding the following chapters which will go into detail about how SQL commands are applied to define and modify data.

We also advise users who are already familiar with SQL to read this chapter carefully because it contains several rules and concepts that are implemented inconsistently among SQL databases or that are specific to PostgreSQL.

4.1. Lexical Structure

SQL input consists of a sequence of *commands*. A command is composed of a sequence of *tokens*, terminated by a semicolon (";"). The end of the input stream also terminates a command. Which tokens are valid depends on the syntax of the particular command.

A token can be a *key word*, an *identifier*, a *quoted identifier*, a *literal* (or constant), or a special character symbol. Tokens are normally separated by whitespace (space, tab, newline), but need not be if there is no ambiguity (which is generally only the case if a special character is adjacent to some other token type).

For example, the following is (syntactically) valid SQL input:

```
SELECT * FROM MY_TABLE;
UPDATE MY_TABLE SET A = 5;
INSERT INTO MY_TABLE VALUES (3, 'hi there');
```

This is a sequence of three commands, one per line (although this is not required; more than one command can be on a line, and commands can usefully be split across lines).

Additionally, *comments* can occur in SQL input. They are not tokens, they are effectively equivalent to whitespace.

The SQL syntax is not very consistent regarding what tokens identify commands and which are operands or parameters. The first few tokens are generally the command name, so in the above example we would usually speak of a "SELECT", an "UPDATE", and an "INSERT" command. But for instance the UPDATE command always requires a SET token to appear in a certain position, and this particular variation of INSERT also requires a VALUES in order to be complete. The precise syntax rules for each command are described in Part VI.

4.1.1. Identifiers and Key Words

Tokens such as SELECT, UPDATE, or VALUES in the example above are examples of *key words*, that is, words that have a fixed meaning in the SQL language. The tokens MY_TABLE and A are examples of *identifiers*. They identify names of tables, columns, or other database objects, depending on the command they are used in. Therefore they are sometimes simply called "names". Key words and identifiers have the same lexical structure, meaning that one cannot know whether a token is an identifier or a key word without knowing the language. A complete list of key words can be found in Appendix C.

SQL identifiers and key words must begin with a letter (a-z, but also letters with diacritical marks and non-Latin letters) or an underscore (_). Subsequent characters in an identifier or key word can be letters, underscores, digits (0-9), or dollar signs ($). Note that dollar signs are not allowed in identifiers according to the letter of the SQL standard, so their use might render applications less portable. The SQL standard will not define a key word that contains digits or starts or ends with an underscore, so identifiers of this form are safe against possible conflict with future extensions of the standard.

The system uses no more than NAMEDATALEN-1 bytes of an identifier; longer names can be written in commands, but they will be truncated. By default, NAMEDATALEN is 64 so the maximum identifier length is 63 bytes. If this limit is problematic, it can be raised by changing the NAMEDATALEN constant in src/include/pg_config_manual.h.

Key words and unquoted identifiers are case insensitive. Therefore:

```
UPDATE MY_TABLE SET A = 5;
```

can equivalently be written as:

```
uPDaTE my_TabLE SeT a = 5;
```

A convention often used is to write key words in upper case and names in lower case, e.g.:

```
UPDATE my_table SET a = 5;
```

There is a second kind of identifier: the *delimited identifier* or *quoted identifier*. It is formed by enclosing an arbitrary sequence of characters in double-quotes ("). A delimited identifier is always an identifier, never a key word. So "select" could be used to refer to a column or table named "select", whereas an unquoted select would be taken as a key word and would therefore provoke a parse error when used where a table or column name is expected. The example can be written with quoted identifiers like this:

```
UPDATE "my_table" SET "a" = 5;
```

Quoted identifiers can contain any character, except the character with code zero. (To include a double quote, write two double quotes.) This allows constructing table or column names that would otherwise not be possible, such as ones containing spaces or ampersands. The length limitation still applies.

A variant of quoted identifiers allows including escaped Unicode characters identified by their code points. This variant starts with U& (upper or lower case U followed by ampersand) immediately before the opening double quote, without any spaces in between, for example U&"foo". (Note that this creates an ambiguity with the operator &. Use spaces around the operator to avoid this problem.) Inside the quotes, Unicode characters can be specified in escaped form by writing a backslash followed by the four-digit hexadecimal code point number or alternatively a backslash followed by a plus sign followed by a six-digit hexadecimal code point number. For example, the identifier "data" could be written as

```
U&"d\0061t\+000061"
```

The following less trivial example writes the Russian word "slon" (elephant) in Cyrillic letters:

```
U&"\0441\043B\043E\043D"
```

If a different escape character than backslash is desired, it can be specified using the UESCAPE clause after the string, for example:

```
U&"d!0061t!+000061" UESCAPE '!'
```

The escape character can be any single character other than a hexadecimal digit, the plus sign, a single quote, a double quote, or a whitespace character. Note that the escape character is written in single quotes, not double quotes.

To include the escape character in the identifier literally, write it twice.

The Unicode escape syntax works only when the server encoding is UTF8. When other server encodings are used, only code points in the ASCII range (up to \007F) can be specified. Both the 4-digit and the 6-digit form can be used to specify UTF-16 surrogate pairs to compose characters with code points larger than U+FFFF, although the availability of the 6-digit form technically makes this unnecessary. (Surrogate pairs are not stored directly, but combined into a single code point that is then encoded in UTF-8.)

Quoting an identifier also makes it case-sensitive, whereas unquoted names are always folded to lower case. For example, the identifiers FOO, foo, and "foo" are considered the same by PostgreSQL, but "Foo" and "FOO" are different from these three and each other. (The folding of unquoted names to lower case in PostgreSQL is incompatible with the SQL standard, which says that unquoted names should be folded to upper case. Thus, foo should be equivalent to "FOO" not "foo" according to the standard. If you want to write portable applications you are advised to always quote a particular name or never quote it.)

4.1.2. Constants

There are three kinds of *implicitly-typed constants* in PostgreSQL: strings, bit strings, and numbers. Constants can also be specified with explicit types, which can enable more accurate representation and more efficient handling by the system. These alternatives are discussed in the following subsections.

4.1.2.1. String Constants

A string constant in SQL is an arbitrary sequence of characters bounded by single quotes ('), for example 'This is a string'. To include a single-quote character within a string constant, write two adjacent single quotes, e.g., 'Dianne''s horse'. Note that this is *not* the same as a double-quote character (").

Two string constants that are only separated by whitespace *with at least one newline* are concatenated and effectively treated as if the string had been written as one constant. For example:

```
SELECT 'foo'
'bar';
```

is equivalent to:

```
SELECT 'foobar';
```

but:

```
SELECT 'foo'      'bar';
```

is not valid syntax. (This slightly bizarre behavior is specified by SQL; PostgreSQL is following the standard.)

4.1.2.2. String Constants with C-style Escapes

PostgreSQL also accepts "escape" string constants, which are an extension to the SQL standard. An escape string constant is specified by writing the letter E (upper or lower case) just before the opening single quote, e.g., E'foo'. (When continuing an escape string constant across lines, write E only before the first opening quote.) Within an escape string, a backslash character (\) begins a C-like *backslash escape* sequence, in which the combination of backslash and following character(s) represent a special byte value, as shown in Table 4-1.

Table 4-1. Backslash Escape Sequences

Backslash Escape Sequence	Interpretation
\b	backspace
\f	form feed
\n	newline
\r	carriage return
\t	tab
\o, \oo, \ooo (o = 0 - 7)	octal byte value
\xh, \xhh (h = 0 - 9, A - F)	hexadecimal byte value
\uxxxx, \Uxxxxxxxx (x = 0 - 9, A - F)	16 or 32-bit hexadecimal Unicode character value

Any other character following a backslash is taken literally. Thus, to include a backslash character, write two backslashes (\\). Also, a single quote can be included in an escape string by writing \', in addition to the normal way of ''.

It is your responsibility that the byte sequences you create, especially when using the octal or hexadecimal escapes, compose valid characters in the server character set encoding. When the server encoding is UTF-8, then the Unicode escapes or the alternative Unicode escape syntax, explained in Section 4.1.2.3, should be used instead. (The alternative would be doing the UTF-8 encoding by hand and writing out the bytes, which would be very cumbersome.)

The Unicode escape syntax works fully only when the server encoding is UTF8. When other server encodings are used, only code points in the ASCII range (up to \u007F) can be specified. Both the 4-digit and the 8-digit form can be used to specify UTF-16 surrogate pairs to compose characters with code points larger than U+FFFF, although the availability of the 8-digit form technically makes this unnecessary. (When surrogate pairs are used when the server encoding is UTF8, they are first combined into a single code point that is then encoded in UTF-8.)

Caution

If the configuration parameter standard_conforming_strings is `off`, then PostgreSQL recognizes backslash escapes in both regular and escape string constants. However, as of PostgreSQL 9.1, the default is `on`, meaning that backslash escapes are recognized only in escape string constants. This behavior is more standards-compliant, but might break applications which rely on the historical behavior, where backslash escapes were always recognized. As a workaround, you can set this parameter to `off`, but it is better to migrate away from using backslash escapes. If you need to use a backslash escape to represent a special character, write the string constant with an `E`.

In addition to `standard_conforming_strings`, the configuration parameters escape_string_warning and backslash_quote govern treatment of backslashes in string constants.

The character with the code zero cannot be in a string constant.

4.1.2.3. String Constants with Unicode Escapes

PostgreSQL also supports another type of escape syntax for strings that allows specifying arbitrary Unicode characters by code point. A Unicode escape string constant starts with `U&` (upper or lower case letter U followed by ampersand) immediately before the opening quote, without any spaces in between, for example `U&'foo'`. (Note that this creates an ambiguity with the operator `&`. Use spaces around the operator to avoid this problem.) Inside the quotes, Unicode characters can be specified in escaped form by writing a backslash followed by the four-digit hexadecimal code point number or alternatively a backslash followed by a plus sign followed by a six-digit hexadecimal code point number. For example, the string `'data'` could be written as

```
U&'d\0061t\+000061'
```

The following less trivial example writes the Russian word "slon" (elephant) in Cyrillic letters:

```
U&'\0441\043B\043E\043D'
```

If a different escape character than backslash is desired, it can be specified using the `UESCAPE` clause after the string, for example:

```
U&'d!0061t!+000061' UESCAPE '!'
```

The escape character can be any single character other than a hexadecimal digit, the plus sign, a single quote, a double quote, or a whitespace character.

The Unicode escape syntax works only when the server encoding is `UTF8`. When other server encodings are used, only code points in the ASCII range (up to `\007F`) can be specified. Both the 4-digit and the 6-digit form can be used to specify UTF-16 surrogate pairs to compose characters with code points larger than U+FFFF, although the availability of the 6-digit form technically makes this unnecessary. (When surrogate pairs are used when the server encoding is `UTF8`, they are first combined into a single code point that is then encoded in UTF-8.)

Also, the Unicode escape syntax for string constants only works when the configuration parameter standard_conforming_strings is turned on. This is because otherwise this syntax could confuse clients that parse the SQL statements to the point that it could lead to SQL injections and similar security issues. If the parameter is set to off, this syntax will be rejected with an error message.

To include the escape character in the string literally, write it twice.

4.1.2.4. Dollar-quoted String Constants

While the standard syntax for specifying string constants is usually convenient, it can be difficult to understand when the desired string contains many single quotes or backslashes, since each of those must be doubled. To allow more readable queries in such situations, PostgreSQL provides another way, called "dollar quoting", to write string constants. A dollar-quoted string constant consists of a dollar sign ($), an optional "tag" of zero or more characters, another dollar sign, an arbitrary sequence of characters that makes up the string content, a dollar sign, the same tag that began this dollar quote, and a dollar sign. For example, here are two different ways to specify the string "Dianne's horse" using dollar quoting:

```
$$Dianne's horse$$
$SomeTag$Dianne's horse$SomeTag$
```

Notice that inside the dollar-quoted string, single quotes can be used without needing to be escaped. Indeed, no characters inside a dollar-quoted string are ever escaped: the string content is always written literally. Backslashes are not special, and neither are dollar signs, unless they are part of a sequence matching the opening tag.

It is possible to nest dollar-quoted string constants by choosing different tags at each nesting level. This is most commonly used in writing function definitions. For example:

```
$function$
BEGIN
    RETURN ($1 ~ $q$[\t\r\n\v\\]$q$);
END;
$function$
```

Here, the sequence q[\t\r\n\v\\]q represents a dollar-quoted literal string [\t\r\n\v\\], which will be recognized when the function body is executed by PostgreSQL. But since the sequence does not match the outer dollar quoting delimiter $function$, it is just some more characters within the constant so far as the outer string is concerned.

The tag, if any, of a dollar-quoted string follows the same rules as an unquoted identifier, except that it cannot contain a dollar sign. Tags are case sensitive, so tagString contenttag is correct, but TAGString contenttag is not.

A dollar-quoted string that follows a keyword or identifier must be separated from it by whitespace; otherwise the dollar quoting delimiter would be taken as part of the preceding identifier.

Dollar quoting is not part of the SQL standard, but it is often a more convenient way to write complicated string literals than the standard-compliant single quote syntax. It is particularly useful when representing string constants inside other constants, as is often needed in procedural function definitions. With single-quote syntax, each backslash in the above example would have to be written as four backslashes, which would be reduced to two backslashes in parsing the original string constant, and then to one when the inner string constant is re-parsed during function execution.

4.1.2.5. Bit-string Constants

Bit-string constants look like regular string constants with a B (upper or lower case) immediately before the opening quote (no intervening whitespace), e.g., B'1001'. The only characters allowed within bit-string constants are 0 and 1.

Alternatively, bit-string constants can be specified in hexadecimal notation, using a leading X (upper or lower case), e.g., X'1FF'. This notation is equivalent to a bit-string constant with four binary digits for each hexadecimal digit.

Both forms of bit-string constant can be continued across lines in the same way as regular string constants. Dollar quoting cannot be used in a bit-string constant.

4.1.2.6. Numeric Constants

Numeric constants are accepted in these general forms:

```
digits
digits.[digits][e[+-]digits]
[digits].digits[e[+-]digits]
digitse[+-]digits
```

where *digits* is one or more decimal digits (0 through 9). At least one digit must be before or after the decimal point, if one is used. At least one digit must follow the exponent marker (e), if one is present. There cannot be any spaces or other characters embedded in the constant. Note that any leading plus or minus sign is not actually considered part of the constant; it is an operator applied to the constant.

These are some examples of valid numeric constants:

```
42
3.5
4.
.001
5e2
1.925e-3
```

A numeric constant that contains neither a decimal point nor an exponent is initially presumed to be type integer if its value fits in type integer (32 bits); otherwise it is presumed to be type bigint if its value fits in type bigint (64 bits); otherwise it is taken to be type numeric. Constants that contain decimal points and/or exponents are always initially presumed to be type numeric.

The initially assigned data type of a numeric constant is just a starting point for the type resolution algorithms. In most cases the constant will be automatically coerced to the most appropriate type depending on context. When necessary, you can force a numeric value to be interpreted as a specific data type by casting it. For example, you can force a numeric value to be treated as type real (float4) by writing:

```
REAL '1.23'   -- string style
1.23::REAL    -- PostgreSQL (historical) style
```

These are actually just special cases of the general casting notations discussed next.

4.1.2.7. Constants of Other Types

A constant of an *arbitrary* type can be entered using any one of the following notations:

```
type 'string'
'string'::type
CAST ( 'string' AS type )
```

The string constant's text is passed to the input conversion routine for the type called `type`. The result is a constant of the indicated type. The explicit type cast can be omitted if there is no ambiguity as to the type the constant must be (for example, when it is assigned directly to a table column), in which case it is automatically coerced.

The string constant can be written using either regular SQL notation or dollar-quoting.

It is also possible to specify a type coercion using a function-like syntax:

```
typename ( 'string' )
```

but not all type names can be used in this way; see Section 4.2.9 for details.

The `::`, `CAST()`, and function-call syntaxes can also be used to specify run-time type conversions of arbitrary expressions, as discussed in Section 4.2.9. To avoid syntactic ambiguity, the `type 'string'` syntax can only be used to specify the type of a simple literal constant. Another restriction on the `type 'string'` syntax is that it does not work for array types; use `::` or `CAST()` to specify the type of an array constant.

The `CAST()` syntax conforms to SQL. The `type 'string'` syntax is a generalization of the standard: SQL specifies this syntax only for a few data types, but PostgreSQL allows it for all types. The syntax with `::` is historical PostgreSQL usage, as is the function-call syntax.

4.1.3. Operators

An operator name is a sequence of up to `NAMEDATALEN`-1 (63 by default) characters from the following list:

```
+ - * / < > = ~ ! @ # % ^ & | ` ?
```

There are a few restrictions on operator names, however:

- `--` and `/*` cannot appear anywhere in an operator name, since they will be taken as the start of a comment.

- A multiple-character operator name cannot end in + or -, unless the name also contains at least one of these characters:

  ```
  ~ ! @ # % ^ & | ` ?
  ```

  For example, `@-` is an allowed operator name, but `*-` is not. This restriction allows PostgreSQL to parse SQL-compliant queries without requiring spaces between tokens.

When working with non-SQL-standard operator names, you will usually need to separate adjacent operators with spaces to avoid ambiguity. For example, if you have defined a left unary operator named @, you cannot write X*@Y; you must write X* @Y to ensure that PostgreSQL reads it as two operator names not one.

4.1.4. Special Characters

Some characters that are not alphanumeric have a special meaning that is different from being an operator. Details on the usage can be found at the location where the respective syntax element is described. This section only exists to advise the existence and summarize the purposes of these characters.

- A dollar sign ($) followed by digits is used to represent a positional parameter in the body of a function definition or a prepared statement. In other contexts the dollar sign can be part of an identifier or a dollar-quoted string constant.
- Parentheses (( )) have their usual meaning to group expressions and enforce precedence. In some cases parentheses are required as part of the fixed syntax of a particular SQL command.
- Brackets ([]) are used to select the elements of an array. See Section 8.15 for more information on arrays.
- Commas (,) are used in some syntactical constructs to separate the elements of a list.
- The semicolon (;) terminates an SQL command. It cannot appear anywhere within a command, except within a string constant or quoted identifier.
- The colon (:) is used to select "slices" from arrays. (See Section 8.15.) In certain SQL dialects (such as Embedded SQL), the colon is used to prefix variable names.
- The asterisk (*) is used in some contexts to denote all the fields of a table row or composite value. It also has a special meaning when used as the argument of an aggregate function, namely that the aggregate does not require any explicit parameter.
- The period (.) is used in numeric constants, and to separate schema, table, and column names.

4.1.5. Comments

A comment is a sequence of characters beginning with double dashes and extending to the end of the line, e.g.:

```
-- This is a standard SQL comment
```

Alternatively, C-style block comments can be used:

```
/* multiline comment
 * with nesting: /* nested block comment */
 */
```

where the comment begins with `/*` and extends to the matching occurrence of `*/`. These block comments nest, as specified in the SQL standard but unlike C, so that one can comment out larger blocks of code that might contain existing block comments.

A comment is removed from the input stream before further syntax analysis and is effectively replaced by whitespace.

4.1.6. Operator Precedence

Table 4-2 shows the precedence and associativity of the operators in PostgreSQL. Most operators have the same precedence and are left-associative. The precedence and associativity of the operators is hard-wired into the parser. This can lead to non-intuitive behavior; for example the Boolean operators < and > have a different precedence than the Boolean operators <= and >=. Also, you will sometimes need to add parentheses when using combinations of binary and unary operators. For instance:

```
SELECT 5 ! - 6;
```

will be parsed as:

```
SELECT 5 ! (- 6);
```

because the parser has no idea — until it is too late — that ! is defined as a postfix operator, not an infix one. To get the desired behavior in this case, you must write:

```
SELECT (5 !) - 6;
```

This is the price one pays for extensibility.

Table 4-2. Operator Precedence (decreasing)

Operator/Element	Associativity	Description
.	left	table/column name separator
::	left	PostgreSQL-style typecast
[ ]	left	array element selection
+ -	right	unary plus, unary minus
^	left	exponentiation
* / %	left	multiplication, division, modulo
+ -	left	addition, subtraction
IS		IS TRUE, IS FALSE, IS NULL, etc
ISNULL		test for null
NOTNULL		test for not null
(any other)	left	all other native and user-defined operators
IN		set membership
BETWEEN		range containment

Operator/Element	Associativity	Description
`OVERLAPS`		time interval overlap
`LIKE ILIKE SIMILAR`		string pattern matching
`< >`		less than, greater than
`=`	right	equality, assignment
`NOT`	right	logical negation
`AND`	left	logical conjunction
`OR`	left	logical disjunction

Note that the operator precedence rules also apply to user-defined operators that have the same names as the built-in operators mentioned above. For example, if you define a "+" operator for some custom data type it will have the same precedence as the built-in "+" operator, no matter what yours does.

When a schema-qualified operator name is used in the `OPERATOR` syntax, as for example in:

```
SELECT 3 OPERATOR(pg_catalog.+) 4;
```

the `OPERATOR` construct is taken to have the default precedence shown in Table 4-2 for "any other" operator. This is true no matter which specific operator appears inside `OPERATOR()`.

4.2. Value Expressions

Value expressions are used in a variety of contexts, such as in the target list of the `SELECT` command, as new column values in `INSERT` or `UPDATE`, or in search conditions in a number of commands. The result of a value expression is sometimes called a *scalar*, to distinguish it from the result of a table expression (which is a table). Value expressions are therefore also called *scalar expressions* (or even simply *expressions*). The expression syntax allows the calculation of values from primitive parts using arithmetic, logical, set, and other operations.

A value expression is one of the following:

- A constant or literal value
- A column reference
- A positional parameter reference, in the body of a function definition or prepared statement
- A subscripted expression
- A field selection expression
- An operator invocation
- A function call
- An aggregate expression
- A window function call
- A type cast
- A collation expression

- A scalar subquery

- An array constructor

- A row constructor

- Another value expression in parentheses (used to group subexpressions and override precedence)

In addition to this list, there are a number of constructs that can be classified as an expression but do not follow any general syntax rules. These generally have the semantics of a function or operator and are explained in the appropriate location in Chapter 9. An example is the IS NULL clause.

We have already discussed constants in Section 4.1.2. The following sections discuss the remaining options.

4.2.1. Column References

A column can be referenced in the form:

```
correlation.columnname
```

correlation is the name of a table (possibly qualified with a schema name), or an alias for a table defined by means of a FROM clause. The correlation name and separating dot can be omitted if the column name is unique across all the tables being used in the current query. (See also Chapter 7.)

4.2.2. Positional Parameters

A positional parameter reference is used to indicate a value that is supplied externally to an SQL statement. Parameters are used in SQL function definitions and in prepared queries. Some client libraries also support specifying data values separately from the SQL command string, in which case parameters are used to refer to the out-of-line data values. The form of a parameter reference is:

```
$number
```

For example, consider the definition of a function, dept, as:

```
CREATE FUNCTION dept(text) RETURNS dept
    AS $$ SELECT * FROM dept WHERE name = $1 $$
    LANGUAGE SQL;
```

Here the $1 references the value of the first function argument whenever the function is invoked.

4.2.3. Subscripts

If an expression yields a value of an array type, then a specific element of the array value can be extracted by writing

```
expression[subscript]
```

or multiple adjacent elements (an "array slice") can be extracted by writing

```
expression[lower_subscript:upper_subscript]
```

(Here, the brackets `[ ]` are meant to appear literally.) Each `subscript` is itself an expression, which must yield an integer value.

In general the array `expression` must be parenthesized, but the parentheses can be omitted when the expression to be subscripted is just a column reference or positional parameter. Also, multiple subscripts can be concatenated when the original array is multidimensional. For example:

```
mytable.arraycolumn[4]
mytable.two_d_column[17][34]
$1[10:42]
(arrayfunction(a,b))[42]
```

The parentheses in the last example are required. See Section 8.15 for more about arrays.

4.2.4. Field Selection

If an expression yields a value of a composite type (row type), then a specific field of the row can be extracted by writing

```
expression.fieldname
```

In general the row `expression` must be parenthesized, but the parentheses can be omitted when the expression to be selected from is just a table reference or positional parameter. For example:

```
mytable.mycolumn
$1.somecolumn
(rowfunction(a,b)).col3
```

(Thus, a qualified column reference is actually just a special case of the field selection syntax.) An important special case is extracting a field from a table column that is of a composite type:

```
(compositecol).somefield
(mytable.compositecol).somefield
```

The parentheses are required here to show that `compositecol` is a column name not a table name, or that `mytable` is a table name not a schema name in the second case.

In a select list (see Section 7.3), you can ask for all fields of a composite value by writing `.*`:

```
(compositecol).*
```

4.2.5. Operator Invocations

There are three possible syntaxes for an operator invocation:

expression operator expression (binary infix operator)
operator expression (unary prefix operator)
expression operator (unary postfix operator)

where the *operator* token follows the syntax rules of Section 4.1.3, or is one of the key words AND, OR, and NOT, or is a qualified operator name in the form:

OPERATOR(*schema.operatorname*)

Which particular operators exist and whether they are unary or binary depends on what operators have been defined by the system or the user. Chapter 9 describes the built-in operators.

4.2.6. Function Calls

The syntax for a function call is the name of a function (possibly qualified with a schema name), followed by its argument list enclosed in parentheses:

function_name ([*expression* [, *expression* ...]])

For example, the following computes the square root of 2:

sqrt(2)

The list of built-in functions is in Chapter 9. Other functions can be added by the user.

The arguments can optionally have names attached. See Section 4.3 for details.

> **Note:** A function that takes a single argument of composite type can optionally be called using field-selection syntax, and conversely field selection can be written in functional style. That is, the notations col(table) and table.col are interchangeable. This behavior is not SQL-standard but is provided in PostgreSQL because it allows use of functions to emulate "computed fields". For more information see Section 35.4.3.

4.2.7. Aggregate Expressions

An *aggregate expression* represents the application of an aggregate function across the rows selected by a query. An aggregate function reduces multiple inputs to a single output value, such as the sum or average of the inputs. The syntax of an aggregate expression is one of the following:

```
aggregate_name (expression [ , ... ] [ order_by_clause ] ) [ FILTER ( WHERE filter_
aggregate_name (ALL expression [ , ... ] [ order_by_clause ] ) [ FILTER ( WHERE fil
aggregate_name (DISTINCT expression [ , ... ] [ order_by_clause ] ) [ FILTER ( WHEF
aggregate_name ( * ) [ FILTER ( WHERE filter_clause ) ]
aggregate_name ( [ expression [ , ... ] ] ) WITHIN GROUP ( order_by_clause ) [ FIL1
```

where `aggregate_name` is a previously defined aggregate (possibly qualified with a schema name) and `expression` is any value expression that does not itself contain an aggregate expression or a window function call. The optional `order_by_clause` and `filter_clause` are described below.

The first form of aggregate expression invokes the aggregate once for each input row. The second form is the same as the first, since `ALL` is the default. The third form invokes the aggregate once for each distinct value of the expression (or distinct set of values, for multiple expressions) found in the input rows. The fourth form invokes the aggregate once for each input row; since no particular input value is specified, it is generally only useful for the `count(*)` aggregate function. The last form is used with *ordered-set* aggregate functions, which are described below.

Most aggregate functions ignore null inputs, so that rows in which one or more of the expression(s) yield null are discarded. This can be assumed to be true, unless otherwise specified, for all built-in aggregates.

For example, `count(*)` yields the total number of input rows; `count(f1)` yields the number of input rows in which `f1` is non-null, since `count` ignores nulls; and `count(distinct f1)` yields the number of distinct non-null values of `f1`.

Ordinarily, the input rows are fed to the aggregate function in an unspecified order. In many cases this does not matter; for example, `min` produces the same result no matter what order it receives the inputs in. However, some aggregate functions (such as `array_agg` and `string_agg`) produce results that depend on the ordering of the input rows. When using such an aggregate, the optional `order_by_clause` can be used to specify the desired ordering. The `order_by_clause` has the same syntax as for a query-level `ORDER BY` clause, as described in Section 7.5, except that its expressions are always just expressions and cannot be output-column names or numbers. For example:

```
SELECT array_agg(a ORDER BY b DESC) FROM table;
```

When dealing with multiple-argument aggregate functions, note that the `ORDER BY` clause goes after all the aggregate arguments. For example, write this:

```
SELECT string_agg(a, ',' ORDER BY a) FROM table;
```

not this:

```
SELECT string_agg(a ORDER BY a, ',') FROM table;  -- incorrect
```

The latter is syntactically valid, but it represents a call of a single-argument aggregate function with two `ORDER BY` keys (the second one being rather useless since it's a constant).

If DISTINCT is specified in addition to an *order_by_clause*, then all the ORDER BY expressions must match regular arguments of the aggregate; that is, you cannot sort on an expression that is not included in the DISTINCT list.

Note: The ability to specify both DISTINCT and ORDER BY in an aggregate function is a PostgreSQL extension.

Placing ORDER BY within the aggregate's regular argument list, as described so far, is used when ordering the input rows for a "normal" aggregate for which ordering is optional. There is a subclass of aggregate functions called *ordered-set aggregates* for which an *order_by_clause* is *required*, usually because the aggregate's computation is only sensible in terms of a specific ordering of its input rows. Typical examples of ordered-set aggregates include rank and percentile calculations. For an ordered-set aggregate, the *order_by_clause* is written inside WITHIN GROUP (...), as shown in the final syntax alternative above. The expressions in the *order_by_clause* are evaluated once per input row just like normal aggregate arguments, sorted as per the *order_by_clause*'s requirements, and fed to the aggregate function as input arguments. (This is unlike the case for a non-WITHIN GROUP *order_by_clause*, which is not treated as argument(s) to the aggregate function.) The argument expressions preceding WITHIN GROUP, if any, are called *direct arguments* to distinguish them from the *aggregated arguments* listed in the *order_by_clause*. Unlike normal aggregate arguments, direct arguments are evaluated only once per aggregate call, not once per input row. This means that they can contain variables only if those variables are grouped by GROUP BY; this restriction is the same as if the direct arguments were not inside an aggregate expression at all. Direct arguments are typically used for things like percentile fractions, which only make sense as a single value per aggregation calculation. The direct argument list can be empty; in this case, write just () not (*). (PostgreSQL will actually accept either spelling, but only the first way conforms to the SQL standard.) An example of an ordered-set aggregate call is:

```
SELECT percentile_disc(0.5) WITHIN GROUP (ORDER BY income) FROM households;
 percentile_disc
-----------------
           50489
```

which obtains the 50th percentile, or median, value of the income column from table households. Here, 0.5 is a direct argument; it would make no sense for the percentile fraction to be a value varying across rows.

If FILTER is specified, then only the input rows for which the *filter_clause* evaluates to true are fed to the aggregate function; other rows are discarded. For example:

```
SELECT
    count(*) AS unfiltered,
    count(*) FILTER (WHERE i < 5) AS filtered
FROM generate_series(1,10) AS s(i);
 unfiltered | filtered
------------+----------
         10 |        4
(1 row)
```

The predefined aggregate functions are described in Section 9.20. Other aggregate functions can be added by the user.

An aggregate expression can only appear in the result list or HAVING clause of a SELECT command. It is forbidden in other clauses, such as WHERE, because those clauses are logically evaluated before the results of aggregates are formed.

When an aggregate expression appears in a subquery (see Section 4.2.11 and Section 9.22), the aggregate is normally evaluated over the rows of the subquery. But an exception occurs if the aggregate's arguments (and *filter_clause* if any) contain only outer-level variables: the aggregate then belongs to the nearest such outer level, and is evaluated over the rows of that query. The aggregate expression as a whole is then an outer reference for the subquery it appears in, and acts as a constant over any one evaluation of that subquery. The restriction about appearing only in the result list or HAVING clause applies with respect to the query level that the aggregate belongs to.

4.2.8. Window Function Calls

A *window function call* represents the application of an aggregate-like function over some portion of the rows selected by a query. Unlike regular aggregate function calls, this is not tied to grouping of the selected rows into a single output row — each row remains separate in the query output. However the window function is able to scan all the rows that would be part of the current row's group according to the grouping specification (PARTITION BY list) of the window function call. The syntax of a window function call is one of the following:

```
function_name ([expression [, expression ... ]]) [ FILTER ( WHERE filter_clause ) ]
function_name ([expression [, expression ... ]]) [ FILTER ( WHERE filter_clause ) ]
function_name ( * ) [ FILTER ( WHERE filter_clause ) ] OVER window_name
function_name ( * ) [ FILTER ( WHERE filter_clause ) ] OVER ( window_definition )
```

where *window_definition* has the syntax

```
[ existing_window_name ]
[ PARTITION BY expression [, ...] ]
[ ORDER BY expression [ ASC | DESC | USING operator ] [ NULLS { FIRST | LAST } ]
[ frame_clause ]
```

and the optional *frame_clause* can be one of

```
{ RANGE | ROWS } frame_start
{ RANGE | ROWS } BETWEEN frame_start AND frame_end
```

where *frame_start* and *frame_end* can be one of

```
UNBOUNDED PRECEDING
value PRECEDING
CURRENT ROW
value FOLLOWING
UNBOUNDED FOLLOWING
```

Here, *expression* represents any value expression that does not itself contain window function calls.

window_name is a reference to a named window specification defined in the query's WINDOW clause. Alternatively, a full *window_definition* can be given within parentheses, using the same syntax as for defining a named window in the WINDOW clause; see the SELECT reference page for details. It's worth pointing out that OVER wname is not exactly equivalent to OVER (wname); the latter implies copying and modifying the window definition, and will be rejected if the referenced window specification includes a frame clause.

The PARTITION BY option groups the rows of the query into *partitions*, which are processed separately by the window function. PARTITION BY works similarly to a query-level GROUP BY clause, except that its expressions are always just expressions and cannot be output-column names or numbers. Without PARTITION BY, all rows produced by the query are treated as a single partition. The ORDER BY option determines the order in which the rows of a partition are processed by the window function. It works similarly to a query-level ORDER BY clause, but likewise cannot use output-column names or numbers. Without ORDER BY, rows are processed in an unspecified order.

The *frame_clause* specifies the set of rows constituting the *window frame*, which is a subset of the current partition, for those window functions that act on the frame instead of the whole partition. The frame can be specified in either RANGE or ROWS mode; in either case, it runs from the *frame_start* to the *frame_end*. If *frame_end* is omitted, it defaults to CURRENT ROW.

A *frame_start* of UNBOUNDED PRECEDING means that the frame starts with the first row of the partition, and similarly a *frame_end* of UNBOUNDED FOLLOWING means that the frame ends with the last row of the partition.

In RANGE mode, a *frame_start* of CURRENT ROW means the frame starts with the current row's first *peer* row (a row that ORDER BY considers equivalent to the current row), while a *frame_end* of CURRENT ROW means the frame ends with the last equivalent ORDER BY peer. In ROWS mode, CURRENT ROW simply means the current row.

The *value* PRECEDING and *value* FOLLOWING cases are currently only allowed in ROWS mode. They indicate that the frame starts or ends the specified number of rows before or after the current row. *value* must be an integer expression not containing any variables, aggregate functions, or window functions. The value must not be null or negative; but it can be zero, which just selects the current row.

The default framing option is RANGE UNBOUNDED PRECEDING, which is the same as RANGE BETWEEN UNBOUNDED PRECEDING AND CURRENT ROW. With ORDER BY, this sets the frame to be all rows from the partition start up through the current row's last ORDER BY peer. Without ORDER BY, all rows of the partition are included in the window frame, since all rows become peers of the current row.

Restrictions are that *frame_start* cannot be UNBOUNDED FOLLOWING, *frame_end* cannot be UNBOUNDED PRECEDING, and the *frame_end* choice cannot appear earlier in the above list than the *frame_start* choice — for example RANGE BETWEEN CURRENT ROW AND *value* PRECEDING is not allowed.

If FILTER is specified, then only the input rows for which the *filter_clause* evaluates to true are fed to the window function; other rows are discarded. Only window functions that are aggregates accept a FILTER clause.

The built-in window functions are described in Table 9-53. Other window functions can be added by the user. Also, any built-in or user-defined normal aggregate function can be used as a window function. Ordered-set aggregates presently cannot be used as window functions, however.

The syntaxes using * are used for calling parameter-less aggregate functions as window functions, for example count(*) OVER (PARTITION BY x ORDER BY y). The asterisk (*) is customarily not used for non-aggregate window functions. Aggregate window functions, unlike normal aggregate functions, do not allow `DISTINCT` or `ORDER BY` to be used within the function argument list.

Window function calls are permitted only in the `SELECT` list and the `ORDER BY` clause of the query.

More information about window functions can be found in Section 3.5, Section 9.21, and Section 7.2.4.

4.2.9. Type Casts

A type cast specifies a conversion from one data type to another. PostgreSQL accepts two equivalent syntaxes for type casts:

```
CAST ( expression AS type )
expression::type
```

The `CAST` syntax conforms to SQL; the syntax with `::` is historical PostgreSQL usage.

When a cast is applied to a value expression of a known type, it represents a run-time type conversion. The cast will succeed only if a suitable type conversion operation has been defined. Notice that this is subtly different from the use of casts with constants, as shown in Section 4.1.2.7. A cast applied to an unadorned string literal represents the initial assignment of a type to a literal constant value, and so it will succeed for any type (if the contents of the string literal are acceptable input syntax for the data type).

An explicit type cast can usually be omitted if there is no ambiguity as to the type that a value expression must produce (for example, when it is assigned to a table column); the system will automatically apply a type cast in such cases. However, automatic casting is only done for casts that are marked "OK to apply implicitly" in the system catalogs. Other casts must be invoked with explicit casting syntax. This restriction is intended to prevent surprising conversions from being applied silently.

It is also possible to specify a type cast using a function-like syntax:

```
typename ( expression )
```

However, this only works for types whose names are also valid as function names. For example, `double precision` cannot be used this way, but the equivalent `float8` can. Also, the names `interval`, `time`, and `timestamp` can only be used in this fashion if they are double-quoted, because of syntactic conflicts. Therefore, the use of the function-like cast syntax leads to inconsistencies and should probably be avoided.

> **Note:** The function-like syntax is in fact just a function call. When one of the two standard cast syntaxes is used to do a run-time conversion, it will internally invoke a registered function to perform the conversion. By convention, these conversion functions have the same name as their output type, and thus the "function-like syntax" is nothing more than a direct invocation of the underlying conversion function. Obviously, this is not something that a portable application should rely on. For further details see CREATE CAST.

4.2.10. Collation Expressions

The COLLATE clause overrides the collation of an expression. It is appended to the expression it applies to:

```
expr COLLATE collation
```

where `collation` is a possibly schema-qualified identifier. The COLLATE clause binds tighter than operators; parentheses can be used when necessary.

If no collation is explicitly specified, the database system either derives a collation from the columns involved in the expression, or it defaults to the default collation of the database if no column is involved in the expression.

The two common uses of the COLLATE clause are overriding the sort order in an ORDER BY clause, for example:

```
SELECT a, b, c FROM tbl WHERE ... ORDER BY a COLLATE "C";
```

and overriding the collation of a function or operator call that has locale-sensitive results, for example:

```
SELECT * FROM tbl WHERE a > 'foo' COLLATE "C";
```

Note that in the latter case the COLLATE clause is attached to an input argument of the operator we wish to affect. It doesn't matter which argument of the operator or function call the COLLATE clause is attached to, because the collation that is applied by the operator or function is derived by considering all arguments, and an explicit COLLATE clause will override the collations of all other arguments. (Attaching non-matching COLLATE clauses to more than one argument, however, is an error. For more details see Section 22.2.) Thus, this gives the same result as the previous example:

```
SELECT * FROM tbl WHERE a COLLATE "C" > 'foo';
```

But this is an error:

```
SELECT * FROM tbl WHERE (a > 'foo') COLLATE "C";
```

because it attempts to apply a collation to the result of the > operator, which is of the non-collatable data type `boolean`.

4.2.11. Scalar Subqueries

A scalar subquery is an ordinary SELECT query in parentheses that returns exactly one row with one column. (See Chapter 7 for information about writing queries.) The SELECT query is executed and the single returned value is used in the surrounding value expression. It is an error to use a query that returns more than one row or more than one column as a scalar subquery. (But if, during a particular execution, the subquery returns no rows, there is no error; the scalar result is taken to be null.) The subquery can refer to variables from the surrounding query, which will act as constants during any one evaluation of the subquery. See also Section 9.22 for other expressions involving subqueries.

For example, the following finds the largest city population in each state:

```
SELECT name, (SELECT max(pop) FROM cities WHERE cities.state = states.name)
```

```
FROM states;
```

4.2.12. Array Constructors

An array constructor is an expression that builds an array value using values for its member elements. A simple array constructor consists of the key word ARRAY, a left square bracket [, a list of expressions (separated by commas) for the array element values, and finally a right square bracket]. For example:

```
SELECT ARRAY[1,2,3+4];
  array
---------
 {1,2,7}
(1 row)
```

By default, the array element type is the common type of the member expressions, determined using the same rules as for UNION or CASE constructs (see Section 10.5). You can override this by explicitly casting the array constructor to the desired type, for example:

```
SELECT ARRAY[1,2,22.7]::integer[];
  array
----------
 {1,2,23}
(1 row)
```

This has the same effect as casting each expression to the array element type individually. For more on casting, see Section 4.2.9.

Multidimensional array values can be built by nesting array constructors. In the inner constructors, the key word ARRAY can be omitted. For example, these produce the same result:

```
SELECT ARRAY[ARRAY[1,2], ARRAY[3,4]];
     array
---------------
 {{1,2},{3,4}}
(1 row)

SELECT ARRAY[[1,2],[3,4]];
     array
---------------
 {{1,2},{3,4}}
(1 row)
```

Since multidimensional arrays must be rectangular, inner constructors at the same level must produce sub-arrays of identical dimensions. Any cast applied to the outer ARRAY constructor propagates automatically to all the inner constructors.

Multidimensional array constructor elements can be anything yielding an array of the proper kind, not only a sub-ARRAY construct. For example:

```
CREATE TABLE arr(f1 int[], f2 int[]);
```

```
INSERT INTO arr VALUES (ARRAY[[1,2],[3,4]], ARRAY[[5,6],[7,8]]);

SELECT ARRAY[f1, f2, '{{9,10},{11,12}}'::int[]] FROM arr;
                    array
---------------------------------------------------
 {{{1,2},{3,4}},{{5,6},{7,8}},{{9,10},{11,12}}}
(1 row)
```

You can construct an empty array, but since it's impossible to have an array with no type, you must explicitly cast your empty array to the desired type. For example:

```
SELECT ARRAY[]::integer[];
 array
-------
 {}
(1 row)
```

It is also possible to construct an array from the results of a subquery. In this form, the array constructor is written with the key word ARRAY followed by a parenthesized (not bracketed) subquery. For example:

```
SELECT ARRAY(SELECT oid FROM pg_proc WHERE proname LIKE 'bytea%');
                                array
----------------------------------------------------------------------
 {2011,1954,1948,1952,1951,1244,1950,2005,1949,1953,2006,31,2412,2413}
(1 row)
```

The subquery must return a single column. The resulting one-dimensional array will have an element for each row in the subquery result, with an element type matching that of the subquery's output column.

The subscripts of an array value built with ARRAY always begin with one. For more information about arrays, see Section 8.15.

4.2.13. Row Constructors

A row constructor is an expression that builds a row value (also called a composite value) using values for its member fields. A row constructor consists of the key word ROW, a left parenthesis, zero or more expressions (separated by commas) for the row field values, and finally a right parenthesis. For example:

```
SELECT ROW(1,2.5,'this is a test');
```

The key word ROW is optional when there is more than one expression in the list.

A row constructor can include the syntax *rowvalue.**, which will be expanded to a list of the elements of the row value, just as occurs when the .* syntax is used at the top level of a SELECT list. For example, if table t has columns f1 and f2, these are the same:

```
SELECT ROW(t.*, 42) FROM t;
SELECT ROW(t.f1, t.f2, 42) FROM t;
```

Note: Before PostgreSQL 8.2, the `.*` syntax was not expanded, so that writing `ROW(t.*, 42)` created a two-field row whose first field was another row value. The new behavior is usually more useful. If you need the old behavior of nested row values, write the inner row value without `.*`, for instance `ROW(t, 42)`.

By default, the value created by a `ROW` expression is of an anonymous record type. If necessary, it can be cast to a named composite type — either the row type of a table, or a composite type created with `CREATE TYPE AS`. An explicit cast might be needed to avoid ambiguity. For example:

```
CREATE TABLE mytable(f1 int, f2 float, f3 text);

CREATE FUNCTION getf1(mytable) RETURNS int AS 'SELECT $1.f1' LANGUAGE SQL;

-- No cast needed since only one getf1() exists
SELECT getf1(ROW(1,2.5,'this is a test'));
 getf1
-------
     1
(1 row)

CREATE TYPE myrowtype AS (f1 int, f2 text, f3 numeric);

CREATE FUNCTION getf1(myrowtype) RETURNS int AS 'SELECT $1.f1' LANGUAGE SQL;

-- Now we need a cast to indicate which function to call:
SELECT getf1(ROW(1,2.5,'this is a test'));
ERROR:  function getf1(record) is not unique

SELECT getf1(ROW(1,2.5,'this is a test')::mytable);
 getf1
-------
     1
(1 row)

SELECT getf1(CAST(ROW(11,'this is a test',2.5) AS myrowtype));
 getf1
-------
    11
(1 row)
```

Row constructors can be used to build composite values to be stored in a composite-type table column, or to be passed to a function that accepts a composite parameter. Also, it is possible to compare two row values or test a row with `IS NULL` or `IS NOT NULL`, for example:

```
SELECT ROW(1,2.5,'this is a test') = ROW(1, 3, 'not the same');

SELECT ROW(table.*) IS NULL FROM table;  -- detect all-null rows
```

For more detail see Section 9.23. Row constructors can also be used in connection with subqueries, as discussed in Section 9.22.

4.2.14. Expression Evaluation Rules

The order of evaluation of subexpressions is not defined. In particular, the inputs of an operator or function are not necessarily evaluated left-to-right or in any other fixed order.

Furthermore, if the result of an expression can be determined by evaluating only some parts of it, then other subexpressions might not be evaluated at all. For instance, if one wrote:

```
SELECT true OR somefunc();
```

then `somefunc()` would (probably) not be called at all. The same would be the case if one wrote:

```
SELECT somefunc() OR true;
```

Note that this is not the same as the left-to-right "short-circuiting" of Boolean operators that is found in some programming languages.

As a consequence, it is unwise to use functions with side effects as part of complex expressions. It is particularly dangerous to rely on side effects or evaluation order in `WHERE` and `HAVING` clauses, since those clauses are extensively reprocessed as part of developing an execution plan. Boolean expressions (`AND`/`OR`/`NOT` combinations) in those clauses can be reorganized in any manner allowed by the laws of Boolean algebra.

When it is essential to force evaluation order, a `CASE` construct (see Section 9.17) can be used. For example, this is an untrustworthy way of trying to avoid division by zero in a `WHERE` clause:

```
SELECT ... WHERE x > 0 AND y/x > 1.5;
```

But this is safe:

```
SELECT ... WHERE CASE WHEN x > 0 THEN y/x > 1.5 ELSE false END;
```

A `CASE` construct used in this fashion will defeat optimization attempts, so it should only be done when necessary. (In this particular example, it would be better to sidestep the problem by writing `y > 1.5*x` instead.)

`CASE` is not a cure-all for such issues, however. One limitation of the technique illustrated above is that it does not prevent early evaluation of constant subexpressions. As described in Section 35.6, functions and operators marked `IMMUTABLE` can be evaluated when the query is planned rather than when it is executed. Thus for example

```
SELECT CASE WHEN x > 0 THEN x ELSE 1/0 END FROM tab;
```

is likely to result in a division-by-zero failure due to the planner trying to simplify the constant subexpression, even if every row in the table has `x > 0` so that the `ELSE` arm would never be entered at run time.

While that particular example might seem silly, related cases that don't obviously involve constants can occur in queries executed within functions, since the values of function arguments and local variables can be inserted into queries as constants for planning purposes. Within PL/pgSQL functions, for example, using an `IF-THEN-ELSE` statement to protect a risky computation is much safer than just nesting it in a `CASE` expression.

Another limitation of the same kind is that a `CASE` cannot prevent evaluation of an aggregate expression contained within it, because aggregate expressions are computed before other expressions in a `SELECT` list or `HAVING` clause are considered. For example, the following query can cause a division-by-zero error despite seemingly having protected against it:

```
SELECT CASE WHEN min(employees) > 0
            THEN avg(expenses / employees)
       END
    FROM departments;
```

The `min()` and `avg()` aggregates are computed concurrently over all the input rows, so if any row has `employees` equal to zero, the division-by-zero error will occur before there is any opportunity to test the result of `min()`. Instead, use a `WHERE` or `FILTER` clause to prevent problematic input rows from reaching an aggregate function in the first place.

4.3. Calling Functions

PostgreSQL allows functions that have named parameters to be called using either *positional* or *named* notation. Named notation is especially useful for functions that have a large number of parameters, since it makes the associations between parameters and actual arguments more explicit and reliable. In positional notation, a function call is written with its argument values in the same order as they are defined in the function declaration. In named notation, the arguments are matched to the function parameters by name and can be written in any order.

In either notation, parameters that have default values given in the function declaration need not be written in the call at all. But this is particularly useful in named notation, since any combination of parameters can be omitted; while in positional notation parameters can only be omitted from right to left.

PostgreSQL also supports *mixed* notation, which combines positional and named notation. In this case, positional parameters are written first and named parameters appear after them.

The following examples will illustrate the usage of all three notations, using the following function definition:

```
CREATE FUNCTION concat_lower_or_upper(a text, b text, uppercase boolean DEFAULT
RETURNS text
AS
$$
  SELECT CASE
        WHEN $3 THEN UPPER($1 || ' ' || $2)
        ELSE LOWER($1 || ' ' || $2)
        END;
$$
LANGUAGE SQL IMMUTABLE STRICT;
```

Function `concat_lower_or_upper` has two mandatory parameters, `a` and `b`. Additionally there is one optional parameter `uppercase` which defaults to `false`. The `a` and `b` inputs will be concatenated, and forced to either upper or lower case depending on the `uppercase` parameter. The remaining details of this function definition are not important here (see Chapter 35 for more information).

4.3.1. Using Positional Notation

Positional notation is the traditional mechanism for passing arguments to functions in PostgreSQL. An example is:

```
SELECT concat_lower_or_upper('Hello', 'World', true);
 concat_lower_or_upper
----------------------
 HELLO WORLD
(1 row)
```

All arguments are specified in order. The result is upper case since `uppercase` is specified as `true`. Another example is:

```
SELECT concat_lower_or_upper('Hello', 'World');
 concat_lower_or_upper
----------------------
 hello world
(1 row)
```

Here, the `uppercase` parameter is omitted, so it receives its default value of `false`, resulting in lower case output. In positional notation, arguments can be omitted from right to left so long as they have defaults.

4.3.2. Using Named Notation

In named notation, each argument's name is specified using `:=` to separate it from the argument expression. For example:

```
SELECT concat_lower_or_upper(a := 'Hello', b := 'World');
 concat_lower_or_upper
----------------------
 hello world
(1 row)
```

Again, the argument `uppercase` was omitted so it is set to `false` implicitly. One advantage of using named notation is that the arguments may be specified in any order, for example:

```
SELECT concat_lower_or_upper(a := 'Hello', b := 'World', uppercase := true);
 concat_lower_or_upper
----------------------
 HELLO WORLD
(1 row)

SELECT concat_lower_or_upper(a := 'Hello', uppercase := true, b := 'World');
 concat_lower_or_upper
----------------------
```

```
HELLO WORLD
(1 row)
```

4.3.3. Using Mixed Notation

The mixed notation combines positional and named notation. However, as already mentioned, named arguments cannot precede positional arguments. For example:

```
SELECT concat_lower_or_upper('Hello', 'World', uppercase := true);
 concat_lower_or_upper
-----------------------
 HELLO WORLD
(1 row)
```

In the above query, the arguments a and b are specified positionally, while uppercase is specified by name. In this example, that adds little except documentation. With a more complex function having numerous parameters that have default values, named or mixed notation can save a great deal of writing and reduce chances for error.

> **Note:** Named and mixed call notations currently cannot be used when calling an aggregate function (but they do work when an aggregate function is used as a window function).

Chapter 5. Data Definition

This chapter covers how one creates the database structures that will hold one's data. In a relational database, the raw data is stored in tables, so the majority of this chapter is devoted to explaining how tables are created and modified and what features are available to control what data is stored in the tables. Subsequently, we discuss how tables can be organized into schemas, and how privileges can be assigned to tables. Finally, we will briefly look at other features that affect the data storage, such as inheritance, views, functions, and triggers.

5.1. Table Basics

A table in a relational database is much like a table on paper: It consists of rows and columns. The number and order of the columns is fixed, and each column has a name. The number of rows is variable — it reflects how much data is stored at a given moment. SQL does not make any guarantees about the order of the rows in a table. When a table is read, the rows will appear in an unspecified order, unless sorting is explicitly requested. This is covered in Chapter 7. Furthermore, SQL does not assign unique identifiers to rows, so it is possible to have several completely identical rows in a table. This is a consequence of the mathematical model that underlies SQL but is usually not desirable. Later in this chapter we will see how to deal with this issue.

Each column has a data type. The data type constrains the set of possible values that can be assigned to a column and assigns semantics to the data stored in the column so that it can be used for computations. For instance, a column declared to be of a numerical type will not accept arbitrary text strings, and the data stored in such a column can be used for mathematical computations. By contrast, a column declared to be of a character string type will accept almost any kind of data but it does not lend itself to mathematical calculations, although other operations such as string concatenation are available.

PostgreSQL includes a sizable set of built-in data types that fit many applications. Users can also define their own data types. Most built-in data types have obvious names and semantics, so we defer a detailed explanation to Chapter 8. Some of the frequently used data types are `integer` for whole numbers, `numeric` for possibly fractional numbers, `text` for character strings, `date` for dates, `time` for time-of-day values, and `timestamp` for values containing both date and time.

To create a table, you use the aptly named CREATE TABLE command. In this command you specify at least a name for the new table, the names of the columns and the data type of each column. For example:

```
CREATE TABLE my_first_table (
    first_column text,
    second_column integer
);
```

This creates a table named `my_first_table` with two columns. The first column is named `first_column` and has a data type of `text`; the second column has the name `second_column` and the type `integer`. The table and column names follow the identifier syntax explained in Section 4.1.1. The type names are usually also identifiers, but there are some exceptions. Note that the column list is comma-separated and surrounded by parentheses.

Of course, the previous example was heavily contrived. Normally, you would give names to your tables and columns that convey what kind of data they store. So let's look at a more realistic example:

```
CREATE TABLE products (
    product_no integer,
    name text,
    price numeric
);
```

(The `numeric` type can store fractional components, as would be typical of monetary amounts.)

> **Tip:** When you create many interrelated tables it is wise to choose a consistent naming pattern for the tables and columns. For instance, there is a choice of using singular or plural nouns for table names, both of which are favored by some theorist or other.

There is a limit on how many columns a table can contain. Depending on the column types, it is between 250 and 1600. However, defining a table with anywhere near this many columns is highly unusual and often a questionable design.

If you no longer need a table, you can remove it using the DROP TABLE command. For example:

```
DROP TABLE my_first_table;
DROP TABLE products;
```

Attempting to drop a table that does not exist is an error. Nevertheless, it is common in SQL script files to unconditionally try to drop each table before creating it, ignoring any error messages, so that the script works whether or not the table exists. (If you like, you can use the DROP TABLE IF EXISTS variant to avoid the error messages, but this is not standard SQL.)

If you need to modify a table that already exists, see Section 5.5 later in this chapter.

With the tools discussed so far you can create fully functional tables. The remainder of this chapter is concerned with adding features to the table definition to ensure data integrity, security, or convenience. If you are eager to fill your tables with data now you can skip ahead to Chapter 6 and read the rest of this chapter later.

5.2. Default Values

A column can be assigned a default value. When a new row is created and no values are specified for some of the columns, those columns will be filled with their respective default values. A data manipulation command can also request explicitly that a column be set to its default value, without having to know what that value is. (Details about data manipulation commands are in Chapter 6.)

If no default value is declared explicitly, the default value is the null value. This usually makes sense because a null value can be considered to represent unknown data.

In a table definition, default values are listed after the column data type. For example:

```
CREATE TABLE products (
    product_no integer,
    name text,
    price numeric DEFAULT 9.99
);
```

The default value can be an expression, which will be evaluated whenever the default value is inserted (*not* when the table is created). A common example is for a `timestamp` column to have a default of `CURRENT_TIMESTAMP`, so that it gets set to the time of row insertion. Another common example is generating a "serial number" for each row. In PostgreSQL this is typically done by something like:

```
CREATE TABLE products (
    product_no integer DEFAULT nextval('products_product_no_seq'),
    ...
);
```

where the `nextval()` function supplies successive values from a *sequence object* (see Section 9.16). This arrangement is sufficiently common that there's a special shorthand for it:

```
CREATE TABLE products (
    product_no SERIAL,
    ...
);
```

The `SERIAL` shorthand is discussed further in Section 8.1.4.

5.3. Constraints

Data types are a way to limit the kind of data that can be stored in a table. For many applications, however, the constraint they provide is too coarse. For example, a column containing a product price should probably only accept positive values. But there is no standard data type that accepts only positive numbers. Another issue is that you might want to constrain column data with respect to other columns or rows. For example, in a table containing product information, there should be only one row for each product number.

To that end, SQL allows you to define constraints on columns and tables. Constraints give you as much control over the data in your tables as you wish. If a user attempts to store data in a column that would violate a constraint, an error is raised. This applies even if the value came from the default value definition.

5.3.1. Check Constraints

A check constraint is the most generic constraint type. It allows you to specify that the value in a certain column must satisfy a Boolean (truth-value) expression. For instance, to require positive product prices, you could use:

```
CREATE TABLE products (
    product_no integer,
    name text,
    price numeric CHECK (price > 0)
);
```

As you see, the constraint definition comes after the data type, just like default value definitions. Default values and constraints can be listed in any order. A check constraint consists of the key word CHECK followed by an expression in parentheses. The check constraint expression should involve the column thus constrained, otherwise the constraint would not make too much sense.

You can also give the constraint a separate name. This clarifies error messages and allows you to refer to the constraint when you need to change it. The syntax is:

```
CREATE TABLE products (
    product_no integer,
    name text,
    price numeric CONSTRAINT positive_price CHECK (price > 0)
);
```

So, to specify a named constraint, use the key word CONSTRAINT followed by an identifier followed by the constraint definition. (If you don't specify a constraint name in this way, the system chooses a name for you.)

A check constraint can also refer to several columns. Say you store a regular price and a discounted price, and you want to ensure that the discounted price is lower than the regular price:

```
CREATE TABLE products (
    product_no integer,
    name text,
    price numeric CHECK (price > 0),
    discounted_price numeric CHECK (discounted_price > 0),
    CHECK (price > discounted_price)
);
```

The first two constraints should look familiar. The third one uses a new syntax. It is not attached to a particular column, instead it appears as a separate item in the comma-separated column list. Column definitions and these constraint definitions can be listed in mixed order.

We say that the first two constraints are column constraints, whereas the third one is a table constraint because it is written separately from any one column definition. Column constraints can also be written as table constraints, while the reverse is not necessarily possible, since a column constraint is supposed to refer to only the column it is attached to. (PostgreSQL doesn't enforce that rule, but you should follow it if you want your table definitions to work with other database systems.) The above example could also be written as:

```
CREATE TABLE products (
    product_no integer,
    name text,
    price numeric,
    CHECK (price > 0),
    discounted_price numeric,
    CHECK (discounted_price > 0),
    CHECK (price > discounted_price)
);
```

or even:

```
CREATE TABLE products (
    product_no integer,
    name text,
    price numeric CHECK (price > 0),
    discounted_price numeric,
    CHECK (discounted_price > 0 AND price > discounted_price)
);
```

It's a matter of taste.

Names can be assigned to table constraints in the same way as column constraints:

```
CREATE TABLE products (
    product_no integer,
    name text,
    price numeric,
    CHECK (price > 0),
    discounted_price numeric,
    CHECK (discounted_price > 0),
    CONSTRAINT valid_discount CHECK (price > discounted_price)
);
```

It should be noted that a check constraint is satisfied if the check expression evaluates to true or the null value. Since most expressions will evaluate to the null value if any operand is null, they will not prevent null values in the constrained columns. To ensure that a column does not contain null values, the not-null constraint described in the next section can be used.

5.3.2. Not-Null Constraints

A not-null constraint simply specifies that a column must not assume the null value. A syntax example:

```
CREATE TABLE products (
    product_no integer NOT NULL,
    name text NOT NULL,
    price numeric
);
```

A not-null constraint is always written as a column constraint. A not-null constraint is functionally equivalent to creating a check constraint CHECK (*column_name* IS NOT NULL), but in PostgreSQL creating an explicit not-null constraint is more efficient. The drawback is that you cannot give explicit names to not-null constraints created this way.

Of course, a column can have more than one constraint. Just write the constraints one after another:

```
CREATE TABLE products (
    product_no integer NOT NULL,
    name text NOT NULL,
    price numeric NOT NULL CHECK (price > 0)
);
```

The order doesn't matter. It does not necessarily determine in which order the constraints are checked.

The NOT NULL constraint has an inverse: the NULL constraint. This does not mean that the column must be null, which would surely be useless. Instead, this simply selects the default behavior that the column might be null. The NULL constraint is not present in the SQL standard and should not be used in portable applications. (It was only added to PostgreSQL to be compatible with some other database systems.) Some users, however, like it because it makes it easy to toggle the constraint in a script file. For example, you could start with:

```
CREATE TABLE products (
    product_no integer NULL,
    name text NULL,
    price numeric NULL
);
```

and then insert the NOT key word where desired.

Tip: In most database designs the majority of columns should be marked not null.

5.3.3. Unique Constraints

Unique constraints ensure that the data contained in a column or a group of columns is unique with respect to all the rows in the table. The syntax is:

```
CREATE TABLE products (
    product_no integer UNIQUE,
    name text,
    price numeric
);
```

when written as a column constraint, and:

```
CREATE TABLE products (
    product_no integer,
    name text,
    price numeric,
    UNIQUE (product_no)
);
```

when written as a table constraint.

If a unique constraint refers to a group of columns, the columns are listed separated by commas:

```
CREATE TABLE example (
    a integer,
    b integer,
    c integer,
    UNIQUE (a, c)
);
```

This specifies that the combination of values in the indicated columns is unique across the whole table, though any one of the columns need not be (and ordinarily isn't) unique.

You can assign your own name for a unique constraint, in the usual way:

```
CREATE TABLE products (
    product_no integer CONSTRAINT must_be_different UNIQUE,
    name text,
    price numeric
);
```

Adding a unique constraint will automatically create a unique btree index on the column or group of columns used in the constraint. A uniqueness constraint on only some rows can be enforced by creating a partial index.

In general, a unique constraint is violated when there is more than one row in the table where the values of all of the columns included in the constraint are equal. However, two null values are not considered equal in this comparison. That means even in the presence of a unique constraint it is possible to store duplicate rows that contain a null value in at least one of the constrained columns. This behavior conforms to the SQL standard, but we have heard that other SQL databases might not follow this rule. So be careful when developing applications that are intended to be portable.

5.3.4. Primary Keys

Technically, a primary key constraint is simply a combination of a unique constraint and a not-null constraint. So, the following two table definitions accept the same data:

```
CREATE TABLE products (
    product_no integer UNIQUE NOT NULL,
    name text,
    price numeric
);

CREATE TABLE products (
    product_no integer PRIMARY KEY,
    name text,
    price numeric
);
```

Primary keys can also constrain more than one column; the syntax is similar to unique constraints:

```
CREATE TABLE example (
    a integer,
    b integer,
    c integer,
    PRIMARY KEY (a, c)
);
```

A primary key indicates that a column or group of columns can be used as a unique identifier for rows in the table. (This is a direct consequence of the definition of a primary key. Note that a unique constraint does not, by itself, provide a unique identifier because it does not exclude null values.) This is useful both for documentation purposes and for client applications. For example, a GUI application that allows modifying row values probably needs to know the primary key of a table to be able to identify rows uniquely.

Adding a primary key will automatically create a unique btree index on the column or group of columns used in the primary key.

A table can have at most one primary key. (There can be any number of unique and not-null constraints, which are functionally the same thing, but only one can be identified as the primary key.) Relational database theory dictates that every table must have a primary key. This rule is not enforced by PostgreSQL, but it is usually best to follow it.

5.3.5. Foreign Keys

A foreign key constraint specifies that the values in a column (or a group of columns) must match the values appearing in some row of another table. We say this maintains the *referential integrity* between two related tables.

Say you have the product table that we have used several times already:

```
CREATE TABLE products (
    product_no integer PRIMARY KEY,
    name text,
    price numeric
);
```

Let's also assume you have a table storing orders of those products. We want to ensure that the orders table only contains orders of products that actually exist. So we define a foreign key constraint in the orders table that references the products table:

```
CREATE TABLE orders (
    order_id integer PRIMARY KEY,
    product_no integer REFERENCES products (product_no),
    quantity integer
);
```

Now it is impossible to create orders with non-NULL product_no entries that do not appear in the products table.

We say that in this situation the orders table is the *referencing* table and the products table is the *referenced* table. Similarly, there are referencing and referenced columns.

You can also shorten the above command to:

```
CREATE TABLE orders (
    order_id integer PRIMARY KEY,
    product_no integer REFERENCES products,
    quantity integer
);
```

because in absence of a column list the primary key of the referenced table is used as the referenced column(s).

A foreign key can also constrain and reference a group of columns. As usual, it then needs to be written in table constraint form. Here is a contrived syntax example:

```
CREATE TABLE t1 (
  a integer PRIMARY KEY,
  b integer,
  c integer,
  FOREIGN KEY (b, c) REFERENCES other_table (c1, c2)
);
```

Of course, the number and type of the constrained columns need to match the number and type of the referenced columns.

You can assign your own name for a foreign key constraint, in the usual way.

A table can have more than one foreign key constraint. This is used to implement many-to-many relationships between tables. Say you have tables about products and orders, but now you want to allow one order to contain possibly many products (which the structure above did not allow). You could use this table structure:

```
CREATE TABLE products (
    product_no integer PRIMARY KEY,
    name text,
    price numeric
);

CREATE TABLE orders (
    order_id integer PRIMARY KEY,
    shipping_address text,
    ...
);

CREATE TABLE order_items (
    product_no integer REFERENCES products,
    order_id integer REFERENCES orders,
    quantity integer,
    PRIMARY KEY (product_no, order_id)
);
```

Notice that the primary key overlaps with the foreign keys in the last table.

We know that the foreign keys disallow creation of orders that do not relate to any products. But what if a product is removed after an order is created that references it? SQL allows you to handle that as well. Intuitively, we have a few options:

- Disallow deleting a referenced product
- Delete the orders as well
- Something else?

To illustrate this, let's implement the following policy on the many-to-many relationship example above: when someone wants to remove a product that is still referenced by an order (via order_items), we disallow it. If someone removes an order, the order items are removed as well:

```
CREATE TABLE products (
    product_no integer PRIMARY KEY,
    name text,
    price numeric
);

CREATE TABLE orders (
    order_id integer PRIMARY KEY,
    shipping_address text,
    ...
);

CREATE TABLE order_items (
    product_no integer REFERENCES products ON DELETE RESTRICT,
    order_id integer REFERENCES orders ON DELETE CASCADE,
    quantity integer,
    PRIMARY KEY (product_no, order_id)
);
```

Restricting and cascading deletes are the two most common options. RESTRICT prevents deletion of a referenced row. NO ACTION means that if any referencing rows still exist when the constraint is checked, an error is raised; this is the default behavior if you do not specify anything. (The essential difference between these two choices is that NO ACTION allows the check to be deferred until later in the transaction, whereas RESTRICT does not.) CASCADE specifies that when a referenced row is deleted, row(s) referencing it should be automatically deleted as well. There are two other options: SET NULL and SET DEFAULT. These cause the referencing column(s) in the referencing row(s) to be set to nulls or their default values, respectively, when the referenced row is deleted. Note that these do not excuse you from observing any constraints. For example, if an action specifies SET DEFAULT but the default value would not satisfy the foreign key constraint, the operation will fail.

Analogous to ON DELETE there is also ON UPDATE which is invoked when a referenced column is changed (updated). The possible actions are the same. In this case, CASCADE means that the updated values of the referenced column(s) should be copied into the referencing row(s).

Normally, a referencing row need not satisfy the foreign key constraint if any of its referencing columns are null. If MATCH FULL is added to the foreign key declaration, a referencing row escapes satisfying the constraint only if all its referencing columns are null (so a mix of null and non-null values is guaranteed to fail a MATCH FULL constraint). If you don't want referencing rows to be able to avoid satisfying the foreign key constraint, declare the referencing column(s) as NOT NULL.

A foreign key must reference columns that either are a primary key or form a unique constraint. This means that the referenced columns always have an index (the one underlying the primary key or unique constraint); so checks on whether a referencing row has a match will be efficient. Since a DELETE of a row from the referenced table or an UPDATE of a referenced column will require a scan of the referencing table for rows matching the old value, it is often a good idea to index the referencing columns too. Because this is not always needed, and there are many choices available on how to index, declaration of a foreign key constraint does not automatically create an index on the referencing columns.

More information about updating and deleting data is in Chapter 6. Also see the description of foreign key constraint syntax in the reference documentation for CREATE TABLE.

5.3.6. Exclusion Constraints

Exclusion constraints ensure that if any two rows are compared on the specified columns or expressions using the specified operators, at least one of these operator comparisons will return false or null. The syntax is:

```
CREATE TABLE circles (
    c circle,
    EXCLUDE USING gist (c WITH &&)
);
```

See also CREATE TABLE ... CONSTRAINT ... EXCLUDE for details.

Adding an exclusion constraint will automatically create an index of the type specified in the constraint declaration.

5.4. System Columns

Every table has several *system columns* that are implicitly defined by the system. Therefore, these names cannot be used as names of user-defined columns. (Note that these restrictions are separate from whether the name is a key word or not; quoting a name will not allow you to escape these restrictions.) You do not really need to be concerned about these columns; just know they exist.

oid

> The object identifier (object ID) of a row. This column is only present if the table was created using WITH OIDS, or if the default_with_oids configuration variable was set at the time. This column is of type oid (same name as the column); see Section 8.18 for more information about the type.

tableoid

> The OID of the table containing this row. This column is particularly handy for queries that select from inheritance hierarchies (see Section 5.8), since without it, it's difficult to tell which individual table a row came from. The tableoid can be joined against the oid column of pg_class to obtain the table name.

xmin

> The identity (transaction ID) of the inserting transaction for this row version. (A row version is an individual state of a row; each update of a row creates a new row version for the same logical row.)

cmin

> The command identifier (starting at zero) within the inserting transaction.

xmax

> The identity (transaction ID) of the deleting transaction, or zero for an undeleted row version. It is possible for this column to be nonzero in a visible row version. That usually indicates that the deleting transaction hasn't committed yet, or that an attempted deletion was rolled back.

cmax

> The command identifier within the deleting transaction, or zero.

ctid

> The physical location of the row version within its table. Note that although the ctid can be used to locate the row version very quickly, a row's ctid will change if it is updated or moved by VACUUM FULL. Therefore ctid is useless as a long-term row identifier. The OID, or even better a user-defined serial number, should be used to identify logical rows.

OIDs are 32-bit quantities and are assigned from a single cluster-wide counter. In a large or long-lived database, it is possible for the counter to wrap around. Hence, it is bad practice to assume that OIDs are unique, unless you take steps to ensure that this is the case. If you need to identify the rows in a table, using a sequence generator is strongly recommended. However, OIDs can be used as well, provided that a few additional precautions are taken:

- A unique constraint should be created on the OID column of each table for which the OID will be used to identify rows. When such a unique constraint (or unique index) exists, the system takes care not to generate an OID matching an already-existing row. (Of course, this is only possible if the table contains fewer than 2^{32} (4 billion) rows, and in practice the table size had better be much less than that, or performance might suffer.)

- OIDs should never be assumed to be unique across tables; use the combination of tableoid and row OID if you need a database-wide identifier.

- Of course, the tables in question must be created WITH OIDS. As of PostgreSQL 8.1, WITHOUT OIDS is the default.

Transaction identifiers are also 32-bit quantities. In a long-lived database it is possible for transaction IDs to wrap around. This is not a fatal problem given appropriate maintenance procedures; see Chapter 23 for details. It is unwise, however, to depend on the uniqueness of transaction IDs over the long term (more than one billion transactions).

Command identifiers are also 32-bit quantities. This creates a hard limit of 2^{32} (4 billion) SQL commands within a single transaction. In practice this limit is not a problem — note that the limit is on the number of SQL commands, not the number of rows processed. Also, only commands that actually modify the database contents will consume a command identifier.

5.5. Modifying Tables

When you create a table and you realize that you made a mistake, or the requirements of the application change, you can drop the table and create it again. But this is not a convenient option if the table is already filled with data, or if the table is referenced by other database objects (for instance a foreign key constraint). Therefore PostgreSQL provides a family of commands to make modifications to existing tables. Note that this is conceptually distinct from altering the data contained in the table: here we are interested in altering the definition, or structure, of the table.

You can:

- Add columns
- Remove columns
- Add constraints
- Remove constraints
- Change default values
- Change column data types
- Rename columns
- Rename tables

All these actions are performed using the ALTER TABLE command, whose reference page contains details beyond those given here.

5.5.1. Adding a Column

To add a column, use a command like:

```
ALTER TABLE products ADD COLUMN description text;
```

The new column is initially filled with whatever default value is given (null if you don't specify a DEFAULT clause).

You can also define constraints on the column at the same time, using the usual syntax:

```
ALTER TABLE products ADD COLUMN description text CHECK (description <> ");
```

In fact all the options that can be applied to a column description in CREATE TABLE can be used here. Keep in mind however that the default value must satisfy the given constraints, or the ADD will fail. Alternatively, you can add constraints later (see below) after you've filled in the new column correctly.

> **Tip:** Adding a column with a default requires updating each row of the table (to store the new column value). However, if no default is specified, PostgreSQL is able to avoid the physical update. So if you intend to fill the column with mostly nondefault values, it's best to add the column with no default, insert the correct values using UPDATE, and then add any desired default as described below.

5.5.2. Removing a Column

To remove a column, use a command like:

```
ALTER TABLE products DROP COLUMN description;
```

Whatever data was in the column disappears. Table constraints involving the column are dropped, too. However, if the column is referenced by a foreign key constraint of another table, PostgreSQL will not silently drop that constraint. You can authorize dropping everything that depends on the column by adding CASCADE:

```
ALTER TABLE products DROP COLUMN description CASCADE;
```

See Section 5.12 for a description of the general mechanism behind this.

5.5.3. Adding a Constraint

To add a constraint, the table constraint syntax is used. For example:

```
ALTER TABLE products ADD CHECK (name <> ");
ALTER TABLE products ADD CONSTRAINT some_name UNIQUE (product_no);
ALTER TABLE products ADD FOREIGN KEY (product_group_id) REFERENCES product_grou
```

To add a not-null constraint, which cannot be written as a table constraint, use this syntax:

```
ALTER TABLE products ALTER COLUMN product_no SET NOT NULL;
```

The constraint will be checked immediately, so the table data must satisfy the constraint before it can be added.

5.5.4. Removing a Constraint

To remove a constraint you need to know its name. If you gave it a name then that's easy. Otherwise the system assigned a generated name, which you need to find out. The psql command \d *tablename* can be helpful here; other interfaces might also provide a way to inspect table details. Then the command is:

```
ALTER TABLE products DROP CONSTRAINT some_name;
```

(If you are dealing with a generated constraint name like $2, don't forget that you'll need to double-quote it to make it a valid identifier.)

As with dropping a column, you need to add CASCADE if you want to drop a constraint that something else depends on. An example is that a foreign key constraint depends on a unique or primary key constraint on the referenced column(s).

This works the same for all constraint types except not-null constraints. To drop a not null constraint use:

```
ALTER TABLE products ALTER COLUMN product_no DROP NOT NULL;
```

(Recall that not-null constraints do not have names.)

5.5.5. Changing a Column's Default Value

To set a new default for a column, use a command like:

```
ALTER TABLE products ALTER COLUMN price SET DEFAULT 7.77;
```

Note that this doesn't affect any existing rows in the table, it just changes the default for future `INSERT` commands.

To remove any default value, use:

```
ALTER TABLE products ALTER COLUMN price DROP DEFAULT;
```

This is effectively the same as setting the default to null. As a consequence, it is not an error to drop a default where one hadn't been defined, because the default is implicitly the null value.

5.5.6. Changing a Column's Data Type

To convert a column to a different data type, use a command like:

```
ALTER TABLE products ALTER COLUMN price TYPE numeric(10,2);
```

This will succeed only if each existing entry in the column can be converted to the new type by an implicit cast. If a more complex conversion is needed, you can add a `USING` clause that specifies how to compute the new values from the old.

PostgreSQL will attempt to convert the column's default value (if any) to the new type, as well as any constraints that involve the column. But these conversions might fail, or might produce surprising results. It's often best to drop any constraints on the column before altering its type, and then add back suitably modified constraints afterwards.

5.5.7. Renaming a Column

To rename a column:

```
ALTER TABLE products RENAME COLUMN product_no TO product_number;
```

5.5.8. Renaming a Table

To rename a table:

```
ALTER TABLE products RENAME TO items;
```

5.6. Privileges

When an object is created, it is assigned an owner. The owner is normally the role that executed the creation statement. For most kinds of objects, the initial state is that only the owner (or a superuser) can do anything with the object. To allow other roles to use it, *privileges* must be granted.

There are different kinds of privileges: SELECT, INSERT, UPDATE, DELETE, TRUNCATE, REFERENCES, TRIGGER, CREATE, CONNECT, TEMPORARY, EXECUTE, and USAGE. The privileges applicable to a particular object vary depending on the object's type (table, function, etc). For complete information on the different types of privileges supported by PostgreSQL, refer to the GRANT reference page. The following sections and chapters will also show you how those privileges are used.

The right to modify or destroy an object is always the privilege of the owner only.

An object can be assigned to a new owner with an ALTER command of the appropriate kind for the object, e.g. ALTER TABLE. Superusers can always do this; ordinary roles can only do it if they are both the current owner of the object (or a member of the owning role) and a member of the new owning role.

To assign privileges, the GRANT command is used. For example, if joe is an existing user, and accounts is an existing table, the privilege to update the table can be granted with:

```
GRANT UPDATE ON accounts TO joe;
```

Writing ALL in place of a specific privilege grants all privileges that are relevant for the object type.

The special "user" name PUBLIC can be used to grant a privilege to every user on the system. Also, "group" roles can be set up to help manage privileges when there are many users of a database — for details see Chapter 20.

To revoke a privilege, use the fittingly named REVOKE command:

```
REVOKE ALL ON accounts FROM PUBLIC;
```

The special privileges of the object owner (i.e., the right to do DROP, GRANT, REVOKE, etc.) are always implicit in being the owner, and cannot be granted or revoked. But the object owner can choose to revoke his own ordinary privileges, for example to make a table read-only for himself as well as others.

Ordinarily, only the object's owner (or a superuser) can grant or revoke privileges on an object. However, it is possible to grant a privilege "with grant option", which gives the recipient the right to grant it in turn to others. If the grant option is subsequently revoked then all who received the privilege from that recipient (directly or through a chain of grants) will lose the privilege. For details see the GRANT and REVOKE reference pages.

5.7. Schemas

A PostgreSQL database cluster contains one or more named databases. Users and groups of users are shared across the entire cluster, but no other data is shared across databases. Any given client connection to the server can access only the data in a single database, the one specified in the connection request.

> **Note:** Users of a cluster do not necessarily have the privilege to access every database in the cluster. Sharing of user names means that there cannot be different users named, say, joe in two databases in the same cluster; but the system can be configured to allow joe access to only some of the databases.

A database contains one or more named *schemas*, which in turn contain tables. Schemas also contain other kinds of named objects, including data types, functions, and operators. The same object name can be used in different schemas without conflict; for example, both schema1 and myschema can contain tables named `mytable`. Unlike databases, schemas are not rigidly separated: a user can access objects in any of the schemas in the database he is connected to, if he has privileges to do so.

There are several reasons why one might want to use schemas:

- To allow many users to use one database without interfering with each other.
- To organize database objects into logical groups to make them more manageable.
- Third-party applications can be put into separate schemas so they do not collide with the names of other objects.

Schemas are analogous to directories at the operating system level, except that schemas cannot be nested.

5.7.1. Creating a Schema

To create a schema, use the CREATE SCHEMA command. Give the schema a name of your choice. For example:

```
CREATE SCHEMA myschema;
```

To create or access objects in a schema, write a *qualified name* consisting of the schema name and table name separated by a dot:

```
schema.table
```

This works anywhere a table name is expected, including the table modification commands and the data access commands discussed in the following chapters. (For brevity we will speak of tables only, but the same ideas apply to other kinds of named objects, such as types and functions.)

Actually, the even more general syntax

```
database.schema.table
```

can be used too, but at present this is just for *pro forma* compliance with the SQL standard. If you write a database name, it must be the same as the database you are connected to.

So to create a table in the new schema, use:

```
CREATE TABLE myschema.mytable (
  ...
);
```

To drop a schema if it's empty (all objects in it have been dropped), use:

```
DROP SCHEMA myschema;
```

To drop a schema including all contained objects, use:

```
DROP SCHEMA myschema CASCADE;
```

See Section 5.12 for a description of the general mechanism behind this.

Often you will want to create a schema owned by someone else (since this is one of the ways to restrict the activities of your users to well-defined namespaces). The syntax for that is:

```
CREATE SCHEMA schemaname AUTHORIZATION username;
```

You can even omit the schema name, in which case the schema name will be the same as the user name. See Section 5.7.6 for how this can be useful.

Schema names beginning with `pg_` are reserved for system purposes and cannot be created by users.

5.7.2. The Public Schema

In the previous sections we created tables without specifying any schema names. By default such tables (and other objects) are automatically put into a schema named "public". Every new database contains such a schema. Thus, the following are equivalent:

```
CREATE TABLE products ( ... );
```

and:

```
CREATE TABLE public.products ( ... );
```

5.7.3. The Schema Search Path

Qualified names are tedious to write, and it's often best not to wire a particular schema name into applications anyway. Therefore tables are often referred to by *unqualified names*, which consist of just the table name. The system determines which table is meant by following a *search path*, which is a list of schemas to look in. The first matching table in the search path is taken to be the one wanted. If there is no match in the search path, an error is reported, even if matching table names exist in other schemas in the database.

The first schema named in the search path is called the current schema. Aside from being the first schema searched, it is also the schema in which new tables will be created if the `CREATE TABLE` command does not specify a schema name.

To show the current search path, use the following command:

```
SHOW search_path;
```

In the default setup this returns:

```
 search_path
--------------
 "$user",public
```

The first element specifies that a schema with the same name as the current user is to be searched. If no such schema exists, the entry is ignored. The second element refers to the public schema that we have seen already.

The first schema in the search path that exists is the default location for creating new objects. That is the reason that by default objects are created in the public schema. When objects are referenced in any other context without schema qualification (table modification, data modification, or query commands) the search path is traversed until a matching object is found. Therefore, in the default configuration, any unqualified access again can only refer to the public schema.

To put our new schema in the path, we use:

```
SET search_path TO myschema,public;
```

(We omit the $user here because we have no immediate need for it.) And then we can access the table without schema qualification:

```
DROP TABLE mytable;
```

Also, since myschema is the first element in the path, new objects would by default be created in it.

We could also have written:

```
SET search_path TO myschema;
```

Then we no longer have access to the public schema without explicit qualification. There is nothing special about the public schema except that it exists by default. It can be dropped, too.

See also Section 9.25 for other ways to manipulate the schema search path.

The search path works in the same way for data type names, function names, and operator names as it does for table names. Data type and function names can be qualified in exactly the same way as table names. If you need to write a qualified operator name in an expression, there is a special provision: you must write

```
OPERATOR(schema.operator)
```

This is needed to avoid syntactic ambiguity. An example is:

```
SELECT 3 OPERATOR(pg_catalog.+) 4;
```

In practice one usually relies on the search path for operators, so as not to have to write anything so ugly as that.

5.7.4. Schemas and Privileges

By default, users cannot access any objects in schemas they do not own. To allow that, the owner of the schema must grant the USAGE privilege on the schema. To allow users to make use of the objects in the schema, additional privileges might need to be granted, as appropriate for the object.

A user can also be allowed to create objects in someone else's schema. To allow that, the CREATE privilege on the schema needs to be granted. Note that by default, everyone has CREATE and USAGE privileges on the schema public. This allows all users that are able to connect to a given database to create objects in its public schema. If you do not want to allow that, you can revoke that privilege:

```
REVOKE CREATE ON SCHEMA public FROM PUBLIC;
```

(The first "public" is the schema, the second "public" means "every user". In the first sense it is an identifier, in the second sense it is a key word, hence the different capitalization; recall the guidelines from Section 4.1.1.)

5.7.5. The System Catalog Schema

In addition to `public` and user-created schemas, each database contains a `pg_catalog` schema, which contains the system tables and all the built-in data types, functions, and operators. `pg_catalog` is always effectively part of the search path. If it is not named explicitly in the path then it is implicitly searched *before* searching the path's schemas. This ensures that built-in names will always be findable. However, you can explicitly place `pg_catalog` at the end of your search path if you prefer to have user-defined names override built-in names.

Since system table names begin with `pg_`, it is best to avoid such names to ensure that you won't suffer a conflict if some future version defines a system table named the same as your table. (With the default search path, an unqualified reference to your table name would then be resolved as the system table instead.) System tables will continue to follow the convention of having names beginning with `pg_`, so that they will not conflict with unqualified user-table names so long as users avoid the `pg_` prefix.

5.7.6. Usage Patterns

Schemas can be used to organize your data in many ways. There are a few usage patterns that are recommended and are easily supported by the default configuration:

- If you do not create any schemas then all users access the public schema implicitly. This simulates the situation where schemas are not available at all. This setup is mainly recommended when there is only a single user or a few cooperating users in a database. This setup also allows smooth transition from the non-schema-aware world.

- You can create a schema for each user with the same name as that user. Recall that the default search path starts with `$user`, which resolves to the user name. Therefore, if each user has a separate schema, they access their own schemas by default.

  If you use this setup then you might also want to revoke access to the public schema (or drop it altogether), so users are truly constrained to their own schemas.

- To install shared applications (tables to be used by everyone, additional functions provided by third parties, etc.), put them into separate schemas. Remember to grant appropriate privileges to allow the other users to access them. Users can then refer to these additional objects by qualifying the names with a schema name, or they can put the additional schemas into their search path, as they choose.

5.7.7. Portability

In the SQL standard, the notion of objects in the same schema being owned by different users does not exist. Moreover, some implementations do not allow you to create schemas that have a different name than their owner. In fact, the concepts of schema and user are nearly equivalent in a database system that implements only the basic schema support specified in the standard. Therefore, many users consider qualified names to really consist of *username.tablename*. This is how PostgreSQL will effectively behave if you create a per-user schema for every user.

Also, there is no concept of a `public` schema in the SQL standard. For maximum conformance to the standard, you should not use (perhaps even remove) the `public` schema.

Of course, some SQL database systems might not implement schemas at all, or provide namespace support by allowing (possibly limited) cross-database access. If you need to work with those systems, then maximum portability would be achieved by not using schemas at all.

5.8. Inheritance

PostgreSQL implements table inheritance, which can be a useful tool for database designers. (SQL:1999 and later define a type inheritance feature, which differs in many respects from the features described here.)

Let's start with an example: suppose we are trying to build a data model for cities. Each state has many cities, but only one capital. We want to be able to quickly retrieve the capital city for any particular state. This can be done by creating two tables, one for state capitals and one for cities that are not capitals. However, what happens when we want to ask for data about a city, regardless of whether it is a capital or not? The inheritance feature can help to resolve this problem. We define the `capitals` table so that it inherits from `cities`:

```
CREATE TABLE cities (
    name            text,
    population      float,
    altitude        int     -- in feet
);

CREATE TABLE capitals (
    state           char(2)
) INHERITS (cities);
```

In this case, the `capitals` table *inherits* all the columns of its parent table, `cities`. State capitals also have an extra column, `state`, that shows their state.

In PostgreSQL, a table can inherit from zero or more other tables, and a query can reference either all rows of a table or all rows of a table plus all of its descendant tables. The latter behavior is the default. For example, the following query finds the names of all cities, including state capitals, that are located at an altitude over 500 feet:

```
SELECT name, altitude
    FROM cities
    WHERE altitude > 500;
```

Given the sample data from the PostgreSQL tutorial (see Section 2.1), this returns:

```
    name      | altitude
```

```
-----------+----------
 Las Vegas  |     2174
 Mariposa   |     1953
 Madison    |      845
```

On the other hand, the following query finds all the cities that are not state capitals and are situated at an altitude over 500 feet:

```
SELECT name, altitude
    FROM ONLY cities
    WHERE altitude > 500;
```

```
   name     | altitude
-----------+----------
 Las Vegas  |     2174
 Mariposa   |     1953
```

Here the ONLY keyword indicates that the query should apply only to cities, and not any tables below cities in the inheritance hierarchy. Many of the commands that we have already discussed — SELECT, UPDATE and DELETE — support the ONLY keyword.

You can also write the table name with a trailing * to explicitly specify that descendant tables are included:

```
SELECT name, altitude
    FROM cities*
    WHERE altitude > 500;
```

Writing * is not necessary, since this behavior is the default (unless you have changed the setting of the sql_inheritance configuration option). However writing * might be useful to emphasize that additional tables will be searched.

In some cases you might wish to know which table a particular row originated from. There is a system column called tableoid in each table which can tell you the originating table:

```
SELECT c.tableoid, c.name, c.altitude
FROM cities c
WHERE c.altitude > 500;
```

which returns:

```
 tableoid |    name     | altitude
----------+-----------+----------
   139793 | Las Vegas  |     2174
   139793 | Mariposa   |     1953
   139798 | Madison    |      845
```

(If you try to reproduce this example, you will probably get different numeric OIDs.) By doing a join with pg_class you can see the actual table names:

```
SELECT p.relname, c.name, c.altitude
FROM cities c, pg_class p
```

```
WHERE c.altitude > 500 AND c.tableoid = p.oid;
```

which returns:

```
relname  |   name    | altitude
---------+-----------+----------
cities   | Las Vegas |    2174
cities   | Mariposa  |    1953
capitals | Madison   |     845
```

Inheritance does not automatically propagate data from `INSERT` or `COPY` commands to other tables in the inheritance hierarchy. In our example, the following `INSERT` statement will fail:

```
INSERT INTO cities (name, population, altitude, state)
VALUES ('New York', NULL, NULL, 'NY');
```

We might hope that the data would somehow be routed to the `capitals` table, but this does not happen: `INSERT` always inserts into exactly the table specified. In some cases it is possible to redirect the insertion using a rule (see Chapter 38). However that does not help for the above case because the `cities` table does not contain the column `state`, and so the command will be rejected before the rule can be applied.

All check constraints and not-null constraints on a parent table are automatically inherited by its children. Other types of constraints (unique, primary key, and foreign key constraints) are not inherited.

A table can inherit from more than one parent table, in which case it has the union of the columns defined by the parent tables. Any columns declared in the child table's definition are added to these. If the same column name appears in multiple parent tables, or in both a parent table and the child's definition, then these columns are "merged" so that there is only one such column in the child table. To be merged, columns must have the same data types, else an error is raised. The merged column will have copies of all the check constraints coming from any one of the column definitions it came from, and will be marked not-null if any of them are.

Table inheritance is typically established when the child table is created, using the `INHERITS` clause of the CREATE TABLE statement. Alternatively, a table which is already defined in a compatible way can have a new parent relationship added, using the `INHERIT` variant of ALTER TABLE. To do this the new child table must already include columns with the same names and types as the columns of the parent. It must also include check constraints with the same names and check expressions as those of the parent. Similarly an inheritance link can be removed from a child using the `NO INHERIT` variant of ALTER TABLE. Dynamically adding and removing inheritance links like this can be useful when the inheritance relationship is being used for table partitioning (see Section 5.9).

One convenient way to create a compatible table that will later be made a new child is to use the `LIKE` clause in `CREATE TABLE`. This creates a new table with the same columns as the source table. If there are any `CHECK` constraints defined on the source table, the `INCLUDING CONSTRAINTS` option to `LIKE` should be specified, as the new child must have constraints matching the parent to be considered compatible.

A parent table cannot be dropped while any of its children remain. Neither can columns or check constraints of child tables be dropped or altered if they are inherited from any parent tables. If you wish to remove a table and all of its descendants, one easy way is to drop the parent table with the `CASCADE` option.

ALTER TABLE will propagate any changes in column data definitions and check constraints down the inheritance hierarchy. Again, dropping columns that are depended on by other tables is only possible when using the CASCADE option. ALTER TABLE follows the same rules for duplicate column merging and rejection that apply during CREATE TABLE.

Note how table access permissions are handled. Querying a parent table can automatically access data in child tables without further access privilege checking. This preserves the appearance that the data is (also) in the parent table. Accessing the child tables directly is, however, not automatically allowed and would require further privileges to be granted.

5.8.1. Caveats

Note that not all SQL commands are able to work on inheritance hierarchies. Commands that are used for data querying, data modification, or schema modification (e.g., SELECT, UPDATE, DELETE, most variants of ALTER TABLE, but not INSERT or ALTER TABLE ... RENAME) typically default to including child tables and support the ONLY notation to exclude them. Commands that do database maintenance and tuning (e.g., REINDEX, VACUUM) typically only work on individual, physical tables and do not support recursing over inheritance hierarchies. The respective behavior of each individual command is documented in its reference page (Reference I, *SQL Commands*).

A serious limitation of the inheritance feature is that indexes (including unique constraints) and foreign key constraints only apply to single tables, not to their inheritance children. This is true on both the referencing and referenced sides of a foreign key constraint. Thus, in the terms of the above example:

- If we declared cities.name to be UNIQUE or a PRIMARY KEY, this would not stop the capitals table from having rows with names duplicating rows in cities. And those duplicate rows would by default show up in queries from cities. In fact, by default capitals would have no unique constraint at all, and so could contain multiple rows with the same name. You could add a unique constraint to capitals, but this would not prevent duplication compared to cities.

- Similarly, if we were to specify that cities.name REFERENCES some other table, this constraint would not automatically propagate to capitals. In this case you could work around it by manually adding the same REFERENCES constraint to capitals.

- Specifying that another table's column REFERENCES cities(name) would allow the other table to contain city names, but not capital names. There is no good workaround for this case.

These deficiencies will probably be fixed in some future release, but in the meantime considerable care is needed in deciding whether inheritance is useful for your application.

5.9. Partitioning

PostgreSQL supports basic table partitioning. This section describes why and how to implement partitioning as part of your database design.

5.9.1. Overview

Partitioning refers to splitting what is logically one large table into smaller physical pieces. Partitioning can provide several benefits:

- Query performance can be improved dramatically in certain situations, particularly when most of the heavily accessed rows of the table are in a single partition or a small number of partitions. The partitioning substitutes for leading columns of indexes, reducing index size and making it more likely that the heavily-used parts of the indexes fit in memory.

- When queries or updates access a large percentage of a single partition, performance can be improved by taking advantage of sequential scan of that partition instead of using an index and random access reads scattered across the whole table.

- Bulk loads and deletes can be accomplished by adding or removing partitions, if that requirement is planned into the partitioning design. `ALTER TABLE NO INHERIT` and `DROP TABLE` are both far faster than a bulk operation. These commands also entirely avoid the `VACUUM` overhead caused by a bulk `DELETE`.

- Seldom-used data can be migrated to cheaper and slower storage media.

The benefits will normally be worthwhile only when a table would otherwise be very large. The exact point at which a table will benefit from partitioning depends on the application, although a rule of thumb is that the size of the table should exceed the physical memory of the database server.

Currently, PostgreSQL supports partitioning via table inheritance. Each partition must be created as a child table of a single parent table. The parent table itself is normally empty; it exists just to represent the entire data set. You should be familiar with inheritance (see Section 5.8) before attempting to set up partitioning.

The following forms of partitioning can be implemented in PostgreSQL:

Range Partitioning

> The table is partitioned into "ranges" defined by a key column or set of columns, with no overlap between the ranges of values assigned to different partitions. For example one might partition by date ranges, or by ranges of identifiers for particular business objects.

List Partitioning

> The table is partitioned by explicitly listing which key values appear in each partition.

5.9.2. Implementing Partitioning

To set up a partitioned table, do the following:

1. Create the "master" table, from which all of the partitions will inherit.

   This table will contain no data. Do not define any check constraints on this table, unless you intend them to be applied equally to all partitions. There is no point in defining any indexes or unique constraints on it, either.

2. Create several "child" tables that each inherit from the master table. Normally, these tables will not add any columns to the set inherited from the master.

   We will refer to the child tables as partitions, though they are in every way normal PostgreSQL tables.

3. Add table constraints to the partition tables to define the allowed key values in each partition.

   Typical examples would be:

   ```
   CHECK ( x = 1 )
   CHECK ( county IN ( 'Oxfordshire', 'Buckinghamshire', 'Warwickshire' ))
   CHECK ( outletID >= 100 AND outletID < 200 )
   ```

   Ensure that the constraints guarantee that there is no overlap between the key values permitted in different partitions. A common mistake is to set up range constraints like:

   ```
   CHECK ( outletID BETWEEN 100 AND 200 )
   CHECK ( outletID BETWEEN 200 AND 300 )
   ```

   This is wrong since it is not clear which partition the key value 200 belongs in.

   Note that there is no difference in syntax between range and list partitioning; those terms are descriptive only.

4. For each partition, create an index on the key column(s), as well as any other indexes you might want. (The key index is not strictly necessary, but in most scenarios it is helpful. If you intend the key values to be unique then you should always create a unique or primary-key constraint for each partition.)

5. Optionally, define a trigger or rule to redirect data inserted into the master table to the appropriate partition.

6. Ensure that the constraint_exclusion configuration parameter is not disabled in `postgresql.conf`. If it is, queries will not be optimized as desired.

For example, suppose we are constructing a database for a large ice cream company. The company measures peak temperatures every day as well as ice cream sales in each region. Conceptually, we want a table like:

```
CREATE TABLE measurement (
    city_id         int not null,
    logdate         date not null,
    peaktemp        int,
    unitsales       int
);
```

We know that most queries will access just the last week's, month's or quarter's data, since the main use of this table will be to prepare online reports for management. To reduce the amount of old data that needs to be stored, we decide to only keep the most recent 3 years worth of data. At the beginning of each month we will remove the oldest month's data.

In this situation we can use partitioning to help us meet all of our different requirements for the measurements table. Following the steps outlined above, partitioning can be set up as follows:

1. The master table is the `measurement` table, declared exactly as above.

2. Next we create one partition for each active month:

   ```
   CREATE TABLE measurement_y2006m02 ( ) INHERITS (measurement);
   CREATE TABLE measurement_y2006m03 ( ) INHERITS (measurement);
   ...
   ```

```
CREATE TABLE measurement_y2007m11 ( ) INHERITS (measurement);
CREATE TABLE measurement_y2007m12 ( ) INHERITS (measurement);
CREATE TABLE measurement_y2008m01 ( ) INHERITS (measurement);
```

Each of the partitions are complete tables in their own right, but they inherit their definitions from the `measurement` table.

This solves one of our problems: deleting old data. Each month, all we will need to do is perform a `DROP TABLE` on the oldest child table and create a new child table for the new month's data.

3. We must provide non-overlapping table constraints. Rather than just creating the partition tables as above, the table creation script should really be:

```
CREATE TABLE measurement_y2006m02 (
    CHECK ( logdate >= DATE '2006-02-01' AND logdate < DATE '2006-03-01' )
) INHERITS (measurement);
CREATE TABLE measurement_y2006m03 (
    CHECK ( logdate >= DATE '2006-03-01' AND logdate < DATE '2006-04-01' )
) INHERITS (measurement);
...
CREATE TABLE measurement_y2007m11 (
    CHECK ( logdate >= DATE '2007-11-01' AND logdate < DATE '2007-12-01' )
) INHERITS (measurement);
CREATE TABLE measurement_y2007m12 (
    CHECK ( logdate >= DATE '2007-12-01' AND logdate < DATE '2008-01-01' )
) INHERITS (measurement);
CREATE TABLE measurement_y2008m01 (
    CHECK ( logdate >= DATE '2008-01-01' AND logdate < DATE '2008-02-01' )
) INHERITS (measurement);
```

4. We probably need indexes on the key columns too:

```
CREATE INDEX measurement_y2006m02_logdate ON measurement_y2006m02 (logdate);
CREATE INDEX measurement_y2006m03_logdate ON measurement_y2006m03 (logdate);
...
CREATE INDEX measurement_y2007m11_logdate ON measurement_y2007m11 (logdate);
CREATE INDEX measurement_y2007m12_logdate ON measurement_y2007m12 (logdate);
CREATE INDEX measurement_y2008m01_logdate ON measurement_y2008m01 (logdate);
```

We choose not to add further indexes at this time.

5. We want our application to be able to say `INSERT INTO measurement ...` and have the data be redirected into the appropriate partition table. We can arrange that by attaching a suitable trigger function to the master table. If data will be added only to the latest partition, we can use a very simple trigger function:

```
CREATE OR REPLACE FUNCTION measurement_insert_trigger()
RETURNS TRIGGER AS $$
BEGIN
    INSERT INTO measurement_y2008m01 VALUES (NEW.*);
    RETURN NULL;
END;
$$
LANGUAGE plpgsql;
```

After creating the function, we create a trigger which calls the trigger function:

```
CREATE TRIGGER insert_measurement_trigger
    BEFORE INSERT ON measurement
    FOR EACH ROW EXECUTE PROCEDURE measurement_insert_trigger();
```

We must redefine the trigger function each month so that it always points to the current partition. The trigger definition does not need to be updated, however.

We might want to insert data and have the server automatically locate the partition into which the row should be added. We could do this with a more complex trigger function, for example:

```
CREATE OR REPLACE FUNCTION measurement_insert_trigger()
RETURNS TRIGGER AS $$
BEGIN
    IF ( NEW.logdate >= DATE '2006-02-01' AND
         NEW.logdate < DATE '2006-03-01' ) THEN
        INSERT INTO measurement_y2006m02 VALUES (NEW.*);
    ELSIF ( NEW.logdate >= DATE '2006-03-01' AND
            NEW.logdate < DATE '2006-04-01' ) THEN
        INSERT INTO measurement_y2006m03 VALUES (NEW.*);
    ...
    ELSIF ( NEW.logdate >= DATE '2008-01-01' AND
            NEW.logdate < DATE '2008-02-01' ) THEN
        INSERT INTO measurement_y2008m01 VALUES (NEW.*);
    ELSE
        RAISE EXCEPTION 'Date out of range.  Fix the measurement_insert_tri(
    END IF;
    RETURN NULL;
END;
$$
LANGUAGE plpgsql;
```

The trigger definition is the same as before. Note that each `IF` test must exactly match the `CHECK` constraint for its partition.

While this function is more complex than the single-month case, it doesn't need to be updated as often, since branches can be added in advance of being needed.

> **Note:** In practice it might be best to check the newest partition first, if most inserts go into that partition. For simplicity we have shown the trigger's tests in the same order as in other parts of this example.

As we can see, a complex partitioning scheme could require a substantial amount of DDL. In the above example we would be creating a new partition each month, so it might be wise to write a script that generates the required DDL automatically.

5.9.3. Managing Partitions

Normally the set of partitions established when initially defining the table are not intended to remain static. It is common to want to remove old partitions of data and periodically add new partitions for new data. One of the most important advantages of partitioning is precisely that it allows this otherwise painful task to be executed nearly instantaneously by manipulating the partition structure, rather than physically moving large amounts of data around.

The simplest option for removing old data is simply to drop the partition that is no longer necessary:

```
DROP TABLE measurement_y2006m02;
```

This can very quickly delete millions of records because it doesn't have to individually delete every record.

Another option that is often preferable is to remove the partition from the partitioned table but retain access to it as a table in its own right:

```
ALTER TABLE measurement_y2006m02 NO INHERIT measurement;
```

This allows further operations to be performed on the data before it is dropped. For example, this is often a useful time to back up the data using COPY, pg_dump, or similar tools. It might also be a useful time to aggregate data into smaller formats, perform other data manipulations, or run reports.

Similarly we can add a new partition to handle new data. We can create an empty partition in the partitioned table just as the original partitions were created above:

```
CREATE TABLE measurement_y2008m02 (
    CHECK ( logdate >= DATE '2008-02-01' AND logdate < DATE '2008-03-01' )
) INHERITS (measurement);
```

As an alternative, it is sometimes more convenient to create the new table outside the partition structure, and make it a proper partition later. This allows the data to be loaded, checked, and transformed prior to it appearing in the partitioned table:

```
CREATE TABLE measurement_y2008m02
  (LIKE measurement INCLUDING DEFAULTS INCLUDING CONSTRAINTS);
ALTER TABLE measurement_y2008m02 ADD CONSTRAINT y2008m02
    CHECK ( logdate >= DATE '2008-02-01' AND logdate < DATE '2008-03-01' );
\copy measurement_y2008m02 from 'measurement_y2008m02'
-- possibly some other data preparation work
ALTER TABLE measurement_y2008m02 INHERIT measurement;
```

5.9.4. Partitioning and Constraint Exclusion

Constraint exclusion is a query optimization technique that improves performance for partitioned tables defined in the fashion described above. As an example:

```
SET constraint_exclusion = on;
SELECT count(*) FROM measurement WHERE logdate >= DATE '2008-01-01';
```

Without constraint exclusion, the above query would scan each of the partitions of the measurement table. With constraint exclusion enabled, the planner will examine the constraints of each partition and try to prove that the partition need not be scanned because it could not contain any rows meeting the query's WHERE clause. When the planner can prove this, it excludes the partition from the query plan.

You can use the EXPLAIN command to show the difference between a plan with constraint_exclusion on and a plan with it off. A typical unoptimized plan for this type of table setup is:

```
SET constraint_exclusion = off;
EXPLAIN SELECT count(*) FROM measurement WHERE logdate >= DATE '2008-01-01';

                                    QUERY PLAN
-----------------------------------------------------------------------------
 Aggregate  (cost=158.66..158.68 rows=1 width=0)
   ->  Append  (cost=0.00..151.88 rows=2715 width=0)
         ->  Seq Scan on measurement  (cost=0.00..30.38 rows=543 width=0)
               Filter: (logdate >= '2008-01-01'::date)
         ->  Seq Scan on measurement_y2006m02 measurement  (cost=0.00..30.38 r(
               Filter: (logdate >= '2008-01-01'::date)
         ->  Seq Scan on measurement_y2006m03 measurement  (cost=0.00..30.38 r(
               Filter: (logdate >= '2008-01-01'::date)

...

         ->  Seq Scan on measurement_y2007m12 measurement  (cost=0.00..30.38 r(
               Filter: (logdate >= '2008-01-01'::date)
         ->  Seq Scan on measurement_y2008m01 measurement  (cost=0.00..30.38 r(
               Filter: (logdate >= '2008-01-01'::date)
```

Some or all of the partitions might use index scans instead of full-table sequential scans, but the point here is that there is no need to scan the older partitions at all to answer this query. When we enable constraint exclusion, we get a significantly cheaper plan that will deliver the same answer:

```
SET constraint_exclusion = on;
EXPLAIN SELECT count(*) FROM measurement WHERE logdate >= DATE '2008-01-01';
                                    QUERY PLAN
-----------------------------------------------------------------------------
 Aggregate  (cost=63.47..63.48 rows=1 width=0)
   ->  Append  (cost=0.00..60.75 rows=1086 width=0)
         ->  Seq Scan on measurement  (cost=0.00..30.38 rows=543 width=0)
               Filter: (logdate >= '2008-01-01'::date)
         ->  Seq Scan on measurement_y2008m01 measurement  (cost=0.00..30.38 r(
               Filter: (logdate >= '2008-01-01'::date)
```

Note that constraint exclusion is driven only by CHECK constraints, not by the presence of indexes. Therefore it isn't necessary to define indexes on the key columns. Whether an index needs to be created for a given partition depends on whether you expect that queries that scan the partition will generally scan a large part of the partition or just a small part. An index will be helpful in the latter case but not the former.

The default (and recommended) setting of constraint_exclusion is actually neither on nor off, but an intermediate setting called partition, which causes the technique to be applied only to queries that are likely to be working on partitioned tables. The on setting causes the planner to examine CHECK constraints in all queries, even simple ones that are unlikely to benefit.

5.9.5. Alternative Partitioning Methods

A different approach to redirecting inserts into the appropriate partition table is to set up rules, instead of a trigger, on the master table. For example:

```
CREATE RULE measurement_insert_y2006m02 AS
```

```
ON INSERT TO measurement WHERE
    ( logdate >= DATE '2006-02-01' AND logdate < DATE '2006-03-01' )
DO INSTEAD
    INSERT INTO measurement_y2006m02 VALUES (NEW.*);
...
CREATE RULE measurement_insert_y2008m01 AS
ON INSERT TO measurement WHERE
    ( logdate >= DATE '2008-01-01' AND logdate < DATE '2008-02-01' )
DO INSTEAD
    INSERT INTO measurement_y2008m01 VALUES (NEW.*);
```

A rule has significantly more overhead than a trigger, but the overhead is paid once per query rather than once per row, so this method might be advantageous for bulk-insert situations. In most cases, however, the trigger method will offer better performance.

Be aware that COPY ignores rules. If you want to use COPY to insert data, you'll need to copy into the correct partition table rather than into the master. COPY does fire triggers, so you can use it normally if you use the trigger approach.

Another disadvantage of the rule approach is that there is no simple way to force an error if the set of rules doesn't cover the insertion date; the data will silently go into the master table instead.

Partitioning can also be arranged using a UNION ALL view, instead of table inheritance. For example,

```
CREATE VIEW measurement AS
          SELECT * FROM measurement_y2006m02
UNION ALL SELECT * FROM measurement_y2006m03
...
UNION ALL SELECT * FROM measurement_y2007m11
UNION ALL SELECT * FROM measurement_y2007m12
UNION ALL SELECT * FROM measurement_y2008m01;
```

However, the need to recreate the view adds an extra step to adding and dropping individual partitions of the data set. In practice this method has little to recommend it compared to using inheritance.

5.9.6. Caveats

The following caveats apply to partitioned tables:

* There is no automatic way to verify that all of the CHECK constraints are mutually exclusive. It is safer to create code that generates partitions and creates and/or modifies associated objects than to write each by hand.

* The schemes shown here assume that the partition key column(s) of a row never change, or at least do not change enough to require it to move to another partition. An UPDATE that attempts to do that will fail because of the CHECK constraints. If you need to handle such cases, you can put suitable update triggers on the partition tables, but it makes management of the structure much more complicated.

* If you are using manual VACUUM or ANALYZE commands, don't forget that you need to run them on each partition individually. A command like:

```
ANALYZE measurement;
```

will only process the master table.

The following caveats apply to constraint exclusion:

- Constraint exclusion only works when the query's WHERE clause contains constants (or externally supplied parameters). For example, a comparison against a non-immutable function such as CURRENT_TIMESTAMP cannot be optimized, since the planner cannot know which partition the function value might fall into at run time.

- Keep the partitioning constraints simple, else the planner may not be able to prove that partitions don't need to be visited. Use simple equality conditions for list partitioning, or simple range tests for range partitioning, as illustrated in the preceding examples. A good rule of thumb is that partitioning constraints should contain only comparisons of the partitioning column(s) to constants using B-tree-indexable operators.

- All constraints on all partitions of the master table are examined during constraint exclusion, so large numbers of partitions are likely to increase query planning time considerably. Partitioning using these techniques will work well with up to perhaps a hundred partitions; don't try to use many thousands of partitions.

5.10. Foreign Data

PostgreSQL implements portions of the SQL/MED specification, allowing you to access data that resides outside PostgreSQL using regular SQL queries. Such data is referred to as *foreign data*. (Note that this usage is not to be confused with foreign keys, which are a type of constraint within the database.)

Foreign data is accessed with help from a *foreign data wrapper*. A foreign data wrapper is a library that can communicate with an external data source, hiding the details of connecting to the data source and obtaining data from it. There are some foreign data wrappers available as contrib modules; see Appendix F. Other kinds of foreign data wrappers might be found as third party products. If none of the existing foreign data wrappers suit your needs, you can write your own; see Chapter 53.

To access foreign data, you need to create a *foreign server* object, which defines how to connect to a particular external data source according to the set of options used by its supporting foreign data wrapper. Then you need to create one or more *foreign tables*, which define the structure of the remote data. A foreign table can be used in queries just like a normal table, but a foreign table has no storage in the PostgreSQL server. Whenever it is used, PostgreSQL asks the foreign data wrapper to fetch data from the external source, or transmit data to the external source in the case of update commands.

Accessing remote data may require authenticating to the external data source. This information can be provided by a *user mapping*, which can provide additional data such as user names and passwords based on the current PostgreSQL role.

For additional information, see CREATE FOREIGN DATA WRAPPER, CREATE SERVER, CREATE USER MAPPING, and CREATE FOREIGN TABLE.

5.11. Other Database Objects

Tables are the central objects in a relational database structure, because they hold your data. But they are not the only objects that exist in a database. Many other kinds of objects can be created to make the use and management of the data more efficient or convenient. They are not discussed in this chapter, but we give you a list here so that you are aware of what is possible:

- Views

- Functions and operators

- Data types and domains

- Triggers and rewrite rules

Detailed information on these topics appears in Part V.

5.12. Dependency Tracking

When you create complex database structures involving many tables with foreign key constraints, views, triggers, functions, etc. you implicitly create a net of dependencies between the objects. For instance, a table with a foreign key constraint depends on the table it references.

To ensure the integrity of the entire database structure, PostgreSQL makes sure that you cannot drop objects that other objects still depend on. For example, attempting to drop the products table we had considered in Section 5.3.5, with the orders table depending on it, would result in an error message such as this:

```
DROP TABLE products;

NOTICE:  constraint orders_product_no_fkey on table orders depends on table prc
ERROR:  cannot drop table products because other objects depend on it
HINT:  Use DROP ... CASCADE to drop the dependent objects too.
```

The error message contains a useful hint: if you do not want to bother deleting all the dependent objects individually, you can run:

```
DROP TABLE products CASCADE;
```

and all the dependent objects will be removed. In this case, it doesn't remove the orders table, it only removes the foreign key constraint. (If you want to check what DROP ... CASCADE will do, run DROP without CASCADE and read the NOTICE messages.)

All drop commands in PostgreSQL support specifying CASCADE. Of course, the nature of the possible dependencies varies with the type of the object. You can also write RESTRICT instead of CASCADE to get the default behavior, which is to prevent the dropping of objects that other objects depend on.

> **Note:** According to the SQL standard, specifying either RESTRICT or CASCADE is required. No database system actually enforces that rule, but whether the default behavior is RESTRICT or CASCADE varies across systems.

Note: Foreign key constraint dependencies and serial column dependencies from PostgreSQL versions prior to 7.3 are *not* maintained or created during the upgrade process. All other dependency types will be properly created during an upgrade from a pre-7.3 database.

Chapter 6. Data Manipulation

The previous chapter discussed how to create tables and other structures to hold your data. Now it is time to fill the tables with data. This chapter covers how to insert, update, and delete table data. The chapter after this will finally explain how to extract your long-lost data from the database.

6.1. Inserting Data

When a table is created, it contains no data. The first thing to do before a database can be of much use is to insert data. Data is conceptually inserted one row at a time. Of course you can also insert more than one row, but there is no way to insert less than one row. Even if you know only some column values, a complete row must be created.

To create a new row, use the INSERT command. The command requires the table name and column values. For example, consider the products table from Chapter 5:

```
CREATE TABLE products (
    product_no integer,
    name text,
    price numeric
);
```

An example command to insert a row would be:

```
INSERT INTO products VALUES (1, 'Cheese', 9.99);
```

The data values are listed in the order in which the columns appear in the table, separated by commas. Usually, the data values will be literals (constants), but scalar expressions are also allowed.

The above syntax has the drawback that you need to know the order of the columns in the table. To avoid this you can also list the columns explicitly. For example, both of the following commands have the same effect as the one above:

```
INSERT INTO products (product_no, name, price) VALUES (1, 'Cheese', 9.99);
INSERT INTO products (name, price, product_no) VALUES ('Cheese', 9.99, 1);
```

Many users consider it good practice to always list the column names.

If you don't have values for all the columns, you can omit some of them. In that case, the columns will be filled with their default values. For example:

```
INSERT INTO products (product_no, name) VALUES (1, 'Cheese');
INSERT INTO products VALUES (1, 'Cheese');
```

The second form is a PostgreSQL extension. It fills the columns from the left with as many values as are given, and the rest will be defaulted.

For clarity, you can also request default values explicitly, for individual columns or for the entire row:

```
INSERT INTO products (product_no, name, price) VALUES (1, 'Cheese', DEFAULT);
INSERT INTO products DEFAULT VALUES;
```

You can insert multiple rows in a single command:

```
INSERT INTO products (product_no, name, price) VALUES
    (1, 'Cheese', 9.99),
    (2, 'Bread', 1.99),
    (3, 'Milk', 2.99);
```

Tip: When inserting a lot of data at the same time, considering using the COPY command. It is not as flexible as the INSERT command, but is more efficient. Refer to Section 14.4 for more information on improving bulk loading performance.

6.2. Updating Data

The modification of data that is already in the database is referred to as updating. You can update individual rows, all the rows in a table, or a subset of all rows. Each column can be updated separately; the other columns are not affected.

To update existing rows, use the UPDATE command. This requires three pieces of information:

1. The name of the table and column to update
2. The new value of the column
3. Which row(s) to update

Recall from Chapter 5 that SQL does not, in general, provide a unique identifier for rows. Therefore it is not always possible to directly specify which row to update. Instead, you specify which conditions a row must meet in order to be updated. Only if you have a primary key in the table (independent of whether you declared it or not) can you reliably address individual rows by choosing a condition that matches the primary key. Graphical database access tools rely on this fact to allow you to update rows individually.

For example, this command updates all products that have a price of 5 to have a price of 10:

```
UPDATE products SET price = 10 WHERE price = 5;
```

This might cause zero, one, or many rows to be updated. It is not an error to attempt an update that does not match any rows.

Let's look at that command in detail. First is the key word UPDATE followed by the table name. As usual, the table name can be schema-qualified, otherwise it is looked up in the path. Next is the key word SET followed by the column name, an equal sign, and the new column value. The new column value can be any scalar expression, not just a constant. For example, if you want to raise the price of all products by 10% you could use:

```
UPDATE products SET price = price * 1.10;
```

As you see, the expression for the new value can refer to the existing value(s) in the row. We also left out the WHERE clause. If it is omitted, it means that all rows in the table are updated. If it is present, only those rows that match the WHERE condition are updated. Note that the equals sign in the SET clause is an assignment while the one in the WHERE clause is a comparison, but this does not create any ambiguity. Of course, the WHERE condition does not have to be an equality test. Many other operators are available (see Chapter 9). But the expression needs to evaluate to a Boolean result.

You can update more than one column in an UPDATE command by listing more than one assignment in the SET clause. For example:

```
UPDATE mytable SET a = 5, b = 3, c = 1 WHERE a > 0;
```

6.3. Deleting Data

So far we have explained how to add data to tables and how to change data. What remains is to discuss how to remove data that is no longer needed. Just as adding data is only possible in whole rows, you can only remove entire rows from a table. In the previous section we explained that SQL does not provide a way to directly address individual rows. Therefore, removing rows can only be done by specifying conditions that the rows to be removed have to match. If you have a primary key in the table then you can specify the exact row. But you can also remove groups of rows matching a condition, or you can remove all rows in the table at once.

You use the DELETE command to remove rows; the syntax is very similar to the UPDATE command. For instance, to remove all rows from the products table that have a price of 10, use:

```
DELETE FROM products WHERE price = 10;
```

If you simply write:

```
DELETE FROM products;
```

then all rows in the table will be deleted! Caveat programmer.

Chapter 7. Queries

The previous chapters explained how to create tables, how to fill them with data, and how to manipulate that data. Now we finally discuss how to retrieve the data from the database.

7.1. Overview

The process of retrieving or the command to retrieve data from a database is called a *query*. In SQL the SELECT command is used to specify queries. The general syntax of the SELECT command is

```
[WITH with_queries] SELECT select_list FROM table_expression [sort_specification]
```

The following sections describe the details of the select list, the table expression, and the sort specification. WITH queries are treated last since they are an advanced feature.

A simple kind of query has the form:

```
SELECT * FROM table1;
```

Assuming that there is a table called table1, this command would retrieve all rows and all user-defined columns from table1. (The method of retrieval depends on the client application. For example, the psql program will display an ASCII-art table on the screen, while client libraries will offer functions to extract individual values from the query result.) The select list specification * means all columns that the table expression happens to provide. A select list can also select a subset of the available columns or make calculations using the columns. For example, if table1 has columns named a, b, and c (and perhaps others) you can make the following query:

```
SELECT a, b + c FROM table1;
```

(assuming that b and c are of a numerical data type). See Section 7.3 for more details.

FROM table1 is a simple kind of table expression: it reads just one table. In general, table expressions can be complex constructs of base tables, joins, and subqueries. But you can also omit the table expression entirely and use the SELECT command as a calculator:

```
SELECT 3 * 4;
```

This is more useful if the expressions in the select list return varying results. For example, you could call a function this way:

```
SELECT random();
```

7.2. Table Expressions

A *table expression* computes a table. The table expression contains a FROM clause that is optionally followed by WHERE, GROUP BY, and HAVING clauses. Trivial table expressions simply refer to a table on disk, a so-called base table, but more complex expressions can be used to modify or combine base tables in various ways.

The optional WHERE, GROUP BY, and HAVING clauses in the table expression specify a pipeline of successive transformations performed on the table derived in the FROM clause. All these transformations produce a virtual table that provides the rows that are passed to the select list to compute the output rows of the query.

7.2.1. The FROM Clause

The *FROM Clause* derives a table from one or more other tables given in a comma-separated table reference list.

```
FROM table_reference [, table_reference [, ...]]
```

A table reference can be a table name (possibly schema-qualified), or a derived table such as a subquery, a JOIN construct, or complex combinations of these. If more than one table reference is listed in the FROM clause, the tables are cross-joined (that is, the Cartesian product of their rows is formed; see below). The result of the FROM list is an intermediate virtual table that can then be subject to transformations by the WHERE, GROUP BY, and HAVING clauses and is finally the result of the overall table expression.

When a table reference names a table that is the parent of a table inheritance hierarchy, the table reference produces rows of not only that table but all of its descendant tables, unless the key word ONLY precedes the table name. However, the reference produces only the columns that appear in the named table — any columns added in subtables are ignored.

Instead of writing ONLY before the table name, you can write * after the table name to explicitly specify that descendant tables are included. Writing * is not necessary since that behavior is the default (unless you have changed the setting of the sql_inheritance configuration option). However writing * might be useful to emphasize that additional tables will be searched.

7.2.1.1. Joined Tables

A joined table is a table derived from two other (real or derived) tables according to the rules of the particular join type. Inner, outer, and cross-joins are available. The general syntax of a joined table is

```
T1 join_type T2 [ join_condition ]
```

Joins of all types can be chained together, or nested: either or both *T1* and *T2* can be joined tables. Parentheses can be used around JOIN clauses to control the join order. In the absence of parentheses, JOIN clauses nest left-to-right.

Join Types

Cross join

```
T1 CROSS JOIN T2
```

For every possible combination of rows from *T1* and *T2* (i.e., a Cartesian product), the joined table will contain a row consisting of all columns in *T1* followed by all columns in *T2*. If the tables have N and M rows respectively, the joined table will have N * M rows.

FROM `T1` CROSS JOIN `T2` is equivalent to FROM `T1` INNER JOIN `T2` ON TRUE (see below). It is also equivalent to FROM `T1`, `T2`.

> **Note:** This latter equivalence does not hold exactly when more than two tables appear, because JOIN binds more tightly than comma. For example FROM `T1` CROSS JOIN `T2` INNER JOIN `T3` ON `condition` is not the same as FROM `T1`, `T2` INNER JOIN `T3` ON `condition` because the `condition` can reference `T1` in the first case but not the second.

Qualified joins

```
T1 { [INNER] | { LEFT | RIGHT | FULL } [OUTER] } JOIN T2 ON boolean_expressio
T1 { [INNER] | { LEFT | RIGHT | FULL } [OUTER] } JOIN T2 USING ( join column
T1 NATURAL { [INNER] | { LEFT | RIGHT | FULL } [OUTER] } JOIN T2
```

The words INNER and OUTER are optional in all forms. INNER is the default; LEFT, RIGHT, and FULL imply an outer join.

The *join condition* is specified in the ON or USING clause, or implicitly by the word NATURAL. The join condition determines which rows from the two source tables are considered to "match", as explained in detail below.

The possible types of qualified join are:

INNER JOIN

For each row R1 of T1, the joined table has a row for each row in T2 that satisfies the join condition with R1.

LEFT OUTER JOIN

First, an inner join is performed. Then, for each row in T1 that does not satisfy the join condition with any row in T2, a joined row is added with null values in columns of T2. Thus, the joined table always has at least one row for each row in T1.

RIGHT OUTER JOIN

First, an inner join is performed. Then, for each row in T2 that does not satisfy the join condition with any row in T1, a joined row is added with null values in columns of T1. This is the converse of a left join: the result table will always have a row for each row in T2.

FULL OUTER JOIN

First, an inner join is performed. Then, for each row in T1 that does not satisfy the join condition with any row in T2, a joined row is added with null values in columns of T2. Also, for each row of T2 that does not satisfy the join condition with any row in T1, a joined row with null values in the columns of T1 is added.

The ON clause is the most general kind of join condition: it takes a Boolean value expression of the same kind as is used in a WHERE clause. A pair of rows from `T1` and `T2` match if the ON expression evaluates to true.

The USING clause is a shorthand that allows you to take advantage of the specific situation where both sides of the join use the same name for the joining column(s). It takes a comma-separated list of the shared column names and forms a join condition that includes an equality comparison for each one. For example, joining *T1* and *T2* with USING (a, b) produces the join condition ON *T1*.a = *T2*.a AND *T1*.b = *T2*.b.

Furthermore, the output of JOIN USING suppresses redundant columns: there is no need to print both of the matched columns, since they must have equal values. While JOIN ON produces all columns from *T1* followed by all columns from *T2*, JOIN USING produces one output column for each of the listed column pairs (in the listed order), followed by any remaining columns from *T1*, followed by any remaining columns from *T2*.

Finally, NATURAL is a shorthand form of USING: it forms a USING list consisting of all column names that appear in both input tables. As with USING, these columns appear only once in the output table. If there are no common column names, NATURAL behaves like CROSS JOIN.

> **Note:** USING is reasonably safe from column changes in the joined relations since only the listed columns are combined. NATURAL is considerably more risky since any schema changes to either relation that cause a new matching column name to be present will cause the join to combine that new column as well.

To put this together, assume we have tables t1:

```
num | name
-----+------
   1 | a
   2 | b
   3 | c
```

and t2:

```
num | value
-----+-------
   1 | xxx
   3 | yyy
   5 | zzz
```

then we get the following results for the various joins:

```
=> SELECT * FROM t1 CROSS JOIN t2;
num | name | num | value
-----+------+-----+-------
   1 | a    |   1 | xxx
   1 | a    |   3 | yyy
   1 | a    |   5 | zzz
   2 | b    |   1 | xxx
   2 | b    |   3 | yyy
   2 | b    |   5 | zzz
   3 | c    |   1 | xxx
   3 | c    |   3 | yyy
   3 | c    |   5 | zzz
(9 rows)
```

```
=> SELECT * FROM t1 INNER JOIN t2 ON t1.num = t2.num;
 num | name | num | value
-----+------+-----+-------
   1 | a    |   1 | xxx
   3 | c    |   3 | yyy
(2 rows)


=> SELECT * FROM t1 INNER JOIN t2 USING (num);
 num | name | value
-----+------+-------
   1 | a    | xxx
   3 | c    | yyy
(2 rows)


=> SELECT * FROM t1 NATURAL INNER JOIN t2;
 num | name | value
-----+------+-------
   1 | a    | xxx
   3 | c    | yyy
(2 rows)


=> SELECT * FROM t1 LEFT JOIN t2 ON t1.num = t2.num;
 num | name | num | value
-----+------+-----+-------
   1 | a    |   1 | xxx
   2 | b    |     |
   3 | c    |   3 | yyy
(3 rows)


=> SELECT * FROM t1 LEFT JOIN t2 USING (num);
 num | name | value
-----+------+-------
   1 | a    | xxx
   2 | b    |
   3 | c    | yyy
(3 rows)


=> SELECT * FROM t1 RIGHT JOIN t2 ON t1.num = t2.num;
 num | name | num | value
-----+------+-----+-------
   1 | a    |   1 | xxx
   3 | c    |   3 | yyy
     |      |   5 | zzz
(3 rows)


=> SELECT * FROM t1 FULL JOIN t2 ON t1.num = t2.num;
 num | name | num | value
-----+------+-----+-------
   1 | a    |   1 | xxx
   2 | b    |     |
   3 | c    |   3 | yyy
     |      |   5 | zzz
```

```
(4 rows)
```

The join condition specified with ON can also contain conditions that do not relate directly to the join. This can prove useful for some queries but needs to be thought out carefully. For example:

```
=> SELECT * FROM t1 LEFT JOIN t2 ON t1.num = t2.num AND t2.value = 'xxx';
 num | name | num | value
-----+------+-----+-------
   1 | a    |   1 | xxx
   2 | b    |     |
   3 | c    |     |
(3 rows)
```

Notice that placing the restriction in the WHERE clause produces a different result:

```
=> SELECT * FROM t1 LEFT JOIN t2 ON t1.num = t2.num WHERE t2.value = 'xxx';
 num | name | num | value
-----+------+-----+-------
   1 | a    |   1 | xxx
(1 row)
```

This is because a restriction placed in the ON clause is processed *before* the join, while a restriction placed in the WHERE clause is processed *after* the join. That does not matter with inner joins, but it matters a lot with outer joins.

7.2.1.2. Table and Column Aliases

A temporary name can be given to tables and complex table references to be used for references to the derived table in the rest of the query. This is called a *table alias*.

To create a table alias, write

```
FROM table_reference AS alias
```

or

```
FROM table_reference alias
```

The AS key word is optional noise. `alias` can be any identifier.

A typical application of table aliases is to assign short identifiers to long table names to keep the join clauses readable. For example:

```
SELECT * FROM some_very_long_table_name s JOIN another_fairly_long_name a ON s.
```

The alias becomes the new name of the table reference so far as the current query is concerned — it is not allowed to refer to the table by the original name elsewhere in the query. Thus, this is not valid:

```
SELECT * FROM my_table AS m WHERE my_table.a > 5;    -- wrong
```

Table aliases are mainly for notational convenience, but it is necessary to use them when joining a table to itself, e.g.:

```
SELECT * FROM people AS mother JOIN people AS child ON mother.id = child.mother
```

Additionally, an alias is required if the table reference is a subquery (see Section 7.2.1.3).

Parentheses are used to resolve ambiguities. In the following example, the first statement assigns the alias b to the second instance of my_table, but the second statement assigns the alias to the result of the join:

```
SELECT * FROM my_table AS a CROSS JOIN my_table AS b ...
SELECT * FROM (my_table AS a CROSS JOIN my_table) AS b ...
```

Another form of table aliasing gives temporary names to the columns of the table, as well as the table itself:

```
FROM table_reference [AS] alias ( column1 [, column2 [, ...]] )
```

If fewer column aliases are specified than the actual table has columns, the remaining columns are not renamed. This syntax is especially useful for self-joins or subqueries.

When an alias is applied to the output of a JOIN clause, the alias hides the original name(s) within the JOIN. For example:

```
SELECT a.* FROM my_table AS a JOIN your_table AS b ON ...
```

is valid SQL, but:

```
SELECT a.* FROM (my_table AS a JOIN your_table AS b ON ...) AS c
```

is not valid; the table alias a is not visible outside the alias c.

7.2.1.3. Subqueries

Subqueries specifying a derived table must be enclosed in parentheses and *must* be assigned a table alias name (as in Section 7.2.1.2). For example:

```
FROM (SELECT * FROM table1) AS alias_name
```

This example is equivalent to FROM table1 AS alias_name. More interesting cases, which cannot be reduced to a plain join, arise when the subquery involves grouping or aggregation.

A subquery can also be a VALUES list:

```
FROM (VALUES ('anne', 'smith'), ('bob', 'jones'), ('joe', 'blow'))
    AS names(first, last)
```

Again, a table alias is required. Assigning alias names to the columns of the VALUES list is optional, but is good practice. For more information see Section 7.7.

7.2.1.4. Table Functions

Table functions are functions that produce a set of rows, made up of either base data types (scalar types) or composite data types (table rows). They are used like a table, view, or subquery in the FROM clause of a query. Columns returned by table functions can be included in SELECT, JOIN, or WHERE clauses in the same manner as columns of a table, view, or subquery.

Table functions may also be combined using the ROWS FROM syntax, with the results returned in parallel columns; the number of result rows in this case is that of the largest function result, with smaller results padded with null values to match.

```
function_call [WITH ORDINALITY] [[AS] table_alias [(column_alias [, ... ])]]
ROWS FROM( function_call [, ... ] ) [WITH ORDINALITY] [[AS] table_alias [(column_a
```

If the WITH ORDINALITY clause is specified, an additional column of type bigint will be added to the function result columns. This column numbers the rows of the function result set, starting from 1. (This is a generalization of the SQL-standard syntax for UNNEST ... WITH ORDINALITY.) By default, the ordinal column is called ordinality, but a different column name can be assigned to it using an AS clause.

The special table function UNNEST may be called with any number of array parameters, and it returns a corresponding number of columns, as if UNNEST (Section 9.18) had been called on each parameter separately and combined using the ROWS FROM construct.

```
UNNEST( array_expression [, ... ] ) [WITH ORDINALITY] [[AS] table_alias [(column_a
```

If no table_alias is specified, the function name is used as the table name; in the case of a ROWS FROM() construct, the first function's name is used.

If column aliases are not supplied, then for a function returning a base data type, the column name is also the same as the function name. For a function returning a composite type, the result columns get the names of the individual attributes of the type.

Some examples:

```
CREATE TABLE foo (fooid int, foosubid int, fooname text);

CREATE FUNCTION getfoo(int) RETURNS SETOF foo AS $$
    SELECT * FROM foo WHERE fooid = $1;
$$ LANGUAGE SQL;

SELECT * FROM getfoo(1) AS t1;

SELECT * FROM foo
    WHERE foosubid IN (
                    SELECT foosubid
                    FROM getfoo(foo.fooid) z
                    WHERE z.fooid = foo.fooid
                );

CREATE VIEW vw_getfoo AS SELECT * FROM getfoo(1);

SELECT * FROM vw_getfoo;
```

In some cases it is useful to define table functions that can return different column sets depending on how they are invoked. To support this, the table function can be declared as returning the pseudotype `record`. When such a function is used in a query, the expected row structure must be specified in the query itself, so that the system can know how to parse and plan the query. This syntax looks like:

```
function_call [AS] alias (column_definition [, ... ])
function_call AS [alias] (column_definition [, ... ])
ROWS FROM( ... function_call AS (column_definition [, ... ]) [, ... ] )
```

When not using the `ROWS FROM()` syntax, the `column_definition` list replaces the column alias list that could otherwise be attached to the `FROM` item; the names in the column definitions serve as column aliases. When using the `ROWS FROM()` syntax, a `column_definition` list can be attached to each member function separately; or if there is only one member function and no `WITH ORDINALITY` clause, a `column_definition` list can be written in place of a column alias list following `ROWS FROM()`.

Consider this example:

```
SELECT *
    FROM dblink('dbname=mydb', 'SELECT proname, prosrc FROM pg_proc')
      AS t1(proname name, prosrc text)
    WHERE proname LIKE 'bytea%';
```

The dblink function (part of the dblink module) executes a remote query. It is declared to return `record` since it might be used for any kind of query. The actual column set must be specified in the calling query so that the parser knows, for example, what * should expand to.

7.2.1.5. LATERAL Subqueries

Subqueries appearing in `FROM` can be preceded by the key word `LATERAL`. This allows them to reference columns provided by preceding `FROM` items. (Without `LATERAL`, each subquery is evaluated independently and so cannot cross-reference any other `FROM` item.)

Table functions appearing in `FROM` can also be preceded by the key word `LATERAL`, but for functions the key word is optional; the function's arguments can contain references to columns provided by preceding `FROM` items in any case.

A `LATERAL` item can appear at top level in the `FROM` list, or within a `JOIN` tree. In the latter case it can also refer to any items that are on the left-hand side of a `JOIN` that it is on the right-hand side of.

When a `FROM` item contains `LATERAL` cross-references, evaluation proceeds as follows: for each row of the `FROM` item providing the cross-referenced column(s), or set of rows of multiple `FROM` items providing the columns, the `LATERAL` item is evaluated using that row or row set's values of the columns. The resulting row(s) are joined as usual with the rows they were computed from. This is repeated for each row or set of rows from the column source table(s).

A trivial example of `LATERAL` is

```
SELECT * FROM foo, LATERAL (SELECT * FROM bar WHERE bar.id = foo.bar_id) ss;
```

This is not especially useful since it has exactly the same result as the more conventional

```
SELECT * FROM foo, bar WHERE bar.id = foo.bar_id;
```

LATERAL is primarily useful when the cross-referenced column is necessary for computing the row(s) to be joined. A common application is providing an argument value for a set-returning function. For example, supposing that vertices(polygon) returns the set of vertices of a polygon, we could identify close-together vertices of polygons stored in a table with:

```
SELECT p1.id, p2.id, v1, v2
FROM polygons p1, polygons p2,
     LATERAL vertices(p1.poly) v1,
     LATERAL vertices(p2.poly) v2
WHERE (v1 <-> v2) < 10 AND p1.id != p2.id;
```

This query could also be written

```
SELECT p1.id, p2.id, v1, v2
FROM polygons p1 CROSS JOIN LATERAL vertices(p1.poly) v1,
     polygons p2 CROSS JOIN LATERAL vertices(p2.poly) v2
WHERE (v1 <-> v2) < 10 AND p1.id != p2.id;
```

or in several other equivalent formulations. (As already mentioned, the LATERAL key word is unnecessary in this example, but we use it for clarity.)

It is often particularly handy to LEFT JOIN to a LATERAL subquery, so that source rows will appear in the result even if the LATERAL subquery produces no rows for them. For example, if get_product_names() returns the names of products made by a manufacturer, but some manufacturers in our table currently produce no products, we could find out which ones those are like this:

```
SELECT m.name
FROM manufacturers m LEFT JOIN LATERAL get_product_names(m.id) pname ON true
WHERE pname IS NULL;
```

7.2.2. The WHERE Clause

The syntax of the *WHERE Clause* is

```
WHERE search_condition
```

where search_condition is any value expression (see Section 4.2) that returns a value of type boolean.

After the processing of the FROM clause is done, each row of the derived virtual table is checked against the search condition. If the result of the condition is true, the row is kept in the output table, otherwise (i.e., if the result is false or null) it is discarded. The search condition typically references at least one column of the table generated in the FROM clause; this is not required, but otherwise the WHERE clause will be fairly useless.

> **Note:** The join condition of an inner join can be written either in the WHERE clause or in the JOIN clause. For example, these table expressions are equivalent:

```
FROM a, b WHERE a.id = b.id AND b.val > 5
```

and:

```
FROM a INNER JOIN b ON (a.id = b.id) WHERE b.val > 5
```

or perhaps even:

```
FROM a NATURAL JOIN b WHERE b.val > 5
```

Which one of these you use is mainly a matter of style. The JOIN syntax in the FROM clause is probably not as portable to other SQL database management systems, even though it is in the SQL standard. For outer joins there is no choice: they must be done in the FROM clause. The ON or USING clause of an outer join is *not* equivalent to a WHERE condition, because it results in the addition of rows (for unmatched input rows) as well as the removal of rows in the final result.

Here are some examples of WHERE clauses:

```
SELECT ... FROM fdt WHERE c1 > 5

SELECT ... FROM fdt WHERE c1 IN (1, 2, 3)

SELECT ... FROM fdt WHERE c1 IN (SELECT c1 FROM t2)

SELECT ... FROM fdt WHERE c1 IN (SELECT c3 FROM t2 WHERE c2 = fdt.c1 + 10)

SELECT ... FROM fdt WHERE c1 BETWEEN (SELECT c3 FROM t2 WHERE c2 = fdt.c1 + 10)

SELECT ... FROM fdt WHERE EXISTS (SELECT c1 FROM t2 WHERE c2 > fdt.c1)
```

fdt is the table derived in the FROM clause. Rows that do not meet the search condition of the WHERE clause are eliminated from fdt. Notice the use of scalar subqueries as value expressions. Just like any other query, the subqueries can employ complex table expressions. Notice also how fdt is referenced in the subqueries. Qualifying c1 as fdt.c1 is only necessary if c1 is also the name of a column in the derived input table of the subquery. But qualifying the column name adds clarity even when it is not needed. This example shows how the column naming scope of an outer query extends into its inner queries.

7.2.3. The GROUP BY and HAVING Clauses

After passing the WHERE filter, the derived input table might be subject to grouping, using the GROUP BY clause, and elimination of group rows using the HAVING clause.

```
SELECT select_list
    FROM ...
    [WHERE ...]
    GROUP BY grouping_column_reference [, grouping_column_reference]...
```

The *GROUP BY Clause* is used to group together those rows in a table that have the same values in all the columns listed. The order in which the columns are listed does not matter. The effect is to combine each set of rows having common values into one group row that represents all rows in the group. This is done to eliminate redundancy in the output and/or compute aggregates that apply to these groups. For instance:

```
=> SELECT * FROM test1;
 x | y
---+---
 a | 3
 c | 2
 b | 5
 a | 1
(4 rows)

=> SELECT x FROM test1 GROUP BY x;
 x
---
 a
 b
 c
(3 rows)
```

In the second query, we could not have written SELECT * FROM test1 GROUP BY x, because there is no single value for the column y that could be associated with each group. The grouped-by columns can be referenced in the select list since they have a single value in each group.

In general, if a table is grouped, columns that are not listed in GROUP BY cannot be referenced except in aggregate expressions. An example with aggregate expressions is:

```
=> SELECT x, sum(y) FROM test1 GROUP BY x;
 x | sum
---+-----
 a |   4
 b |   5
 c |   2
(3 rows)
```

Here sum is an aggregate function that computes a single value over the entire group. More information about the available aggregate functions can be found in Section 9.20.

> **Tip:** Grouping without aggregate expressions effectively calculates the set of distinct values in a column. This can also be achieved using the DISTINCT clause (see Section 7.3.3).

Here is another example: it calculates the total sales for each product (rather than the total sales of all products):

```
SELECT product_id, p.name, (sum(s.units) * p.price) AS sales
    FROM products p LEFT JOIN sales s USING (product_id)
    GROUP BY product_id, p.name, p.price;
```

In this example, the columns product_id, p.name, and p.price must be in the GROUP BY clause since they are referenced in the query select list (but see below). The column s.units does not have to be in the GROUP BY list since it is only used in an aggregate expression (sum(...)), which represents the sales of a product. For each product, the query returns a summary row about all sales of the product.

If the products table is set up so that, say, product_id is the primary key, then it would be enough to group by product_id in the above example, since name and price would be *functionally dependent* on the product ID, and so there would be no ambiguity about which name and price value to return for each product ID group.

In strict SQL, GROUP BY can only group by columns of the source table but PostgreSQL extends this to also allow GROUP BY to group by columns in the select list. Grouping by value expressions instead of simple column names is also allowed.

If a table has been grouped using GROUP BY, but only certain groups are of interest, the HAVING clause can be used, much like a WHERE clause, to eliminate groups from the result. The syntax is:

```
SELECT select_list FROM ... [WHERE ...] GROUP BY ... HAVING boolean_expression
```

Expressions in the HAVING clause can refer both to grouped expressions and to ungrouped expressions (which necessarily involve an aggregate function).

Example:

```
=> SELECT x, sum(y) FROM test1 GROUP BY x HAVING sum(y) > 3;
 x | sum
---+-----
 a |   4
 b |   5
(2 rows)
```

```
=> SELECT x, sum(y) FROM test1 GROUP BY x HAVING x < 'c';
 x | sum
---+-----
 a |   4
 b |   5
(2 rows)
```

Again, a more realistic example:

```
SELECT product_id, p.name, (sum(s.units) * (p.price - p.cost)) AS profit
    FROM products p LEFT JOIN sales s USING (product_id)
    WHERE s.date > CURRENT_DATE - INTERVAL '4 weeks'
    GROUP BY product_id, p.name, p.price, p.cost
    HAVING sum(p.price * s.units) > 5000;
```

In the example above, the WHERE clause is selecting rows by a column that is not grouped (the expression is only true for sales during the last four weeks), while the HAVING clause restricts the output to groups with total gross sales over 5000. Note that the aggregate expressions do not necessarily need to be the same in all parts of the query.

If a query contains aggregate function calls, but no GROUP BY clause, grouping still occurs: the result is a single group row (or perhaps no rows at all, if the single row is then eliminated by HAVING). The same is true if it contains a HAVING clause, even without any aggregate function calls or GROUP BY clause.

7.2.4. Window Function Processing

If the query contains any window functions (see Section 3.5, Section 9.21 and Section 4.2.8), these functions are evaluated after any grouping, aggregation, and HAVING filtering is performed. That is, if the query uses any aggregates, GROUP BY, or HAVING, then the rows seen by the window functions are the group rows instead of the original table rows from FROM/WHERE.

When multiple window functions are used, all the window functions having syntactically equivalent PARTITION BY and ORDER BY clauses in their window definitions are guaranteed to be evaluated in a single pass over the data. Therefore they will see the same sort ordering, even if the ORDER BY does not uniquely determine an ordering. However, no guarantees are made about the evaluation of functions having different PARTITION BY or ORDER BY specifications. (In such cases a sort step is typically required between the passes of window function evaluations, and the sort is not guaranteed to preserve ordering of rows that its ORDER BY sees as equivalent.)

Currently, window functions always require presorted data, and so the query output will be ordered according to one or another of the window functions' PARTITION BY/ORDER BY clauses. It is not recommended to rely on this, however. Use an explicit top-level ORDER BY clause if you want to be sure the results are sorted in a particular way.

7.3. Select Lists

As shown in the previous section, the table expression in the SELECT command constructs an intermediate virtual table by possibly combining tables, views, eliminating rows, grouping, etc. This table is finally passed on to processing by the *select list*. The select list determines which *columns* of the intermediate table are actually output.

7.3.1. Select-List Items

The simplest kind of select list is * which emits all columns that the table expression produces. Otherwise, a select list is a comma-separated list of value expressions (as defined in Section 4.2). For instance, it could be a list of column names:

```
SELECT a, b, c FROM ...
```

The columns names a, b, and c are either the actual names of the columns of tables referenced in the FROM clause, or the aliases given to them as explained in Section 7.2.1.2. The name space available in the select list is the same as in the WHERE clause, unless grouping is used, in which case it is the same as in the HAVING clause.

If more than one table has a column of the same name, the table name must also be given, as in:

```
SELECT tbl1.a, tbl2.a, tbl1.b FROM ...
```

When working with multiple tables, it can also be useful to ask for all the columns of a particular table:

```
SELECT tbl1.*, tbl2.a FROM ...
```

(See also Section 7.2.2.)

If an arbitrary value expression is used in the select list, it conceptually adds a new virtual column to the returned table. The value expression is evaluated once for each result row, with the row's values substituted for any column references. But the expressions in the select list do not have to reference any columns in the table expression of the FROM clause; they can be constant arithmetic expressions, for instance.

7.3.2. Column Labels

The entries in the select list can be assigned names for subsequent processing, such as for use in an ORDER BY clause or for display by the client application. For example:

```
SELECT a AS value, b + c AS sum FROM ...
```

If no output column name is specified using AS, the system assigns a default column name. For simple column references, this is the name of the referenced column. For function calls, this is the name of the function. For complex expressions, the system will generate a generic name.

The AS keyword is optional, but only if the new column name does not match any PostgreSQL keyword (see Appendix C). To avoid an accidental match to a keyword, you can double-quote the column name. For example, VALUE is a keyword, so this does not work:

```
SELECT a value, b + c AS sum FROM ...
```

but this does:

```
SELECT a "value", b + c AS sum FROM ...
```

For protection against possible future keyword additions, it is recommended that you always either write AS or double-quote the output column name.

> **Note:** The naming of output columns here is different from that done in the FROM clause (see Section 7.2.1.2). It is possible to rename the same column twice, but the name assigned in the select list is the one that will be passed on.

7.3.3. DISTINCT

After the select list has been processed, the result table can optionally be subject to the elimination of duplicate rows. The DISTINCT key word is written directly after SELECT to specify this:

```
SELECT DISTINCT select_list ...
```

(Instead of DISTINCT the key word ALL can be used to specify the default behavior of retaining all rows.)

Obviously, two rows are considered distinct if they differ in at least one column value. Null values are considered equal in this comparison.

Alternatively, an arbitrary expression can determine what rows are to be considered distinct:

```
SELECT DISTINCT ON (expression [, expression ...]) select_list ...
```

Here `expression` is an arbitrary value expression that is evaluated for all rows. A set of rows for which all the expressions are equal are considered duplicates, and only the first row of the set is kept in the output. Note that the "first row" of a set is unpredictable unless the query is sorted on enough columns to guarantee a unique ordering of the rows arriving at the `DISTINCT` filter. (`DISTINCT ON` processing occurs after `ORDER BY` sorting.)

The `DISTINCT ON` clause is not part of the SQL standard and is sometimes considered bad style because of the potentially indeterminate nature of its results. With judicious use of `GROUP BY` and subqueries in `FROM`, this construct can be avoided, but it is often the most convenient alternative.

7.4. Combining Queries

The results of two queries can be combined using the set operations union, intersection, and difference. The syntax is

```
query1 UNION [ALL] query2
query1 INTERSECT [ALL] query2
query1 EXCEPT [ALL] query2
```

`query1` and `query2` are queries that can use any of the features discussed up to this point. Set operations can also be nested and chained, for example

```
query1 UNION query2 UNION query3
```

which is executed as:

```
(query1 UNION query2) UNION query3
```

`UNION` effectively appends the result of `query2` to the result of `query1` (although there is no guarantee that this is the order in which the rows are actually returned). Furthermore, it eliminates duplicate rows from its result, in the same way as `DISTINCT`, unless `UNION ALL` is used.

`INTERSECT` returns all rows that are both in the result of `query1` and in the result of `query2`. Duplicate rows are eliminated unless `INTERSECT ALL` is used.

`EXCEPT` returns all rows that are in the result of `query1` but not in the result of `query2`. (This is sometimes called the *difference* between two queries.) Again, duplicates are eliminated unless `EXCEPT ALL` is used.

In order to calculate the union, intersection, or difference of two queries, the two queries must be "union compatible", which means that they return the same number of columns and the corresponding columns have compatible data types, as described in Section 10.5.

7.5. Sorting Rows

After a query has produced an output table (after the select list has been processed) it can optionally be sorted. If sorting is not chosen, the rows will be returned in an unspecified order. The actual order in that case will depend on the scan and join plan types and the order on disk, but it must not be relied on. A particular output ordering can only be guaranteed if the sort step is explicitly chosen.

The ORDER BY clause specifies the sort order:

```
SELECT select_list
    FROM table_expression
    ORDER BY sort_expression1 [ASC | DESC] [NULLS { FIRST | LAST }]
             [, sort_expression2 [ASC | DESC] [NULLS { FIRST | LAST }] ...]
```

The sort expression(s) can be any expression that would be valid in the query's select list. An example is:

```
SELECT a, b FROM table1 ORDER BY a + b, c;
```

When more than one expression is specified, the later values are used to sort rows that are equal according to the earlier values. Each expression can be followed by an optional ASC or DESC keyword to set the sort direction to ascending or descending. ASC order is the default. Ascending order puts smaller values first, where "smaller" is defined in terms of the $<$ operator. Similarly, descending order is determined with the $>$ operator. [1]

The NULLS FIRST and NULLS LAST options can be used to determine whether nulls appear before or after non-null values in the sort ordering. By default, null values sort as if larger than any non-null value; that is, NULLS FIRST is the default for DESC order, and NULLS LAST otherwise.

Note that the ordering options are considered independently for each sort column. For example ORDER BY x, y DESC means ORDER BY x ASC, y DESC, which is not the same as ORDER BY x DESC, y DESC.

A *sort_expression* can also be the column label or number of an output column, as in:

```
SELECT a + b AS sum, c FROM table1 ORDER BY sum;
SELECT a, max(b) FROM table1 GROUP BY a ORDER BY 1;
```

both of which sort by the first output column. Note that an output column name has to stand alone, that is, it cannot be used in an expression — for example, this is *not* correct:

```
SELECT a + b AS sum, c FROM table1 ORDER BY sum + c;          -- wrong
```

This restriction is made to reduce ambiguity. There is still ambiguity if an ORDER BY item is a simple name that could match either an output column name or a column from the table expression. The output column is used in such cases. This would only cause confusion if you use AS to rename an output column to match some other table column's name.

ORDER BY can be applied to the result of a UNION, INTERSECT, or EXCEPT combination, but in this case it is only permitted to sort by output column names or numbers, not by expressions.

---

1. Actually, PostgreSQL uses the *default B-tree operator class* for the expression's data type to determine the sort ordering for ASC and DESC. Conventionally, data types will be set up so that the $<$ and $>$ operators correspond to this sort ordering, but a user-defined data type's designer could choose to do something different.

7.6. `LIMIT` and `OFFSET`

`LIMIT` and `OFFSET` allow you to retrieve just a portion of the rows that are generated by the rest of the query:

```
SELECT select_list
    FROM table_expression
    [ ORDER BY ... ]
    [ LIMIT { number | ALL } ] [ OFFSET number ]
```

If a limit count is given, no more than that many rows will be returned (but possibly less, if the query itself yields less rows). `LIMIT ALL` is the same as omitting the `LIMIT` clause.

`OFFSET` says to skip that many rows before beginning to return rows. `OFFSET 0` is the same as omitting the `OFFSET` clause, and `LIMIT NULL` is the same as omitting the `LIMIT` clause. If both `OFFSET` and `LIMIT` appear, then `OFFSET` rows are skipped before starting to count the `LIMIT` rows that are returned.

When using `LIMIT`, it is important to use an `ORDER BY` clause that constrains the result rows into a unique order. Otherwise you will get an unpredictable subset of the query's rows. You might be asking for the tenth through twentieth rows, but tenth through twentieth in what ordering? The ordering is unknown, unless you specified `ORDER BY`.

The query optimizer takes `LIMIT` into account when generating query plans, so you are very likely to get different plans (yielding different row orders) depending on what you give for `LIMIT` and `OFFSET`. Thus, using different `LIMIT`/`OFFSET` values to select different subsets of a query result *will give inconsistent results* unless you enforce a predictable result ordering with `ORDER BY`. This is not a bug; it is an inherent consequence of the fact that SQL does not promise to deliver the results of a query in any particular order unless `ORDER BY` is used to constrain the order.

The rows skipped by an `OFFSET` clause still have to be computed inside the server; therefore a large `OFFSET` might be inefficient.

7.7. `VALUES` Lists

`VALUES` provides a way to generate a "constant table" that can be used in a query without having to actually create and populate a table on-disk. The syntax is

```
VALUES ( expression [, ...] ) [, ...]
```

Each parenthesized list of expressions generates a row in the table. The lists must all have the same number of elements (i.e., the number of columns in the table), and corresponding entries in each list must have compatible data types. The actual data type assigned to each column of the result is determined using the same rules as for `UNION` (see Section 10.5).

As an example:

```
VALUES (1, 'one'), (2, 'two'), (3, 'three');
```

will return a table of two columns and three rows. It's effectively equivalent to:

```
SELECT 1 AS column1, 'one' AS column2
UNION ALL
SELECT 2, 'two'
UNION ALL
SELECT 3, 'three';
```

By default, PostgreSQL assigns the names `column1`, `column2`, etc. to the columns of a `VALUES` table. The column names are not specified by the SQL standard and different database systems do it differently, so it's usually better to override the default names with a table alias list, like this:

```
=> SELECT * FROM (VALUES (1, 'one'), (2, 'two'), (3, 'three')) AS t (num,letter
 num | letter
-----+--------
   1 | one
   2 | two
   3 | three
(3 rows)
```

Syntactically, `VALUES` followed by expression lists is treated as equivalent to:

```
SELECT select_list FROM table_expression
```

and can appear anywhere a `SELECT` can. For example, you can use it as part of a `UNION`, or attach a *sort_specification* (`ORDER BY`, `LIMIT`, and/or `OFFSET`) to it. `VALUES` is most commonly used as the data source in an `INSERT` command, and next most commonly as a subquery.

For more information see VALUES.

7.8. `WITH` Queries (Common Table Expressions)

`WITH` provides a way to write auxiliary statements for use in a larger query. These statements, which are often referred to as Common Table Expressions or CTEs, can be thought of as defining temporary tables that exist just for one query. Each auxiliary statement in a `WITH` clause can be a `SELECT`, `INSERT`, `UPDATE`, or `DELETE`; and the `WITH` clause itself is attached to a primary statement that can also be a `SELECT`, `INSERT`, `UPDATE`, or `DELETE`.

7.8.1. `SELECT` in `WITH`

The basic value of `SELECT` in `WITH` is to break down complicated queries into simpler parts. An example is:

```
WITH regional_sales AS (
        SELECT region, SUM(amount) AS total_sales
        FROM orders
        GROUP BY region
    ), top_regions AS (
        SELECT region
        FROM regional_sales
```

```
      WHERE total_sales > (SELECT SUM(total_sales)/10 FROM regional_sales)
    )
SELECT region,
       product,
       SUM(quantity) AS product_units,
       SUM(amount) AS product_sales
FROM orders
WHERE region IN (SELECT region FROM top_regions)
GROUP BY region, product;
```

which displays per-product sales totals in only the top sales regions. The WITH clause defines two auxiliary statements named regional_sales and top_regions, where the output of regional_sales is used in top_regions and the output of top_regions is used in the primary SELECT query. This example could have been written without WITH, but we'd have needed two levels of nested sub-SELECTs. It's a bit easier to follow this way.

The optional RECURSIVE modifier changes WITH from a mere syntactic convenience into a feature that accomplishes things not otherwise possible in standard SQL. Using RECURSIVE, a WITH query can refer to its own output. A very simple example is this query to sum the integers from 1 through 100:

```
WITH RECURSIVE t(n) AS (
    VALUES (1)
  UNION ALL
    SELECT n+1 FROM t WHERE n < 100
)
SELECT sum(n) FROM t;
```

The general form of a recursive WITH query is always a *non-recursive term*, then UNION (or UNION ALL), then a *recursive term*, where only the recursive term can contain a reference to the query's own output. Such a query is executed as follows:

Recursive Query Evaluation

1. Evaluate the non-recursive term. For UNION (but not UNION ALL), discard duplicate rows. Include all remaining rows in the result of the recursive query, and also place them in a temporary *working table*.

2. So long as the working table is not empty, repeat these steps:

   a. Evaluate the recursive term, substituting the current contents of the working table for the recursive self-reference. For UNION (but not UNION ALL), discard duplicate rows and rows that duplicate any previous result row. Include all remaining rows in the result of the recursive query, and also place them in a temporary *intermediate table*.

   b. Replace the contents of the working table with the contents of the intermediate table, then empty the intermediate table.

Note: Strictly speaking, this process is iteration not recursion, but RECURSIVE is the terminology chosen by the SQL standards committee.

In the example above, the working table has just a single row in each step, and it takes on the values from 1 through 100 in successive steps. In the 100th step, there is no output because of the WHERE clause, and so the query terminates.

Recursive queries are typically used to deal with hierarchical or tree-structured data. A useful example is this query to find all the direct and indirect sub-parts of a product, given only a table that shows immediate inclusions:

```
WITH RECURSIVE included_parts(sub_part, part, quantity) AS (
    SELECT sub_part, part, quantity FROM parts WHERE part = 'our_product'
  UNION ALL
    SELECT p.sub_part, p.part, p.quantity
    FROM included_parts pr, parts p
    WHERE p.part = pr.sub_part
  )
SELECT sub_part, SUM(quantity) as total_quantity
FROM included_parts
GROUP BY sub_part
```

When working with recursive queries it is important to be sure that the recursive part of the query will eventually return no tuples, or else the query will loop indefinitely. Sometimes, using UNION instead of UNION ALL can accomplish this by discarding rows that duplicate previous output rows. However, often a cycle does not involve output rows that are completely duplicate: it may be necessary to check just one or a few fields to see if the same point has been reached before. The standard method for handling such situations is to compute an array of the already-visited values. For example, consider the following query that searches a table graph using a link field:

```
WITH RECURSIVE search_graph(id, link, data, depth) AS (
        SELECT g.id, g.link, g.data, 1
        FROM graph g
      UNION ALL
        SELECT g.id, g.link, g.data, sg.depth + 1
        FROM graph g, search_graph sg
        WHERE g.id = sg.link
)
SELECT * FROM search_graph;
```

This query will loop if the link relationships contain cycles. Because we require a "depth" output, just changing UNION ALL to UNION would not eliminate the looping. Instead we need to recognize whether we have reached the same row again while following a particular path of links. We add two columns path and cycle to the loop-prone query:

```
WITH RECURSIVE search_graph(id, link, data, depth, path, cycle) AS (
        SELECT g.id, g.link, g.data, 1,
          ARRAY[g.id],
          false
        FROM graph g
      UNION ALL
        SELECT g.id, g.link, g.data, sg.depth + 1,
          path || g.id,
          g.id = ANY(path)
```

```
        FROM graph g, search_graph sg
        WHERE g.id = sg.link AND NOT cycle
)
SELECT * FROM search_graph;
```

Aside from preventing cycles, the array value is often useful in its own right as representing the "path" taken to reach any particular row.

In the general case where more than one field needs to be checked to recognize a cycle, use an array of rows. For example, if we needed to compare fields f1 and f2:

```
WITH RECURSIVE search_graph(id, link, data, depth, path, cycle) AS (
        SELECT g.id, g.link, g.data, 1,
          ARRAY[ROW(g.f1, g.f2)],
          false
        FROM graph g
    UNION ALL
        SELECT g.id, g.link, g.data, sg.depth + 1,
          path || ROW(g.f1, g.f2),
          ROW(g.f1, g.f2) = ANY(path)
        FROM graph g, search_graph sg
        WHERE g.id = sg.link AND NOT cycle
)
SELECT * FROM search_graph;
```

> **Tip:** Omit the ROW() syntax in the common case where only one field needs to be checked to recognize a cycle. This allows a simple array rather than a composite-type array to be used, gaining efficiency.

> **Tip:** The recursive query evaluation algorithm produces its output in breadth-first search order. You can display the results in depth-first search order by making the outer query ORDER BY a "path" column constructed in this way.

A helpful trick for testing queries when you are not certain if they might loop is to place a LIMIT in the parent query. For example, this query would loop forever without the LIMIT:

```
WITH RECURSIVE t(n) AS (
    SELECT 1
  UNION ALL
    SELECT n+1 FROM t
)
SELECT n FROM t LIMIT 100;
```

This works because PostgreSQL's implementation evaluates only as many rows of a WITH query as are actually fetched by the parent query. Using this trick in production is not recommended, because other systems might work differently. Also, it usually won't work if you make the outer query sort the recursive query's results or join them to some other table, because in such cases the outer query will usually try to fetch all of the WITH query's output anyway.

A useful property of WITH queries is that they are evaluated only once per execution of the parent query, even if they are referred to more than once by the parent query or sibling WITH queries. Thus, expensive calculations that are needed in multiple places can be placed within a WITH query to avoid redundant work. Another possible application is to prevent unwanted multiple evaluations of functions with side-effects. However, the other side of this coin is that the optimizer is less able to push restrictions from the parent query down into a WITH query than an ordinary sub-query. The WITH query will generally be evaluated as written, without suppression of rows that the parent query might discard afterwards. (But, as mentioned above, evaluation might stop early if the reference(s) to the query demand only a limited number of rows.)

The examples above only show WITH being used with SELECT, but it can be attached in the same way to INSERT, UPDATE, or DELETE. In each case it effectively provides temporary table(s) that can be referred to in the main command.

7.8.2. Data-Modifying Statements in WITH

You can use data-modifying statements (INSERT, UPDATE, or DELETE) in WITH. This allows you to perform several different operations in the same query. An example is:

```
WITH moved_rows AS (
    DELETE FROM products
    WHERE
        "date" >= '2010-10-01' AND
        "date" < '2010-11-01'
    RETURNING *
)
INSERT INTO products_log
SELECT * FROM moved_rows;
```

This query effectively moves rows from products to products_log. The DELETE in WITH deletes the specified rows from products, returning their contents by means of its RETURNING clause; and then the primary query reads that output and inserts it into products_log.

A fine point of the above example is that the WITH clause is attached to the INSERT, not the sub-SELECT within the INSERT. This is necessary because data-modifying statements are only allowed in WITH clauses that are attached to the top-level statement. However, normal WITH visibility rules apply, so it is possible to refer to the WITH statement's output from the sub-SELECT.

Data-modifying statements in WITH usually have RETURNING clauses, as seen in the example above. It is the output of the RETURNING clause, *not* the target table of the data-modifying statement, that forms the temporary table that can be referred to by the rest of the query. If a data-modifying statement in WITH lacks a RETURNING clause, then it forms no temporary table and cannot be referred to in the rest of the query. Such a statement will be executed nonetheless. A not-particularly-useful example is:

```
WITH t AS (
    DELETE FROM foo
)
DELETE FROM bar;
```

This example would remove all rows from tables foo and bar. The number of affected rows reported to the client would only include rows removed from bar.

Recursive self-references in data-modifying statements are not allowed. In some cases it is possible to work around this limitation by referring to the output of a recursive `WITH`, for example:

```
WITH RECURSIVE included_parts(sub_part, part) AS (
    SELECT sub_part, part FROM parts WHERE part = 'our_product'
  UNION ALL
    SELECT p.sub_part, p.part
    FROM included_parts pr, parts p
    WHERE p.part = pr.sub_part
  )
DELETE FROM parts
  WHERE part IN (SELECT part FROM included_parts);
```

This query would remove all direct and indirect subparts of a product.

Data-modifying statements in `WITH` are executed exactly once, and always to completion, independently of whether the primary query reads all (or indeed any) of their output. Notice that this is different from the rule for `SELECT` in `WITH`: as stated in the previous section, execution of a `SELECT` is carried only as far as the primary query demands its output.

The sub-statements in `WITH` are executed concurrently with each other and with the main query. Therefore, when using data-modifying statements in `WITH`, the order in which the specified updates actually happen is unpredictable. All the statements are executed with the same *snapshot* (see Chapter 13), so they cannot "see" one another's effects on the target tables. This alleviates the effects of the unpredictability of the actual order of row updates, and means that `RETURNING` data is the only way to communicate changes between different `WITH` sub-statements and the main query. An example of this is that in

```
WITH t AS (
    UPDATE products SET price = price * 1.05
    RETURNING *
)
SELECT * FROM products;
```

the outer `SELECT` would return the original prices before the action of the `UPDATE`, while in

```
WITH t AS (
    UPDATE products SET price = price * 1.05
    RETURNING *
)
SELECT * FROM t;
```

the outer `SELECT` would return the updated data.

Trying to update the same row twice in a single statement is not supported. Only one of the modifications takes place, but it is not easy (and sometimes not possible) to reliably predict which one. This also applies to deleting a row that was already updated in the same statement: only the update is performed. Therefore you should generally avoid trying to modify a single row twice in a single statement. In particular avoid writing `WITH` sub-statements that could affect the same rows changed by the main statement or a sibling sub-statement. The effects of such a statement will not be predictable.

At present, any table used as the target of a data-modifying statement in `WITH` must not have a conditional rule, nor an `ALSO` rule, nor an `INSTEAD` rule that expands to multiple statements.

Chapter 8. Data Types

PostgreSQL has a rich set of native data types available to users. Users can add new types to PostgreSQL using the CREATE TYPE command.

Table 8-1 shows all the built-in general-purpose data types. Most of the alternative names listed in the "Aliases" column are the names used internally by PostgreSQL for historical reasons. In addition, some internally used or deprecated types are available, but are not listed here.

Table 8-1. Data Types

Name	Aliases	Description
`bigint`	`int8`	signed eight-byte integer
`bigserial`	`serial8`	autoincrementing eight-byte integer
`bit [ (n) ]`		fixed-length bit string
`bit varying [ (n) ]`	`varbit`	variable-length bit string
`boolean`	`bool`	logical Boolean (true/false)
`box`		rectangular box on a plane
`bytea`		binary data ("byte array")
`character [ (n) ]`	`char [ (n) ]`	fixed-length character string
`character varying [ (n) ]`	`varchar [ (n) ]`	variable-length character string
`cidr`		IPv4 or IPv6 network address
`circle`		circle on a plane
`date`		calendar date (year, month, day)
`double precision`	`float8`	double precision floating-point number (8 bytes)
`inet`		IPv4 or IPv6 host address
`integer`	`int, int4`	signed four-byte integer
`interval [ fields ] [ (p) ]`		time span
`json`		textual JSON data
`jsonb`		binary JSON data, decomposed
`line`		infinite line on a plane
`lseg`		line segment on a plane
`macaddr`		MAC (Media Access Control) address
`money`		currency amount
`numeric [ (p, s) ]`	`decimal [ (p, s) ]`	exact numeric of selectable precision
`path`		geometric path on a plane

Name	Aliases	Description
`pg_lsn`		PostgreSQL Log Sequence Number
`point`		geometric point on a plane
`polygon`		closed geometric path on a plane
`real`	`float4`	single precision floating-point number (4 bytes)
`smallint`	`int2`	signed two-byte integer
`smallserial`	`serial2`	autoincrementing two-byte integer
`serial`	`serial4`	autoincrementing four-byte integer
`text`		variable-length character string
`time [ (p) ] [ without time zone ]`		time of day (no time zone)
`time [ (p) ] with time zone`	`timetz`	time of day, including time zone
`timestamp [ (p) ] [ without time zone ]`		date and time (no time zone)
`timestamp [ (p) ] with time zone`	`timestamptz`	date and time, including time zone
`tsquery`		text search query
`tsvector`		text search document
`txid_snapshot`		user-level transaction ID snapshot
`uuid`		universally unique identifier
`xml`		XML data

Compatibility: The following types (or spellings thereof) are specified by SQL: `bigint`, `bit`, `bit varying`, `boolean`, `char`, `character varying`, `character`, `varchar`, `date`, `double precision`, `integer`, `interval`, `numeric`, `decimal`, `real`, `smallint`, `time` (with or without time zone), `timestamp` (with or without time zone), `xml`.

Each data type has an external representation determined by its input and output functions. Many of the built-in types have obvious external formats. However, several types are either unique to PostgreSQL, such as geometric paths, or have several possible formats, such as the date and time types. Some of the input and output functions are not invertible, i.e., the result of an output function might lose accuracy when compared to the original input.

8.1. Numeric Types

Numeric types consist of two-, four-, and eight-byte integers, four- and eight-byte floating-point numbers, and selectable-precision decimals. Table 8-2 lists the available types.

Table 8-2. Numeric Types

Name	Storage Size	Description	Range
smallint	2 bytes	small-range integer	-32768 to +32767
integer	4 bytes	typical choice for integer	-2147483648 to +2147483647
bigint	8 bytes	large-range integer	-9223372036854775808 to +9223372036854775807
decimal	variable	user-specified precision, exact	up to 131072 digits before the decimal point; up to 16383 digits after the decimal point
numeric	variable	user-specified precision, exact	up to 131072 digits before the decimal point; up to 16383 digits after the decimal point
real	4 bytes	variable-precision, inexact	6 decimal digits precision
double precision	8 bytes	variable-precision, inexact	15 decimal digits precision
smallserial	2 bytes	small autoincrementing integer	1 to 32767
serial	4 bytes	autoincrementing integer	1 to 2147483647
bigserial	8 bytes	large autoincrementing integer	1 to 9223372036854775807

The syntax of constants for the numeric types is described in Section 4.1.2. The numeric types have a full set of corresponding arithmetic operators and functions. Refer to Chapter 9 for more information. The following sections describe the types in detail.

8.1.1. Integer Types

The types smallint, integer, and bigint store whole numbers, that is, numbers without fractional components, of various ranges. Attempts to store values outside of the allowed range will result in an error.

The type integer is the common choice, as it offers the best balance between range, storage size, and performance. The smallint type is generally only used if disk space is at a premium. The bigint type is designed to be used when the range of the integer type is insufficient.

SQL only specifies the integer types integer (or int), smallint, and bigint. The type names int2, int4, and int8 are extensions, which are also used by some other SQL database systems.

8.1.2. Arbitrary Precision Numbers

The type `numeric` can store numbers with a very large number of digits and perform calculations exactly. It is especially recommended for storing monetary amounts and other quantities where exactness is required. However, arithmetic on `numeric` values is very slow compared to the integer types, or to the floating-point types described in the next section.

We use the following terms below: The *scale* of a `numeric` is the count of decimal digits in the fractional part, to the right of the decimal point. The *precision* of a `numeric` is the total count of significant digits in the whole number, that is, the number of digits to both sides of the decimal point. So the number 23.5141 has a precision of 6 and a scale of 4. Integers can be considered to have a scale of zero.

Both the maximum precision and the maximum scale of a `numeric` column can be configured. To declare a column of type `numeric` use the syntax:

```
NUMERIC(precision, scale)
```

The precision must be positive, the scale zero or positive. Alternatively:

```
NUMERIC(precision)
```

selects a scale of 0. Specifying:

```
NUMERIC
```

without any precision or scale creates a column in which numeric values of any precision and scale can be stored, up to the implementation limit on precision. A column of this kind will not coerce input values to any particular scale, whereas `numeric` columns with a declared scale will coerce input values to that scale. (The SQL standard requires a default scale of 0, i.e., coercion to integer precision. We find this a bit useless. If you're concerned about portability, always specify the precision and scale explicitly.)

> **Note:** The maximum allowed precision when explicitly specified in the type declaration is 1000; `NUMERIC` without a specified precision is subject to the limits described in Table 8-2.

If the scale of a value to be stored is greater than the declared scale of the column, the system will round the value to the specified number of fractional digits. Then, if the number of digits to the left of the decimal point exceeds the declared precision minus the declared scale, an error is raised.

Numeric values are physically stored without any extra leading or trailing zeroes. Thus, the declared precision and scale of a column are maximums, not fixed allocations. (In this sense the `numeric` type is more akin to `varchar(n)` than to `char(n)`.) The actual storage requirement is two bytes for each group of four decimal digits, plus three to eight bytes overhead.

In addition to ordinary numeric values, the `numeric` type allows the special value NaN, meaning "not-a-number". Any operation on NaN yields another NaN. When writing this value as a constant in an SQL command, you must put quotes around it, for example `UPDATE table SET x = 'NaN'`. On input, the string NaN is recognized in a case-insensitive manner.

> **Note:** In most implementations of the "not-a-number" concept, NaN is not considered equal to any other numeric value (including NaN). In order to allow `numeric` values to be sorted and used in tree-based indexes, PostgreSQL treats NaN values as equal, and greater than all non-NaN values.

The types `decimal` and `numeric` are equivalent. Both types are part of the SQL standard.

8.1.3. Floating-Point Types

The data types `real` and `double precision` are inexact, variable-precision numeric types. In practice, these types are usually implementations of IEEE Standard 754 for Binary Floating-Point Arithmetic (single and double precision, respectively), to the extent that the underlying processor, operating system, and compiler support it.

Inexact means that some values cannot be converted exactly to the internal format and are stored as approximations, so that storing and retrieving a value might show slight discrepancies. Managing these errors and how they propagate through calculations is the subject of an entire branch of mathematics and computer science and will not be discussed here, except for the following points:

- If you require exact storage and calculations (such as for monetary amounts), use the `numeric` type instead.

- If you want to do complicated calculations with these types for anything important, especially if you rely on certain behavior in boundary cases (infinity, underflow), you should evaluate the implementation carefully.

- Comparing two floating-point values for equality might not always work as expected.

On most platforms, the `real` type has a range of at least 1E-37 to 1E+37 with a precision of at least 6 decimal digits. The `double precision` type typically has a range of around 1E-307 to 1E+308 with a precision of at least 15 digits. Values that are too large or too small will cause an error. Rounding might take place if the precision of an input number is too high. Numbers too close to zero that are not representable as distinct from zero will cause an underflow error.

> **Note:** The extra_float_digits setting controls the number of extra significant digits included when a floating point value is converted to text for output. With the default value of 0, the output is the same on every platform supported by PostgreSQL. Increasing it will produce output that more accurately represents the stored value, but may be unportable.

In addition to ordinary numeric values, the floating-point types have several special values:

```
Infinity
-Infinity
NaN
```

These represent the IEEE 754 special values "infinity", "negative infinity", and "not-a-number", respectively. (On a machine whose floating-point arithmetic does not follow IEEE 754, these values will probably not work as expected.) When writing these values as constants in an SQL command, you must put quotes around them, for example `UPDATE table SET x = 'Infinity'`. On input, these strings are recognized in a case-insensitive manner.

Note: IEEE754 specifies that NaN should not compare equal to any other floating-point value (including NaN). In order to allow floating-point values to be sorted and used in tree-based indexes, PostgreSQL treats NaN values as equal, and greater than all non-NaN values.

PostgreSQL also supports the SQL-standard notations float and float(p) for specifying inexact numeric types. Here, *p* specifies the minimum acceptable precision in *binary* digits. PostgreSQL accepts float(1) to float(24) as selecting the real type, while float(25) to float(53) select double precision. Values of *p* outside the allowed range draw an error. float with no precision specified is taken to mean double precision.

Note: The assumption that real and double precision have exactly 24 and 53 bits in the mantissa respectively is correct for IEEE-standard floating point implementations. On non-IEEE platforms it might be off a little, but for simplicity the same ranges of *p* are used on all platforms.

8.1.4. Serial Types

The data types smallserial, serial and bigserial are not true types, but merely a notational convenience for creating unique identifier columns (similar to the AUTO_INCREMENT property supported by some other databases). In the current implementation, specifying:

```
CREATE TABLE tablename (
    colname SERIAL
);
```

is equivalent to specifying:

```
CREATE SEQUENCE tablename_colname_seq;
CREATE TABLE tablename (
    colname integer NOT NULL DEFAULT nextval('tablename_colname_seq')
);
ALTER SEQUENCE tablename_colname_seq OWNED BY tablename.colname;
```

Thus, we have created an integer column and arranged for its default values to be assigned from a sequence generator. A NOT NULL constraint is applied to ensure that a null value cannot be inserted. (In most cases you would also want to attach a UNIQUE or PRIMARY KEY constraint to prevent duplicate values from being inserted by accident, but this is not automatic.) Lastly, the sequence is marked as "owned by" the column, so that it will be dropped if the column or table is dropped.

Note: Because smallserial, serial and bigserial are implemented using sequences, there may be "holes" or gaps in the sequence of values which appears in the column, even if no rows are ever deleted. A value allocated from the sequence is still "used up" even if a row containing that value is never successfully inserted into the table column. This may happen, for example, if the inserting transaction rolls back. See nextval() in Section 9.16 for details.

To insert the next value of the sequence into the `serial` column, specify that the `serial` column should be assigned its default value. This can be done either by excluding the column from the list of columns in the `INSERT` statement, or through the use of the `DEFAULT` key word.

The type names `serial` and `serial4` are equivalent: both create `integer` columns. The type names `bigserial` and `serial8` work the same way, except that they create a `bigint` column. `bigserial` should be used if you anticipate the use of more than 2^{31} identifiers over the lifetime of the table. The type names `smallserial` and `serial2` also work the same way, except that they create a `smallint` column.

The sequence created for a `serial` column is automatically dropped when the owning column is dropped. You can drop the sequence without dropping the column, but this will force removal of the column default expression.

8.2. Monetary Types

The `money` type stores a currency amount with a fixed fractional precision; see Table 8-3. The fractional precision is determined by the database's lc_monetary setting. The range shown in the table assumes there are two fractional digits. Input is accepted in a variety of formats, including integer and floating-point literals, as well as typical currency formatting, such as `'$1,000.00'`. Output is generally in the latter form but depends on the locale.

Table 8-3. Monetary Types

Name	Storage Size	Description	Range
money	8 bytes	currency amount	-92233720368547758.08 to +92233720368547758.07

Since the output of this data type is locale-sensitive, it might not work to load `money` data into a database that has a different setting of `lc_monetary`. To avoid problems, before restoring a dump into a new database make sure `lc_monetary` has the same or equivalent value as in the database that was dumped.

Values of the `numeric`, `int`, and `bigint` data types can be cast to `money`. Conversion from the `real` and `double precision` data types can be done by casting to `numeric` first, for example:

```
SELECT '12.34'::float8::numeric::money;
```

However, this is not recommended. Floating point numbers should not be used to handle money due to the potential for rounding errors.

A `money` value can be cast to `numeric` without loss of precision. Conversion to other types could potentially lose precision, and must also be done in two stages:

```
SELECT '52093.89'::money::numeric::float8;
```

When a `money` value is divided by another `money` value, the result is `double precision` (i.e., a pure number, not money); the currency units cancel each other out in the division.

8.3. Character Types

Table 8-4. Character Types

Name	Description
`character varying(n)`, `varchar(n)`	variable-length with limit
`character(n)`, `char(n)`	fixed-length, blank padded
`text`	variable unlimited length

Table 8-4 shows the general-purpose character types available in PostgreSQL.

SQL defines two primary character types: `character varying(n)` and `character(n)`, where n is a positive integer. Both of these types can store strings up to n characters (not bytes) in length. An attempt to store a longer string into a column of these types will result in an error, unless the excess characters are all spaces, in which case the string will be truncated to the maximum length. (This somewhat bizarre exception is required by the SQL standard.) If the string to be stored is shorter than the declared length, values of type `character` will be space-padded; values of type `character varying` will simply store the shorter string.

If one explicitly casts a value to `character varying(n)` or `character(n)`, then an over-length value will be truncated to n characters without raising an error. (This too is required by the SQL standard.)

The notations `varchar(n)` and `char(n)` are aliases for `character varying(n)` and `character(n)`, respectively. `character` without length specifier is equivalent to `character(1)`. If `character varying` is used without length specifier, the type accepts strings of any size. The latter is a PostgreSQL extension.

In addition, PostgreSQL provides the `text` type, which stores strings of any length. Although the type `text` is not in the SQL standard, several other SQL database management systems have it as well.

Values of type `character` are physically padded with spaces to the specified width n, and are stored and displayed that way. However, trailing spaces are treated as semantically insignificant and disregarded when comparing two values of type `character`. In collations where whitespace is significant, this behavior can produce unexpected results, e.g. `SELECT 'a '::CHAR(2) collate "C" < 'a\n'::CHAR(2)` returns true. Trailing spaces are removed when converting a `character` value to one of the other string types. Note that trailing spaces *are* semantically significant in `character varying` and `text` values, and when using pattern matching, e.g. `LIKE`, regular expressions.

The storage requirement for a short string (up to 126 bytes) is 1 byte plus the actual string, which includes the space padding in the case of `character`. Longer strings have 4 bytes of overhead instead of 1. Long strings are compressed by the system automatically, so the physical requirement on disk might be less. Very long values are also stored in background tables so that they do not interfere with rapid access to shorter column values. In any case, the longest possible character string that can be stored is about 1 GB. (The maximum value that will be allowed for n in the data type declaration is less than that. It wouldn't be useful to change this because with multibyte character encodings the number of characters and bytes can be quite different. If you desire to store long strings with no specific upper limit, use `text` or `character varying` without a length specifier, rather than making up an arbitrary length limit.)

> **Tip:** There is no performance difference among these three types, apart from increased storage space when using the blank-padded type, and a few extra CPU cycles to check the length when storing into a length-constrained column. While `character(n)` has performance advantages in some other database systems, there is no such advantage in PostgreSQL; in fact `character(n)` is usually the slowest of the three because of its additional storage costs. In most situations `text` or `character varying` should be used instead.

Refer to Section 4.1.2.1 for information about the syntax of string literals, and to Chapter 9 for information about available operators and functions. The database character set determines the character set used to store textual values; for more information on character set support, refer to Section 22.3.

Example 8-1. Using the Character Types

```
CREATE TABLE test1 (a character(4));
INSERT INTO test1 VALUES ('ok');
SELECT a, char_length(a) FROM test1; -- ❶
  a   | char_length
------+-------------
 ok   |           2


CREATE TABLE test2 (b varchar(5));
INSERT INTO test2 VALUES ('ok');
INSERT INTO test2 VALUES ('good      ');
INSERT INTO test2 VALUES ('too long');
ERROR:  value too long for type character varying(5)
INSERT INTO test2 VALUES ('too long'::varchar(5)); -- explicit truncation
SELECT b, char_length(b) FROM test2;
   b   | char_length
-------+-------------
 ok    |           2
 good  |           5
 too l |           5
```

❶ The `char_length` function is discussed in Section 9.4.

There are two other fixed-length character types in PostgreSQL, shown in Table 8-5. The `name` type exists *only* for the storage of identifiers in the internal system catalogs and is not intended for use by the general user. Its length is currently defined as 64 bytes (63 usable characters plus terminator) but should be referenced using the constant NAMEDATALEN in C source code. The length is set at compile time (and is therefore adjustable for special uses); the default maximum length might change in a future release. The type `"char"` (note the quotes) is different from `char(1)` in that it only uses one byte of storage. It is internally used in the system catalogs as a simplistic enumeration type.

Table 8-5. Special Character Types

Name	Storage Size	Description
`"char"`	1 byte	single-byte internal type
`name`	64 bytes	internal type for object names

8.4. Binary Data Types

The `bytea` data type allows storage of binary strings; see Table 8-6.

Table 8-6. Binary Data Types

Name	Storage Size	Description
`bytea`	1 or 4 bytes plus the actual binary string	variable-length binary string

A binary string is a sequence of octets (or bytes). Binary strings are distinguished from character strings in two ways. First, binary strings specifically allow storing octets of value zero and other "non-printable" octets (usually, octets outside the range 32 to 126). Character strings disallow zero octets, and also disallow any other octet values and sequences of octet values that are invalid according to the database's selected character set encoding. Second, operations on binary strings process the actual bytes, whereas the processing of character strings depends on locale settings. In short, binary strings are appropriate for storing data that the programmer thinks of as "raw bytes", whereas character strings are appropriate for storing text.

The `bytea` type supports two external formats for input and output: PostgreSQL's historical "escape" format, and "hex" format. Both of these are always accepted on input. The output format depends on the configuration parameter bytea_output; the default is hex. (Note that the hex format was introduced in PostgreSQL 9.0; earlier versions and some tools don't understand it.)

The SQL standard defines a different binary string type, called `BLOB` or `BINARY LARGE OBJECT`. The input format is different from `bytea`, but the provided functions and operators are mostly the same.

8.4.1. `bytea` Hex Format

The "hex" format encodes binary data as 2 hexadecimal digits per byte, most significant nibble first. The entire string is preceded by the sequence \x (to distinguish it from the escape format). In some contexts, the initial backslash may need to be escaped by doubling it, in the same cases in which backslashes have to be doubled in escape format; details appear below. The hexadecimal digits can be either upper or lower case, and whitespace is permitted between digit pairs (but not within a digit pair nor in the starting \x sequence). The hex format is compatible with a wide range of external applications and protocols, and it tends to be faster to convert than the escape format, so its use is preferred.

Example:

```
SELECT E'\\xDEADBEEF';
```

8.4.2. `bytea` Escape Format

The "escape" format is the traditional PostgreSQL format for the `bytea` type. It takes the approach of representing a binary string as a sequence of ASCII characters, while converting those bytes that cannot be represented as an ASCII character into special escape sequences. If, from the point of view of the application, representing bytes as characters makes sense, then this representation can be convenient. But in practice it is usually confusing because it fuzzes up the distinction between binary strings and character strings, and also the particular escape mechanism that was chosen is somewhat unwieldy. So this format should probably be avoided for most new applications.

When entering `bytea` values in escape format, octets of certain values *must* be escaped, while all octet values *can* be escaped. In general, to escape an octet, convert it into its three-digit octal value and precede it by a backslash (or two backslashes, if writing the value as a literal using escape string syntax). Backslash itself (octet value 92) can alternatively be represented by double backslashes. Table 8-7 shows the characters that must be escaped, and gives the alternative escape sequences where applicable.

Table 8-7. `bytea` Literal Escaped Octets

Decimal Octet Value	Description	Escaped Input Representation	Example	Output Representation
0	zero octet	`E'\\000'`	`SELECT E'\\000'::bytea;`	`\000`
39	single quote	`''''` or `E'\\047'`	`SELECT E'\''::bytea;`	`'`
92	backslash	`E'\\\\'` or `E'\\134'`	`SELECT E'\\\\'::bytea;`	`\\`
0 to 31 and 127 to 255	"non-printable" octets	`E'\\xxx'` (octal value)	`SELECT E'\\001'::bytea;`	`\001`

The requirement to escape *non-printable* octets varies depending on locale settings. In some instances you can get away with leaving them unescaped. Note that the result in each of the examples in Table 8-7 was exactly one octet in length, even though the output representation is sometimes more than one character.

The reason multiple backslashes are required, as shown in Table 8-7, is that an input string written as a string literal must pass through two parse phases in the PostgreSQL server. The first backslash of each pair is interpreted as an escape character by the string-literal parser (assuming escape string syntax is used) and is therefore consumed, leaving the second backslash of the pair. (Dollar-quoted strings can be used to avoid this level of escaping.) The remaining backslash is then recognized by the `bytea` input function as starting either a three digit octal value or escaping another backslash. For example, a string literal passed to the server as `E'\\001'` becomes `\001` after passing through the escape string parser. The `\001` is then sent to the `bytea` input function, where it is converted to a single octet with a decimal value of 1. Note that the single-quote character is not treated specially by `bytea`, so it follows the normal rules for string literals. (See also Section 4.1.2.1.)

`Bytea` octets are sometimes escaped when output. In general, each "non-printable" octet is converted into its equivalent three-digit octal value and preceded by one backslash. Most "printable" octets are represented by their standard representation in the client character set. The octet with decimal value 92 (backslash) is doubled in the output. Details are in Table 8-8.

Table 8-8. `bytea` Output Escaped Octets

Decimal Octet Value	Description	Escaped Output Representation	Example	Output Result
92	backslash	\\	SELECT E'\\134'::bytea;	\\
0 to 31 and 127 to 255	"non-printable" octets	\xxx (octal value)	SELECT E'\\001'::bytea;	\001
32 to 126	"printable" octets	client character set representation	SELECT E'\\176'::bytea;	~

Depending on the front end to PostgreSQL you use, you might have additional work to do in terms of escaping and unescaping `bytea` strings. For example, you might also have to escape line feeds and carriage returns if your interface automatically translates these.

8.5. Date/Time Types

PostgreSQL supports the full set of SQL date and time types, shown in Table 8-9. The operations available on these data types are described in Section 9.9. Dates are counted according to the Gregorian calendar, even in years before that calendar was introduced (see Section B.4 for more information).

Table 8-9. Date/Time Types

Name	Storage Size	Description	Low Value	High Value	Resolution
timestamp [(p)] [without time zone]	8 bytes	both date and time (no time zone)	4713 BC	294276 AD	1 microsecond / 14 digits
timestamp [(p)] with time zone	8 bytes	both date and time, with time zone	4713 BC	294276 AD	1 microsecond / 14 digits
date	4 bytes	date (no time of day)	4713 BC	5874897 AD	1 day
time [(p)] [without time zone]	8 bytes	time of day (no date)	00:00:00	24:00:00	1 microsecond / 14 digits
time [(p)] with time zone	12 bytes	times of day only, with time zone	00:00:00+1459	24:00:00-1459	1 microsecond / 14 digits

Name	Storage Size	Description	Low Value	High Value	Resolution
interval [fields] [(p)]	16 bytes	time interval	-178000000 years	178000000 years	1 microsecond / 14 digits

Note: The SQL standard requires that writing just `timestamp` be equivalent to `timestamp without time zone`, and PostgreSQL honors that behavior. `timestamptz` is accepted as an abbreviation for `timestamp with time zone`; this is a PostgreSQL extension.

`time`, `timestamp`, and `interval` accept an optional precision value p which specifies the number of fractional digits retained in the seconds field. By default, there is no explicit bound on precision. The allowed range of p is from 0 to 6 for the `timestamp` and `interval` types.

Note: When `timestamp` values are stored as eight-byte integers (currently the default), microsecond precision is available over the full range of values. When `timestamp` values are stored as double precision floating-point numbers instead (a deprecated compile-time option), the effective limit of precision might be less than 6. `timestamp` values are stored as seconds before or after midnight 2000-01-01. When `timestamp` values are implemented using floating-point numbers, microsecond precision is achieved for dates within a few years of 2000-01-01, but the precision degrades for dates further away. Note that using floating-point datetimes allows a larger range of `timestamp` values to be represented than shown above: from 4713 BC up to 5874897 AD.

The same compile-time option also determines whether `time` and `interval` values are stored as floating-point numbers or eight-byte integers. In the floating-point case, large `interval` values degrade in precision as the size of the interval increases.

For the `time` types, the allowed range of p is from 0 to 6 when eight-byte integer storage is used, or from 0 to 10 when floating-point storage is used.

The `interval` type has an additional option, which is to restrict the set of stored fields by writing one of these phrases:

```
YEAR
MONTH
DAY
HOUR
MINUTE
SECOND
YEAR TO MONTH
DAY TO HOUR
DAY TO MINUTE
DAY TO SECOND
HOUR TO MINUTE
HOUR TO SECOND
MINUTE TO SECOND
```

Note that if both `fields` and p are specified, the `fields` must include SECOND, since the precision applies only to the seconds.

The type `time with time zone` is defined by the SQL standard, but the definition exhibits properties which lead to questionable usefulness. In most cases, a combination of `date`, `time`, `timestamp without time zone`, and `timestamp with time zone` should provide a complete range of date/time functionality required by any application.

The types `abstime` and `reltime` are lower precision types which are used internally. You are discouraged from using these types in applications; these internal types might disappear in a future release.

8.5.1. Date/Time Input

Date and time input is accepted in almost any reasonable format, including ISO 8601, SQL-compatible, traditional POSTGRES, and others. For some formats, ordering of day, month, and year in date input is ambiguous and there is support for specifying the expected ordering of these fields. Set the DateStyle parameter to `MDY` to select month-day-year interpretation, `DMY` to select day-month-year interpretation, or `YMD` to select year-month-day interpretation.

PostgreSQL is more flexible in handling date/time input than the SQL standard requires. See Appendix B for the exact parsing rules of date/time input and for the recognized text fields including months, days of the week, and time zones.

Remember that any date or time literal input needs to be enclosed in single quotes, like text strings. Refer to Section 4.1.2.7 for more information. SQL requires the following syntax

```
type [ (p) ] 'value'
```

where p is an optional precision specification giving the number of fractional digits in the seconds field. Precision can be specified for `time`, `timestamp`, and `interval` types. The allowed values are mentioned above. If no precision is specified in a constant specification, it defaults to the precision of the literal value.

8.5.1.1. Dates

Table 8-10 shows some possible inputs for the `date` type.

Table 8-10. Date Input

Example	Description
1999-01-08	ISO 8601; January 8 in any mode (recommended format)
January 8, 1999	unambiguous in any `datestyle` input mode
1/8/1999	January 8 in `MDY` mode; August 1 in `DMY` mode
1/18/1999	January 18 in `MDY` mode; rejected in other modes
01/02/03	January 2, 2003 in `MDY` mode; February 1, 2003 in `DMY` mode; February 3, 2001 in `YMD` mode
1999-Jan-08	January 8 in any mode
Jan-08-1999	January 8 in any mode
08-Jan-1999	January 8 in any mode
99-Jan-08	January 8 in `YMD` mode, else error

Example	Description
08-Jan-99	January 8, except error in YMD mode
Jan-08-99	January 8, except error in YMD mode
19990108	ISO 8601; January 8, 1999 in any mode
990108	ISO 8601; January 8, 1999 in any mode
1999.008	year and day of year
J2451187	Julian date
January 8, 99 BC	year 99 BC

8.5.1.2. Times

The time-of-day types are `time [ (p) ] without time zone` and `time [ (p) ] with time zone`. `time` alone is equivalent to `time without time zone`.

Valid input for these types consists of a time of day followed by an optional time zone. (See Table 8-11 and Table 8-12.) If a time zone is specified in the input for `time without time zone`, it is silently ignored. You can also specify a date but it will be ignored, except when you use a time zone name that involves a daylight-savings rule, such as `America/New_York`. In this case specifying the date is required in order to determine whether standard or daylight-savings time applies. The appropriate time zone offset is recorded in the `time with time zone` value.

Table 8-11. Time Input

Example	Description
04:05:06.789	ISO 8601
04:05:06	ISO 8601
04:05	ISO 8601
040506	ISO 8601
04:05 AM	same as 04:05; AM does not affect value
04:05 PM	same as 16:05; input hour must be <= 12
04:05:06.789-8	ISO 8601
04:05:06-08:00	ISO 8601
04:05-08:00	ISO 8601
040506-08	ISO 8601
04:05:06 PST	time zone specified by abbreviation
2003-04-12 04:05:06 America/New_York	time zone specified by full name

Table 8-12. Time Zone Input

Example	Description
PST	Abbreviation (for Pacific Standard Time)
America/New_York	Full time zone name

Example	Description
PST8PDT	POSIX-style time zone specification
-8:00	ISO-8601 offset for PST
-800	ISO-8601 offset for PST
-8	ISO-8601 offset for PST
zulu	Military abbreviation for UTC
z	Short form of zulu

Refer to Section 8.5.3 for more information on how to specify time zones.

8.5.1.3. Time Stamps

Valid input for the time stamp types consists of the concatenation of a date and a time, followed by an optional time zone, followed by an optional AD or BC. (Alternatively, AD/BC can appear before the time zone, but this is not the preferred ordering.) Thus:

```
1999-01-08 04:05:06
```

and:

```
1999-01-08 04:05:06 -8:00
```

are valid values, which follow the ISO 8601 standard. In addition, the common format:

```
January 8 04:05:06 1999 PST
```

is supported.

The SQL standard differentiates timestamp without time zone and timestamp with time zone literals by the presence of a "+" or "-" symbol and time zone offset after the time. Hence, according to the standard,

```
TIMESTAMP '2004-10-19 10:23:54'
```

is a timestamp without time zone, while

```
TIMESTAMP '2004-10-19 10:23:54+02'
```

is a timestamp with time zone. PostgreSQL never examines the content of a literal string before determining its type, and therefore will treat both of the above as timestamp without time zone. To ensure that a literal is treated as timestamp with time zone, give it the correct explicit type:

```
TIMESTAMP WITH TIME ZONE '2004-10-19 10:23:54+02'
```

In a literal that has been determined to be timestamp without time zone, PostgreSQL will silently ignore any time zone indication. That is, the resulting value is derived from the date/time fields in the input value, and is not adjusted for time zone.

For timestamp with time zone, the internally stored value is always in UTC (Universal Coordinated Time, traditionally known as Greenwich Mean Time, GMT). An input value that has an explicit time zone specified is converted to UTC using the appropriate offset for that time zone. If no time zone is stated in the input string, then it is assumed to be in the time zone indicated by the system's TimeZone parameter, and is converted to UTC using the offset for the `timezone` zone.

When a `timestamp with time zone` value is output, it is always converted from UTC to the current `timezone` zone, and displayed as local time in that zone. To see the time in another time zone, either change `timezone` or use the `AT TIME ZONE` construct (see Section 9.9.3).

Conversions between `timestamp without time zone` and `timestamp with time zone` normally assume that the `timestamp without time zone` value should be taken or given as `timezone` local time. A different time zone can be specified for the conversion using `AT TIME ZONE`.

8.5.1.4. Special Values

PostgreSQL supports several special date/time input values for convenience, as shown in Table 8-13. The values `infinity` and `-infinity` are specially represented inside the system and will be displayed unchanged; but the others are simply notational shorthands that will be converted to ordinary date/time values when read. (In particular, `now` and related strings are converted to a specific time value as soon as they are read.) All of these values need to be enclosed in single quotes when used as constants in SQL commands.

Table 8-13. Special Date/Time Inputs

Input String	Valid Types	Description
epoch	date, timestamp	1970-01-01 00:00:00+00 (Unix system time zero)
infinity	date, timestamp	later than all other time stamps
-infinity	date, timestamp	earlier than all other time stamps
now	date, time, timestamp	current transaction's start time
today	date, timestamp	midnight today
tomorrow	date, timestamp	midnight tomorrow
yesterday	date, timestamp	midnight yesterday
allballs	time	00:00:00.00 UTC

The following SQL-compatible functions can also be used to obtain the current time value for the corresponding data type: `CURRENT_DATE`, `CURRENT_TIME`, `CURRENT_TIMESTAMP`, `LOCALTIME`, `LOCALTIMESTAMP`. The latter four accept an optional subsecond precision specification. (See Section 9.9.4.) Note that these are SQL functions and are *not* recognized in data input strings.

8.5.2. Date/Time Output

The output format of the date/time types can be set to one of the four styles ISO 8601, SQL (Ingres), traditional POSTGRES (Unix date format), or German. The default is the ISO format. (The SQL standard requires the use of the ISO 8601 format. The name of the "SQL" output format is a historical accident.) Table 8-14 shows examples of each output style. The output of the `date` and `time` types is generally only the date or time part in accordance with the given examples. However, the POSTGRES style outputs date-only values in ISO format.

Table 8-14. Date/Time Output Styles

Style Specification	Description	Example
ISO	ISO 8601, SQL standard	1997-12-17 07:37:16-08
SQL	traditional style	12/17/1997 07:37:16.00 PST
Postgres	original style	Wed Dec 17 07:37:16 1997 PST
German	regional style	17.12.1997 07:37:16.00 PST

> **Note:** ISO 8601 specifies the use of uppercase letter T to separate the date and time. PostgreSQL accepts that format on input, but on output it uses a space rather than T, as shown above. This is for readability and for consistency with RFC 3339 as well as some other database systems.

In the SQL and POSTGRES styles, day appears before month if DMY field ordering has been specified, otherwise month appears before day. (See Section 8.5.1 for how this setting also affects interpretation of input values.) Table 8-15 shows examples.

Table 8-15. Date Order Conventions

datestyle Setting	Input Ordering	Example Output
SQL, DMY	*day/month/year*	17/12/1997 15:37:16.00 CET
SQL, MDY	*month/day/year*	12/17/1997 07:37:16.00 PST
Postgres, DMY	*day/month/year*	Wed 17 Dec 07:37:16 1997 PST

The date/time style can be selected by the user using the SET datestyle command, the DateStyle parameter in the postgresql.conf configuration file, or the PGDATESTYLE environment variable on the server or client.

The formatting function to_char (see Section 9.8) is also available as a more flexible way to format date/time output.

8.5.3. Time Zones

Time zones, and time-zone conventions, are influenced by political decisions, not just earth geometry. Time zones around the world became somewhat standardized during the 1900s, but continue to be prone to arbitrary changes, particularly with respect to daylight-savings rules. PostgreSQL uses the widely-used IANA (Olson) time zone database for information about historical time zone rules. For times in the future, the assumption is that the latest known rules for a given time zone will continue to be observed indefinitely far into the future.

PostgreSQL endeavors to be compatible with the SQL standard definitions for typical usage. However, the SQL standard has an odd mix of date and time types and capabilities. Two obvious problems are:

- Although the `date` type cannot have an associated time zone, the `time` type can. Time zones in the real world have little meaning unless associated with a date as well as a time, since the offset can vary through the year with daylight-saving time boundaries.

- The default time zone is specified as a constant numeric offset from UTC. It is therefore impossible to adapt to daylight-saving time when doing date/time arithmetic across DST boundaries.

To address these difficulties, we recommend using date/time types that contain both date and time when using time zones. We do *not* recommend using the type `time with time zone` (though it is supported by PostgreSQL for legacy applications and for compliance with the SQL standard). PostgreSQL assumes your local time zone for any type containing only date or time.

All timezone-aware dates and times are stored internally in UTC. They are converted to local time in the zone specified by the TimeZone configuration parameter before being displayed to the client.

PostgreSQL allows you to specify time zones in three different forms:

- A full time zone name, for example `America/New_York`. The recognized time zone names are listed in the `pg_timezone_names` view (see Section 48.72). PostgreSQL uses the widely-used IANA time zone data for this purpose, so the same time zone names are also recognized by much other software.

- A time zone abbreviation, for example `PST`. Such a specification merely defines a particular offset from UTC, in contrast to full time zone names which can imply a set of daylight savings transition-date rules as well. The recognized abbreviations are listed in the `pg_timezone_abbrevs` view (see Section 48.71). You cannot set the configuration parameters TimeZone or log_timezone to a time zone abbreviation, but you can use abbreviations in date/time input values and with the `AT TIME ZONE` operator.

- In addition to the timezone names and abbreviations, PostgreSQL will accept POSIX-style time zone specifications of the form *STDoffset* or *STDoffsetDST*, where *STD* is a zone abbreviation, *offset* is a numeric offset in hours west from UTC, and *DST* is an optional daylight-savings zone abbreviation, assumed to stand for one hour ahead of the given offset. For example, if `EST5EDT` were not already a recognized zone name, it would be accepted and would be functionally equivalent to United States East Coast time. In this syntax, a zone abbreviation can be a string of letters, or an arbitrary string surrounded by angle brackets (`<>`). When a daylight-savings zone abbreviation is present, it is assumed to be used according to the same daylight-savings transition rules used in the IANA time zone database's `posixrules` entry. In a standard PostgreSQL installation, `posixrules` is the same as `US/Eastern`, so that POSIX-style time zone specifications follow USA daylight-savings rules. If needed, you can adjust this behavior by replacing the `posixrules` file.

In short, this is the difference between abbreviations and full names: abbreviations represent a specific offset from UTC, whereas many of the full names imply a local daylight-savings time rule, and so have two possible UTC offsets. As an example, `2014-06-04 12:00 America/New_York` represents noon local time in New York, which for this particular date was Eastern Daylight Time (UTC-4). So `2014-06-04 12:00 EDT` specifies that same time instant. But `2014-06-04 12:00 EST` specifies noon Eastern Standard Time (UTC-5), regardless of whether daylight savings was nominally in effect on that date.

To complicate matters, some jurisdictions have used the same timezone abbreviation to mean different UTC offsets at different times; for example, in Moscow MSK has meant UTC+3 in some years and UTC+4 in others. PostgreSQL interprets such abbreviations according to whatever they meant (or had most recently meant) on the specified date; but, as with the EST example above, this is not necessarily the same as local civil time on that date.

One should be wary that the POSIX-style time zone feature can lead to silently accepting bogus input, since there is no check on the reasonableness of the zone abbreviations. For example, SET TIMEZONE TO FOOBAR0 will work, leaving the system effectively using a rather peculiar abbreviation for UTC. Another issue to keep in mind is that in POSIX time zone names, positive offsets are used for locations *west* of Greenwich. Everywhere else, PostgreSQL follows the ISO-8601 convention that positive timezone offsets are *east* of Greenwich.

In all cases, timezone names and abbreviations are recognized case-insensitively. (This is a change from PostgreSQL versions prior to 8.2, which were case-sensitive in some contexts but not others.)

Neither timezone names nor abbreviations are hard-wired into the server; they are obtained from configuration files stored under .../share/timezone/ and .../share/timezonesets/ of the installation directory (see Section B.3).

The TimeZone configuration parameter can be set in the file postgresql.conf, or in any of the other standard ways described in Chapter 18. There are also some special ways to set it:

- The SQL command SET TIME ZONE sets the time zone for the session. This is an alternative spelling of SET TIMEZONE TO with a more SQL-spec-compatible syntax.

- The PGTZ environment variable is used by libpq clients to send a SET TIME ZONE command to the server upon connection.

8.5.4. Interval Input

interval values can be written using the following verbose syntax:

```
[@] quantity unit [quantity unit...] [direction]
```

where quantity is a number (possibly signed); unit is microsecond, millisecond, second, minute, hour, day, week, month, year, decade, century, millennium, or abbreviations or plurals of these units; direction can be ago or empty. The at sign (@) is optional noise. The amounts of the different units are implicitly added with appropriate sign accounting. ago negates all the fields. This syntax is also used for interval output, if IntervalStyle is set to postgres_verbose.

Quantities of days, hours, minutes, and seconds can be specified without explicit unit markings. For example, '1 12:59:10' is read the same as '1 day 12 hours 59 min 10 sec'. Also, a combination of years and months can be specified with a dash; for example '200-10' is read the same as '200 years 10 months'. (These shorter forms are in fact the only ones allowed by the SQL standard, and are used for output when IntervalStyle is set to sql_standard.)

Interval values can also be written as ISO 8601 time intervals, using either the "format with designators" of the standard's section 4.4.3.2 or the "alternative format" of section 4.4.3.3. The format with designators looks like this:

```
P quantity unit [ quantity unit ...] [ T [ quantity unit ...]]
```

The string must start with a P, and may include a T that introduces the time-of-day units. The available unit abbreviations are given in Table 8-16. Units may be omitted, and may be specified in any order, but units smaller than a day must appear after T. In particular, the meaning of M depends on whether it is before or after T.

Table 8-16. ISO 8601 Interval Unit Abbreviations

Abbreviation	Meaning
Y	Years
M	Months (in the date part)
W	Weeks
D	Days
H	Hours
M	Minutes (in the time part)
S	Seconds

In the alternative format:

```
P [ years-months-days ] [ T hours:minutes:seconds ]
```

the string must begin with P, and a T separates the date and time parts of the interval. The values are given as numbers similar to ISO 8601 dates.

When writing an interval constant with a `fields` specification, or when assigning a string to an interval column that was defined with a `fields` specification, the interpretation of unmarked quantities depends on the `fields`. For example INTERVAL '1' YEAR is read as 1 year, whereas INTERVAL '1' means 1 second. Also, field values "to the right" of the least significant field allowed by the `fields` specification are silently discarded. For example, writing INTERVAL '1 day 2:03:04' HOUR TO MINUTE results in dropping the seconds field, but not the day field.

According to the SQL standard all fields of an interval value must have the same sign, so a leading negative sign applies to all fields; for example the negative sign in the interval literal '-1 2:03:04' applies to both the days and hour/minute/second parts. PostgreSQL allows the fields to have different signs, and traditionally treats each field in the textual representation as independently signed, so that the hour/minute/second part is considered positive in this example. If `IntervalStyle` is set to `sql_standard` then a leading sign is considered to apply to all fields (but only if no additional signs appear). Otherwise the traditional PostgreSQL interpretation is used. To avoid ambiguity, it's recommended to attach an explicit sign to each field if any field is negative.

Internally `interval` values are stored as months, days, and seconds. This is done because the number of days in a month varies, and a day can have 23 or 25 hours if a daylight savings time adjustment is involved. The months and days fields are integers while the seconds field can store fractions. Because intervals are usually created from constant strings or `timestamp` subtraction, this storage method works well in most cases. Functions `justify_days` and `justify_hours` are available for adjusting days and hours that overflow their normal ranges.

In the verbose input format, and in some fields of the more compact input formats, field values can have fractional parts; for example '1.5 week' or '01:02:03.45'. Such input is converted to the appropriate number of months, days, and seconds for storage. When this would result in a fractional number of months or days, the fraction is added to the lower-order fields using the conversion factors 1 month = 30 days and 1 day = 24 hours. For example, `'1.5 month'` becomes 1 month and 15 days. Only seconds will ever be shown as fractional on output.

Table 8-17 shows some examples of valid `interval` input.

Table 8-17. Interval Input

Example	Description
1-2	SQL standard format: 1 year 2 months
3 4:05:06	SQL standard format: 3 days 4 hours 5 minutes 6 seconds
1 year 2 months 3 days 4 hours 5 minutes 6 seconds	Traditional Postgres format: 1 year 2 months 3 days 4 hours 5 minutes 6 seconds
P1Y2M3DT4H5M6S	ISO 8601 "format with designators": same meaning as above
P0001-02-03T04:05:06	ISO 8601 "alternative format": same meaning as above

8.5.5. Interval Output

The output format of the interval type can be set to one of the four styles `sql_standard`, `postgres`, `postgres_verbose`, or `iso_8601`, using the command `SET intervalstyle`. The default is the `postgres` format. Table 8-18 shows examples of each output style.

The `sql_standard` style produces output that conforms to the SQL standard's specification for interval literal strings, if the interval value meets the standard's restrictions (either year-month only or day-time only, with no mixing of positive and negative components). Otherwise the output looks like a standard year-month literal string followed by a day-time literal string, with explicit signs added to disambiguate mixed-sign intervals.

The output of the `postgres` style matches the output of PostgreSQL releases prior to 8.4 when the DateStyle parameter was set to `ISO`.

The output of the `postgres_verbose` style matches the output of PostgreSQL releases prior to 8.4 when the `DateStyle` parameter was set to non-`ISO` output.

The output of the `iso_8601` style matches the "format with designators" described in section 4.4.3.2 of the ISO 8601 standard.

Table 8-18. Interval Output Style Examples

Style Specification	Year-Month Interval	Day-Time Interval	Mixed Interval
sql_standard	1-2	3 4:05:06	-1-2 +3 -4:05:06
postgres	1 year 2 mons	3 days 04:05:06	-1 year -2 mons +3 days -04:05:06

Style Specification	Year-Month Interval	Day-Time Interval	Mixed Interval
postgres_verbose	@ 1 year 2 mons	@ 3 days 4 hours 5 mins 6 secs	@ 1 year 2 mons -3 days 4 hours 5 mins 6 secs ago
iso_8601	P1Y2M	P3DT4H5M6S	P-1Y-2M3DT-4H-5M-6S

8.6. Boolean Type

PostgreSQL provides the standard SQL type boolean; see Table 8-19. The boolean type can have several states: "true", "false", and a third state, "unknown", which is represented by the SQL null value.

Table 8-19. Boolean Data Type

Name	Storage Size	Description
boolean	1 byte	state of true or false

Valid literal values for the "true" state are:

```
TRUE
't'
'true'
'y'
'yes'
'on'
'1'
```

For the "false" state, the following values can be used:

```
FALSE
'f'
'false'
'n'
'no'
'off'
'0'
```

Leading or trailing whitespace is ignored, and case does not matter. The key words TRUE and FALSE are the preferred (SQL-compliant) usage.

Example 8-2 shows that boolean values are output using the letters t and f.

Example 8-2. Using the boolean Type

```
CREATE TABLE test1 (a boolean, b text);
```

```
INSERT INTO test1 VALUES (TRUE, 'sic est');
INSERT INTO test1 VALUES (FALSE, 'non est');
SELECT * FROM test1;
 a |    b
---+---------
 t | sic est
 f | non est


SELECT * FROM test1 WHERE a;
 a |    b
---+---------
 t | sic est
```

8.7. Enumerated Types

Enumerated (enum) types are data types that comprise a static, ordered set of values. They are equivalent to the enum types supported in a number of programming languages. An example of an enum type might be the days of the week, or a set of status values for a piece of data.

8.7.1. Declaration of Enumerated Types

Enum types are created using the CREATE TYPE command, for example:

```
CREATE TYPE mood AS ENUM ('sad', 'ok', 'happy');
```

Once created, the enum type can be used in table and function definitions much like any other type:

```
CREATE TYPE mood AS ENUM ('sad', 'ok', 'happy');
CREATE TABLE person (
    name text,
    current_mood mood
);
INSERT INTO person VALUES ('Moe', 'happy');
SELECT * FROM person WHERE current_mood = 'happy';
 name | current_mood
------+--------------
 Moe  | happy
(1 row)
```

8.7.2. Ordering

The ordering of the values in an enum type is the order in which the values were listed when the type was created. All standard comparison operators and related aggregate functions are supported for enums. For example:

```
INSERT INTO person VALUES ('Larry', 'sad');
```

```
INSERT INTO person VALUES ('Curly', 'ok');
SELECT * FROM person WHERE current_mood > 'sad';
 name  | current_mood
-------+--------------
 Moe   | happy
 Curly | ok
(2 rows)

SELECT * FROM person WHERE current_mood > 'sad' ORDER BY current_mood;
 name  | current_mood
-------+--------------
 Curly | ok
 Moe   | happy
(2 rows)

SELECT name
FROM person
WHERE current_mood = (SELECT MIN(current_mood) FROM person);
 name
-------
 Larry
(1 row)
```

8.7.3. Type Safety

Each enumerated data type is separate and cannot be compared with other enumerated types. See this example:

```
CREATE TYPE happiness AS ENUM ('happy', 'very happy', 'ecstatic');
CREATE TABLE holidays (
    num_weeks integer,
    happiness happiness
);
INSERT INTO holidays(num_weeks,happiness) VALUES (4, 'happy');
INSERT INTO holidays(num_weeks,happiness) VALUES (6, 'very happy');
INSERT INTO holidays(num_weeks,happiness) VALUES (8, 'ecstatic');
INSERT INTO holidays(num_weeks,happiness) VALUES (2, 'sad');
ERROR:  invalid input value for enum happiness: "sad"
SELECT person.name, holidays.num_weeks FROM person, holidays
  WHERE person.current_mood = holidays.happiness;
ERROR:  operator does not exist: mood = happiness
```

If you really need to do something like that, you can either write a custom operator or add explicit casts to your query:

```
SELECT person.name, holidays.num_weeks FROM person, holidays
  WHERE person.current_mood::text = holidays.happiness::text;
 name | num_weeks
```

```
------+----------
 Moe  |         4
(1 row)
```

8.7.4. Implementation Details

An enum value occupies four bytes on disk. The length of an enum value's textual label is limited by the NAMEDATALEN setting compiled into PostgreSQL; in standard builds this means at most 63 bytes.

Enum labels are case sensitive, so 'happy' is not the same as 'HAPPY'. White space in the labels is significant too.

The translations from internal enum values to textual labels are kept in the system catalog pg_enum. Querying this catalog directly can be useful.

8.8. Geometric Types

Geometric data types represent two-dimensional spatial objects. Table 8-20 shows the geometric types available in PostgreSQL.

Table 8-20. Geometric Types

Name	Storage Size	Description	Representation
point	16 bytes	Point on a plane	(x,y)
line	32 bytes	Infinite line	{A,B,C}
lseg	32 bytes	Finite line segment	((x1,y1),(x2,y2))
box	32 bytes	Rectangular box	((x1,y1),(x2,y2))
path	16+16n bytes	Closed path (similar to polygon)	((x1,y1),...)
path	16+16n bytes	Open path	[(x1,y1),...]
polygon	40+16n bytes	Polygon (similar to closed path)	((x1,y1),...)
circle	24 bytes	Circle	<(x,y),r> (center point and radius)

A rich set of functions and operators is available to perform various geometric operations such as scaling, translation, rotation, and determining intersections. They are explained in Section 9.11.

8.8.1. Points

Points are the fundamental two-dimensional building block for geometric types. Values of type point are specified using either of the following syntaxes:

```
( x , y )
  x , y
```

where x and y are the respective coordinates, as floating-point numbers.

Points are output using the first syntax.

8.8.2. Lines

Lines are represented by the linear equation $Ax + By + C = 0$, where A and B are not both zero. Values of type `line` are input and output in the following form:

```
{ A, B, C }
```

Alternatively, any of the following forms can be used for input:

```
[ ( x1 , y1 ) , ( x2 , y2 ) ]
( ( x1 , y1 ) , ( x2 , y2 ) )
  ( x1 , y1 ) , ( x2 , y2 )
    x1 , y1   ,   x2 , y2
```

where $(x1,y1)$ and $(x2,y2)$ are two different points on the line.

8.8.3. Line Segments

Line segments are represented by pairs of points that are the endpoints of the segment. Values of type `lseg` are specified using any of the following syntaxes:

```
[ ( x1 , y1 ) , ( x2 , y2 ) ]
( ( x1 , y1 ) , ( x2 , y2 ) )
  ( x1 , y1 ) , ( x2 , y2 )
    x1 , y1   ,   x2 , y2
```

where $(x1,y1)$ and $(x2,y2)$ are the end points of the line segment.

Line segments are output using the first syntax.

8.8.4. Boxes

Boxes are represented by pairs of points that are opposite corners of the box. Values of type `box` are specified using any of the following syntaxes:

```
( ( x1 , y1 ) , ( x2 , y2 ) )
  ( x1 , y1 ) , ( x2 , y2 )
    x1 , y1   ,   x2 , y2
```

where $(x1,y1)$ and $(x2,y2)$ are any two opposite corners of the box.

Boxes are output using the second syntax.

Any two opposite corners can be supplied on input, but the values will be reordered as needed to store the upper right and lower left corners, in that order.

8.8.5. Paths

Paths are represented by lists of connected points. Paths can be *open*, where the first and last points in the list are considered not connected, or *closed*, where the first and last points are considered connected.

Values of type `path` are specified using any of the following syntaxes:

```
[ ( x1 , y1 ) , ... , ( xn , yn ) ]
( ( x1 , y1 ) , ... , ( xn , yn ) )
  ( x1 , y1 ) , ... , ( xn , yn )
  ( x1 , y1  , ... ,   xn , yn )
    x1 , y1  , ... ,   xn , yn
```

where the points are the end points of the line segments comprising the path. Square brackets (`[]`) indicate an open path, while parentheses (`()`) indicate a closed path. When the outermost parentheses are omitted, as in the third through fifth syntaxes, a closed path is assumed.

Paths are output using the first or second syntax, as appropriate.

8.8.6. Polygons

Polygons are represented by lists of points (the vertexes of the polygon). Polygons are very similar to closed paths, but are stored differently and have their own set of support routines.

Values of type `polygon` are specified using any of the following syntaxes:

```
( ( x1 , y1 ) , ... , ( xn , yn ) )
  ( x1 , y1 ) , ... , ( xn , yn )
  ( x1 , y1  , ... ,   xn , yn )
    x1 , y1  , ... ,   xn , yn
```

where the points are the end points of the line segments comprising the boundary of the polygon.

Polygons are output using the first syntax.

8.8.7. Circles

Circles are represented by a center point and radius. Values of type `circle` are specified using any of the following syntaxes:

```
< ( x , y ) , r >
( ( x , y ) , r )
  ( x , y ) , r
    x , y   , r
```

where (x, y) is the center point and r is the radius of the circle.

Circles are output using the first syntax.

8.9. Network Address Types

PostgreSQL offers data types to store IPv4, IPv6, and MAC addresses, as shown in Table 8-21. It is better to use these types instead of plain text types to store network addresses, because these types offer input error checking and specialized operators and functions (see Section 9.12).

Table 8-21. Network Address Types

Name	Storage Size	Description
cidr	7 or 19 bytes	IPv4 and IPv6 networks
inet	7 or 19 bytes	IPv4 and IPv6 hosts and networks
macaddr	6 bytes	MAC addresses

When sorting inet or cidr data types, IPv4 addresses will always sort before IPv6 addresses, including IPv4 addresses encapsulated or mapped to IPv6 addresses, such as ::10.2.3.4 or ::ffff:10.4.3.2.

8.9.1. inet

The inet type holds an IPv4 or IPv6 host address, and optionally its subnet, all in one field. The subnet is represented by the number of network address bits present in the host address (the "netmask"). If the netmask is 32 and the address is IPv4, then the value does not indicate a subnet, only a single host. In IPv6, the address length is 128 bits, so 128 bits specify a unique host address. Note that if you want to accept only networks, you should use the cidr type rather than inet.

The input format for this type is *address/y* where *address* is an IPv4 or IPv6 address and *y* is the number of bits in the netmask. If the */y* portion is missing, the netmask is 32 for IPv4 and 128 for IPv6, so the value represents just a single host. On display, the */y* portion is suppressed if the netmask specifies a single host.

8.9.2. cidr

The cidr type holds an IPv4 or IPv6 network specification. Input and output formats follow Classless Internet Domain Routing conventions. The format for specifying networks is *address/y* where *address* is the network represented as an IPv4 or IPv6 address, and *y* is the number of bits in the netmask. If *y* is omitted, it is calculated using assumptions from the older classful network numbering system, except it will be at least large enough to include all of the octets written in the input. It is an error to specify a network address that has bits set to the right of the specified netmask.

Table 8-22 shows some examples.

Table 8-22. cidr Type Input Examples

cidr **Input**	cidr **Output**	abbrev(cidr)
192.168.100.128/25	192.168.100.128/25	192.168.100.128/25
192.168/24	192.168.0.0/24	192.168.0/24
192.168/25	192.168.0.0/25	192.168.0.0/25
192.168.1	192.168.1.0/24	192.168.1/24
192.168	192.168.0.0/24	192.168.0/24
128.1	128.1.0.0/16	128.1/16
128	128.0.0.0/16	128.0/16
128.1.2	128.1.2.0/24	128.1.2/24
10.1.2	10.1.2.0/24	10.1.2/24
10.1	10.1.0.0/16	10.1/16
10	10.0.0.0/8	10/8
10.1.2.3/32	10.1.2.3/32	10.1.2.3/32
2001:4f8:3:ba::/64	2001:4f8:3:ba::/64	2001:4f8:3:ba::/64
2001:4f8:3:ba:2e0:81ff:fe22:d1f1/128	2001:4f8:3:ba:2e0:81ff:fe22:d1f1/128	2001:4f8:3:ba:2e0:81ff:fe22:d1f1
::ffff:1.2.3.0/120	::ffff:1.2.3.0/120	::ffff:1.2.3/120
::ffff:1.2.3.0/128	::ffff:1.2.3.0/128	::ffff:1.2.3.0/128

8.9.3. inet VS. cidr

The essential difference between inet and cidr data types is that inet accepts values with nonzero bits to the right of the netmask, whereas cidr does not.

> **Tip:** If you do not like the output format for inet or cidr values, try the functions host, text, and abbrev.

8.9.4. macaddr

The macaddr type stores MAC addresses, known for example from Ethernet card hardware addresses (although MAC addresses are used for other purposes as well). Input is accepted in the following formats:

```
'08:00:2b:01:02:03'
'08-00-2b-01-02-03'
'08002b:010203'
'08002b-010203'
'0800.2b01.0203'
'08002b010203'
```

These examples would all specify the same address. Upper and lower case is accepted for the digits a through f. Output is always in the first of the forms shown.

IEEE Std 802-2001 specifies the second shown form (with hyphens) as the canonical form for MAC addresses, and specifies the first form (with colons) as the bit-reversed notation, so that 08-00-2b-01-02-03 = 01:00:4D:08:04:0C. This convention is widely ignored nowadays, and it is relevant only for obsolete network protocols (such as Token Ring). PostgreSQL makes no provisions for bit reversal, and all accepted formats use the canonical LSB order.

The remaining four input formats are not part of any standard.

8.10. Bit String Types

Bit strings are strings of 1's and 0's. They can be used to store or visualize bit masks. There are two SQL bit types: bit(n) and bit varying(n), where n is a positive integer.

bit type data must match the length n exactly; it is an error to attempt to store shorter or longer bit strings. bit varying data is of variable length up to the maximum length n; longer strings will be rejected. Writing bit without a length is equivalent to bit(1), while bit varying without a length specification means unlimited length.

> **Note:** If one explicitly casts a bit-string value to bit(n), it will be truncated or zero-padded on the right to be exactly n bits, without raising an error. Similarly, if one explicitly casts a bit-string value to bit varying(n), it will be truncated on the right if it is more than n bits.

Refer to Section 4.1.2.5 for information about the syntax of bit string constants. Bit-logical operators and string manipulation functions are available; see Section 9.6.

Example 8-3. Using the Bit String Types

```
CREATE TABLE test (a BIT(3), b BIT VARYING(5));
INSERT INTO test VALUES (B'101', B'00');
INSERT INTO test VALUES (B'10', B'101');
ERROR:  bit string length 2 does not match type bit(3)
INSERT INTO test VALUES (B'10'::bit(3), B'101');
SELECT * FROM test;
  a  |  b
-----+-----
 101 | 00
 100 | 101
```

A bit string value requires 1 byte for each group of 8 bits, plus 5 or 8 bytes overhead depending on the length of the string (but long values may be compressed or moved out-of-line, as explained in Section 8.3 for character strings).

8.11. Text Search Types

PostgreSQL provides two data types that are designed to support full text search, which is the activity of searching through a collection of natural-language *documents* to locate those that best match a *query*. The `tsvector` type represents a document in a form optimized for text search; the `tsquery` type similarly represents a text query. Chapter 12 provides a detailed explanation of this facility, and Section 9.13 summarizes the related functions and operators.

8.11.1. `tsvector`

A `tsvector` value is a sorted list of distinct *lexemes*, which are words that have been *normalized* to merge different variants of the same word (see Chapter 12 for details). Sorting and duplicate-elimination are done automatically during input, as shown in this example:

```
SELECT 'a fat cat sat on a mat and ate a fat rat'::tsvector;
                    tsvector
----------------------------------------------------
 'a' 'and' 'ate' 'cat' 'fat' 'mat' 'on' 'rat' 'sat'
```

To represent lexemes containing whitespace or punctuation, surround them with quotes:

```
SELECT $$the lexeme '    ' contains spaces$$::tsvector;
                  tsvector
-------------------------------------------
 '    ' 'contains' 'lexeme' 'spaces' 'the'
```

(We use dollar-quoted string literals in this example and the next one to avoid the confusion of having to double quote marks within the literals.) Embedded quotes and backslashes must be doubled:

```
SELECT $$the lexeme 'Joe''s' contains a quote$$::tsvector;
                  tsvector
------------------------------------------------
 'Joe''s' 'a' 'contains' 'lexeme' 'quote' 'the'
```

Optionally, integer *positions* can be attached to lexemes:

```
SELECT 'a:1 fat:2 cat:3 sat:4 on:5 a:6 mat:7 and:8 ate:9 a:10 fat:11 rat:12'::t
                            tsvector
-------------------------------------------------------------------------------
 'a':1,6,10 'and':8 'ate':9 'cat':3 'fat':2,11 'mat':7 'on':5 'rat':12 'sat':4
```

A position normally indicates the source word's location in the document. Positional information can be used for *proximity ranking*. Position values can range from 1 to 16383; larger numbers are silently set to 16383. Duplicate positions for the same lexeme are discarded.

Lexemes that have positions can further be labeled with a *weight*, which can be A, B, C, or D. D is the default and hence is not shown on output:

```
SELECT 'a:1A fat:2B,4C cat:5D'::tsvector;
          tsvector
----------------------------
 'a':1A 'cat':5 'fat':2B,4C
```

Weights are typically used to reflect document structure, for example by marking title words differently from body words. Text search ranking functions can assign different priorities to the different weight markers.

It is important to understand that the `tsvector` type itself does not perform any normalization; it assumes the words it is given are normalized appropriately for the application. For example,

```
select 'The Fat Rats'::tsvector;
      tsvector
--------------------
 'Fat' 'Rats' 'The'
```

For most English-text-searching applications the above words would be considered non-normalized, but `tsvector` doesn't care. Raw document text should usually be passed through `to_tsvector` to normalize the words appropriately for searching:

```
SELECT to_tsvector('english', 'The Fat Rats');
   to_tsvector
-----------------
 'fat':2 'rat':3
```

Again, see Chapter 12 for more detail.

8.11.2. `tsquery`

A `tsquery` value stores lexemes that are to be searched for, and combines them honoring the Boolean operators `&` (AND), `|` (OR), and `!` (NOT). Parentheses can be used to enforce grouping of the operators:

```
SELECT 'fat & rat'::tsquery;
    tsquery
---------------
 'fat' & 'rat'

SELECT 'fat & (rat | cat)'::tsquery;
         tsquery
-------------------------
 'fat' & ( 'rat' | 'cat' )

SELECT 'fat & rat & ! cat'::tsquery;
       tsquery
-----------------------
 'fat' & 'rat' & !'cat'
```

In the absence of parentheses, `!` (NOT) binds most tightly, and `&` (AND) binds more tightly than `|` (OR).

Optionally, lexemes in a `tsquery` can be labeled with one or more weight letters, which restricts them to match only `tsvector` lexemes with matching weights:

```
SELECT 'fat:ab & cat'::tsquery;
    tsquery
------------------
 'fat':AB & 'cat'
```

Also, lexemes in a `tsquery` can be labeled with `*` to specify prefix matching:

```
SELECT 'super:*'::tsquery;
  tsquery
-----------
 'super':*
```

This query will match any word in a `tsvector` that begins with "super". Note that prefixes are first processed by text search configurations, which means this comparison returns true:

```
SELECT to_tsvector( 'postgraduate' ) @@ to_tsquery( 'postgres:*' );
 ?column?
----------
 t
(1 row)
```

because `postgres` gets stemmed to `postgr`:

```
SELECT to_tsquery('postgres:*');
 to_tsquery
------------
 'postgr':*
(1 row)
```

which then matches `postgraduate`.

Quoting rules for lexemes are the same as described previously for lexemes in `tsvector`; and, as with `tsvector`, any required normalization of words must be done before converting to the `tsquery` type. The `to_tsquery` function is convenient for performing such normalization:

```
SELECT to_tsquery('Fat:ab & Cats');
    to_tsquery
------------------
 'fat':AB & 'cat'
```

8.12. UUID Type

The data type `uuid` stores Universally Unique Identifiers (UUID) as defined by RFC 4122, ISO/IEC 9834-8:2005, and related standards. (Some systems refer to this data type as a globally unique identifier, or GUID, instead.) This identifier is a 128-bit quantity that is generated by an algorithm chosen to make it very unlikely that the same identifier will be generated by anyone else in the known universe using the same algorithm. Therefore, for distributed systems, these identifiers provide a better uniqueness guarantee than sequence generators, which are only unique within a single database.

A UUID is written as a sequence of lower-case hexadecimal digits, in several groups separated by hyphens, specifically a group of 8 digits followed by three groups of 4 digits followed by a group of 12 digits, for a total of 32 digits representing the 128 bits. An example of a UUID in this standard form is:

```
a0eebc99-9c0b-4ef8-bb6d-6bb9bd380a11
```

PostgreSQL also accepts the following alternative forms for input: use of upper-case digits, the standard format surrounded by braces, omitting some or all hyphens, adding a hyphen after any group of four digits. Examples are:

```
A0EEBC99-9C0B-4EF8-BB6D-6BB9BD380A11
{a0eebc99-9c0b-4ef8-bb6d-6bb9bd380a11}
a0eebc999c0b4ef8bb6d6bb9bd380a11
a0ee-bc99-9c0b-4ef8-bb6d-6bb9-bd38-0a11
{a0eebc99-9c0b4ef8-bb6d6bb9-bd380a11}
```

Output is always in the standard form.

PostgreSQL provides storage and comparison functions for UUIDs, but the core database does not include any function for generating UUIDs, because no single algorithm is well suited for every application. The uuid-ossp module provides functions that implement several standard algorithms. The pgcrypto module also provides a generation function for random UUIDs. Alternatively, UUIDs could be generated by client applications or other libraries invoked through a server-side function.

8.13. XML Type

The `xml` data type can be used to store XML data. Its advantage over storing XML data in a `text` field is that it checks the input values for well-formedness, and there are support functions to perform type-safe operations on it; see Section 9.14. Use of this data type requires the installation to have been built with `configure --with-libxml`.

The `xml` type can store well-formed "documents", as defined by the XML standard, as well as "content" fragments, which are defined by the production XMLDecl? content in the XML standard. Roughly, this means that content fragments can have more than one top-level element or character node. The expression *xmlvalue* IS DOCUMENT can be used to evaluate whether a particular `xml` value is a full document or only a content fragment.

8.13.1. Creating XML Values

To produce a value of type `xml` from character data, use the function `xmlparse`:

```
XMLPARSE ( { DOCUMENT | CONTENT } value)
```

Examples:

```
XMLPARSE (DOCUMENT '<?xml version="1.0"?><book><title>Manual</title><chapter>..
XMLPARSE (CONTENT 'abc<foo>bar</foo><bar>foo</bar>')
```

While this is the only way to convert character strings into XML values according to the SQL standard, the PostgreSQL-specific syntaxes:

```
xml '<foo>bar</foo>'
'<foo>bar</foo>'::xml
```

can also be used.

The xml type does not validate input values against a document type declaration (DTD), even when the input value specifies a DTD. There is also currently no built-in support for validating against other XML schema languages such as XML Schema.

The inverse operation, producing a character string value from xml, uses the function xmlserialize:

```
XMLSERIALIZE ( { DOCUMENT | CONTENT } value AS type )
```

type can be character, character varying, or text (or an alias for one of those). Again, according to the SQL standard, this is the only way to convert between type xml and character types, but PostgreSQL also allows you to simply cast the value.

When a character string value is cast to or from type xml without going through XMLPARSE or XMLSERIALIZE, respectively, the choice of DOCUMENT versus CONTENT is determined by the "XML option" session configuration parameter, which can be set using the standard command:

```
SET XML OPTION { DOCUMENT | CONTENT };
```

or the more PostgreSQL-like syntax

```
SET xmloption TO { DOCUMENT | CONTENT };
```

The default is CONTENT, so all forms of XML data are allowed.

> **Note:** With the default XML option setting, you cannot directly cast character strings to type xml if they contain a document type declaration, because the definition of XML content fragment does not accept them. If you need to do that, either use XMLPARSE or change the XML option.

8.13.2. Encoding Handling

Care must be taken when dealing with multiple character encodings on the client, server, and in the XML data passed through them. When using the text mode to pass queries to the server and query results to the client (which is the normal mode), PostgreSQL converts all character data passed between the client and the server and vice versa to the character encoding of the respective end; see Section 22.3. This includes string representations of XML values, such as in the above examples. This would ordinarily mean that encoding declarations contained in XML data can become invalid as the character data is converted to other encodings while traveling between client and server, because the embedded encoding declaration is not changed. To cope with this behavior, encoding declarations contained in character strings presented for input to the xml type are *ignored*, and content is assumed to be in the current server encoding. Consequently, for correct processing, character strings of XML data must be sent from the client in the current client encoding. It is the responsibility of the client to either convert documents to the current client encoding before sending them to the server, or to adjust the client encoding appropriately. On output, values of type xml will not have an encoding declaration, and clients should assume all data is in the current client encoding.

When using binary mode to pass query parameters to the server and query results back to the client, no character set conversion is performed, so the situation is different. In this case, an encoding declaration in the XML data will be observed, and if it is absent, the data will be assumed to be in UTF-8 (as required by the XML standard; note that PostgreSQL does not support UTF-16). On output, data will have an encoding declaration specifying the client encoding, unless the client encoding is UTF-8, in which case it will be omitted.

Needless to say, processing XML data with PostgreSQL will be less error-prone and more efficient if the XML data encoding, client encoding, and server encoding are the same. Since XML data is internally processed in UTF-8, computations will be most efficient if the server encoding is also UTF-8.

Caution

Some XML-related functions may not work at all on non-ASCII data when the server encoding is not UTF-8. This is known to be an issue for xpath() in particular.

8.13.3. Accessing XML Values

The xml data type is unusual in that it does not provide any comparison operators. This is because there is no well-defined and universally useful comparison algorithm for XML data. One consequence of this is that you cannot retrieve rows by comparing an xml column against a search value. XML values should therefore typically be accompanied by a separate key field such as an ID. An alternative solution for comparing XML values is to convert them to character strings first, but note that character string comparison has little to do with a useful XML comparison method.

Since there are no comparison operators for the xml data type, it is not possible to create an index directly on a column of this type. If speedy searches in XML data are desired, possible workarounds include casting the expression to a character string type and indexing that, or indexing an XPath expression. Of course, the actual query would have to be adjusted to search by the indexed expression.

The text-search functionality in PostgreSQL can also be used to speed up full-document searches of XML data. The necessary preprocessing support is, however, not yet available in the PostgreSQL distribution.

8.14. JSON Types

JSON data types are for storing JSON (JavaScript Object Notation) data, as specified in RFC 7159[1]. Such data can also be stored as text, but the JSON data types have the advantage of enforcing that each stored value is valid according to the JSON rules. There are also assorted JSON-specific functions and operators available for data stored in these data types; see Section 9.15.

There are two JSON data types: json and jsonb. They accept *almost* identical sets of values as input. The major practical difference is one of efficiency. The json data type stores an exact copy of the input text, which processing functions must reparse on each execution; while jsonb data is stored in a decomposed binary format that makes it slightly slower to input due to added conversion overhead, but significantly faster to process, since no reparsing is needed. jsonb also supports indexing, which can be a significant advantage.

---

1. http://rfc7159.net/rfc7159

Because the `json` type stores an exact copy of the input text, it will preserve semantically-insignificant white space between tokens, as well as the order of keys within JSON objects. Also, if a JSON object within the value contains the same key more than once, all the key/value pairs are kept. (The processing functions consider the last value as the operative one.) By contrast, `jsonb` does not preserve white space, does not preserve the order of object keys, and does not keep duplicate object keys. If duplicate keys are specified in the input, only the last value is kept.

In general, most applications should prefer to store JSON data as `jsonb`, unless there are quite specialized needs, such as legacy assumptions about ordering of object keys.

PostgreSQL allows only one character set encoding per database. It is therefore not possible for the JSON types to conform rigidly to the JSON specification unless the database encoding is UTF8. Attempts to directly include characters that cannot be represented in the database encoding will fail; conversely, characters that can be represented in the database encoding but not in UTF8 will be allowed.

RFC 7159 permits JSON strings to contain Unicode escape sequences denoted by `\u`*XXXX*. In the input function for the `json` type, Unicode escapes are allowed regardless of the database encoding, and are checked only for syntactic correctness (that is, that four hex digits follow `\u`). However, the input function for `jsonb` is stricter: it disallows Unicode escapes for non-ASCII characters (those above `U+007F`) unless the database encoding is UTF8. The `jsonb` type also rejects `\u0000` (because that cannot be represented in PostgreSQL's `text` type), and it insists that any use of Unicode surrogate pairs to designate characters outside the Unicode Basic Multilingual Plane be correct. Valid Unicode escapes are converted to the equivalent ASCII or UTF8 character for storage; this includes folding surrogate pairs into a single character.

> **Note:** Many of the JSON processing functions described in Section 9.15 will convert Unicode escapes to regular characters, and will therefore throw the same types of errors just described even if their input is of type `json` not `jsonb`. The fact that the `json` input function does not make these checks may be considered a historical artifact, although it does allow for simple storage (without processing) of JSON Unicode escapes in a non-UTF8 database encoding. In general, it is best to avoid mixing Unicode escapes in JSON with a non-UTF8 database encoding, if possible.

When converting textual JSON input into `jsonb`, the primitive types described by RFC 7159 are effectively mapped onto native PostgreSQL types, as shown in Table 8-23. Therefore, there are some minor additional constraints on what constitutes valid `jsonb` data that do not apply to the `json` type, nor to JSON in the abstract, corresponding to limits on what can be represented by the underlying data type. Notably, `jsonb` will reject numbers that are outside the range of the PostgreSQL `numeric` data type, while `json` will not. Such implementation-defined restrictions are permitted by RFC 7159. However, in practice such problems are far more likely to occur in other implementations, as it is common to represent JSON's `number` primitive type as IEEE 754 double precision floating point (which RFC 7159 explicitly anticipates and allows for). When using JSON as an interchange format with such systems, the danger of losing numeric precision compared to data originally stored by PostgreSQL should be considered.

Conversely, as noted in the table there are some minor restrictions on the input format of JSON primitive types that do not apply to the corresponding PostgreSQL types.

Table 8-23. JSON primitive types and corresponding PostgreSQL types

JSON primitive type	PostgreSQL type	Notes

JSON primitive type	PostgreSQL type	Notes
string	text	\u0000 is disallowed, as are non-ASCII Unicode escapes if database encoding is not UTF8
number	numeric	NaN and infinity values are disallowed
boolean	boolean	Only lowercase true and false spellings are accepted
null	(none)	SQL NULL is a different concept

8.14.1. JSON Input and Output Syntax

The input/output syntax for the JSON data types is as specified in RFC 7159.

The following are all valid json (or jsonb) expressions:

```
-- Simple scalar/primitive value
-- Primitive values can be numbers, quoted strings, true, false, or null
SELECT '5'::json;

-- Array of zero or more elements (elements need not be of same type)
SELECT '[1, 2, "foo", null]'::json;

-- Object containing pairs of keys and values
-- Note that object keys must always be quoted strings
SELECT '{"bar": "baz", "balance": 7.77, "active": false}'::json;

-- Arrays and objects can be nested arbitrarily
SELECT '{"foo": [true, "bar"], "tags": {"a": 1, "b": null}}'::json;
```

As previously stated, when a JSON value is input and then printed without any additional processing, json outputs the same text that was input, while jsonb does not preserve semantically-insignificant details such as whitespace. For example, note the differences here:

```
SELECT '{"bar": "baz", "balance": 7.77, "active":false}'::json;
                     json
------------------------------------------------
 {"bar": "baz", "balance": 7.77, "active":false}
(1 row)

SELECT '{"bar": "baz", "balance": 7.77, "active":false}'::jsonb;
                     jsonb
------------------------------------------------
 {"bar": "baz", "active": false, "balance": 7.77}
(1 row)
```

One semantically-insignificant detail worth noting is that in jsonb, numbers will be printed according to the behavior of the underlying numeric type. In practice this means that numbers entered with E notation will be printed without it, for example:

```
SELECT '{"reading": 1.230e-5}'::json, '{"reading": 1.230e-5}'::jsonb;
        json           |           jsonb
-----------------------+-------------------------
 {"reading": 1.230e-5} | {"reading": 0.00001230}
(1 row)
```

However, `jsonb` will preserve trailing fractional zeroes, as seen in this example, even though those are semantically insignificant for purposes such as equality checks.

8.14.2. Designing JSON documents effectively

Representing data as JSON can be considerably more flexible than the traditional relational data model, which is compelling in environments where requirements are fluid. It is quite possible for both approaches to co-exist and complement each other within the same application. However, even for applications where maximal flexibility is desired, it is still recommended that JSON documents have a somewhat fixed structure. The structure is typically unenforced (though enforcing some business rules declaratively is possible), but having a predictable structure makes it easier to write queries that usefully summarize a set of "documents" (datums) in a table.

JSON data is subject to the same concurrency-control considerations as any other data type when stored in a table. Although storing large documents is practicable, keep in mind that any update acquires a row-level lock on the whole row. Consider limiting JSON documents to a manageable size in order to decrease lock contention among updating transactions. Ideally, JSON documents should each represent an atomic datum that business rules dictate cannot reasonably be further subdivided into smaller datums that could be modified independently.

8.14.3. `jsonb` Containment and Existence

Testing *containment* is an important capability of `jsonb`. There is no parallel set of facilities for the `json` type. Containment tests whether one `jsonb` document has contained within it another one. These examples return true except as noted:

```
-- Simple scalar/primitive values contain only the identical value:
SELECT '"foo"'::jsonb @> '"foo"'::jsonb;

-- The array on the right side is contained within the one on the left:
SELECT '[1, 2, 3]'::jsonb @> '[1, 3]'::jsonb;

-- Order of array elements is not significant, so this is also true:
SELECT '[1, 2, 3]'::jsonb @> '[3, 1]'::jsonb;

-- Duplicate array elements don't matter either:
SELECT '[1, 2, 3]'::jsonb @> '[1, 2, 2]'::jsonb;

-- The object with a single pair on the right side is contained
-- within the object on the left side:
SELECT '{"product": "PostgreSQL", "version": 9.4, "jsonb":true}'::jsonb @> '{"v

-- The array on the right side is not considered contained within the
```

```
-- array on the left, even though a similar array is nested within it:
SELECT '[1, 2, [1, 3]]'::jsonb @> '[1, 3]'::jsonb;  -- yields false

-- But with a layer of nesting, it is contained:
SELECT '[1, 2, [1, 3]]'::jsonb @> '[[1, 3]]'::jsonb;

-- Similarly, containment is not reported here:
SELECT '{"foo": {"bar": "baz"}}'::jsonb @> '{"bar": "baz"}'::jsonb;  -- yields
```

The general principle is that the contained object must match the containing object as to structure and data contents, possibly after discarding some non-matching array elements or object key/value pairs from the containing object. But remember that the order of array elements is not significant when doing a containment match, and duplicate array elements are effectively considered only once.

As a special exception to the general principle that the structures must match, an array may contain a primitive value:

```
-- This array contains the primitive string value:
SELECT '["foo", "bar"]'::jsonb @> '"bar"'::jsonb;

-- This exception is not reciprocal -- non-containment is reported here:
SELECT '"bar"'::jsonb @> '["bar"]'::jsonb;  -- yields false
```

jsonb also has an *existence* operator, which is a variation on the theme of containment: it tests whether a string (given as a text value) appears as an object key or array element at the top level of the jsonb value. These examples return true except as noted:

```
-- String exists as array element:
SELECT '["foo", "bar", "baz"]'::jsonb ? 'bar';

-- String exists as object key:
SELECT '{"foo": "bar"}'::jsonb ? 'foo';

-- Object values are not considered:
SELECT '{"foo": "bar"}'::jsonb ? 'bar';  -- yields false

-- As with containment, existence must match at the top level:
SELECT '{"foo": {"bar": "baz"}}'::jsonb ? 'bar'; -- yields false

-- A string is considered to exist if it matches a primitive JSON string:
SELECT '"foo"'::jsonb ? 'foo';
```

JSON objects are better suited than arrays for testing containment or existence when there are many keys or elements involved, because unlike arrays they are internally optimized for searching, and do not need to be searched linearly.

The various containment and existence operators, along with all other JSON operators and functions are documented in Section 9.15.

8.14.4. `jsonb` Indexing

GIN indexes can be used to efficiently search for keys or key/value pairs occurring within a large number of `jsonb` documents (datums). Two GIN "operator classes" are provided, offering different performance and flexibility trade-offs.

The default GIN operator class for `jsonb` supports queries with the `@>`, `?`, `?&` and `?|` operators. (For details of the semantics that these operators implement, see Table 9-41.) An example of creating an index with this operator class is:

```
CREATE INDEX idxgin ON api USING gin (jdoc);
```

The non-default GIN operator class `jsonb_path_ops` supports indexing the `@>` operator only. An example of creating an index with this operator class is:

```
CREATE INDEX idxginp ON api USING gin (jdoc jsonb_path_ops);
```

Consider the example of a table that stores JSON documents retrieved from a third-party web service, with a documented schema definition. A typical document is:

```
{
    "guid": "9c36adc1-7fb5-4d5b-83b4-90356a46061a",
    "name": "Angela Barton",
    "is_active": true,
    "company": "Magnafone",
    "address": "178 Howard Place, Gulf, Washington, 702",
    "registered": "2009-11-07T08:53:22 +08:00",
    "latitude": 19.793713,
    "longitude": 86.513373,
    "tags": [
        "enim",
        "aliquip",
        "qui"
    ]
}
```

We store these documents in a table named `api`, in a `jsonb` column named `jdoc`. If a GIN index is created on this column, queries like the following can make use of the index:

```
-- Find documents in which the key "company" has value "Magnafone"
SELECT jdoc->'guid', jdoc->'name' FROM api WHERE jdoc @> '{"company": "Magnafo
```

However, the index could not be used for queries like the following, because though the operator `?` is indexable, it is not applied directly to the indexed column `jdoc`:

```
-- Find documents in which the key "tags" contains key or array element "qui"
SELECT jdoc->'guid', jdoc->'name' FROM api WHERE jdoc -> 'tags' ? 'qui';
```

Still, with appropriate use of expression indexes, the above query can use an index. If querying for particular items within the `"tags"` key is common, defining an index like this may be worthwhile:

```
CREATE INDEX idxgintags ON api USING gin ((jdoc -> 'tags'));
```

Now, the `WHERE` clause `jdoc -> 'tags' ? 'qui'` will be recognized as an application of the index-able operator `?` to the indexed expression `jdoc -> 'tags'`. (More information on expression indexes can be found in Section 11.7.)

Another approach to querying is to exploit containment, for example:

```
-- Find documents in which the key "tags" contains array element "qui"
SELECT jdoc->'guid', jdoc->'name' FROM api WHERE jdoc @> '{"tags": ["qui"]}';
```

A simple GIN index on the `jdoc` column can support this query. But note that such an index will store copies of every key and value in the `jdoc` column, whereas the expression index of the previous example stores only data found under the `tags` key. While the simple-index approach is far more flexible (since it supports queries about any key), targeted expression indexes are likely to be smaller and faster to search than a simple index.

Although the `jsonb_path_ops` operator class supports only queries with the `@>` operator, it has notable performance advantages over the default operator class `jsonb_ops`. A `jsonb_path_ops` index is usually much smaller than a `jsonb_ops` index over the same data, and the specificity of searches is better, particularly when queries contain keys that appear frequently in the data. Therefore search operations typically perform better than with the default operator class.

The technical difference between a `jsonb_ops` and a `jsonb_path_ops` GIN index is that the former creates independent index items for each key and value in the data, while the latter creates index items only for each value in the data. [2] Basically, each `jsonb_path_ops` index item is a hash of the value and the key(s) leading to it; for example to index `{"foo": {"bar": "baz"}}`, a single index item would be created incorporating all three of `foo`, `bar`, and `baz` into the hash value. Thus a containment query looking for this structure would result in an extremely specific index search; but there is no way at all to find out whether `foo` appears as a key. On the other hand, a `jsonb_ops` index would create three index items representing `foo`, `bar`, and `baz` separately; then to do the containment query, it would look for rows containing all three of these items. While GIN indexes can perform such an AND search fairly efficiently, it will still be less specific and slower than the equivalent `jsonb_path_ops` search, especially if there are a very large number of rows containing any single one of the three index items.

A disadvantage of the `jsonb_path_ops` approach is that it produces no index entries for JSON structures not containing any values, such as `{"a": {}}`. If a search for documents containing such a structure is requested, it will require a full-index scan, which is quite slow. `jsonb_path_ops` is therefore ill-suited for applications that often perform such searches.

`jsonb` also supports `btree` and `hash` indexes. These are usually useful only if it's important to check equality of complete JSON documents. The `btree` ordering for `jsonb` datums is seldom of great interest, but for completeness it is:

```
Object > Array > Boolean > Number > String > Null

Object with n pairs > object with n - 1 pairs

Array with n elements > array with n - 1 elements
```

Objects with equal numbers of pairs are compared in the order:

```
key-1, value-1, key-2 ...
```

---

2. For this purpose, the term "value" includes array elements, though JSON terminology sometimes considers array elements distinct from values within objects.

Note that object keys are compared in their storage order; in particular, since shorter keys are stored before longer keys, this can lead to results that might be unintuitive, such as:

```
{ "aa": 1, "c": 1} > {"b": 1, "d": 1}
```

Similarly, arrays with equal numbers of elements are compared in the order:

```
element-1, element-2 ...
```

Primitive JSON values are compared using the same comparison rules as for the underlying PostgreSQL data type. Strings are compared using the default database collation.

8.15. Arrays

PostgreSQL allows columns of a table to be defined as variable-length multidimensional arrays. Arrays of any built-in or user-defined base type, enum type, or composite type can be created. Arrays of domains are not yet supported.

8.15.1. Declaration of Array Types

To illustrate the use of array types, we create this table:

```
CREATE TABLE sal_emp (
    name            text,
    pay_by_quarter  integer[],
    schedule        text[][]
);
```

As shown, an array data type is named by appending square brackets (`[]`) to the data type name of the array elements. The above command will create a table named `sal_emp` with a column of type `text` (`name`), a one-dimensional array of type `integer` (`pay_by_quarter`), which represents the employee's salary by quarter, and a two-dimensional array of `text` (`schedule`), which represents the employee's weekly schedule.

The syntax for `CREATE TABLE` allows the exact size of arrays to be specified, for example:

```
CREATE TABLE tictactoe (
    squares    integer[3][3]
);
```

However, the current implementation ignores any supplied array size limits, i.e., the behavior is the same as for arrays of unspecified length.

The current implementation does not enforce the declared number of dimensions either. Arrays of a particular element type are all considered to be of the same type, regardless of size or number of dimensions. So, declaring the array size or number of dimensions in `CREATE TABLE` is simply documentation; it does not affect run-time behavior.

An alternative syntax, which conforms to the SQL standard by using the keyword `ARRAY`, can be used for one-dimensional arrays. `pay_by_quarter` could have been defined as:

```
    pay_by_quarter  integer ARRAY[4],
```

Or, if no array size is to be specified:

```
    pay_by_quarter  integer ARRAY,
```

As before, however, PostgreSQL does not enforce the size restriction in any case.

8.15.2. Array Value Input

To write an array value as a literal constant, enclose the element values within curly braces and separate them by commas. (If you know C, this is not unlike the C syntax for initializing structures.) You can put double quotes around any element value, and must do so if it contains commas or curly braces. (More details appear below.) Thus, the general format of an array constant is the following:

```
'{ val1 delim val2 delim ... }'
```

where `delim` is the delimiter character for the type, as recorded in its `pg_type` entry. Among the standard data types provided in the PostgreSQL distribution, all use a comma (`,`), except for type `box` which uses a semicolon (`;`). Each `val` is either a constant of the array element type, or a subarray. An example of an array constant is:

```
'{{1,2,3},{4,5,6},{7,8,9}}'
```

This constant is a two-dimensional, 3-by-3 array consisting of three subarrays of integers.

To set an element of an array constant to NULL, write `NULL` for the element value. (Any upper- or lower-case variant of `NULL` will do.) If you want an actual string value "NULL", you must put double quotes around it.

(These kinds of array constants are actually only a special case of the generic type constants discussed in Section 4.1.2.7. The constant is initially treated as a string and passed to the array input conversion routine. An explicit type specification might be necessary.)

Now we can show some `INSERT` statements:

```
INSERT INTO sal_emp
    VALUES ('Bill',
    '{10000, 10000, 10000, 10000}',
    '{{"meeting", "lunch"}, {"training", "presentation"}}');

INSERT INTO sal_emp
    VALUES ('Carol',
    '{20000, 25000, 25000, 25000}',
    '{{"breakfast", "consulting"}, {"meeting", "lunch"}}');
```

The result of the previous two inserts looks like this:

```
SELECT * FROM sal_emp;
 name  |      pay_by_quarter     |                   schedule
-------+-------------------------+---------------------------------------------
```

```
Bill  | {10000,10000,10000,10000} | {{meeting,lunch},{training,presentation}}
Carol | {20000,25000,25000,25000} | {{breakfast,consulting},{meeting,lunch}}
(2 rows)
```

Multidimensional arrays must have matching extents for each dimension. A mismatch causes an error, for example:

```
INSERT INTO sal_emp
    VALUES ('Bill',
    '{10000, 10000, 10000, 10000}',
    '{{"meeting", "lunch"}, {"meeting"}}');
ERROR:  multidimensional arrays must have array expressions with matching dimer
```

The `ARRAY` constructor syntax can also be used:

```
INSERT INTO sal_emp
    VALUES ('Bill',
    ARRAY[10000, 10000, 10000, 10000],
    ARRAY[['meeting', 'lunch'], ['training', 'presentation']]);

INSERT INTO sal_emp
    VALUES ('Carol',
    ARRAY[20000, 25000, 25000, 25000],
    ARRAY[['breakfast', 'consulting'], ['meeting', 'lunch']]);
```

Notice that the array elements are ordinary SQL constants or expressions; for instance, string literals are single quoted, instead of double quoted as they would be in an array literal. The `ARRAY` constructor syntax is discussed in more detail in Section 4.2.12.

8.15.3. Accessing Arrays

Now, we can run some queries on the table. First, we show how to access a single element of an array. This query retrieves the names of the employees whose pay changed in the second quarter:

```
SELECT name FROM sal_emp WHERE pay_by_quarter[1] <> pay_by_quarter[2];
```

```
 name
-------
 Carol
(1 row)
```

The array subscript numbers are written within square brackets. By default PostgreSQL uses a one-based numbering convention for arrays, that is, an array of *n* elements starts with `array[1]` and ends with `array[n]`.

This query retrieves the third quarter pay of all employees:

```
SELECT pay_by_quarter[3] FROM sal_emp;
```

```
pay_by_quarter
----------------
          10000
          25000
(2 rows)
```

We can also access arbitrary rectangular slices of an array, or subarrays. An array slice is denoted by writing *lower-bound*:*upper-bound* for one or more array dimensions. For example, this query retrieves the first item on Bill's schedule for the first two days of the week:

```
SELECT schedule[1:2][1:1] FROM sal_emp WHERE name = 'Bill';
```

```
        schedule
------------------------
 {{meeting},{training}}
(1 row)
```

If any dimension is written as a slice, i.e., contains a colon, then all dimensions are treated as slices. Any dimension that has only a single number (no colon) is treated as being from 1 to the number specified. For example, `[2]` is treated as `[1:2]`, as in this example:

```
SELECT schedule[1:2][2] FROM sal_emp WHERE name = 'Bill';
```

```
                    schedule
-------------------------------------------
 {{meeting,lunch},{training,presentation}}
(1 row)
```

To avoid confusion with the non-slice case, it's best to use slice syntax for all dimensions, e.g., `[1:2][1:1]`, not `[2][1:1]`.

An array subscript expression will return null if either the array itself or any of the subscript expressions are null. Also, null is returned if a subscript is outside the array bounds (this case does not raise an error). For example, if `schedule` currently has the dimensions `[1:3][1:2]` then referencing `schedule[3][3]` yields NULL. Similarly, an array reference with the wrong number of subscripts yields a null rather than an error.

An array slice expression likewise yields null if the array itself or any of the subscript expressions are null. However, in other cases such as selecting an array slice that is completely outside the current array bounds, a slice expression yields an empty (zero-dimensional) array instead of null. (This does not match non-slice behavior and is done for historical reasons.) If the requested slice partially overlaps the array bounds, then it is silently reduced to just the overlapping region instead of returning null.

The current dimensions of any array value can be retrieved with the `array_dims` function:

```
SELECT array_dims(schedule) FROM sal_emp WHERE name = 'Carol';
```

```
 array_dims
------------
 [1:2][1:2]
```

```
(1 row)
```

array_dims produces a text result, which is convenient for people to read but perhaps inconvenient for programs. Dimensions can also be retrieved with array_upper and array_lower, which return the upper and lower bound of a specified array dimension, respectively:

```
SELECT array_upper(schedule, 1) FROM sal_emp WHERE name = 'Carol';

 array_upper
-------------
           2
(1 row)
```

array_length will return the length of a specified array dimension:

```
SELECT array_length(schedule, 1) FROM sal_emp WHERE name = 'Carol';

 array_length
--------------
            2
(1 row)
```

cardinality returns the total number of elements in an array across all dimensions. It is effectively the number of rows a call to unnest would yield:

```
SELECT cardinality(schedule) FROM sal_emp WHERE name = 'Carol';

 cardinality
-------------
           4
(1 row)
```

8.15.4. Modifying Arrays

An array value can be replaced completely:

```
UPDATE sal_emp SET pay_by_quarter = '{25000,25000,27000,27000}'
    WHERE name = 'Carol';
```

or using the ARRAY expression syntax:

```
UPDATE sal_emp SET pay_by_quarter = ARRAY[25000,25000,27000,27000]
    WHERE name = 'Carol';
```

An array can also be updated at a single element:

```
UPDATE sal_emp SET pay_by_quarter[4] = 15000
    WHERE name = 'Bill';
```

or updated in a slice:

```
UPDATE sal_emp SET pay_by_quarter[1:2] = '{27000,27000}'
    WHERE name = 'Carol';
```

A stored array value can be enlarged by assigning to elements not already present. Any positions between those previously present and the newly assigned elements will be filled with nulls. For example, if array `myarray` currently has 4 elements, it will have six elements after an update that assigns to `myarray[6]`; `myarray[5]` will contain null. Currently, enlargement in this fashion is only allowed for one-dimensional arrays, not multidimensional arrays.

Subscripted assignment allows creation of arrays that do not use one-based subscripts. For example one might assign to `myarray[-2:7]` to create an array with subscript values from -2 to 7.

New array values can also be constructed using the concatenation operator, `||`:

```
SELECT ARRAY[1,2] || ARRAY[3,4];
 ?column?
-----------
 {1,2,3,4}
(1 row)

SELECT ARRAY[5,6] || ARRAY[[1,2],[3,4]];
      ?column?
---------------------
 {{5,6},{1,2},{3,4}}
(1 row)
```

The concatenation operator allows a single element to be pushed onto the beginning or end of a one-dimensional array. It also accepts two *N*-dimensional arrays, or an *N*-dimensional and an *N+1*-dimensional array.

When a single element is pushed onto either the beginning or end of a one-dimensional array, the result is an array with the same lower bound subscript as the array operand. For example:

```
SELECT array_dims(1 || '[0:1]={2,3}'::int[]);
 array_dims
------------
 [0:2]
(1 row)

SELECT array_dims(ARRAY[1,2] || 3);
 array_dims
------------
 [1:3]
(1 row)
```

When two arrays with an equal number of dimensions are concatenated, the result retains the lower bound subscript of the left-hand operand's outer dimension. The result is an array comprising every element of the left-hand operand followed by every element of the right-hand operand. For example:

```
SELECT array_dims(ARRAY[1,2] || ARRAY[3,4,5]);
 array_dims
------------
 [1:5]
(1 row)

SELECT array_dims(ARRAY[[1,2],[3,4]] || ARRAY[[5,6],[7,8],[9,0]]);
 array_dims
------------
 [1:5][1:2]
(1 row)
```

When an *N*-dimensional array is pushed onto the beginning or end of an *N+1*-dimensional array, the result is analogous to the element-array case above. Each *N*-dimensional sub-array is essentially an element of the *N+1*-dimensional array's outer dimension. For example:

```
SELECT array_dims(ARRAY[1,2] || ARRAY[[3,4],[5,6]]);
 array_dims
------------
 [1:3][1:2]
(1 row)
```

An array can also be constructed by using the functions `array_prepend`, `array_append`, or `array_cat`. The first two only support one-dimensional arrays, but `array_cat` supports multidimensional arrays. Note that the concatenation operator discussed above is preferred over direct use of these functions. In fact, these functions primarily exist for use in implementing the concatenation operator. However, they might be directly useful in the creation of user-defined aggregates. Some examples:

```
SELECT array_prepend(1, ARRAY[2,3]);
 array_prepend
---------------
 {1,2,3}
(1 row)

SELECT array_append(ARRAY[1,2], 3);
 array_append
--------------
 {1,2,3}
(1 row)

SELECT array_cat(ARRAY[1,2], ARRAY[3,4]);
 array_cat
-----------
 {1,2,3,4}
(1 row)

SELECT array_cat(ARRAY[[1,2],[3,4]], ARRAY[5,6]);
      array_cat
```

```
--------------------
 {{1,2},{3,4},{5,6}}
(1 row)

SELECT array_cat(ARRAY[5,6], ARRAY[[1,2],[3,4]]);
      array_cat
--------------------
 {{5,6},{1,2},{3,4}}
```

8.15.5. Searching in Arrays

To search for a value in an array, each value must be checked. This can be done manually, if you know the size of the array. For example:

```
SELECT * FROM sal_emp WHERE pay_by_quarter[1] = 10000 OR
                            pay_by_quarter[2] = 10000 OR
                            pay_by_quarter[3] = 10000 OR
                            pay_by_quarter[4] = 10000;
```

However, this quickly becomes tedious for large arrays, and is not helpful if the size of the array is unknown. An alternative method is described in Section 9.23. The above query could be replaced by:

```
SELECT * FROM sal_emp WHERE 10000 = ANY (pay_by_quarter);
```

In addition, you can find rows where the array has all values equal to 10000 with:

```
SELECT * FROM sal_emp WHERE 10000 = ALL (pay_by_quarter);
```

Alternatively, the generate_subscripts function can be used. For example:

```
SELECT * FROM
   (SELECT pay_by_quarter,
           generate_subscripts(pay_by_quarter, 1) AS s
     FROM sal_emp) AS foo
 WHERE pay_by_quarter[s] = 10000;
```

This function is described in Table 9-55.

You can also search an array using the && operator, which checks whether the left operand overlaps with the right operand. For instance:

```
SELECT * FROM sal_emp WHERE pay_by_quarter && ARRAY[10000];
```

This and other array operators are further described in Section 9.18. It can be accelerated by an appropriate index, as described in Section 11.2.

> **Tip:** Arrays are not sets; searching for specific array elements can be a sign of database misdesign. Consider using a separate table with a row for each item that would be an array element. This will be easier to search, and is likely to scale better for a large number of elements.

8.15.6. Array Input and Output Syntax

The external text representation of an array value consists of items that are interpreted according to the I/O conversion rules for the array's element type, plus decoration that indicates the array structure. The decoration consists of curly braces ({ and }) around the array value plus delimiter characters between adjacent items. The delimiter character is usually a comma (,) but can be something else: it is determined by the `typdelim` setting for the array's element type. Among the standard data types provided in the PostgreSQL distribution, all use a comma, except for type `box`, which uses a semicolon (;). In a multidimensional array, each dimension (row, plane, cube, etc.) gets its own level of curly braces, and delimiters must be written between adjacent curly-braced entities of the same level.

The array output routine will put double quotes around element values if they are empty strings, contain curly braces, delimiter characters, double quotes, backslashes, or white space, or match the word NULL. Double quotes and backslashes embedded in element values will be backslash-escaped. For numeric data types it is safe to assume that double quotes will never appear, but for textual data types one should be prepared to cope with either the presence or absence of quotes.

By default, the lower bound index value of an array's dimensions is set to one. To represent arrays with other lower bounds, the array subscript ranges can be specified explicitly before writing the array contents. This decoration consists of square brackets ([]) around each array dimension's lower and upper bounds, with a colon (:) delimiter character in between. The array dimension decoration is followed by an equal sign (=). For example:

```
SELECT f1[1][-2][3] AS e1, f1[1][-1][5] AS e2
 FROM (SELECT '[1:1][-2:-1][3:5]={{{1,2,3},{4,5,6}}}'::int[] AS f1) AS ss;

 e1 | e2
----+----
  1 |  6
(1 row)
```

The array output routine will include explicit dimensions in its result only when there are one or more lower bounds different from one.

If the value written for an element is NULL (in any case variant), the element is taken to be NULL. The presence of any quotes or backslashes disables this and allows the literal string value "NULL" to be entered. Also, for backward compatibility with pre-8.2 versions of PostgreSQL, the array_nulls configuration parameter can be turned `off` to suppress recognition of NULL as a NULL.

As shown previously, when writing an array value you can use double quotes around any individual array element. You *must* do so if the element value would otherwise confuse the array-value parser. For example, elements containing curly braces, commas (or the data type's delimiter character), double quotes, backslashes, or leading or trailing whitespace must be double-quoted. Empty strings and strings matching the word NULL must be quoted, too. To put a double quote or backslash in a quoted array element value, use escape string syntax and precede it with a backslash. Alternatively, you can avoid quotes and use backslash-escaping to protect all data characters that would otherwise be taken as array syntax.

You can add whitespace before a left brace or after a right brace. You can also add whitespace before or after any individual item string. In all of these cases the whitespace will be ignored. However, whitespace within double-quoted elements, or surrounded on both sides by non-whitespace characters of an element, is not ignored.

> **Note:** Remember that what you write in an SQL command will first be interpreted as a string literal, and then as an array. This doubles the number of backslashes you need. For example, to insert a `text` array value containing a backslash and a double quote, you'd need to write:
>
> ```
> INSERT ... VALUES (E'{"\\\\","\\""}');
> ```
>
> The escape string processor removes one level of backslashes, so that what arrives at the array-value parser looks like `{"\\","\""}`. In turn, the strings fed to the `text` data type's input routine become `\` and `"` respectively. (If we were working with a data type whose input routine also treated backslashes specially, `bytea` for example, we might need as many as eight backslashes in the command to get one backslash into the stored array element.) Dollar quoting (see Section 4.1.2.4) can be used to avoid the need to double backslashes.

> **Tip:** The `ARRAY` constructor syntax (see Section 4.2.12) is often easier to work with than the array-literal syntax when writing array values in SQL commands. In `ARRAY`, individual element values are written the same way they would be written when not members of an array.

8.16. Composite Types

A *composite type* represents the structure of a row or record; it is essentially just a list of field names and their data types. PostgreSQL allows composite types to be used in many of the same ways that simple types can be used. For example, a column of a table can be declared to be of a composite type.

8.16.1. Declaration of Composite Types

Here are two simple examples of defining composite types:

```
CREATE TYPE complex AS (
    r           double precision,
    i           double precision
);

CREATE TYPE inventory_item AS (
    name            text,
    supplier_id     integer,
    price           numeric
);
```

The syntax is comparable to `CREATE TABLE`, except that only field names and types can be specified; no constraints (such as `NOT NULL`) can presently be included. Note that the `AS` keyword is essential; without it, the system will think a different kind of CREATE TYPE command is meant, and you will get odd syntax errors.

Having defined the types, we can use them to create tables:

```
CREATE TABLE on_hand (
    item        inventory_item,
    count       integer
);

INSERT INTO on_hand VALUES (ROW('fuzzy dice', 42, 1.99), 1000);
```

or functions:

```
CREATE FUNCTION price_extension(inventory_item, integer) RETURNS numeric
AS 'SELECT $1.price * $2' LANGUAGE SQL;

SELECT price_extension(item, 10) FROM on_hand;
```

Whenever you create a table, a composite type is also automatically created, with the same name as the table, to represent the table's row type. For example, had we said:

```
CREATE TABLE inventory_item (
    name            text,
    supplier_id     integer REFERENCES suppliers,
    price           numeric CHECK (price > 0)
);
```

then the same inventory_item composite type shown above would come into being as a byproduct, and could be used just as above. Note however an important restriction of the current implementation: since no constraints are associated with a composite type, the constraints shown in the table definition *do not apply* to values of the composite type outside the table. (A partial workaround is to use domain types as members of composite types.)

8.16.2. Composite Value Input

To write a composite value as a literal constant, enclose the field values within parentheses and separate them by commas. You can put double quotes around any field value, and must do so if it contains commas or parentheses. (More details appear below.) Thus, the general format of a composite constant is the following:

```
'( val1 , val2 , ... )'
```

An example is:

```
'("fuzzy dice",42,1.99)'
```

which would be a valid value of the inventory_item type defined above. To make a field be NULL, write no characters at all in its position in the list. For example, this constant specifies a NULL third field:

```
' ("fuzzy dice",42,)'
```

If you want an empty string rather than NULL, write double quotes:

```
' ("",42,)'
```

Here the first field is a non-NULL empty string, the third is NULL.

(These constants are actually only a special case of the generic type constants discussed in Section 4.1.2.7. The constant is initially treated as a string and passed to the composite-type input conversion routine. An explicit type specification might be necessary.)

The ROW expression syntax can also be used to construct composite values. In most cases this is considerably simpler to use than the string-literal syntax since you don't have to worry about multiple layers of quoting. We already used this method above:

```
ROW('fuzzy dice', 42, 1.99)
ROW(", 42, NULL)
```

The ROW keyword is actually optional as long as you have more than one field in the expression, so these can simplify to:

```
('fuzzy dice', 42, 1.99)
(", 42, NULL)
```

The ROW expression syntax is discussed in more detail in Section 4.2.13.

8.16.3. Accessing Composite Types

To access a field of a composite column, one writes a dot and the field name, much like selecting a field from a table name. In fact, it's so much like selecting from a table name that you often have to use parentheses to keep from confusing the parser. For example, you might try to select some subfields from our on_hand example table with something like:

```
SELECT item.name FROM on_hand WHERE item.price > 9.99;
```

This will not work since the name item is taken to be a table name, not a column name of on_hand, per SQL syntax rules. You must write it like this:

```
SELECT (item).name FROM on_hand WHERE (item).price > 9.99;
```

or if you need to use the table name as well (for instance in a multitable query), like this:

```
SELECT (on_hand.item).name FROM on_hand WHERE (on_hand.item).price > 9.99;
```

Now the parenthesized object is correctly interpreted as a reference to the item column, and then the subfield can be selected from it.

Similar syntactic issues apply whenever you select a field from a composite value. For instance, to select just one field from the result of a function that returns a composite value, you'd need to write something like:

```
SELECT (my_func(...)).field FROM ...
```

Without the extra parentheses, this will generate a syntax error.

8.16.4. Modifying Composite Types

Here are some examples of the proper syntax for inserting and updating composite columns. First, inserting or updating a whole column:

```
INSERT INTO mytab (complex_col) VALUES((1.1,2.2));

UPDATE mytab SET complex_col = ROW(1.1,2.2) WHERE ...;
```

The first example omits ROW, the second uses it; we could have done it either way.

We can update an individual subfield of a composite column:

```
UPDATE mytab SET complex_col.r = (complex_col).r + 1 WHERE ...;
```

Notice here that we don't need to (and indeed cannot) put parentheses around the column name appearing just after SET, but we do need parentheses when referencing the same column in the expression to the right of the equal sign.

And we can specify subfields as targets for INSERT, too:

```
INSERT INTO mytab (complex_col.r, complex_col.i) VALUES(1.1, 2.2);
```

Had we not supplied values for all the subfields of the column, the remaining subfields would have been filled with null values.

8.16.5. Composite Type Input and Output Syntax

The external text representation of a composite value consists of items that are interpreted according to the I/O conversion rules for the individual field types, plus decoration that indicates the composite structure. The decoration consists of parentheses ((and)) around the whole value, plus commas (,) between adjacent items. Whitespace outside the parentheses is ignored, but within the parentheses it is considered part of the field value, and might or might not be significant depending on the input conversion rules for the field data type. For example, in:

```
'(  42)'
```

the whitespace will be ignored if the field type is integer, but not if it is text.

As shown previously, when writing a composite value you can write double quotes around any individual field value. You *must* do so if the field value would otherwise confuse the composite-value parser. In particular, fields containing parentheses, commas, double quotes, or backslashes must be double-quoted. To put a double quote or backslash in a quoted composite field value, precede it with a backslash. (Also, a pair of double quotes within a double-quoted field value is taken to represent a double quote character, analogously to the rules for single quotes in SQL literal strings.) Alternatively, you can avoid quoting and use backslash-escaping to protect all data characters that would otherwise be taken as composite syntax.

A completely empty field value (no characters at all between the commas or parentheses) represents a NULL. To write a value that is an empty string rather than NULL, write "".

The composite output routine will put double quotes around field values if they are empty strings or contain parentheses, commas, double quotes, backslashes, or white space. (Doing so for white space is not essential, but aids legibility.) Double quotes and backslashes embedded in field values will be doubled.

> **Note:** Remember that what you write in an SQL command will first be interpreted as a string literal, and then as a composite. This doubles the number of backslashes you need (assuming escape string syntax is used). For example, to insert a `text` field containing a double quote and a backslash in a composite value, you'd need to write:
>
> ```
> INSERT ... VALUES (E'("\\"\\\\")');
> ```
>
> The string-literal processor removes one level of backslashes, so that what arrives at the composite-value parser looks like `("\"\\")`. In turn, the string fed to the `text` data type's input routine becomes `"\`. (If we were working with a data type whose input routine also treated backslashes specially, `bytea` for example, we might need as many as eight backslashes in the command to get one backslash into the stored composite field.) Dollar quoting (see Section 4.1.2.4) can be used to avoid the need to double backslashes.

> **Tip:** The `ROW` constructor syntax is usually easier to work with than the composite-literal syntax when writing composite values in SQL commands. In `ROW`, individual field values are written the same way they would be written when not members of a composite.

8.17. Range Types

Range types are data types representing a range of values of some element type (called the range's *subtype*). For instance, ranges of `timestamp` might be used to represent the ranges of time that a meeting room is reserved. In this case the data type is `tsrange` (short for "timestamp range"), and `timestamp` is the subtype. The subtype must have a total order so that it is well-defined whether element values are within, before, or after a range of values.

Range types are useful because they represent many element values in a single range value, and because concepts such as overlapping ranges can be expressed clearly. The use of time and date ranges for scheduling purposes is the clearest example; but price ranges, measurement ranges from an instrument, and so forth can also be useful.

8.17.1. Built-in Range Types

PostgreSQL comes with the following built-in range types:

- `int4range` — Range of `integer`
- `int8range` — Range of `bigint`
- `numrange` — Range of `numeric`

- tsrange — Range of `timestamp without time zone`
- tstzrange — Range of `timestamp with time zone`
- daterange — Range of `date`

In addition, you can define your own range types; see CREATE TYPE for more information.

8.17.2. Examples

```
CREATE TABLE reservation (room int, during tsrange);
INSERT INTO reservation VALUES
    (1108, '[2010-01-01 14:30, 2010-01-01 15:30)');

-- Containment
SELECT int4range(10, 20) @> 3;

-- Overlaps
SELECT numrange(11.1, 22.2) && numrange(20.0, 30.0);

-- Extract the upper bound
SELECT upper(int8range(15, 25));

-- Compute the intersection
SELECT int4range(10, 20) * int4range(15, 25);

-- Is the range empty?
SELECT isempty(numrange(1, 5));
```

See Table 9-47 and Table 9-48 for complete lists of operators and functions on range types.

8.17.3. Inclusive and Exclusive Bounds

Every non-empty range has two bounds, the lower bound and the upper bound. All points between these values are included in the range. An inclusive bound means that the boundary point itself is included in the range as well, while an exclusive bound means that the boundary point is not included in the range.

In the text form of a range, an inclusive lower bound is represented by " [" while an exclusive lower bound is represented by " (". Likewise, an inclusive upper bound is represented by "]", while an exclusive upper bound is represented by ")". (See Section 8.17.5 for more details.)

The functions `lower_inc` and `upper_inc` test the inclusivity of the lower and upper bounds of a range value, respectively.

8.17.4. Infinite (Unbounded) Ranges

The lower bound of a range can be omitted, meaning that all points less than the upper bound are included in the range. Likewise, if the upper bound of the range is omitted, then all points greater than the lower bound are included in the range. If both lower and upper bounds are omitted, all values of the element type are considered to be in the range.

This is equivalent to considering that the lower bound is "minus infinity", or the upper bound is "plus infinity", respectively. But note that these infinite values are never values of the range's element type, and can never be part of the range. (So there is no such thing as an inclusive infinite bound — if you try to write one, it will automatically be converted to an exclusive bound.)

Also, some element types have a notion of "infinity", but that is just another value so far as the range type mechanisms are concerned. For example, in timestamp ranges, `[today,]` means the same thing as `[today,)`. But `[today,infinity]` means something different from `[today,infinity)` — the latter excludes the special `timestamp` value `infinity`.

The functions `lower_inf` and `upper_inf` test for infinite lower and upper bounds of a range, respectively.

8.17.5. Range Input/Output

The input for a range value must follow one of the following patterns:

```
(lower-bound,upper-bound)
(lower-bound,upper-bound]
[lower-bound,upper-bound)
[lower-bound,upper-bound]
empty
```

The parentheses or brackets indicate whether the lower and upper bounds are exclusive or inclusive, as described previously. Notice that the final pattern is `empty`, which represents an empty range (a range that contains no points).

The *lower-bound* may be either a string that is valid input for the subtype, or empty to indicate no lower bound. Likewise, *upper-bound* may be either a string that is valid input for the subtype, or empty to indicate no upper bound.

Each bound value can be quoted using `"` (double quote) characters. This is necessary if the bound value contains parentheses, brackets, commas, double quotes, or backslashes, since these characters would otherwise be taken as part of the range syntax. To put a double quote or backslash in a quoted bound value, precede it with a backslash. (Also, a pair of double quotes within a double-quoted bound value is taken to represent a double quote character, analogously to the rules for single quotes in SQL literal strings.) Alternatively, you can avoid quoting and use backslash-escaping to protect all data characters that would otherwise be taken as range syntax. Also, to write a bound value that is an empty string, write `""`, since writing nothing means an infinite bound.

Whitespace is allowed before and after the range value, but any whitespace between the parentheses or brackets is taken as part of the lower or upper bound value. (Depending on the element type, it might or might not be significant.)

> **Note:** These rules are very similar to those for writing field values in composite-type literals. See Section 8.16.5 for additional commentary.

Examples:

```
-- includes 3, does not include 7, and does include all points in between
SELECT '[3,7)'::int4range;

-- does not include either 3 or 7, but includes all points in between
SELECT '(3,7)'::int4range;

-- includes only the single point 4
SELECT '[4,4]'::int4range;

-- includes no points (and will be normalized to 'empty')
SELECT '[4,4)'::int4range;
```

8.17.6. Constructing Ranges

Each range type has a constructor function with the same name as the range type. Using the constructor function is frequently more convenient than writing a range literal constant, since it avoids the need for extra quoting of the bound values. The constructor function accepts two or three arguments. The two-argument form constructs a range in standard form (lower bound inclusive, upper bound exclusive), while the three-argument form constructs a range with bounds of the form specified by the third argument. The third argument must be one of the strings "()", "(]", "[)", or "[]". For example:

```
-- The full form is: lower bound, upper bound, and text argument indicating
-- inclusivity/exclusivity of bounds.
SELECT numrange(1.0, 14.0, '(]');

-- If the third argument is omitted, '[)' is assumed.
SELECT numrange(1.0, 14.0);

-- Although '(]' is specified here, on display the value will be converted to
-- canonical form, since int8range is a discrete range type (see below).
SELECT int8range(1, 14, '(]');

-- Using NULL for either bound causes the range to be unbounded on that side.
SELECT numrange(NULL, 2.2);
```

8.17.7. Discrete Range Types

A discrete range is one whose element type has a well-defined "step", such as integer or date. In these types two elements can be said to be adjacent, when there are no valid values between them. This contrasts with continuous ranges, where it's always (or almost always) possible to identify other element values between two given values. For example, a range over the numeric type is continuous, as is a range over timestamp. (Even though timestamp has limited precision, and so could theoretically be treated as discrete, it's better to consider it continuous since the step size is normally not of interest.)

Another way to think about a discrete range type is that there is a clear idea of a "next" or "previous" value for each element value. Knowing that, it is possible to convert between inclusive and exclusive representations of a range's bounds, by choosing the next or previous element value instead of the one originally given. For example, in an integer range type [4,8] and (3,9) denote the same set of values; but this would not be so for a range over numeric.

A discrete range type should have a *canonicalization* function that is aware of the desired step size for the element type. The canonicalization function is charged with converting equivalent values of the range type to have identical representations, in particular consistently inclusive or exclusive bounds. If a canonicalization function is not specified, then ranges with different formatting will always be treated as unequal, even though they might represent the same set of values in reality.

The built-in range types int4range, int8range, and daterange all use a canonical form that includes the lower bound and excludes the upper bound; that is, [). User-defined range types can use other conventions, however.

8.17.8. Defining New Range Types

Users can define their own range types. The most common reason to do this is to use ranges over subtypes not provided among the built-in range types. For example, to define a new range type of subtype float8:

```
CREATE TYPE floatrange AS RANGE (
    subtype = float8,
    subtype_diff = float8mi
);

SELECT '[1.234, 5.678]'::floatrange;
```

Because float8 has no meaningful "step", we do not define a canonicalization function in this example.

If the subtype is considered to have discrete rather than continuous values, the CREATE TYPE command should specify a canonical function. The canonicalization function takes an input range value, and must return an equivalent range value that may have different bounds and formatting. The canonical output for two ranges that represent the same set of values, for example the integer ranges [1, 7] and [1, 8), must be identical. It doesn't matter which representation you choose to be the canonical one, so long as two equivalent values with different formattings are always mapped to the same value with the same formatting. In addition to adjusting the inclusive/exclusive bounds format, a canonicalization function might round off boundary values, in case the desired step size is larger than what the subtype is capable of storing. For instance, a range type over timestamp could be defined to have a step size of an hour, in which case the canonicalization function would need to round off bounds that weren't a multiple of an hour, or perhaps throw an error instead.

Defining your own range type also allows you to specify a different subtype B-tree operator class or collation to use, so as to change the sort ordering that determines which values fall into a given range.

In addition, any range type that is meant to be used with GiST or SP-GiST indexes should define a subtype difference, or subtype_diff, function. (the index will still work without subtype_diff, but it is likely to be considerably less efficient than if a difference function is provided.) The subtype difference function takes two input values of the subtype, and returns their difference (i.e., X minus Y) represented as a float8 value. In our example above, the function that underlies the regular float8 minus operator can be used; but for any other subtype, some type conversion would be necessary. Some creative thought about how to represent differences as numbers might be needed, too. To the greatest extent possible, the `subtype_diff` function should agree with the sort ordering implied by the selected operator class and collation; that is, its result should be positive whenever its first argument is greater than its second according to the sort ordering.

See CREATE TYPE for more information about creating range types.

8.17.9. Indexing

GiST and SP-GiST indexes can be created for table columns of range types. For instance, to create a GiST index:

```
CREATE INDEX reservation_idx ON reservation USING gist (during);
```

A GiST or SP-GiST index can accelerate queries involving these range operators: =, &&, <@, @>, <<, >>, -|-, &<, and &> (see Table 9-47 for more information).

In addition, B-tree and hash indexes can be created for table columns of range types. For these index types, basically the only useful range operation is equality. There is a B-tree sort ordering defined for range values, with corresponding < and > operators, but the ordering is rather arbitrary and not usually useful in the real world. Range types' B-tree and hash support is primarily meant to allow sorting and hashing internally in queries, rather than creation of actual indexes.

8.17.10. Constraints on Ranges

While UNIQUE is a natural constraint for scalar values, it is usually unsuitable for range types. Instead, an exclusion constraint is often more appropriate (see CREATE TABLE ... CONSTRAINT ... EXCLUDE). Exclusion constraints allow the specification of constraints such as "non-overlapping" on a range type. For example:

```
CREATE TABLE reservation (
    during tsrange,
    EXCLUDE USING gist (during WITH &&)
);
```

That constraint will prevent any overlapping values from existing in the table at the same time:

```
INSERT INTO reservation VALUES
    ('[2010-01-01 11:30, 2010-01-01 15:00)');
INSERT 0 1

INSERT INTO reservation VALUES
    ('[2010-01-01 14:45, 2010-01-01 15:45)');
ERROR:  conflicting key value violates exclusion constraint "reservation_durinc
DETAIL:  Key (during)=(["2010-01-01 14:45:00","2010-01-01 15:45:00")) conflicts
with existing key (during)=(["2010-01-01 11:30:00","2010-01-01 15:00:00")).
```

You can use the `btree_gist` extension to define exclusion constraints on plain scalar data types, which can then be combined with range exclusions for maximum flexibility. For example, after `btree_gist` is installed, the following constraint will reject overlapping ranges only if the meeting room numbers are equal:

```
CREATE EXTENSION btree_gist;
CREATE TABLE room_reservation (
    room text,
    during tsrange,
    EXCLUDE USING gist (room WITH =, during WITH &&)
);

INSERT INTO room_reservation VALUES
    ('123A', '[2010-01-01 14:00, 2010-01-01 15:00)');
INSERT 0 1

INSERT INTO room_reservation VALUES
    ('123A', '[2010-01-01 14:30, 2010-01-01 15:30)');
ERROR:  conflicting key value violates exclusion constraint "room_reservation_r
DETAIL:  Key (room, during)=(123A, ["2010-01-01 14:30:00","2010-01-01 15:30:00"
with existing key (room, during)=(123A, ["2010-01-01 14:00:00","2010-01-01 15:0

INSERT INTO room_reservation VALUES
    ('123B', '[2010-01-01 14:30, 2010-01-01 15:30)');
INSERT 0 1
```

8.18. Object Identifier Types

Object identifiers (OIDs) are used internally by PostgreSQL as primary keys for various system tables. OIDs are not added to user-created tables, unless `WITH OIDS` is specified when the table is created, or the default_with_oids configuration variable is enabled. Type `oid` represents an object identifier. There are also several alias types for `oid`: `regproc`, `regprocedure`, `regoper`, `regoperator`, `regclass`, `regtype`, `regconfig`, and `regdictionary`. Table 8-24 shows an overview.

The `oid` type is currently implemented as an unsigned four-byte integer. Therefore, it is not large enough to provide database-wide uniqueness in large databases, or even in large individual tables. So, using a user-created table's OID column as a primary key is discouraged. OIDs are best used only for references to system tables.

The `oid` type itself has few operations beyond comparison. It can be cast to integer, however, and then manipulated using the standard integer operators. (Beware of possible signed-versus-unsigned confusion if you do this.)

The OID alias types have no operations of their own except for specialized input and output routines. These routines are able to accept and display symbolic names for system objects, rather than the raw numeric value that type `oid` would use. The alias types allow simplified lookup of OID values for objects. For example, to examine the `pg_attribute` rows related to a table `mytable`, one could write:

```
SELECT * FROM pg_attribute WHERE attrelid = 'mytable'::regclass;
```

rather than:

```
SELECT * FROM pg_attribute
  WHERE attrelid = (SELECT oid FROM pg_class WHERE relname = 'mytable');
```

While that doesn't look all that bad by itself, it's still oversimplified. A far more complicated sub-select would be needed to select the right OID if there are multiple tables named mytable in different schemas. The regclass input converter handles the table lookup according to the schema path setting, and so it does the "right thing" automatically. Similarly, casting a table's OID to regclass is handy for symbolic display of a numeric OID.

Table 8-24. Object Identifier Types

Name	References	Description	Value Example
oid	any	numeric object identifier	564182
regproc	pg_proc	function name	sum
regprocedure	pg_proc	function with argument types	sum(int4)
regoper	pg_operator	operator name	+
regoperator	pg_operator	operator with argument types	*(integer,integer) or -(NONE,integer)
regclass	pg_class	relation name	pg_type
regtype	pg_type	data type name	integer
regconfig	pg_ts_config	text search configuration	english
regdictionary	pg_ts_dict	text search dictionary	simple

All of the OID alias types accept schema-qualified names, and will display schema-qualified names on output if the object would not be found in the current search path without being qualified. The regproc and regoper alias types will only accept input names that are unique (not overloaded), so they are of limited use; for most uses regprocedure or regoperator are more appropriate. For regoperator, unary operators are identified by writing NONE for the unused operand.

An additional property of the OID alias types is the creation of dependencies. If a constant of one of these types appears in a stored expression (such as a column default expression or view), it creates a dependency on the referenced object. For example, if a column has a default expression nextval('my_seq'::regclass), PostgreSQL understands that the default expression depends on the sequence my_seq; the system will not let the sequence be dropped without first removing the default expression.

Another identifier type used by the system is xid, or transaction (abbreviated xact) identifier. This is the data type of the system columns xmin and xmax. Transaction identifiers are 32-bit quantities.

A third identifier type used by the system is cid, or command identifier. This is the data type of the system columns cmin and cmax. Command identifiers are also 32-bit quantities.

A final identifier type used by the system is `tid`, or tuple identifier (row identifier). This is the data type of the system column `ctid`. A tuple ID is a pair (block number, tuple index within block) that identifies the physical location of the row within its table.

(The system columns are further explained in Section 5.4.)

8.19. pg_lsn Type

The `pg_lsn` data type can be used to store LSN (Log Sequence Number) data which is a pointer to a location in the XLOG. This type is a representation of `XLogRecPtr` and an internal system type of PostgreSQL.

Internally, an LSN is a 64-bit integer, representing a byte position in the write-ahead log stream. It is printed as two hexadecimal numbers of up to 8 digits each, separated by a slash; for example, `16/B374D848`. The `pg_lsn` type supports the standard comparison operators, like = and >. Two LSNs can be subtracted using the – operator; the result is the number of bytes separating those write-ahead log positions.

8.20. Pseudo-Types

The PostgreSQL type system contains a number of special-purpose entries that are collectively called *pseudo-types*. A pseudo-type cannot be used as a column data type, but it can be used to declare a function's argument or result type. Each of the available pseudo-types is useful in situations where a function's behavior does not correspond to simply taking or returning a value of a specific SQL data type. Table 8-25 lists the existing pseudo-types.

Table 8-25. Pseudo-Types

Name	Description
`any`	Indicates that a function accepts any input data type.
`anyelement`	Indicates that a function accepts any data type (see Section 35.2.5).
`anyarray`	Indicates that a function accepts any array data type (see Section 35.2.5).
`anynonarray`	Indicates that a function accepts any non-array data type (see Section 35.2.5).
`anyenum`	Indicates that a function accepts any enum data type (see Section 35.2.5 and Section 8.7).
`anyrange`	Indicates that a function accepts any range data type (see Section 35.2.5 and Section 8.17).
`cstring`	Indicates that a function accepts or returns a null-terminated C string.

Name	Description
`internal`	Indicates that a function accepts or returns a server-internal data type.
`language_handler`	A procedural language call handler is declared to return `language_handler`.
`fdw_handler`	A foreign-data wrapper handler is declared to return `fdw_handler`.
`record`	Identifies a function returning an unspecified row type.
`trigger`	A trigger function is declared to return `trigger`.
`void`	Indicates that a function returns no value.
`opaque`	An obsolete type name that formerly served all the above purposes.

Functions coded in C (whether built-in or dynamically loaded) can be declared to accept or return any of these pseudo data types. It is up to the function author to ensure that the function will behave safely when a pseudo-type is used as an argument type.

Functions coded in procedural languages can use pseudo-types only as allowed by their implementation languages. At present the procedural languages all forbid use of a pseudo-type as argument type, and allow only `void` and `record` as a result type (plus `trigger` when the function is used as a trigger). Some also support polymorphic functions using the types `anyelement`, `anyarray`, `anynonarray`, `anyenum`, and `anyrange`.

The `internal` pseudo-type is used to declare functions that are meant only to be called internally by the database system, and not by direct invocation in an SQL query. If a function has at least one `internal`-type argument then it cannot be called from SQL. To preserve the type safety of this restriction it is important to follow this coding rule: do not create any function that is declared to return `internal` unless it has at least one `internal` argument.

Chapter 9. Functions and Operators

PostgreSQL provides a large number of functions and operators for the built-in data types. Users can also define their own functions and operators, as described in Part V. The psql commands `\df` and `\do` can be used to list all available functions and operators, respectively.

If you are concerned about portability then note that most of the functions and operators described in this chapter, with the exception of the most trivial arithmetic and comparison operators and some explicitly marked functions, are not specified by the SQL standard. Some of this extended functionality is present in other SQL database management systems, and in many cases this functionality is compatible and consistent between the various implementations. This chapter is also not exhaustive; additional functions appear in relevant sections of the manual.

9.1. Logical Operators

The usual logical operators are available:

```
AND
OR
NOT
```

SQL uses a three-valued logic system with true, false, and `null`, which represents "unknown". Observe the following truth tables:

a	b	a **AND** b	a **OR** b
TRUE	TRUE	TRUE	TRUE
TRUE	FALSE	FALSE	TRUE
TRUE	NULL	NULL	TRUE
FALSE	FALSE	FALSE	FALSE
FALSE	NULL	FALSE	NULL
NULL	NULL	NULL	NULL

a	**NOT** a
TRUE	FALSE
FALSE	TRUE
NULL	NULL

The operators AND and OR are commutative, that is, you can switch the left and right operand without affecting the result. But see Section 4.2.14 for more information about the order of evaluation of subexpressions.

9.2. Comparison Operators

The usual comparison operators are available, shown in Table 9-1.

Table 9-1. Comparison Operators

Operator	Description
<	less than
>	greater than
<=	less than or equal to
>=	greater than or equal to
=	equal
<> or !=	not equal

> **Note:** The != operator is converted to <> in the parser stage. It is not possible to implement != and <> operators that do different things.

Comparison operators are available for all relevant data types. All comparison operators are binary operators that return values of type `boolean`; expressions like 1 < 2 < 3 are not valid (because there is no < operator to compare a Boolean value with 3).

In addition to the comparison operators, the special BETWEEN construct is available:

```
a BETWEEN x AND y
```

is equivalent to

```
a >= x AND a <= y
```

Notice that BETWEEN treats the endpoint values as included in the range. NOT BETWEEN does the opposite comparison:

```
a NOT BETWEEN x AND y
```

is equivalent to

```
a < x OR a > y
```

BETWEEN SYMMETRIC is the same as BETWEEN except there is no requirement that the argument to the left of AND be less than or equal to the argument on the right. If it is not, those two arguments are automatically swapped, so that a nonempty range is always implied.

To check whether a value is or is not null, use the constructs:

```
expression IS NULL
expression IS NOT NULL
```

or the equivalent, but nonstandard, constructs:

```
expression ISNULL
```

```
expression NOTNULL
```

Do *not* write `expression = NULL` because `NULL` is not "equal to" `NULL`. (The null value represents an unknown value, and it is not known whether two unknown values are equal.) This behavior conforms to the SQL standard.

> **Tip:** Some applications might expect that `expression = NULL` returns true if `expression` evaluates to the null value. It is highly recommended that these applications be modified to comply with the SQL standard. However, if that cannot be done the transform_null_equals configuration variable is available. If it is enabled, PostgreSQL will convert `x = NULL` clauses to `x IS NULL`.

> **Note:** If the `expression` is row-valued, then `IS NULL` is true when the row expression itself is null or when all the row's fields are null, while `IS NOT NULL` is true when the row expression itself is non-null and all the row's fields are non-null. Because of this behavior, `IS NULL` and `IS NOT NULL` do not always return inverse results for row-valued expressions, i.e., a row-valued expression that contains both NULL and non-null values will return false for both tests. This definition conforms to the SQL standard, and is a change from the inconsistent behavior exhibited by PostgreSQL versions prior to 8.2.

Ordinary comparison operators yield null (signifying "unknown"), not true or false, when either input is null. For example, `7 = NULL` yields null, as does `7 <> NULL`. When this behavior is not suitable, use the `IS [ NOT ] DISTINCT FROM` constructs:

```
expression IS DISTINCT FROM expression
expression IS NOT DISTINCT FROM expression
```

For non-null inputs, `IS DISTINCT FROM` is the same as the `<>` operator. However, if both inputs are null it returns false, and if only one input is null it returns true. Similarly, `IS NOT DISTINCT FROM` is identical to `=` for non-null inputs, but it returns true when both inputs are null, and false when only one input is null. Thus, these constructs effectively act as though null were a normal data value, rather than "unknown".

Boolean values can also be tested using the constructs

```
expression IS TRUE
expression IS NOT TRUE
expression IS FALSE
expression IS NOT FALSE
expression IS UNKNOWN
expression IS NOT UNKNOWN
```

These will always return true or false, never a null value, even when the operand is null. A null input is treated as the logical value "unknown". Notice that `IS UNKNOWN` and `IS NOT UNKNOWN` are effectively the same as `IS NULL` and `IS NOT NULL`, respectively, except that the input expression must be of Boolean type.

9.3. Mathematical Functions and Operators

Mathematical operators are provided for many PostgreSQL types. For types without standard mathematical conventions (e.g., date/time types) we describe the actual behavior in subsequent sections.

Table 9-2 shows the available mathematical operators.

Table 9-2. Mathematical Operators

Operator	Description	Example	Result
+	addition	`2 + 3`	`5`
-	subtraction	`2 - 3`	`-1`
*	multiplication	`2 * 3`	`6`
/	division (integer division truncates the result)	`4 / 2`	`2`
%	modulo (remainder)	`5 % 4`	`1`
^	exponentiation	`2.0 ^ 3.0`	`8`
|/	square root	`|/ 25.0`	`5`
||/	cube root	`||/ 27.0`	`3`
!	factorial	`5 !`	`120`
!!	factorial (prefix operator)	`!! 5`	`120`
@	absolute value	`@ -5.0`	`5`
&	bitwise AND	`91 & 15`	`11`
|	bitwise OR	`32 | 3`	`35`
#	bitwise XOR	`17 # 5`	`20`
~	bitwise NOT	`~1`	`-2`
<<	bitwise shift left	`1 << 4`	`16`
>>	bitwise shift right	`8 >> 2`	`2`

The bitwise operators work only on integral data types, whereas the others are available for all numeric data types. The bitwise operators are also available for the bit string types `bit` and `bit varying`, as shown in Table 9-11.

Table 9-3 shows the available mathematical functions. In the table, `dp` indicates `double precision`. Many of these functions are provided in multiple forms with different argument types. Except where noted, any given form of a function returns the same data type as its argument. The functions working with `double precision` data are mostly implemented on top of the host system's C library; accuracy and behavior in boundary cases can therefore vary depending on the host system.

Table 9-3. Mathematical Functions

Function	Return Type	Description	Example	Result
`abs(x)`	(same as input)	absolute value	`abs(-17.4)`	`17.4`

Function	Return Type	Description	Example	Result
`cbrt(dp)`	dp	cube root	`cbrt(27.0)`	3
`ceil(dp or numeric)`	(same as input)	smallest integer not less than argument	`ceil(-42.8)`	-42
`ceiling(dp or numeric)`	(same as input)	smallest integer not less than argument (alias for `ceil`)	`ceiling(-95.3)`	-95
`degrees(dp)`	dp	radians to degrees	`degrees(0.5)`	28.6478897565412
`div(y numeric, x numeric)`	numeric	integer quotient of y/x	`div(9,4)`	2
`exp(dp or numeric)`	(same as input)	exponential	`exp(1.0)`	2.7182818284590
`floor(dp or numeric)`	(same as input)	largest integer not greater than argument	`floor(-42.8)`	-43
`ln(dp or numeric)`	(same as input)	natural logarithm	`ln(2.0)`	0.6931471805599
`log(dp or numeric)`	(same as input)	base 10 logarithm	`log(100.0)`	2
`log(b numeric, x numeric)`	numeric	logarithm to base b	`log(2.0, 64.0)`	6.0000000000
`mod(y, x)`	(same as argument types)	remainder of y/x	`mod(9,4)`	1
`pi()`	dp	"π" constant	`pi()`	3.1415926535897
`power(a dp, b dp)`	dp	a raised to the power of b	`power(9.0, 3.0)`	729
`power(a numeric, b numeric)`	numeric	a raised to the power of b	`power(9.0, 3.0)`	729
`radians(dp)`	dp	degrees to radians	`radians(45.0)`	0.7853981633974
`round(dp or numeric)`	(same as input)	round to nearest integer	`round(42.4)`	42
`round(v numeric, s int)`	numeric	round to s decimal places	`round(42.4382, 2)`	42.44
`sign(dp or numeric)`	(same as input)	sign of the argument (-1, 0, +1)	`sign(-8.4)`	-1
`sqrt(dp or numeric)`	(same as input)	square root	`sqrt(2.0)`	1.4142135623731
`trunc(dp or numeric)`	(same as input)	truncate toward zero	`trunc(42.8)`	42

Function	Return Type	Description	Example	Result
trunc(v numeric, s int)	numeric	truncate to s decimal places	trunc(42.4382, 2)	42.43
width_bucket(op numeric, b1 numeric, b2 numeric, count int)	int	return the bucket to which operand would be assigned in an equidepth histogram with count buckets, in the range b1 to b2	width_bucket(5.35, 0.024, 10.06, 5)	3
width_bucket(op dp, b1 dp, b2 dp, count int)	int	return the bucket to which operand would be assigned in an equidepth histogram with count buckets, in the range b1 to b2	width_bucket(5.35, 0.024, 10.06, 5)	3

Table 9-4 shows functions for generating random numbers.

Table 9-4. Random Functions

Function	Return Type	Description
random()	dp	random value in the range 0.0 <= x < 1.0
setseed(dp)	void	set seed for subsequent random() calls (value between -1.0 and 1.0, inclusive)

The characteristics of the values returned by random() depend on the system implementation. It is not suitable for cryptographic applications; see pgcrypto module for an alternative.

Finally, Table 9-5 shows the available trigonometric functions. All trigonometric functions take arguments and return values of type double precision. Trigonometric functions arguments are expressed in radians. Inverse functions return values are expressed in radians. See unit transformation functions radians() and degrees() above.

Table 9-5. Trigonometric Functions

Function	Description
acos(x)	inverse cosine
asin(x)	inverse sine
atan(x)	inverse tangent
atan2(y, x)	inverse tangent of y / x
cos(x)	cosine
cot(x)	cotangent

Function	Description
`sin(x)`	sine
`tan(x)`	tangent

9.4. String Functions and Operators

This section describes functions and operators for examining and manipulating string values. Strings in this context include values of the types `character`, `character varying`, and `text`. Unless otherwise noted, all of the functions listed below work on all of these types, but be wary of potential effects of automatic space-padding when using the `character` type. Some functions also exist natively for the bit-string types.

SQL defines some string functions that use key words, rather than commas, to separate arguments. Details are in Table 9-6. PostgreSQL also provides versions of these functions that use the regular function invocation syntax (see Table 9-7).

> **Note:** Before PostgreSQL 8.3, these functions would silently accept values of several non-string data types as well, due to the presence of implicit coercions from those data types to `text`. Those coercions have been removed because they frequently caused surprising behaviors. However, the string concatenation operator (||) still accepts non-string input, so long as at least one input is of a string type, as shown in Table 9-6. For other cases, insert an explicit coercion to `text` if you need to duplicate the previous behavior.

Table 9-6. SQL String Functions and Operators

Function	Return Type	Description	Example	Result
`string || string`	`text`	String concatenation	`'Post' || 'greSQL'`	`PostgreSQL`
`string || non-string` or `non-string || string`	`text`	String concatenation with one non-string input	`'Value: ' || 42`	`Value: 42`
`bit_length(string)`	`int`	Number of bits in string	`bit_length('jose')`	`32`
`char_length(string)` or `character_length(string)`	`int`	Number of characters in string	`char_length('jose')`	`4`
`lower(string)`	`text`	Convert string to lower case	`lower('TOM')`	`tom`

Function	Return Type	Description	Example	Result
`octet_length(string)`	`int`	Number of bytes in string	`octet_length('jose')`	4
`overlay(string placing string from int [for int])`	`text`	Replace substring	`overlay('Txxxxas placing 'hom' from 2 for 4)`	Thomas
`position(substring in string)`	`int`	Location of specified substring	`position('om' in 'Thomas')`	3
`substring(string [from int] [for int])`	`text`	Extract substring	`substring('Thomas from 2 for 3)`	hom
`substring(string from pattern)`	`text`	Extract substring matching POSIX regular expression. See Section 9.7 for more information on pattern matching.	`substring('Thomas from '...$')`	mas
`substring(string from pattern for escape)`	`text`	Extract substring matching SQL regular expression. See Section 9.7 for more information on pattern matching.	`substring('Thomas from '%#"o_a#"_' for '#')`	oma
`trim([leading | trailing | both] [characters] from string)`	`text`	Remove the longest string containing only the `characters` (a space by default) from the start/end/both ends of the `string`	`trim(both 'x' from 'xTomxx')`	Tom
`trim([leading | trailing | both] [from] string [, characters] )`	`text`	Non-standard version of `trim()`	`trim(both from 'xTomxx', 'x')`	Tom
`upper(string)`	`text`	Convert string to upper case	`upper('tom')`	TOM

Additional string manipulation functions are available and are listed in Table 9-7. Some of them are used internally to implement the SQL-standard string functions listed in Table 9-6.

Table 9-7. Other String Functions

Function	Return Type	Description	Example	Result
`ascii(string)`	`int`	ASCII code of the first character of the argument. For UTF8 returns the Unicode code point of the character. For other multibyte encodings, the argument must be an ASCII character.	`ascii('x')`	`120`
`btrim(string text [, characters text])`	`text`	Remove the longest string consisting only of characters in `characters` (a space by default) from the start and end of `string`	`btrim('xyxtrimyyx', 'xy')`	`trim`
`chr(int)`	`text`	Character with the given code. For UTF8 the argument is treated as a Unicode code point. For other multibyte encodings the argument must designate an ASCII character. The NULL (0) character is not allowed because text data types cannot store such bytes.	`chr(65)`	`A`
`concat(str "any" [, str "any" [, ...] ])`	`text`	Concatenate the text representations of all the arguments. NULL arguments are ignored.	`concat('abcde', 2, NULL, 22)`	`abcde222`

Function	Return Type	Description	Example	Result
`concat_ws(sep text, str "any" [, str "any" [, ...] ])`	text	Concatenate all but the first argument with separators. The first argument is used as the separator string. NULL arguments are ignored.	`concat_ws(',', 'abcde', 2, NULL, 22)`	abcde,2,22
`convert(string bytea, src_encoding name, dest_encoding name)`	bytea	Convert string to `dest_encoding`. The original encoding is specified by `src_encoding`. The `string` must be valid in this encoding. Conversions can be defined by `CREATE CONVERSION`. Also there are some predefined conversions. See Table 9-8 for available conversions.	`convert('text_in_utf8', 'UTF8', 'LATIN1')`	text_in_utf8 represented in Latin-1 encoding (ISO 8859-1)
`convert_from(string bytea, src_encoding name)`	text	Convert string to the database encoding. The original encoding is specified by `src_encoding`. The `string` must be valid in this encoding.	`convert_from('text_in_utf8', 'UTF8')`	text_in_utf8 represented in the current database encoding
`convert_to(string text, dest_encoding name)`	bytea	Convert string to `dest_encoding`.	`convert_to('some text', 'UTF8')`	some text represented in the UTF8 encoding

Function	Return Type	Description	Example	Result
decode(string text, format text)	bytea	Decode binary data from textual representation in string. Options for format are same as in encode.	decode('MTIzAAE=', 'base64')	\x3132330001
encode(data bytea, format text)	text	Encode binary data into a textual representation. Supported formats are: base64, hex, escape. escape converts zero bytes and high-bit-set bytes to octal sequences (\nnn) and doubles backslashes.	encode(E'123\\000\\001', 'base64')	MTIzAAE=
format(formatstr text [, formatarg "any" [, ...]])	text	Format arguments according to a format string. This function is similar to the C function sprintf. See Section 9.4.1.	format('Hello %s, %1$s', 'World')	Hello World, World
initcap(string)	text	Convert the first letter of each word to upper case and the rest to lower case. Words are sequences of alphanumeric characters separated by non-alphanumeric characters.	initcap('hi THOMAS')	Hi Thomas
left(str text, n int)	text	Return first *n* characters in the string. When *n* is negative, return all but last |*n*| characters.	left('abcde', 2)	ab

Function	Return Type	Description	Example	Result
`length(string)`	`int`	Number of characters in `string`	`length('jose')`	4
`length(string bytea, encoding name )`	`int`	Number of characters in `string` in the given `encoding`. The `string` must be valid in this encoding.	`length('jose', 'UTF8')`	4
`lpad(string text, length int [, fill text])`	`text`	Fill up the `string` to length `length` by prepending the characters `fill` (a space by default). If the `string` is already longer than `length` then it is truncated (on the right).	`lpad('hi', 5, 'xy')`	xyxhi
`ltrim(string text [, characters text])`	`text`	Remove the longest string containing only characters from `characters` (a space by default) from the start of `string`	`ltrim('zzzytrim', 'xyz')`	trim
`md5(string)`	`text`	Calculates the MD5 hash of `string`, returning the result in hexadecimal	`md5('abc')`	900150983cd24fb0 d6963f7d28e17f72
`pg_client_encoding()`	`name`	Current client encoding name	`pg_client_encoding()`	SQL_ASCII

Function	Return Type	Description	Example	Result
`quote_ident(string text)`	text	Return the given string suitably quoted to be used as an identifier in an SQL statement string. Quotes are added only if necessary (i.e., if the string contains non-identifier characters or would be case-folded). Embedded quotes are properly doubled. See also Example 40-1.	`quote_ident('Foo bar')`	`"Foo bar"`
`quote_literal(string text)`	text	Return the given string suitably quoted to be used as a string literal in an SQL statement string. Embedded single-quotes and backslashes are properly doubled. Note that `quote_literal` returns null on null input; if the argument might be null, `quote_nullable` is often more suitable. See also Example 40-1.	`quote_literal(E'O\'Reilly')`	`'O''Reilly'`
`quote_literal(value anyelement)`	text	Coerce the given value to text and then quote it as a literal. Embedded single-quotes and backslashes are properly doubled.	`quote_literal(42.5)`	`'42.5'`

Function	Return Type	Description	Example	Result
`quote_nullable(string text)`	`text`	Return the given string suitably quoted to be used as a string literal in an SQL statement string; or, if the argument is null, return NULL. Embedded single-quotes and backslashes are properly doubled. See also Example 40-1.	`quote_nullable(NULL)`	`NULL`
`quote_nullable(value anyelement)`	`text`	Coerce the given value to text and then quote it as a literal; or, if the argument is null, return NULL. Embedded single-quotes and backslashes are properly doubled.	`quote_nullable(42.5)`	`'42.5'`
`regexp_matches(string text, pattern text [, flags text])`	`setof text[]`	Return all captured substrings resulting from matching a POSIX regular expression against the `string`. See Section 9.7.3 for more information.	`regexp_matches('foobarbequebaz', '(bar)(beque)')`	`{bar,beque}`
`regexp_replace(string text, pattern text, replacement text [, flags text])`	`text`	Replace substring(s) matching a POSIX regular expression. See Section 9.7.3 for more information.	`regexp_replace('Thomas', '.[mN]a.', 'M')`	`ThM`

Function	Return Type	Description	Example	Result
`regexp_split_to_array(string text, pattern text [, flags text ])`	`text[]`	Split `string` using a POSIX regular expression as the delimiter. See Section 9.7.3 for more information.	`regexp_split_to world', E'\\s+')`	`{hello,world}`
`regexp_split_to_table(string text, pattern text [, flags text])`	`setof text`	Split `string` using a POSIX regular expression as the delimiter. See Section 9.7.3 for more information.	`regexp_split_to world', E'\\s+')`	`hello world (2 rows)`
`repeat(string text, number int)`	`text`	Repeat `string` the specified `number` of times	`repeat('Pg', 4)`	`PgPgPgPg`
`replace(string text, from text, to text)`	`text`	Replace all occurrences in `string` of substring `from` with substring `to`	`replace('abcdefabcdef', 'cd', 'XX')`	`abXXefabXXef`
`reverse(str)`	`text`	Return reversed string.	`reverse('abcde')`	`edcba`
`right(str text, n int)`	`text`	Return last *n* characters in the string. When *n* is negative, return all but first |*n*| characters.	`right('abcde', 2)`	`de`
`rpad(string text, length int [, fill text])`	`text`	Fill up the `string` to length `length` by appending the characters `fill` (a space by default). If the `string` is already longer than `length` then it is truncated.	`rpad('hi', 5, 'xy')`	`hixyx`

Function	Return Type	Description	Example	Result
`rtrim(string text [, characters text])`	`text`	Remove the longest string containing only characters from `characters` (a space by default) from the end of `string`	`rtrim('trimxxxx', 'x')`	`trim`
`split_part(string text, delimiter text, field int)`	`text`	Split `string` on `delimiter` and return the given field (counting from one)	`split_part('abc~@~def~@~ghi', '~@~', 2)`	`def`
`strpos(string, substring)`	`int`	Location of specified substring (same as `position(substring in string)`, but note the reversed argument order)	`strpos('high', 'ig')`	`2`
`substr(string, from [, count])`	`text`	Extract substring (same as `substring(string from from for count)`)	`substr('alphabet', 3, 2)`	`ph`
`to_ascii(string text [, encoding text])`	`text`	Convert `string` to ASCII from another encoding (only supports conversion from `LATIN1`, `LATIN2`, `LATIN9`, and `WIN1250` encodings)	`to_ascii('Karel')`	`Karel`
`to_hex(number int or bigint)`	`text`	Convert `number` to its equivalent hexadecimal representation	`to_hex(2147483647)`	`7fffffff`

Function	Return Type	Description	Example	Result
`translate(string text, from text, to text)`	text	Any character in `string` that matches a character in the `from` set is replaced by the corresponding character in the `to` set. If `from` is longer than `to`, occurrences of the extra characters in `from` are removed.	`translate('12345', '143', 'ax')`	`a2x5`

The `concat`, `concat_ws` and `format` functions are variadic, so it is possible to pass the values to be concatenated or formatted as an array marked with the `VARIADIC` keyword (see Section 35.4.5). The array's elements are treated as if they were separate ordinary arguments to the function. If the variadic array argument is NULL, `concat` and `concat_ws` return NULL, but `format` treats a NULL as a zero-element array.

See also the aggregate function `string_agg` in Section 9.20.

Table 9-8. Built-in Conversions

Conversion Name [a]	Source Encoding	Destination Encoding
`ascii_to_mic`	SQL_ASCII	MULE_INTERNAL
`ascii_to_utf8`	SQL_ASCII	UTF8
`big5_to_euc_tw`	BIG5	EUC_TW
`big5_to_mic`	BIG5	MULE_INTERNAL
`big5_to_utf8`	BIG5	UTF8
`euc_cn_to_mic`	EUC_CN	MULE_INTERNAL
`euc_cn_to_utf8`	EUC_CN	UTF8
`euc_jp_to_mic`	EUC_JP	MULE_INTERNAL
`euc_jp_to_sjis`	EUC_JP	SJIS
`euc_jp_to_utf8`	EUC_JP	UTF8
`euc_kr_to_mic`	EUC_KR	MULE_INTERNAL
`euc_kr_to_utf8`	EUC_KR	UTF8
`euc_tw_to_big5`	EUC_TW	BIG5
`euc_tw_to_mic`	EUC_TW	MULE_INTERNAL
`euc_tw_to_utf8`	EUC_TW	UTF8
`gb18030_to_utf8`	GB18030	UTF8
`gbk_to_utf8`	GBK	UTF8

Conversion Name a	Source Encoding	Destination Encoding
iso_8859_10_to_utf8	LATIN6	UTF8
iso_8859_13_to_utf8	LATIN7	UTF8
iso_8859_14_to_utf8	LATIN8	UTF8
iso_8859_15_to_utf8	LATIN9	UTF8
iso_8859_16_to_utf8	LATIN10	UTF8
iso_8859_1_to_mic	LATIN1	MULE_INTERNAL
iso_8859_1_to_utf8	LATIN1	UTF8
iso_8859_2_to_mic	LATIN2	MULE_INTERNAL
iso_8859_2_to_utf8	LATIN2	UTF8
iso_8859_2_to_windows_1250	LATIN2	WIN1250
iso_8859_3_to_mic	LATIN3	MULE_INTERNAL
iso_8859_3_to_utf8	LATIN3	UTF8
iso_8859_4_to_mic	LATIN4	MULE_INTERNAL
iso_8859_4_to_utf8	LATIN4	UTF8
iso_8859_5_to_koi8_r	ISO_8859_5	KOI8R
iso_8859_5_to_mic	ISO_8859_5	MULE_INTERNAL
iso_8859_5_to_utf8	ISO_8859_5	UTF8
iso_8859_5_to_windows_1251	ISO_8859_5	WIN1251
iso_8859_5_to_windows_866	ISO_8859_5	WIN866
iso_8859_6_to_utf8	ISO_8859_6	UTF8
iso_8859_7_to_utf8	ISO_8859_7	UTF8
iso_8859_8_to_utf8	ISO_8859_8	UTF8
iso_8859_9_to_utf8	LATIN5	UTF8
johab_to_utf8	JOHAB	UTF8
koi8_r_to_iso_8859_5	KOI8R	ISO_8859_5
koi8_r_to_mic	KOI8R	MULE_INTERNAL
koi8_r_to_utf8	KOI8R	UTF8
koi8_r_to_windows_1251	KOI8R	WIN1251
koi8_r_to_windows_866	KOI8R	WIN866
koi8_u_to_utf8	KOI8U	UTF8
mic_to_ascii	MULE_INTERNAL	SQL_ASCII
mic_to_big5	MULE_INTERNAL	BIG5
mic_to_euc_cn	MULE_INTERNAL	EUC_CN
mic_to_euc_jp	MULE_INTERNAL	EUC_JP
mic_to_euc_kr	MULE_INTERNAL	EUC_KR
mic_to_euc_tw	MULE_INTERNAL	EUC_TW

Conversion Name ᵃ	Source Encoding	Destination Encoding
mic_to_iso_8859_1	MULE_INTERNAL	LATIN1
mic_to_iso_8859_2	MULE_INTERNAL	LATIN2
mic_to_iso_8859_3	MULE_INTERNAL	LATIN3
mic_to_iso_8859_4	MULE_INTERNAL	LATIN4
mic_to_iso_8859_5	MULE_INTERNAL	ISO_8859_5
mic_to_koi8_r	MULE_INTERNAL	KOI8R
mic_to_sjis	MULE_INTERNAL	SJIS
mic_to_windows_1250	MULE_INTERNAL	WIN1250
mic_to_windows_1251	MULE_INTERNAL	WIN1251
mic_to_windows_866	MULE_INTERNAL	WIN866
sjis_to_euc_jp	SJIS	EUC_JP
sjis_to_mic	SJIS	MULE_INTERNAL
sjis_to_utf8	SJIS	UTF8
tcvn_to_utf8	WIN1258	UTF8
uhc_to_utf8	UHC	UTF8
utf8_to_ascii	UTF8	SQL_ASCII
utf8_to_big5	UTF8	BIG5
utf8_to_euc_cn	UTF8	EUC_CN
utf8_to_euc_jp	UTF8	EUC_JP
utf8_to_euc_kr	UTF8	EUC_KR
utf8_to_euc_tw	UTF8	EUC_TW
utf8_to_gb18030	UTF8	GB18030
utf8_to_gbk	UTF8	GBK
utf8_to_iso_8859_1	UTF8	LATIN1
utf8_to_iso_8859_10	UTF8	LATIN6
utf8_to_iso_8859_13	UTF8	LATIN7
utf8_to_iso_8859_14	UTF8	LATIN8
utf8_to_iso_8859_15	UTF8	LATIN9
utf8_to_iso_8859_16	UTF8	LATIN10
utf8_to_iso_8859_2	UTF8	LATIN2
utf8_to_iso_8859_3	UTF8	LATIN3
utf8_to_iso_8859_4	UTF8	LATIN4
utf8_to_iso_8859_5	UTF8	ISO_8859_5
utf8_to_iso_8859_6	UTF8	ISO_8859_6
utf8_to_iso_8859_7	UTF8	ISO_8859_7
utf8_to_iso_8859_8	UTF8	ISO_8859_8
utf8_to_iso_8859_9	UTF8	LATIN5
utf8_to_johab	UTF8	JOHAB

Conversion Name [a]	Source Encoding	Destination Encoding
utf8_to_koi8_r	UTF8	KOI8R
utf8_to_koi8_u	UTF8	KOI8U
utf8_to_sjis	UTF8	SJIS
utf8_to_tcvn	UTF8	WIN1258
utf8_to_uhc	UTF8	UHC
utf8_to_windows_1250	UTF8	WIN1250
utf8_to_windows_1251	UTF8	WIN1251
utf8_to_windows_1252	UTF8	WIN1252
utf8_to_windows_1253	UTF8	WIN1253
utf8_to_windows_1254	UTF8	WIN1254
utf8_to_windows_1255	UTF8	WIN1255
utf8_to_windows_1256	UTF8	WIN1256
utf8_to_windows_1257	UTF8	WIN1257
utf8_to_windows_866	UTF8	WIN866
utf8_to_windows_874	UTF8	WIN874
windows_1250_to_iso_8859_2	WIN1250	LATIN2
windows_1250_to_mic	WIN1250	MULE_INTERNAL
windows_1250_to_utf8	WIN1250	UTF8
windows_1251_to_iso_8859_5	WIN1251	ISO_8859_5
windows_1251_to_koi8_r	WIN1251	KOI8R
windows_1251_to_mic	WIN1251	MULE_INTERNAL
windows_1251_to_utf8	WIN1251	UTF8
windows_1251_to_windows_866	WIN1251	WIN866
windows_1252_to_utf8	WIN1252	UTF8
windows_1256_to_utf8	WIN1256	UTF8
windows_866_to_iso_8859_5	WIN866	ISO_8859_5
windows_866_to_koi8_r	WIN866	KOI8R
windows_866_to_mic	WIN866	MULE_INTERNAL
windows_866_to_utf8	WIN866	UTF8
windows_866_to_windows_1251	WIN866	WIN
windows_874_to_utf8	WIN874	UTF8
euc_jis_2004_to_utf8	EUC_JIS_2004	UTF8
utf8_to_euc_jis_2004	UTF8	EUC_JIS_2004
shift_jis_2004_to_utf8	SHIFT_JIS_2004	UTF8

Conversion Name a	Source Encoding	Destination Encoding
utf8_to_shift_jis_2004	UTF8	SHIFT_JIS_2004
euc_jis_2004_to_shift_jis_2004	EUC_JIS_2004	SHIFT_JIS_2004
shift_jis_2004_to_euc_jis_2004	SHIFT_JIS_2004	EUC_JIS_2004

Notes:

a. The conversion names follow a standard naming scheme: The official name of the source encoding with all non-alphanumeric characters replaced by underscores, followed by _to_, followed by the similarly processed destination encoding name. Therefore, the names might deviate from the customary encoding names.

9.4.1. `format`

The function `format` produces output formatted according to a format string, in a style similar to the C function `sprintf`.

```
format(formatstr text [, formatarg "any" [, ...] ])
```

formatstr is a format string that specifies how the result should be formatted. Text in the format string is copied directly to the result, except where *format specifiers* are used. Format specifiers act as placeholders in the string, defining how subsequent function arguments should be formatted and inserted into the result. Each *formatarg* argument is converted to text according to the usual output rules for its data type, and then formatted and inserted into the result string according to the format specifier(s).

Format specifiers are introduced by a `%` character and have the form

```
%[position][flags][width]type
```

where the component fields are:

position (optional)

A string of the form *n*$ where *n* is the index of the argument to print. Index 1 means the first argument after *formatstr*. If the *position* is omitted, the default is to use the next argument in sequence.

flags (optional)

Additional options controlling how the format specifier's output is formatted. Currently the only supported flag is a minus sign (–) which will cause the format specifier's output to be left-justified. This has no effect unless the *width* field is also specified.

width (optional)

Specifies the *minimum* number of characters to use to display the format specifier's output. The output is padded on the left or right (depending on the – flag) with spaces as needed to fill the width. A too-small width does not cause truncation of the output, but is simply ignored. The width may be specified using any of the following: a positive integer; an asterisk (*) to use the next function argument as the width; or a string of the form *n*$ to use the *n*th function argument as the width.

If the width comes from a function argument, that argument is consumed before the argument that is used for the format specifier's value. If the width argument is negative, the result is left aligned (as if the – flag had been specified) within a field of length abs(*width*).

type (required)

The type of format conversion to use to produce the format specifier's output. The following types are supported:

- s formats the argument value as a simple string. A null value is treated as an empty string.
- I treats the argument value as an SQL identifier, double-quoting it if necessary. It is an error for the value to be null.
- L quotes the argument value as an SQL literal. A null value is displayed as the string NULL, without quotes.

In addition to the format specifiers described above, the special sequence %% may be used to output a literal % character.

Here are some examples of the basic format conversions:

```
SELECT format('Hello %s', 'World');
Result: Hello World

SELECT format('Testing %s, %s, %s, %%', 'one', 'two', 'three');
Result: Testing one, two, three, %

SELECT format('INSERT INTO %I VALUES(%L)', 'Foo bar', E'O\'Reilly');
Result: INSERT INTO "Foo bar" VALUES('O''Reilly')

SELECT format('INSERT INTO %I VALUES(%L)', 'locations', E'C:\\Program Files');
Result: INSERT INTO locations VALUES(E'C:\\Program Files')
```

Here are examples using *width* fields and the – flag:

```
SELECT format('|%10s|', 'foo');
Result: |       foo|

SELECT format('|%-10s|', 'foo');
Result: |foo       |

SELECT format('|%*s|', 10, 'foo');
Result: |       foo|

SELECT format('|%*s|', -10, 'foo');
Result: |foo       |

SELECT format('|%-*s|', 10, 'foo');
Result: |foo       |
```

```
SELECT format('|%-*s|', -10, 'foo');
Result: |foo       |
```

These examples show use of *position* fields:

```
SELECT format('Testing %3$s, %2$s, %1$s', 'one', 'two', 'three');
Result: Testing three, two, one
```

```
SELECT format('|%*2$s|', 'foo', 10, 'bar');
Result: |       bar|
```

```
SELECT format('|%1$*2$s|', 'foo', 10, 'bar');
Result: |       foo|
```

Unlike the standard C function `sprintf`, PostgreSQL's `format` function allows format specifiers with and without *position* fields to be mixed in the same format string. A format specifier without a *position* field always uses the next argument after the last argument consumed. In addition, the `format` function does not require all function arguments to be used in the format string. For example:

```
SELECT format('Testing %3$s, %2$s, %s', 'one', 'two', 'three');
Result: Testing three, two, three
```

The `%I` and `%L` format specifiers are particularly useful for safely constructing dynamic SQL statements. See Example 40-1.

9.5. Binary String Functions and Operators

This section describes functions and operators for examining and manipulating values of type `bytea`.

SQL defines some string functions that use key words, rather than commas, to separate arguments. Details are in Table 9-9. PostgreSQL also provides versions of these functions that use the regular function invocation syntax (see Table 9-10).

> **Note:** The sample results shown on this page assume that the server parameter `bytea_output` is set to `escape` (the traditional PostgreSQL format).

Table 9-9. SQL Binary String Functions and Operators

Function	Return Type	Description	Example	Result

Function	Return Type	Description	Example	Result
`string || string`	`bytea`	String concatenation	`E'\\\\\Post'::bytea || E'\\047gres\\000'::bytea`	`\Post'gres\000`
`octet_length(string)`	`int`	Number of bytes in binary string	`octet_length(E'jo\\000se'::bytea)`	`5`
`overlay(string placing string from int [for int])`	`bytea`	Replace substring	`overlay(E'Th\\000omas'::bytea placing E'\\002\\003'::bytea from 2 for 3)`	`T\\002\\003mas`
`position(substring in string)`	`int`	Location of specified substring	`position(E'\\000om'::bytea in E'Th\\000omas'::bytea)`	`3`
`substring(string [from int] [for int])`	`bytea`	Extract substring	`substring(E'Th\\000omas'::bytea from 2 for 3)`	`h\\000o`
`trim([both] bytes from string)`	`bytea`	Remove the longest string containing only the bytes in `bytes` from the start and end of `string`	`trim(E'\\000'::bytea from E'\\000Tom\\000'::bytea)`	`Tom`

Additional binary string manipulation functions are available and are listed in Table 9-10. Some of them are used internally to implement the SQL-standard string functions listed in Table 9-9.

Table 9-10. Other Binary String Functions

Function	Return Type	Description	Example	Result
`btrim(string bytea, bytes bytea)`	`bytea`	Remove the longest string consisting only of bytes in `bytes` from the start and end of `string`	`btrim(E'\\000trim\\000'::bytea, E'\\000'::bytea)`	`trim`
`decode(string text, format text)`	`bytea`	Decode binary data from textual representation in `string`. Options for `format` are same as in `encode`.	`decode(E'123\\000456'::bytea, 'escape')`	`123\000456`

Function	Return Type	Description	Example	Result
`encode(data bytea, format text)`	`text`	Encode binary data into a textual representation. Supported formats are: `base64`, `hex`, `escape`. `escape` converts zero bytes and high-bit-set bytes to octal sequences (`\nnn`) and doubles backslashes.	`encode(E'123\\000456'::bytea, 'escape')`	`123\000456`
`get_bit(string, offset)`	`int`	Extract bit from string	`get_bit(E'Th\\000omas'::bytea, 45)`	`1`
`get_byte(string, offset)`	`int`	Extract byte from string	`get_byte(E'Th\\000omas'::bytea, 4)`	`109`
`length(string)`	`int`	Length of binary string	`length(E'jo\\000se'::bytea)`	`5`
`md5(string)`	`text`	Calculates the MD5 hash of `string`, returning the result in hexadecimal	`md5(E'Th\\000omas'::bytea)`	`8ab2d3c9689aaf18 b4958c334c82d8b1`
`set_bit(string, offset, newvalue)`	`bytea`	Set bit in string	`set_bit(E'Th\\000omas'::bytea, 45, 0)`	`Th\000omAs`
`set_byte(string, offset, newvalue)`	`bytea`	Set byte in string	`set_byte(E'Th\\000omas'::bytea, 4, 64)`	`Th\000o@as`

`get_byte` and `set_byte` number the first byte of a binary string as byte 0. `get_bit` and `set_bit` number bits from the right within each byte; for example bit 0 is the least significant bit of the first byte, and bit 15 is the most significant bit of the second byte.

See also the aggregate function `string_agg` in Section 9.20 and the large object functions in Section 32.4.

9.6. Bit String Functions and Operators

This section describes functions and operators for examining and manipulating bit strings, that is values of the types `bit` and `bit varying`. Aside from the usual comparison operators, the operators shown in Table 9-11 can be used. Bit string operands of `&`, `|`, and `#` must be of equal length. When bit shifting, the original length of the string is preserved, as shown in the examples.

Table 9-11. Bit String Operators

Operator	Description	Example	Result
||	concatenation	B'10001' || B'011'	10001011
&	bitwise AND	B'10001' & B'01101'	00001
|	bitwise OR	B'10001' | B'01101'	11101
#	bitwise XOR	B'10001' # B'01101'	11100
~	bitwise NOT	~ B'10001'	01110
<<	bitwise shift left	B'10001' << 3	01000
>>	bitwise shift right	B'10001' >> 2	00100

The following SQL-standard functions work on bit strings as well as character strings: `length`, `bit_length`, `octet_length`, `position`, `substring`, `overlay`.

The following functions work on bit strings as well as binary strings: `get_bit`, `set_bit`. When working with a bit string, these functions number the first (leftmost) bit of the string as bit 0.

In addition, it is possible to cast integral values to and from type `bit`. Some examples:

```
44::bit(10)              0000101100
44::bit(3)               100
cast(-44 as bit(12))     111111010100
'1110'::bit(4)::integer  14
```

Note that casting to just "bit" means casting to `bit(1)`, and so will deliver only the least significant bit of the integer.

> **Note:** Casting an integer to `bit(n)` copies the rightmost n bits. Casting an integer to a bit string width wider than the integer itself will sign-extend on the left.

9.7. Pattern Matching

There are three separate approaches to pattern matching provided by PostgreSQL: the traditional SQL `LIKE` operator, the more recent `SIMILAR TO` operator (added in SQL:1999), and POSIX-style regular expressions. Aside from the basic "does this string match this pattern?" operators, functions are available to extract or replace matching substrings and to split a string at matching locations.

> **Tip:** If you have pattern matching needs that go beyond this, consider writing a user-defined function in Perl or Tcl.

9.7.1. `LIKE`

```
string LIKE pattern [ESCAPE escape-character]
string NOT LIKE pattern [ESCAPE escape-character]
```

The `LIKE` expression returns true if the *string* matches the supplied *pattern*. (As expected, the `NOT LIKE` expression returns false if `LIKE` returns true, and vice versa. An equivalent expression is `NOT` (*string* `LIKE` *pattern*).)

If *pattern* does not contain percent signs or underscores, then the pattern only represents the string itself; in that case `LIKE` acts like the equals operator. An underscore (_) in *pattern* stands for (matches) any single character; a percent sign (%) matches any sequence of zero or more characters.

Some examples:

```
'abc' LIKE 'abc'      true
'abc' LIKE 'a%'       true
'abc' LIKE '_b_'      true
'abc' LIKE 'c'        false
```

`LIKE` pattern matching always covers the entire string. Therefore, if it's desired to match a sequence anywhere within a string, the pattern must start and end with a percent sign.

To match a literal underscore or percent sign without matching other characters, the respective character in *pattern* must be preceded by the escape character. The default escape character is the backslash but a different one can be selected by using the `ESCAPE` clause. To match the escape character itself, write two escape characters.

> **Note:** If you have standard_conforming_strings turned off, any backslashes you write in literal string constants will need to be doubled. See Section 4.1.2.1 for more information.

It's also possible to select no escape character by writing `ESCAPE ''`. This effectively disables the escape mechanism, which makes it impossible to turn off the special meaning of underscore and percent signs in the pattern.

The key word `ILIKE` can be used instead of `LIKE` to make the match case-insensitive according to the active locale. This is not in the SQL standard but is a PostgreSQL extension.

The operator `~~` is equivalent to `LIKE`, and `~~*` corresponds to `ILIKE`. There are also `!~~` and `!~~*` operators that represent `NOT LIKE` and `NOT ILIKE`, respectively. All of these operators are PostgreSQL-specific.

9.7.2. `SIMILAR TO` Regular Expressions

```
string SIMILAR TO pattern [ESCAPE escape-character]
string NOT SIMILAR TO pattern [ESCAPE escape-character]
```

The SIMILAR TO operator returns true or false depending on whether its pattern matches the given string. It is similar to LIKE, except that it interprets the pattern using the SQL standard's definition of a regular expression. SQL regular expressions are a curious cross between LIKE notation and common regular expression notation.

Like LIKE, the SIMILAR TO operator succeeds only if its pattern matches the entire string; this is unlike common regular expression behavior where the pattern can match any part of the string. Also like LIKE, SIMILAR TO uses _ and % as wildcard characters denoting any single character and any string, respectively (these are comparable to . and .* in POSIX regular expressions).

In addition to these facilities borrowed from LIKE, SIMILAR TO supports these pattern-matching metacharacters borrowed from POSIX regular expressions:

- | denotes alternation (either of two alternatives).

- * denotes repetition of the previous item zero or more times.

- + denotes repetition of the previous item one or more times.

- ? denotes repetition of the previous item zero or one time.

- {*m*} denotes repetition of the previous item exactly *m* times.

- {*m*, } denotes repetition of the previous item *m* or more times.

- {*m*, *n*} denotes repetition of the previous item at least *m* and not more than *n* times.

- Parentheses () can be used to group items into a single logical item.

- A bracket expression [...] specifies a character class, just as in POSIX regular expressions.

Notice that the period (.) is not a metacharacter for SIMILAR TO.

As with LIKE, a backslash disables the special meaning of any of these metacharacters; or a different escape character can be specified with ESCAPE.

Some examples:

```
'abc' SIMILAR TO 'abc'        true
'abc' SIMILAR TO 'a'          false
'abc' SIMILAR TO '%(b|d)%'    true
'abc' SIMILAR TO '(b|c)%'     false
```

The substring function with three parameters, substring(*string* from *pattern* for *escape-character*), provides extraction of a substring that matches an SQL regular expression pattern. As with SIMILAR TO, the specified pattern must match the entire data string, or else the function fails and returns null. To indicate the part of the pattern that should be returned on success, the pattern must contain two occurrences of the escape character followed by a double quote ("). The text matching the portion of the pattern between these markers is returned.

Some examples, with #" delimiting the return string:

```
substring('foobar' from '%#"o_b#"%' for '#')    oob
substring('foobar' from '#"o_b#"%' for '#')      NULL
```

9.7.3. POSIX Regular Expressions

Table 9-12 lists the available operators for pattern matching using POSIX regular expressions.

Table 9-12. Regular Expression Match Operators

Operator	Description	Example
~	Matches regular expression, case sensitive	`'thomas' ~ '.*thomas.*'`
~*	Matches regular expression, case insensitive	`'thomas' ~* '.*Thomas.*'`
!~	Does not match regular expression, case sensitive	`'thomas' !~ '.*Thomas.*'`
!~*	Does not match regular expression, case insensitive	`'thomas' !~* '.*vadim.*'`

POSIX regular expressions provide a more powerful means for pattern matching than the `LIKE` and `SIMILAR TO` operators. Many Unix tools such as `egrep`, `sed`, or `awk` use a pattern matching language that is similar to the one described here.

A regular expression is a character sequence that is an abbreviated definition of a set of strings (a *regular set*). A string is said to match a regular expression if it is a member of the regular set described by the regular expression. As with `LIKE`, pattern characters match string characters exactly unless they are special characters in the regular expression language — but regular expressions use different special characters than `LIKE` does. Unlike `LIKE` patterns, a regular expression is allowed to match anywhere within a string, unless the regular expression is explicitly anchored to the beginning or end of the string.

Some examples:

```
'abc' ~ 'abc'        true
'abc' ~ '^a'         true
'abc' ~ '(b|d)'      true
'abc' ~ '^(b|c)'    false
```

The POSIX pattern language is described in much greater detail below.

The `substring` function with two parameters, `substring(string from pattern)`, provides extraction of a substring that matches a POSIX regular expression pattern. It returns null if there is no match, otherwise the portion of the text that matched the pattern. But if the pattern contains any parentheses, the portion of the text that matched the first parenthesized subexpression (the one whose left parenthesis comes first) is returned. You can put parentheses around the whole expression if you want to use parentheses within it without triggering this exception. If you need parentheses in the pattern before the subexpression you want to extract, see the non-capturing parentheses described below.

Some examples:

```
substring('foobar' from 'o.b')     oob
substring('foobar' from 'o(.)b')    o
```

The `regexp_replace` function provides substitution of new text for substrings that match POSIX regular expression patterns. It has the syntax `regexp_replace(`*source, pattern, replacement* [*, flags* `])`. The *source* string is returned unchanged if there is no match to the *pattern*. If there is a match, the *source* string is returned with the *replacement* string substituted for the matching substring. The *replacement* string can contain *n*, where *n* is 1 through 9, to indicate that the source substring matching the *n*'th parenthesized subexpression of the pattern should be inserted, and it can contain \& to indicate that the substring matching the entire pattern should be inserted. Write \\ if you need to put a literal backslash in the replacement text. The *flags* parameter is an optional text string containing zero or more single-letter flags that change the function's behavior. Flag `i` specifies case-insensitive matching, while flag `g` specifies replacement of each matching substring rather than only the first one. Supported flags (though not `g`) are described in Table 9-20.

Some examples:

```
regexp_replace('foobarbaz', 'b..', 'X')
                                  fooXbaz
regexp_replace('foobarbaz', 'b..', 'X', 'g')
                                  fooXX
regexp_replace('foobarbaz', 'b(..)', E'X\\1Y', 'g')
                                  fooXarYXazY
```

The `regexp_matches` function returns a text array of all of the captured substrings resulting from matching a POSIX regular expression pattern. It has the syntax `regexp_matches(`*string, pattern* [*, flags* `])`. The function can return no rows, one row, or multiple rows (see the `g` flag below). If the *pattern* does not match, the function returns no rows. If the pattern contains no parenthesized subexpressions, then each row returned is a single-element text array containing the substring matching the whole pattern. If the pattern contains parenthesized subexpressions, the function returns a text array whose *n*'th element is the substring matching the *n*'th parenthesized subexpression of the pattern (not counting "non-capturing" parentheses; see below for details). The *flags* parameter is an optional text string containing zero or more single-letter flags that change the function's behavior. Flag `g` causes the function to find each match in the string, not only the first one, and return a row for each such match. Supported flags (though not `g`) are described in Table 9-20.

Some examples:

```
SELECT regexp_matches('foobarbequebaz', '(bar)(beque)');
 regexp_matches
----------------
 {bar,beque}
(1 row)

SELECT regexp_matches('foobarbequebazilbarfbonk', '(b[^b]+)(b[^b]+)', 'g');
 regexp_matches
----------------
 {bar,beque}
 {bazil,barf}
(2 rows)

SELECT regexp_matches('foobarbequebaz', 'barbeque');
 regexp_matches
```

```
----------------
 {barbeque}
(1 row)
```

It is possible to force `regexp_matches()` to always return one row by using a sub-select; this is particularly useful in a `SELECT` target list when you want all rows returned, even non-matching ones:

```
SELECT col1, (SELECT regexp_matches(col2, '(bar)(beque)')) FROM tab;
```

The `regexp_split_to_table` function splits a string using a POSIX regular expression pattern as a delimiter. It has the syntax `regexp_split_to_table(string, pattern [, flags ])`. If there is no match to the *pattern*, the function returns the *string*. If there is at least one match, for each match it returns the text from the end of the last match (or the beginning of the string) to the beginning of the match. When there are no more matches, it returns the text from the end of the last match to the end of the string. The *flags* parameter is an optional text string containing zero or more single-letter flags that change the function's behavior. `regexp_split_to_table` supports the flags described in Table 9-20.

The `regexp_split_to_array` function behaves the same as `regexp_split_to_table`, except that `regexp_split_to_array` returns its result as an array of `text`. It has the syntax `regexp_split_to_array(string, pattern [, flags ])`. The parameters are the same as for `regexp_split_to_table`.

Some examples:

```
SELECT foo FROM regexp_split_to_table('the quick brown fox jumps over the lazy
  foo
-------
 the
 quick
 brown
 fox
 jumps
 over
 the
 lazy
 dog
(9 rows)

SELECT regexp_split_to_array('the quick brown fox jumps over the lazy dog', E'\
            regexp_split_to_array
-------------------------------------------------
 {the,quick,brown,fox,jumps,over,the,lazy,dog}
(1 row)

SELECT foo FROM regexp_split_to_table('the quick brown fox', E'\\s*') AS foo;
 foo
-----
 t
 h
 e
```

```
q
u
i
c
k
b
r
o
w
n
f
o
x
(16 rows)
```

As the last example demonstrates, the regexp split functions ignore zero-length matches that occur at the start or end of the string or immediately after a previous match. This is contrary to the strict definition of regexp matching that is implemented by `regexp_matches`, but is usually the most convenient behavior in practice. Other software systems such as Perl use similar definitions.

9.7.3.1. Regular Expression Details

PostgreSQL's regular expressions are implemented using a software package written by Henry Spencer. Much of the description of regular expressions below is copied verbatim from his manual.

Regular expressions (REs), as defined in POSIX 1003.2, come in two forms: *extended* REs or EREs (roughly those of `egrep`), and *basic* REs or BREs (roughly those of `ed`). PostgreSQL supports both forms, and also implements some extensions that are not in the POSIX standard, but have become widely used due to their availability in programming languages such as Perl and Tcl. REs using these non-POSIX extensions are called *advanced* REs or AREs in this documentation. AREs are almost an exact superset of EREs, but BREs have several notational incompatibilities (as well as being much more limited). We first describe the ARE and ERE forms, noting features that apply only to AREs, and then describe how BREs differ.

> **Note:** PostgreSQL always initially presumes that a regular expression follows the ARE rules. However, the more limited ERE or BRE rules can be chosen by prepending an *embedded option* to the RE pattern, as described in Section 9.7.3.4. This can be useful for compatibility with applications that expect exactly the POSIX 1003.2 rules.

A regular expression is defined as one or more *branches*, separated by `|`. It matches anything that matches one of the branches.

A branch is zero or more *quantified atoms* or *constraints*, concatenated. It matches a match for the first, followed by a match for the second, etc; an empty branch matches the empty string.

A quantified atom is an *atom* possibly followed by a single *quantifier*. Without a quantifier, it matches a match for the atom. With a quantifier, it can match some number of matches of the atom. An *atom* can be any of the possibilities shown in Table 9-13. The possible quantifiers and their meanings are shown in Table 9-14.

A *constraint* matches an empty string, but matches only when specific conditions are met. A constraint can be used where an atom could be used, except it cannot be followed by a quantifier. The simple constraints are shown in Table 9-15; some more constraints are described later.

Table 9-13. Regular Expression Atoms

Atom	Description
`(re)`	(where `re` is any regular expression) matches a match for `re`, with the match noted for possible reporting
`(?:re)`	as above, but the match is not noted for reporting (a "non-capturing" set of parentheses) (AREs only)
`.`	matches any single character
`[chars]`	a *bracket expression*, matching any one of the `chars` (see Section 9.7.3.2 for more detail)
`\k`	(where *k* is a non-alphanumeric character) matches that character taken as an ordinary character, e.g., `\\` matches a backslash character
`\c`	where *c* is alphanumeric (possibly followed by other characters) is an *escape*, see Section 9.7.3.3 (AREs only; in EREs and BREs, this matches *c*)
`{`	when followed by a character other than a digit, matches the left-brace character `{`; when followed by a digit, it is the beginning of a *bound* (see below)
x	where *x* is a single character with no other significance, matches that character

An RE cannot end with a backslash (\).

> **Note:** If you have standard_conforming_strings turned off, any backslashes you write in literal string constants will need to be doubled. See Section 4.1.2.1 for more information.

Table 9-14. Regular Expression Quantifiers

Quantifier	Matches
`*`	a sequence of 0 or more matches of the atom
`+`	a sequence of 1 or more matches of the atom
`?`	a sequence of 0 or 1 matches of the atom
`{m}`	a sequence of exactly *m* matches of the atom
`{m, }`	a sequence of *m* or more matches of the atom

Quantifier	Matches
{*m*, *n*}	a sequence of *m* through *n* (inclusive) matches of the atom; *m* cannot exceed *n*
*?	non-greedy version of *
+?	non-greedy version of +
??	non-greedy version of ?
{*m*}?	non-greedy version of {*m*}
{*m*, }?	non-greedy version of {*m*, }
{*m*, *n*}?	non-greedy version of {*m*, *n*}

The forms using { . . . } are known as *bounds*. The numbers *m* and *n* within a bound are unsigned decimal integers with permissible values from 0 to 255 inclusive.

Non-greedy quantifiers (available in AREs only) match the same possibilities as their corresponding normal (*greedy*) counterparts, but prefer the smallest number rather than the largest number of matches. See Section 9.7.3.5 for more detail.

Note: A quantifier cannot immediately follow another quantifier, e.g., ** is invalid. A quantifier cannot begin an expression or subexpression or follow ^ or |.

Table 9-15. Regular Expression Constraints

Constraint	Description
^	matches at the beginning of the string
$	matches at the end of the string
(?=*re*)	*positive lookahead* matches at any point where a substring matching *re* begins (AREs only)
(?!*re*)	*negative lookahead* matches at any point where no substring matching *re* begins (AREs only)

Lookahead constraints cannot contain *back references* (see Section 9.7.3.3), and all parentheses within them are considered non-capturing.

9.7.3.2. Bracket Expressions

A *bracket expression* is a list of characters enclosed in [ ]. It normally matches any single character from the list (but see below). If the list begins with ^, it matches any single character *not* from the rest of the list. If two characters in the list are separated by -, this is shorthand for the full range of characters between those two (inclusive) in the collating sequence, e.g., [0-9] in ASCII matches any decimal digit. It is illegal for two ranges to share an endpoint, e.g., a-c-e. Ranges are very collating-sequence-dependent, so portable programs should avoid relying on them.

To include a literal] in the list, make it the first character (after ^, if that is used). To include a literal -, make it the first or last character, or the second endpoint of a range. To use a literal - as the first endpoint of a range, enclose it in [. and .] to make it a collating element (see below). With the exception of these characters, some combinations using [(see next paragraphs), and escapes (AREs only), all other special characters lose their special significance within a bracket expression. In particular, \ is not special when following ERE or BRE rules, though it is special (as introducing an escape) in AREs.

Within a bracket expression, a collating element (a character, a multiple-character sequence that collates as if it were a single character, or a collating-sequence name for either) enclosed in [. and .] stands for the sequence of characters of that collating element. The sequence is treated as a single element of the bracket expression's list. This allows a bracket expression containing a multiple-character collating element to match more than one character, e.g., if the collating sequence includes a ch collating element, then the RE [[.ch.]]*c matches the first five characters of chchcc.

> **Note:** PostgreSQL currently does not support multi-character collating elements. This information describes possible future behavior.

Within a bracket expression, a collating element enclosed in [= and =] is an *equivalence class*, standing for the sequences of characters of all collating elements equivalent to that one, including itself. (If there are no other equivalent collating elements, the treatment is as if the enclosing delimiters were [. and .].) For example, if o and ^ are the members of an equivalence class, then [[=o=]], [[=^=]], and [o^] are all synonymous. An equivalence class cannot be an endpoint of a range.

Within a bracket expression, the name of a character class enclosed in [: and :] stands for the list of all characters belonging to that class. Standard character class names are: alnum, alpha, blank, cntrl, digit, graph, lower, print, punct, space, upper, xdigit. These stand for the character classes defined in ctype. A locale can provide others. A character class cannot be used as an endpoint of a range.

There are two special cases of bracket expressions: the bracket expressions [[:<:]] and [[:>:]] are constraints, matching empty strings at the beginning and end of a word respectively. A word is defined as a sequence of word characters that is neither preceded nor followed by word characters. A word character is an alnum character (as defined by ctype) or an underscore. This is an extension, compatible with but not specified by POSIX 1003.2, and should be used with caution in software intended to be portable to other systems. The constraint escapes described below are usually preferable; they are no more standard, but are easier to type.

9.7.3.3. Regular Expression Escapes

Escapes are special sequences beginning with \ followed by an alphanumeric character. Escapes come in several varieties: character entry, class shorthands, constraint escapes, and back references. A \ followed by an alphanumeric character but not constituting a valid escape is illegal in AREs. In EREs, there are no escapes: outside a bracket expression, a \ followed by an alphanumeric character merely stands for that character as an ordinary character, and inside a bracket expression, \ is an ordinary character. (The latter is the one actual incompatibility between EREs and AREs.)

Character-entry escapes exist to make it easier to specify non-printing and other inconvenient characters in REs. They are shown in Table 9-16.

Class-shorthand escapes provide shorthands for certain commonly-used character classes. They are shown in Table 9-17.

A *constraint escape* is a constraint, matching the empty string if specific conditions are met, written as an escape. They are shown in Table 9-18.

A *back reference* (\n) matches the same string matched by the previous parenthesized subexpression specified by the number *n* (see Table 9-19). For example, ([bc])\1 matches bb or cc but not bc or cb. The subexpression must entirely precede the back reference in the RE. Subexpressions are numbered in the order of their leading parentheses. Non-capturing parentheses do not define subexpressions.

> **Note:** Keep in mind that an escape's leading \ will need to be doubled when entering the pattern as an SQL string constant. For example:
>
> '123' ~ E'^\\d{3}' *true*

Table 9-16. Regular Expression Character-entry Escapes

Escape	Description
\a	alert (bell) character, as in C
\b	backspace, as in C
\B	synonym for backslash (\) to help reduce the need for backslash doubling
\c*X*	(where *X* is any character) the character whose low-order 5 bits are the same as those of *X*, and whose other bits are all zero
\e	the character whose collating-sequence name is ESC, or failing that, the character with octal value 033
\f	form feed, as in C
\n	newline, as in C
\r	carriage return, as in C
\t	horizontal tab, as in C
\u*wxyz*	(where *wxyz* is exactly four hexadecimal digits) the UTF16 (Unicode, 16-bit) character U+*wxyz* in the local byte ordering
\U*stuvwxyz*	(where *stuvwxyz* is exactly eight hexadecimal digits) reserved for a hypothetical Unicode extension to 32 bits
\v	vertical tab, as in C
\x*hhh*	(where *hhh* is any sequence of hexadecimal digits) the character whose hexadecimal value is 0x*hhh* (a single character no matter how many hexadecimal digits are used)
\0	the character whose value is 0 (the null byte)

Escape	Description
\xy	(where *xy* is exactly two octal digits, and is not a *back reference*) the character whose octal value is 0*xy*
\xyz	(where *xyz* is exactly three octal digits, and is not a *back reference*) the character whose octal value is 0*xyz*

Hexadecimal digits are 0-9, a-f, and A-F. Octal digits are 0-7.

The character-entry escapes are always taken as ordinary characters. For example, \135 is] in ASCII, but \135 does not terminate a bracket expression.

Table 9-17. Regular Expression Class-shorthand Escapes

Escape	Description
\d	[[:digit:]]
\s	[[:space:]]
\w	[[:alnum:]_] (note underscore is included)
\D	[^[:digit:]]
\S	[^[:space:]]
\W	[^[:alnum:]_] (note underscore is included)

Within bracket expressions, \d, \s, and \w lose their outer brackets, and \D, \S, and \W are illegal. (So, for example, [a-c\d] is equivalent to [a-c[:digit:]]. Also, [a-c\D], which is equivalent to [a-c^[:digit:]], is illegal.)

Table 9-18. Regular Expression Constraint Escapes

Escape	Description
\A	matches only at the beginning of the string (see Section 9.7.3.5 for how this differs from ^)
\m	matches only at the beginning of a word
\M	matches only at the end of a word
\y	matches only at the beginning or end of a word
\Y	matches only at a point that is not the beginning or end of a word
\Z	matches only at the end of the string (see Section 9.7.3.5 for how this differs from $)

A word is defined as in the specification of [[:<:]] and [[:>:]] above. Constraint escapes are illegal within bracket expressions.

Table 9-19. Regular Expression Back References

Escape	Description

Escape	Description
\m	(where m is a nonzero digit) a back reference to the m'th subexpression
\mnn	(where m is a nonzero digit, and nn is some more digits, and the decimal value mnn is not greater than the number of closing capturing parentheses seen so far) a back reference to the mnn'th subexpression

Note: There is an inherent ambiguity between octal character-entry escapes and back references, which is resolved by the following heuristics, as hinted at above. A leading zero always indicates an octal escape. A single non-zero digit, not followed by another digit, is always taken as a back reference. A multi-digit sequence not starting with a zero is taken as a back reference if it comes after a suitable subexpression (i.e., the number is in the legal range for a back reference), and otherwise is taken as octal.

9.7.3.4. Regular Expression Metasyntax

In addition to the main syntax described above, there are some special forms and miscellaneous syntactic facilities available.

An RE can begin with one of two special *director* prefixes. If an RE begins with ***:, the rest of the RE is taken as an ARE. (This normally has no effect in PostgreSQL, since REs are assumed to be AREs; but it does have an effect if ERE or BRE mode had been specified by the `flags` parameter to a regex function.) If an RE begins with ***=, the rest of the RE is taken to be a literal string, with all characters considered ordinary characters.

An ARE can begin with *embedded options*: a sequence (?xyz) (where xyz is one or more alphabetic characters) specifies options affecting the rest of the RE. These options override any previously determined options — in particular, they can override the case-sensitivity behavior implied by a regex operator, or the `flags` parameter to a regex function. The available option letters are shown in Table 9-20. Note that these same option letters are used in the `flags` parameters of regex functions.

Table 9-20. ARE Embedded-option Letters

Option	Description
b	rest of RE is a BRE
c	case-sensitive matching (overrides operator type)
e	rest of RE is an ERE
i	case-insensitive matching (see Section 9.7.3.5) (overrides operator type)
m	historical synonym for n
n	newline-sensitive matching (see Section 9.7.3.5)

Option	Description
p	partial newline-sensitive matching (see Section 9.7.3.5)
q	rest of RE is a literal ("quoted") string, all ordinary characters
s	non-newline-sensitive matching (default)
t	tight syntax (default; see below)
w	inverse partial newline-sensitive ("weird") matching (see Section 9.7.3.5)
x	expanded syntax (see below)

Embedded options take effect at the) terminating the sequence. They can appear only at the start of an ARE (after the ***: director if any).

In addition to the usual (*tight*) RE syntax, in which all characters are significant, there is an *expanded* syntax, available by specifying the embedded x option. In the expanded syntax, white-space characters in the RE are ignored, as are all characters between a # and the following newline (or the end of the RE). This permits paragraphing and commenting a complex RE. There are three exceptions to that basic rule:

- a white-space character or # preceded by \ is retained

- white space or # within a bracket expression is retained

- white space and comments cannot appear within multi-character symbols, such as (?:

For this purpose, white-space characters are blank, tab, newline, and any character that belongs to the *space* character class.

Finally, in an ARE, outside bracket expressions, the sequence (?#*ttt*) (where *ttt* is any text not containing a)) is a comment, completely ignored. Again, this is not allowed between the characters of multi-character symbols, like (?:. Such comments are more a historical artifact than a useful facility, and their use is deprecated; use the expanded syntax instead.

None of these metasyntax extensions is available if an initial ***= director has specified that the user's input be treated as a literal string rather than as an RE.

9.7.3.5. Regular Expression Matching Rules

In the event that an RE could match more than one substring of a given string, the RE matches the one starting earliest in the string. If the RE could match more than one substring starting at that point, either the longest possible match or the shortest possible match will be taken, depending on whether the RE is *greedy* or *non-greedy*.

Whether an RE is greedy or not is determined by the following rules:

- Most atoms, and all constraints, have no greediness attribute (because they cannot match variable amounts of text anyway).

- Adding parentheses around an RE does not change its greediness.

- A quantified atom with a fixed-repetition quantifier (`{m}` or `{m}?`) has the same greediness (possibly none) as the atom itself.

- A quantified atom with other normal quantifiers (including `{m, n}` with m equal to n) is greedy (prefers longest match).

- A quantified atom with a non-greedy quantifier (including `{m, n}?` with m equal to n) is non-greedy (prefers shortest match).

- A branch — that is, an RE that has no top-level `|` operator — has the same greediness as the first quantified atom in it that has a greediness attribute.

- An RE consisting of two or more branches connected by the `|` operator is always greedy.

The above rules associate greediness attributes not only with individual quantified atoms, but with branches and entire REs that contain quantified atoms. What that means is that the matching is done in such a way that the branch, or whole RE, matches the longest or shortest possible substring *as a whole*. Once the length of the entire match is determined, the part of it that matches any particular subexpression is determined on the basis of the greediness attribute of that subexpression, with subexpressions starting earlier in the RE taking priority over ones starting later.

An example of what this means:

```
SELECT SUBSTRING('XY1234Z', 'Y*([0-9]{1,3})');
Result: 123
SELECT SUBSTRING('XY1234Z', 'Y*?([0-9]{1,3})');
Result: 1
```

In the first case, the RE as a whole is greedy because `Y*` is greedy. It can match beginning at the `Y`, and it matches the longest possible string starting there, i.e., `Y123`. The output is the parenthesized part of that, or `123`. In the second case, the RE as a whole is non-greedy because `Y*?` is non-greedy. It can match beginning at the `Y`, and it matches the shortest possible string starting there, i.e., `Y1`. The subexpression `[0-9]{1,3}` is greedy but it cannot change the decision as to the overall match length; so it is forced to match just `1`.

In short, when an RE contains both greedy and non-greedy subexpressions, the total match length is either as long as possible or as short as possible, according to the attribute assigned to the whole RE. The attributes assigned to the subexpressions only affect how much of that match they are allowed to "eat" relative to each other.

The quantifiers `{1,1}` and `{1,1}?` can be used to force greediness or non-greediness, respectively, on a subexpression or a whole RE.

Match lengths are measured in characters, not collating elements. An empty string is considered longer than no match at all. For example: `bb*` matches the three middle characters of `abbbc`; `(week|wee)(night|knights)` matches all ten characters of `weeknights`; when `(.*).*` is matched against `abc` the parenthesized subexpression matches all three characters; and when `(a*)*` is matched against `bc` both the whole RE and the parenthesized subexpression match an empty string.

If case-independent matching is specified, the effect is much as if all case distinctions had vanished from the alphabet. When an alphabetic that exists in multiple cases appears as an ordinary character outside a bracket expression, it is effectively transformed into a bracket expression containing both cases, e.g., `x` becomes [xX]. When it appears inside a bracket expression, all case counterparts of it are added to the bracket expression, e.g., [x] becomes [xX] and [^x] becomes [^xX].

If newline-sensitive matching is specified, . and bracket expressions using ^ will never match the newline character (so that matches will never cross newlines unless the RE explicitly arranges it) and ^ and $ will match the empty string after and before a newline respectively, in addition to matching at beginning and end of string respectively. But the ARE escapes \A and \Z continue to match beginning or end of string *only*.

If partial newline-sensitive matching is specified, this affects . and bracket expressions as with newline-sensitive matching, but not ^ and $.

If inverse partial newline-sensitive matching is specified, this affects ^ and $ as with newline-sensitive matching, but not . and bracket expressions. This isn't very useful but is provided for symmetry.

9.7.3.6. Limits and Compatibility

No particular limit is imposed on the length of REs in this implementation. However, programs intended to be highly portable should not employ REs longer than 256 bytes, as a POSIX-compliant implementation can refuse to accept such REs.

The only feature of AREs that is actually incompatible with POSIX EREs is that \ does not lose its special significance inside bracket expressions. All other ARE features use syntax which is illegal or has undefined or unspecified effects in POSIX EREs; the *** syntax of directors likewise is outside the POSIX syntax for both BREs and EREs.

Many of the ARE extensions are borrowed from Perl, but some have been changed to clean them up, and a few Perl extensions are not present. Incompatibilities of note include \b, \B, the lack of special treatment for a trailing newline, the addition of complemented bracket expressions to the things affected by newline-sensitive matching, the restrictions on parentheses and back references in lookahead constraints, and the longest/shortest-match (rather than first-match) matching semantics.

Two significant incompatibilities exist between AREs and the ERE syntax recognized by pre-7.4 releases of PostgreSQL:

- In AREs, \ followed by an alphanumeric character is either an escape or an error, while in previous releases, it was just another way of writing the alphanumeric. This should not be much of a problem because there was no reason to write such a sequence in earlier releases.

- In AREs, \ remains a special character within [], so a literal \ within a bracket expression must be written \\.

9.7.3.7. Basic Regular Expressions

BREs differ from EREs in several respects. In BREs, |, +, and ? are ordinary characters and there is no equivalent for their functionality. The delimiters for bounds are \{ and \}, with { and } by themselves ordinary characters. The parentheses for nested subexpressions are \(and \), with (and) by themselves ordinary characters. ^ is an ordinary character except at the beginning of the RE or the beginning of a parenthesized subexpression, $ is an ordinary character except at the end of the RE or the end of a parenthesized subexpression, and `*` is an ordinary character if it appears at the beginning of the RE or the beginning of a parenthesized subexpression (after a possible leading `^`). Finally, single-digit back references are available, and `\<` and `\>` are synonyms for `[[:<:]]` and `[[:>:]]` respectively; no other escapes are available in BREs.

9.8. Data Type Formatting Functions

The PostgreSQL formatting functions provide a powerful set of tools for converting various data types (date/time, integer, floating point, numeric) to formatted strings and for converting from formatted strings to specific data types. Table 9-21 lists them. These functions all follow a common calling convention: the first argument is the value to be formatted and the second argument is a template that defines the output or input format.

A single-argument `to_timestamp` function is also available; it accepts a `double precision` argument and converts from Unix epoch (seconds since 1970-01-01 00:00:00+00) to `timestamp with time zone`. (`Integer` Unix epochs are implicitly cast to `double precision`.)

Table 9-21. Formatting Functions

Function	Return Type	Description	Example
`to_char(timestamp, text)`	`text`	convert time stamp to string	`to_char(current_time 'HH12:MI:SS')`
`to_char(interval, text)`	`text`	convert interval to string	`to_char(interval '15h 2m 12s', 'HH24:MI:SS')`
`to_char(int, text)`	`text`	convert integer to string	`to_char(125, '999')`
`to_char(double precision, text)`	`text`	convert real/double precision to string	`to_char(125.8::real, '999D9')`
`to_char(numeric, text)`	`text`	convert numeric to string	`to_char(-125.8, '999D99S')`
`to_date(text, text)`	`date`	convert string to date	`to_date('05 Dec 200( 'DD Mon YYYY')`
`to_number(text, text)`	`numeric`	convert string to numeric	`to_number('12,454.8 '99G999D9S')`
`to_timestamp(text, text)`	`timestamp with time zone`	convert string to time stamp	`to_timestamp('05 De( 'DD Mon YYYY')`
`to_timestamp(double precision)`	`timestamp with time zone`	convert Unix epoch to time stamp	`to_timestamp(128435:`

In a `to_char` output template string, there are certain patterns that are recognized and replaced with appropriately-formatted data based on the given value. Any text that is not a template pattern is simply copied verbatim. Similarly, in an input template string (for the other functions), template patterns identify the values to be supplied by the input data string.

Table 9-22 shows the template patterns available for formatting date and time values.

Table 9-22. Template Patterns for Date/Time Formatting

Pattern	Description
HH	hour of day (01-12)
HH12	hour of day (01-12)
HH24	hour of day (00-23)
MI	minute (00-59)
SS	second (00-59)
MS	millisecond (000-999)
US	microsecond (000000-999999)
SSSS	seconds past midnight (0-86399)
AM, am, PM or pm	meridiem indicator (without periods)
A.M., a.m., P.M. or p.m.	meridiem indicator (with periods)
Y,YYY	year (4 or more digits) with comma
YYYY	year (4 or more digits)
YYY	last 3 digits of year
YY	last 2 digits of year
Y	last digit of year
IYYY	ISO 8601 week-numbering year (4 or more digits)
IYY	last 3 digits of ISO 8601 week-numbering year
IY	last 2 digits of ISO 8601 week-numbering year
I	last digit of ISO 8601 week-numbering year
BC, bc, AD or ad	era indicator (without periods)
B.C., b.c., A.D. or a.d.	era indicator (with periods)
MONTH	full upper case month name (blank-padded to 9 chars)
Month	full capitalized month name (blank-padded to 9 chars)
month	full lower case month name (blank-padded to 9 chars)
MON	abbreviated upper case month name (3 chars in English, localized lengths vary)
Mon	abbreviated capitalized month name (3 chars in English, localized lengths vary)
mon	abbreviated lower case month name (3 chars in English, localized lengths vary)
MM	month number (01-12)
DAY	full upper case day name (blank-padded to 9 chars)

Pattern	Description
Day	full capitalized day name (blank-padded to 9 chars)
day	full lower case day name (blank-padded to 9 chars)
DY	abbreviated upper case day name (3 chars in English, localized lengths vary)
Dy	abbreviated capitalized day name (3 chars in English, localized lengths vary)
dy	abbreviated lower case day name (3 chars in English, localized lengths vary)
DDD	day of year (001-366)
IDDD	day of ISO 8601 week-numbering year (001-371; day 1 of the year is Monday of the first ISO week)
DD	day of month (01-31)
D	day of the week, Sunday (1) to Saturday (7)
ID	ISO 8601 day of the week, Monday (1) to Sunday (7)
W	week of month (1-5) (the first week starts on the first day of the month)
WW	week number of year (1-53) (the first week starts on the first day of the year)
IW	week number of ISO 8601 week-numbering year (01-53; the first Thursday of the year is in week 1)
CC	century (2 digits) (the twenty-first century starts on 2001-01-01)
J	Julian Day (integer days since November 24, 4714 BC at midnight UTC)
Q	quarter (ignored by to_date and to_timestamp)
RM	month in upper case Roman numerals (I-XII; I=January)
rm	month in lower case Roman numerals (i-xii; i=January)
TZ	upper case time-zone name
tz	lower case time-zone name
OF	time-zone offset

Modifiers can be applied to any template pattern to alter its behavior. For example, FMMonth is the Month pattern with the FM modifier. Table 9-23 shows the modifier patterns for date/time formatting.

Table 9-23. Template Pattern Modifiers for Date/Time Formatting

Modifier	Description	Example
`FM` prefix	fill mode (suppress padding blanks and trailing zeroes)	`FMMonth`
`TH` suffix	upper case ordinal number suffix	`DDTH`, e.g., `12TH`
`th` suffix	lower case ordinal number suffix	`DDth`, e.g., `12th`
`FX` prefix	fixed format global option (see usage notes)	`FX Month DD Day`
`TM` prefix	translation mode (print localized day and month names based on lc_time)	`TMMonth`
`SP` suffix	spell mode (not implemented)	`DDSP`

Usage notes for date/time formatting:

- `FM` suppresses leading zeroes and trailing blanks that would otherwise be added to make the output of a pattern be fixed-width. In PostgreSQL, `FM` modifies only the next specification, while in Oracle `FM` affects all subsequent specifications, and repeated `FM` modifiers toggle fill mode on and off.

- `TM` does not include trailing blanks.

- `to_timestamp` and `to_date` skip multiple blank spaces in the input string unless the `FX` option is used. For example, `to_timestamp('2000    JUN', 'YYYY MON')` works, but `to_timestamp('2000    JUN', 'FXYYYY MON')` returns an error because `to_timestamp` expects one space only. `FX` must be specified as the first item in the template.

- `to_timestamp` and `to_date` exist to handle input formats that cannot be converted by simple casting. These functions interpret input liberally, with minimal error checking. While they produce valid output, the conversion can yield unexpected results. For example, input to these functions is not restricted by normal ranges, thus `to_date('20096040','YYYYMMDD')` returns `2014-01-17` rather than causing an error. Casting does not have this behavior.

- Ordinary text is allowed in `to_char` templates and will be output literally. You can put a substring in double quotes to force it to be interpreted as literal text even if it contains pattern key words. For example, in `'"Hello Year "YYYY'`, the `YYYY` will be replaced by the year data, but the single `Y` in `Year` will not be. In `to_date`, `to_number`, and `to_timestamp`, double-quoted strings skip the number of input characters contained in the string, e.g. `"XX"` skips two input characters.

- If you want to have a double quote in the output you must precede it with a backslash, for example `'\"YYYY Month\"'`.

- If the year format specification is less than four digits, e.g. `YYY`, and the supplied year is less than four digits, the year will be adjusted to be nearest to the year 2020, e.g. `95` becomes 1995.

- The `YYYY` conversion from string to `timestamp` or `date` has a restriction when processing years with more than 4 digits. You must use some non-digit character or template after `YYYY`, otherwise the year is always interpreted as 4 digits. For example (with the year 20000): `to_date('200001131', 'YYYYMMDD')` will be interpreted as a 4-digit year; instead use a non-digit separator after the year, like `to_date('20000-1131', 'YYYY-MMDD')` or `to_date('20000Nov31', 'YYYYMonDD')`.

- In conversions from string to `timestamp` or `date`, the `CC` (century) field is ignored if there is a `YYY`, `YYYY` or `Y,YYY` field. If `CC` is used with `YY` or `Y` then the year is computed as the year in the specified century. If the century is specified but the year is not, the first year of the century is assumed.

- An ISO 8601 week-numbering date (as distinct from a Gregorian date) can be specified to `to_timestamp` and `to_date` in one of two ways:

  - Year, week number, and weekday: for example `to_date('2006-42-4', 'IYYY-IW-ID')` returns the date `2006-10-19`. If you omit the weekday it is assumed to be 1 (Monday).

  - Year and day of year: for example `to_date('2006-291', 'IYYY-IDDD')` also returns `2006-10-19`.

Attempting to enter a date using a mixture of ISO 8601 week-numbering fields and Gregorian date fields is nonsensical, and will cause an error. In the context of an ISO 8601 week-numbering year, the concept of a "month" or "day of month" has no meaning. In the context of a Gregorian year, the ISO week has no meaning.

Caution

While `to_date` will reject a mixture of Gregorian and ISO week-numbering date fields, `to_char` will not, since output format specifications like `YYYY-MM-DD (IYYY-IDDD)` can be useful. But avoid writing something like `IYYY-MM-DD`; that would yield surprising results near the start of the year. (See Section 9.9.1 for more information.)

- In a conversion from string to `timestamp`, millisecond (`MS`) or microsecond (`US`) values are used as the seconds digits after the decimal point. For example `to_timestamp('12:3', 'SS:MS')` is not 3 milliseconds, but 300, because the conversion counts it as 12 + 0.3 seconds. This means for the format `SS:MS`, the input values `12:3`, `12:30`, and `12:300` specify the same number of milliseconds. To get three milliseconds, one must use `12:003`, which the conversion counts as 12 + 0.003 = 12.003 seconds.

  Here is a more complex example: `to_timestamp('15:12:02.020.001230', 'HH:MI:SS.MS.US')` is 15 hours, 12 minutes, and 2 seconds + 20 milliseconds + 1230 microseconds = 2.021230 seconds.

- `to_char(..., 'ID')`'s day of the week numbering matches the `extract(isodow from ...)` function, but `to_char(..., 'D')`'s does not match `extract(dow from ...)`'s day numbering.

- `to_char(interval)` formats `HH` and `HH12` as shown on a 12-hour clock, i.e. zero hours and 36 hours output as `12`, while `HH24` outputs the full hour value, which can exceed 23 for intervals.

Table 9-24 shows the template patterns available for formatting numeric values.

Table 9-24. Template Patterns for Numeric Formatting

Pattern	Description
9	value with the specified number of digits
0	value with leading zeros

Pattern	Description
. (period)	decimal point
, (comma)	group (thousand) separator
PR	negative value in angle brackets
S	sign anchored to number (uses locale)
L	currency symbol (uses locale)
D	decimal point (uses locale)
G	group separator (uses locale)
MI	minus sign in specified position (if number < 0)
PL	plus sign in specified position (if number > 0)
SG	plus/minus sign in specified position
RN	Roman numeral (input between 1 and 3999)
TH or th	ordinal number suffix
V	shift specified number of digits (see notes)
EEEE	exponent for scientific notation

Usage notes for numeric formatting:

- A sign formatted using SG, PL, or MI is not anchored to the number; for example, to_char(-12, 'MI9999') produces '- 12' but to_char(-12, 'S9999') produces ' -12'. The Oracle implementation does not allow the use of MI before 9, but rather requires that 9 precede MI.

- 9 results in a value with the same number of digits as there are 9s. If a digit is not available it outputs a space.

- TH does not convert values less than zero and does not convert fractional numbers.

- PL, SG, and TH are PostgreSQL extensions.

- V effectively multiplies the input values by 10^n, where n is the number of digits following V. to_char does not support the use of V combined with a decimal point (e.g., 99.9V99 is not allowed).

- EEEE (scientific notation) cannot be used in combination with any of the other formatting patterns or modifiers other than digit and decimal point patterns, and must be at the end of the format string (e.g., 9.99EEEE is a valid pattern).

Certain modifiers can be applied to any template pattern to alter its behavior. For example, FM9999 is the 9999 pattern with the FM modifier. Table 9-25 shows the modifier patterns for numeric formatting.

Table 9-25. Template Pattern Modifiers for Numeric Formatting

Modifier	Description	Example
FM prefix	fill mode (suppress padding blanks and trailing zeroes)	FM9999
TH suffix	upper case ordinal number suffix	999TH

Modifier	Description	Example
`th` suffix	lower case ordinal number suffix	`999th`

Table 9-26 shows some examples of the use of the `to_char` function.

Table 9-26. `to_char` Examples

Expression	Result
`to_char(current_timestamp,` `'Day, DD  HH12:MI:SS')`	`'Tuesday  , 06  05:39:18'`
`to_char(current_timestamp,` `'FMDay, FMDD  HH12:MI:SS')`	`'Tuesday, 6  05:39:18'`
`to_char(-0.1, '99.99')`	`'  -.10'`
`to_char(-0.1, 'FM9.99')`	`'-.1'`
`to_char(0.1, '0.9')`	`' 0.1'`
`to_char(12, '9990999.9')`	`'    0012.0'`
`to_char(12, 'FM9990999.9')`	`'0012.'`
`to_char(485, '999')`	`' 485'`
`to_char(-485, '999')`	`'-485'`
`to_char(485, '9 9 9')`	`' 4 8 5'`
`to_char(1485, '9,999')`	`' 1,485'`
`to_char(1485, '9G999')`	`' 1 485'`
`to_char(148.5, '999.999')`	`' 148.500'`
`to_char(148.5, 'FM999.999')`	`'148.5'`
`to_char(148.5, 'FM999.990')`	`'148.500'`
`to_char(148.5, '999D999')`	`' 148,500'`
`to_char(3148.5, '9G999D999')`	`' 3 148,500'`
`to_char(-485, '999S')`	`'485-'`
`to_char(-485, '999MI')`	`'485-'`
`to_char(485, '999MI')`	`'485 '`
`to_char(485, 'FM999MI')`	`'485'`
`to_char(485, 'PL999')`	`'+485'`
`to_char(485, 'SG999')`	`'+485'`
`to_char(-485, 'SG999')`	`'-485'`
`to_char(-485, '9SG99')`	`'4-85'`
`to_char(-485, '999PR')`	`'<485>'`
`to_char(485, 'L999')`	`'DM 485`
`to_char(485, 'RN')`	`'           CDLXXXV'`
`to_char(485, 'FMRN')`	`'CDLXXXV'`
`to_char(5.2, 'FMRN')`	`'V'`
`to_char(482, '999th')`	`' 482nd'`

Expression	Result
`to_char(485, '"Good number:"999')`	`'Good number: 485'`
`to_char(485.8,` `'"Pre:"999" Post:" .999')`	`'Pre: 485 Post: .800'`
`to_char(12, '99V999')`	`' 12000'`
`to_char(12.4, '99V999')`	`' 12400'`
`to_char(12.45, '99V9')`	`' 125'`
`to_char(0.0004859, '9.99EEEE')`	`' 4.86e-04'`

9.9. Date/Time Functions and Operators

Table 9-28 shows the available functions for date/time value processing, with details appearing in the following subsections. Table 9-27 illustrates the behaviors of the basic arithmetic operators (+, *, etc.). For formatting functions, refer to Section 9.8. You should be familiar with the background information on date/time data types from Section 8.5.

All the functions and operators described below that take `time` or `timestamp` inputs actually come in two variants: one that takes `time with time zone` or `timestamp with time zone`, and one that takes `time without time zone` or `timestamp without time zone`. For brevity, these variants are not shown separately. Also, the + and * operators come in commutative pairs (for example both date + integer and integer + date); we show only one of each such pair.

Table 9-27. Date/Time Operators

Operator	Example	Result
+	`date '2001-09-28' +` `integer '7'`	`date '2001-10-05'`
+	`date '2001-09-28' +` `interval '1 hour'`	`timestamp '2001-09-28` `01:00:00'`
+	`date '2001-09-28' + time` `'03:00'`	`timestamp '2001-09-28` `03:00:00'`
+	`interval '1 day' +` `interval '1 hour'`	`interval '1 day` `01:00:00'`

+	`timestamp '2001-09-28`
	`01:00' + interval '23`
	`hours'`
		`timestamp '2001-09-29`
		`00:00:00'`

+	`time '01:00' + interval` `'3 hours'`	`time '04:00:00'`
−	`- interval '23 hours'`	`interval '-23:00:00'`
−	`date '2001-10-01' - date` `'2001-09-28'`	`integer '3'` (days)
−	`date '2001-10-01' -` `integer '7'`	`date '2001-09-24'`

Operator	Example	Result
-	date '2001-09-28' - interval '1 hour'	timestamp '2001-09-27 23:00:00'
-	time '05:00' - time '03:00'	interval '02:00:00'
-	time '05:00' - interval '2 hours'	time '03:00:00'
-	timestamp '2001-09-28 23:00' - interval '23 hours'	timestamp '2001-09-28 00:00:00'
-	interval '1 day' - interval '1 hour'	interval '1 day -01:00:00'
-	timestamp '2001-09-29 03:00' - timestamp '2001-09-27 12:00'	interval '1 day 15:00:00'
*	900 * interval '1 second'	interval '00:15:00'
*	21 * interval '1 day'	interval '21 days'
*	double precision '3.5' * interval '1 hour'	interval '03:30:00'
/	interval '1 hour' / double precision '1.5'	interval '00:40:00'

Table 9-28. Date/Time Functions

Function	Return Type	Description	Example	Result
age(timestamp, timestamp)	interval	Subtract arguments, producing a "symbolic" result that uses years and months, rather than just days	age(timestamp '2001-04-10', timestamp '1957-06-13')	43 years 9 mons 27 days
age(timestamp)	interval	Subtract from current_date (at midnight)	age(timestamp '1957-06-13')	43 years 8 mons 3 days
clock_timestamp()	timestamp with time zone	Current date and time (changes during statement execution); see Section 9.9.4		
current_date	date	Current date; see Section 9.9.4		

Function	Return Type	Description	Example	Result
`current_time`	time with time zone	Current time of day; see Section 9.9.4		
`current_timestamp`	timestamp with time zone	Current date and time (start of current transaction); see Section 9.9.4		
`date_part(text, timestamp)`	double precision	Get subfield (equivalent to `extract`); see Section 9.9.1	`date_part('hour', timestamp '2001-02-16 20:38:40')`	20
`date_part(text, interval)`	double precision	Get subfield (equivalent to `extract`); see Section 9.9.1	`date_part('month', interval '2 years 3 months')`	3
`date_trunc(text, timestamp)`	timestamp	Truncate to specified precision; see also Section 9.9.2	`date_trunc('hour', timestamp '2001-02-16 20:38:40')`	2001-02-16 20:00:00
`date_trunc(text, interval)`	interval	Truncate to specified precision; see also Section 9.9.2	`date_trunc('hour', interval '2 days 3 hours 40 minutes')`	2 days 03:00:00
`extract(field from timestamp)`	double precision	Get subfield; see Section 9.9.1	`extract(hour from timestamp '2001-02-16 20:38:40')`	20
`extract(field from interval)`	double precision	Get subfield; see Section 9.9.1	`extract(month from interval '2 years 3 months')`	3
`isfinite(date)`	boolean	Test for finite date (not +/-infinity)	`isfinite(date '2001-02-16')`	true
`isfinite(timestamp)`	boolean	Test for finite time stamp (not +/-infinity)	`isfinite(timestamp '2001-02-16 21:28:30')`	true
`isfinite(interval)`	boolean	Test for finite interval	`isfinite(interval '4 hours')`	true
`justify_days(interval)`	interval	Adjust interval so 30-day time periods are represented as months	`justify_days(interval '35 days')`	1 mon 5 days

Function	Return Type	Description	Example	Result
justify_hours(interval)	interval	Adjust interval so 24-hour time periods are represented as days	justify_hours(interval '27 hours')	1 day 03:00:00
justify_interval(interval)	interval	Adjust interval using justify_days and justify_hours, with additional sign adjustments	justify_interval(interval '1 mon -1 hour')	29 days 23:00:00
localtime	time	Current time of day; see Section 9.9.4		
localtimestamp	timestamp	Current date and time (start of current transaction); see Section 9.9.4		
make_date(year int, month int, day int)	date	Create date from year, month and day fields	make_date(2013, 7, 15)	2013-07-15
make_interval(years int DEFAULT 0, months int DEFAULT 0, weeks int DEFAULT 0, days int DEFAULT 0, hours int DEFAULT 0, mins int DEFAULT 0, secs double precision DEFAULT 0.0)	interval	Create interval from years, months, weeks, days, hours, minutes and seconds fields	make_interval(days := 10)	10 days
make_time(hour int, min int, sec double precision)	time	Create time from hour, minute and seconds fields	make_time(8, 15, 23.5)	08:15:23.5

Function	Return Type	Description	Example	Result
`make_timestamp(year int, month int, day int, hour int, min int, sec double precision)`	`timestamp`	Create timestamp from year, month, day, hour, minute and seconds fields	`make_timestamp(2013, 7, 15, 8, 15, 23.5)`	`2013-07-15 08:15:23.5`
`make_timestamptz(year int, month int, day int, hour int, min int, sec double precision, [ timezone text ])`	`timestamp with time zone`	Create timestamp with time zone from year, month, day, hour, minute and seconds fields. When `timezone` is not specified, then current time zone is used.	`make_timestamptz(2013, 7, 15, 8, 15, 23.5)`	`2013-07-15 08:15:23.5+01`
`now()`	`timestamp with time zone`	Current date and time (start of current transaction); see Section 9.9.4		
`statement_timestamp()`	`timestamp with time zone`	Current date and time (start of current statement); see Section 9.9.4		
`timeofday()`	`text`	Current date and time (like `clock_timestamp`, but as a `text` string); see Section 9.9.4		
`transaction_timestamp()`	`timestamp with time zone`	Current date and time (start of current transaction); see Section 9.9.4		

In addition to these functions, the SQL OVERLAPS operator is supported:

```
(start1, end1) OVERLAPS (start2, end2)
(start1, length1) OVERLAPS (start2, length2)
```

This expression yields true when two time periods (defined by their endpoints) overlap, false when they do not overlap. The endpoints can be specified as pairs of dates, times, or time stamps; or as a date, time, or time stamp followed by an interval. When a pair of values is provided, either the start or the end can be written first; OVERLAPS automatically takes the earlier value of the pair as the start. Each time period is considered to represent the half-open interval *start <= time < end*, unless *start* and *end* are equal in which case it represents that single time instant. This means for instance that two time periods with only an endpoint in common do not overlap.

```
SELECT (DATE '2001-02-16', DATE '2001-12-21') OVERLAPS
       (DATE '2001-10-30', DATE '2002-10-30');
Result: true
SELECT (DATE '2001-02-16', INTERVAL '100 days') OVERLAPS
       (DATE '2001-10-30', DATE '2002-10-30');
Result: false
SELECT (DATE '2001-10-29', DATE '2001-10-30') OVERLAPS
       (DATE '2001-10-30', DATE '2001-10-31');
Result: false
SELECT (DATE '2001-10-30', DATE '2001-10-30') OVERLAPS
       (DATE '2001-10-30', DATE '2001-10-31');
Result: true
```

When adding an `interval` value to (or subtracting an `interval` value from) a `timestamp with time zone` value, the days component advances or decrements the date of the `timestamp with time zone` by the indicated number of days. Across daylight saving time changes (when the session time zone is set to a time zone that recognizes DST), this means `interval '1 day'` does not necessarily equal `interval '24 hours'`. For example, with the session time zone set to `CST7CDT`, `timestamp with time zone '2005-04-02 12:00-07'` + `interval '1 day'` will produce `timestamp with time zone '2005-04-03 12:00-06'`, while adding `interval '24 hours'` to the same initial `timestamp with time zone` produces `timestamp with time zone '2005-04-03 13:00-06'`, as there is a change in daylight saving time at `2005-04-03 02:00` in time zone `CST7CDT`.

Note there can be ambiguity in the `months` field returned by `age` because different months have different numbers of days. PostgreSQL's approach uses the month from the earlier of the two dates when calculating partial months. For example, `age('2004-06-01', '2004-04-30')` uses April to yield `1 mon 1 day`, while using May would yield `1 mon 2 days` because May has 31 days, while April has only 30.

Subtraction of dates and timestamps can also be complex. One conceptually simple way to perform subtraction is to convert each value to a number of seconds using `EXTRACT(EPOCH FROM ...)`, then subtract the results; this produces the number of *seconds* between the two values. This will adjust for the number of days in each month, timezone changes, and daylight saving time adjustments. Subtraction of date or timestamp values with the "–" operator returns the number of days (24-hours) and hours/minutes/seconds between the values, making the same adjustments. The `age` function returns years, months, days, and hours/minutes/seconds, performing field-by-field subtraction and then adjusting for negative field values. The following queries illustrate the differences in these approaches. The sample results were produced with `timezone = 'US/Eastern'`; there is a daylight saving time change between the two dates used:

```
SELECT EXTRACT(EPOCH FROM timestamptz '2013-07-01 12:00:00') -
       EXTRACT(EPOCH FROM timestamptz '2013-03-01 12:00:00');
Result: 10537200
SELECT (EXTRACT(EPOCH FROM timestamptz '2013-07-01 12:00:00') -
       EXTRACT(EPOCH FROM timestamptz '2013-03-01 12:00:00'))
       / 60 / 60 / 24;
Result: 121.958333333333
SELECT timestamptz '2013-07-01 12:00:00' - timestamptz '2013-03-01 12:00:00';
Result: 121 days 23:00:00
SELECT age(timestamptz '2013-07-01 12:00:00', timestamptz '2013-03-01 12:00:00'
```

Result: 4 mons

9.9.1. **EXTRACT, date_part**

EXTRACT(*field* FROM *source*)

The extract function retrieves subfields such as year or hour from date/time values. *source* must be a value expression of type timestamp, time, or interval. (Expressions of type date are cast to timestamp and can therefore be used as well.) *field* is an identifier or string that selects what field to extract from the source value. The extract function returns values of type double precision. The following are valid field names:

century

> The century
>
> ```
> SELECT EXTRACT(CENTURY FROM TIMESTAMP '2000-12-16 12:21:13');
> Result: 20
> SELECT EXTRACT(CENTURY FROM TIMESTAMP '2001-02-16 20:38:40');
> Result: 21
> ```
>
> The first century starts at 0001-01-01 00:00:00 AD, although they did not know it at the time. This definition applies to all Gregorian calendar countries. There is no century number 0, you go from -1 century to 1 century. If you disagree with this, please write your complaint to: Pope, Cathedral Saint-Peter of Roma, Vatican.

day

> For timestamp values, the day (of the month) field (1 - 31) ; for interval values, the number of days
>
> ```
> SELECT EXTRACT(DAY FROM TIMESTAMP '2001-02-16 20:38:40');
> Result: 16
> ```
>
> ```
> SELECT EXTRACT(DAY FROM INTERVAL '40 days 1 minute');
> Result: 40
> ```

decade

> The year field divided by 10
>
> ```
> SELECT EXTRACT(DECADE FROM TIMESTAMP '2001-02-16 20:38:40');
> Result: 200
> ```

dow

> The day of the week as Sunday (0) to Saturday (6)
>
> ```
> SELECT EXTRACT(DOW FROM TIMESTAMP '2001-02-16 20:38:40');
> Result: 5
> ```
>
> Note that extract's day of the week numbering differs from that of the to_char(..., 'D') function.

doy

> The day of the year (1 - 365/366)
>
> ```
> SELECT EXTRACT(DOY FROM TIMESTAMP '2001-02-16 20:38:40');
> Result: 47
> ```

epoch

> For `timestamp with time zone` values, the number of seconds since 1970-01-01 00:00:00 UTC (can be negative); for `date` and `timestamp` values, the number of seconds since 1970-01-01 00:00:00 local time; for `interval` values, the total number of seconds in the interval
>
> ```
> SELECT EXTRACT(EPOCH FROM TIMESTAMP WITH TIME ZONE '2001-02-16 20:38:40.12-
> Result: 982384720.12
> ```
>
> ```
> SELECT EXTRACT(EPOCH FROM INTERVAL '5 days 3 hours');
> Result: 442800
> ```
>
> Here is how you can convert an epoch value back to a time stamp:
>
> ```
> SELECT TIMESTAMP WITH TIME ZONE 'epoch' + 982384720.12 * INTERVAL '1 second
> ```
>
> (The `to_timestamp` function encapsulates the above conversion.)

hour

> The hour field (0 - 23)
>
> ```
> SELECT EXTRACT(HOUR FROM TIMESTAMP '2001-02-16 20:38:40');
> Result: 20
> ```

isodow

> The day of the week as Monday (1) to Sunday (7)
>
> ```
> SELECT EXTRACT(ISODOW FROM TIMESTAMP '2001-02-18 20:38:40');
> Result: 7
> ```
>
> This is identical to `dow` except for Sunday. This matches the ISO 8601 day of the week numbering.

isoyear

> The ISO 8601 week-numbering year that the date falls in (not applicable to intervals)
>
> ```
> SELECT EXTRACT(ISOYEAR FROM DATE '2006-01-01');
> Result: 2005
> SELECT EXTRACT(ISOYEAR FROM DATE '2006-01-02');
> Result: 2006
> ```
>
> Each ISO 8601 week-numbering year begins with the Monday of the week containing the 4th of January, so in early January or late December the ISO year may be different from the Gregorian year. See the `week` field for more information.
>
> This field is not available in PostgreSQL releases prior to 8.3.

microseconds

> The seconds field, including fractional parts, multiplied by 1 000 000; note that this includes full seconds
>
> ```
> SELECT EXTRACT(MICROSECONDS FROM TIME '17:12:28.5');
> Result: 28500000
> ```

`millennium`

The millennium

```
SELECT EXTRACT(MILLENNIUM FROM TIMESTAMP '2001-02-16 20:38:40');
Result: 3
```

Years in the 1900s are in the second millennium. The third millennium started January 1, 2001.

`milliseconds`

The seconds field, including fractional parts, multiplied by 1000. Note that this includes full seconds.

```
SELECT EXTRACT(MILLISECONDS FROM TIME '17:12:28.5');
Result: 28500
```

`minute`

The minutes field (0 - 59)

```
SELECT EXTRACT(MINUTE FROM TIMESTAMP '2001-02-16 20:38:40');
Result: 38
```

`month`

For `timestamp` values, the number of the month within the year (1 - 12) ; for `interval` values, the number of months, modulo 12 (0 - 11)

```
SELECT EXTRACT(MONTH FROM TIMESTAMP '2001-02-16 20:38:40');
Result: 2
```

```
SELECT EXTRACT(MONTH FROM INTERVAL '2 years 3 months');
Result: 3
```

```
SELECT EXTRACT(MONTH FROM INTERVAL '2 years 13 months');
Result: 1
```

`quarter`

The quarter of the year (1 - 4) that the date is in

```
SELECT EXTRACT(QUARTER FROM TIMESTAMP '2001-02-16 20:38:40');
Result: 1
```

`second`

The seconds field, including fractional parts (0 - 59[1])

```
SELECT EXTRACT(SECOND FROM TIMESTAMP '2001-02-16 20:38:40');
Result: 40
```

```
SELECT EXTRACT(SECOND FROM TIME '17:12:28.5');
Result: 28.5
```

`timezone`

The time zone offset from UTC, measured in seconds. Positive values correspond to time zones east of UTC, negative values to zones west of UTC. (Technically, PostgreSQL uses UT1 because leap seconds are not handled.)

---

[1] 60 if leap seconds are implemented by the operating system

```
timezone_hour
```

The hour component of the time zone offset

```
timezone_minute
```

The minute component of the time zone offset

```
week
```

The number of the ISO 8601 week-numbering week of the year. By definition, ISO weeks start on Mondays and the first week of a year contains January 4 of that year. In other words, the first Thursday of a year is in week 1 of that year.

In the ISO week-numbering system, it is possible for early-January dates to be part of the 52nd or 53rd week of the previous year, and for late-December dates to be part of the first week of the next year. For example, `2005-01-01` is part of the 53rd week of year 2004, and `2006-01-01` is part of the 52nd week of year 2005, while `2012-12-31` is part of the first week of 2013. It's recommended to use the `isoyear` field together with `week` to get consistent results.

```
SELECT EXTRACT(WEEK FROM TIMESTAMP '2001-02-16 20:38:40');
Result: 7
```

```
year
```

The year field. Keep in mind there is no `0 AD`, so subtracting `BC` years from `AD` years should be done with care.

```
SELECT EXTRACT(YEAR FROM TIMESTAMP '2001-02-16 20:38:40');
Result: 2001
```

The `extract` function is primarily intended for computational processing. For formatting date/time values for display, see Section 9.8.

The `date_part` function is modeled on the traditional Ingres equivalent to the SQL-standard function `extract`:

```
date_part('field', source)
```

Note that here the `field` parameter needs to be a string value, not a name. The valid field names for `date_part` are the same as for `extract`.

```
SELECT date_part('day', TIMESTAMP '2001-02-16 20:38:40');
Result: 16
```

```
SELECT date_part('hour', INTERVAL '4 hours 3 minutes');
Result: 4
```

9.9.2. `date_trunc`

The function `date_trunc` is conceptually similar to the `trunc` function for numbers.

```
date_trunc('field', source)
```

source is a value expression of type `timestamp` or `interval`. (Values of type `date` and `time` are cast automatically to `timestamp` or `interval`, respectively.) *field* selects to which precision to truncate the input value. The return value is of type `timestamp` or `interval` with all fields that are less significant than the selected one set to zero (or one, for day and month).

Valid values for *field* are:

```
microseconds
milliseconds
second
minute
hour
day
week
month
quarter
year
decade
century
millennium
```

Examples:

```
SELECT date_trunc('hour', TIMESTAMP '2001-02-16 20:38:40');
Result: 2001-02-16 20:00:00

SELECT date_trunc('year', TIMESTAMP '2001-02-16 20:38:40');
Result: 2001-01-01 00:00:00
```

9.9.3. `AT TIME ZONE`

The `AT TIME ZONE` construct allows conversions of time stamps to different time zones. Table 9-29 shows its variants.

Table 9-29. `AT TIME ZONE` Variants

Expression	Return Type	Description
`timestamp without time zone AT TIME ZONE zone`	`timestamp with time zone`	Treat given time stamp *without time zone* as located in the specified time zone
`timestamp with time zone AT TIME ZONE zone`	`timestamp without time zone`	Convert given time stamp *with time zone* to the new time zone, with no time zone designation

Expression	Return Type	Description
`time with time zone AT TIME ZONE` *zone*	`time with time zone`	Convert given time *with time zone* to the new time zone

In these expressions, the desired time zone *zone* can be specified either as a text string (e.g., `'PST'`) or as an interval (e.g., `INTERVAL '-08:00'`). In the text case, a time zone name can be specified in any of the ways described in Section 8.5.3.

Examples (assuming the local time zone is `PST8PDT`):

```
SELECT TIMESTAMP '2001-02-16 20:38:40' AT TIME ZONE 'MST';
Result: 2001-02-16 19:38:40-08

SELECT TIMESTAMP WITH TIME ZONE '2001-02-16 20:38:40-05' AT TIME ZONE 'MST';
Result: 2001-02-16 18:38:40
```

The first example takes a time stamp without time zone and interprets it as MST time (UTC-7), which is then converted to PST (UTC-8) for display. The second example takes a time stamp specified in EST (UTC-5) and converts it to local time in MST (UTC-7).

The function `timezone(zone, timestamp)` is equivalent to the SQL-conforming construct `timestamp AT TIME ZONE zone`.

9.9.4. Current Date/Time

PostgreSQL provides a number of functions that return values related to the current date and time. These SQL-standard functions all return values based on the start time of the current transaction:

```
CURRENT_DATE
CURRENT_TIME
CURRENT_TIMESTAMP
CURRENT_TIME(precision)
CURRENT_TIMESTAMP(precision)
LOCALTIME
LOCALTIMESTAMP
LOCALTIME(precision)
LOCALTIMESTAMP(precision)
```

`CURRENT_TIME` and `CURRENT_TIMESTAMP` deliver values with time zone; `LOCALTIME` and `LOCALTIMESTAMP` deliver values without time zone.

`CURRENT_TIME`, `CURRENT_TIMESTAMP`, `LOCALTIME`, and `LOCALTIMESTAMP` can optionally take a precision parameter, which causes the result to be rounded to that many fractional digits in the seconds field. Without a precision parameter, the result is given to the full available precision.

Some examples:

```
SELECT CURRENT_TIME;
Result: 14:39:53.662522-05

SELECT CURRENT_DATE;
```

```
Result: 2001-12-23
```

```
SELECT CURRENT_TIMESTAMP;
```
Result: 2001-12-23 14:39:53.662522-05

```
SELECT CURRENT_TIMESTAMP(2);
```
Result: 2001-12-23 14:39:53.66-05

```
SELECT LOCALTIMESTAMP;
```
Result: 2001-12-23 14:39:53.662522

Since these functions return the start time of the current transaction, their values do not change during the transaction. This is considered a feature: the intent is to allow a single transaction to have a consistent notion of the "current" time, so that multiple modifications within the same transaction bear the same time stamp.

> **Note:** Other database systems might advance these values more frequently.

PostgreSQL also provides functions that return the start time of the current statement, as well as the actual current time at the instant the function is called. The complete list of non-SQL-standard time functions is:

```
transaction_timestamp()
statement_timestamp()
clock_timestamp()
timeofday()
now()
```

`transaction_timestamp()` is equivalent to `CURRENT_TIMESTAMP`, but is named to clearly reflect what it returns. `statement_timestamp()` returns the start time of the current statement (more specifically, the time of receipt of the latest command message from the client). `statement_timestamp()` and `transaction_timestamp()` return the same value during the first command of a transaction, but might differ during subsequent commands. `clock_timestamp()` returns the actual current time, and therefore its value changes even within a single SQL command. `timeofday()` is a historical PostgreSQL function. Like `clock_timestamp()`, it returns the actual current time, but as a formatted `text` string rather than a `timestamp with time zone` value. `now()` is a traditional PostgreSQL equivalent to `transaction_timestamp()`.

All the date/time data types also accept the special literal value `now` to specify the current date and time (again, interpreted as the transaction start time). Thus, the following three all return the same result:

```
SELECT CURRENT_TIMESTAMP;
SELECT now();
SELECT TIMESTAMP 'now';  -- incorrect for use with DEFAULT
```

Tip: You do not want to use the third form when specifying a `DEFAULT` clause while creating a table. The system will convert `now` to a `timestamp` as soon as the constant is parsed, so that when the default value is needed, the time of the table creation would be used! The first two forms will not be evaluated until the default value is used, because they are function calls. Thus they will give the desired behavior of defaulting to the time of row insertion.

9.9.5. Delaying Execution

The following functions are available to delay execution of the server process:

```
pg_sleep(seconds)
pg_sleep_for(interval)
pg_sleep_until(timestamp with time zone)
```

`pg_sleep` makes the current session's process sleep until *seconds* seconds have elapsed. *seconds* is a value of type `double precision`, so fractional-second delays can be specified. `pg_sleep_for` is a convenience function for larger sleep times specified as an `interval`. `pg_sleep_until` is a convenience function for when a specific wake-up time is desired. For example:

```
SELECT pg_sleep(1.5);
SELECT pg_sleep_for('5 minutes');
SELECT pg_sleep_until('tomorrow 03:00');
```

Note: The effective resolution of the sleep interval is platform-specific; 0.01 seconds is a common value. The sleep delay will be at least as long as specified. It might be longer depending on factors such as server load. In particular, `pg_sleep_until` is not guaranteed to wake up exactly at the specified time, but it will not wake up any earlier.

Warning

Make sure that your session does not hold more locks than necessary when calling `pg_sleep` or its variants. Otherwise other sessions might have to wait for your sleeping process, slowing down the entire system.

9.10. Enum Support Functions

For enum types (described in Section 8.7), there are several functions that allow cleaner programming without hard-coding particular values of an enum type. These are listed in Table 9-30. The examples assume an enum type created as:

```
CREATE TYPE rainbow AS ENUM ('red', 'orange', 'yellow', 'green', 'blue', 'purpl
```

Table 9-30. Enum Support Functions

Function	Description	Example	Example Result
`enum_first(anyenum)`	Returns the first value of the input enum type	`enum_first(null::rainbow)`	red
`enum_last(anyenum)`	Returns the last value of the input enum type	`enum_last(null::rainbow)`	purple
`enum_range(anyenum)`	Returns all values of the input enum type in an ordered array	`enum_range(null::rainbow)`	{red,orange,yellow,…}
`enum_range(anyenum, anyenum)`	Returns the range between the two given enum values, as an ordered array. The values must be from the same enum type. If the first parameter is null, the result will start with the first value of the enum type. If the second parameter is null, the result will end with the last value of the enum type.	`enum_range('orange', 'green'::rainbow)`	{orange,yellow,green}
		`enum_range(NULL, 'green'::rainbow)`	{red,orange,yellow,…}
		`enum_range('orange', NULL)`	{orange,yellow,green…}

Notice that except for the two-argument form of `enum_range`, these functions disregard the specific value passed to them; they care only about its declared data type. Either null or a specific value of the type can be passed, with the same result. It is more common to apply these functions to a table column or function argument than to a hardwired type name as suggested by the examples.

9.11. Geometric Functions and Operators

The geometric types `point`, `box`, `lseg`, `line`, `path`, `polygon`, and `circle` have a large set of native support functions and operators, shown in Table 9-31, Table 9-32, and Table 9-33.

> # Caution
>
> Note that the "same as" operator, ~=, represents the usual notion of equality for the `point`, `box`, `polygon`, and `circle` types. Some of these types also have an = operator, but = compares for equal *areas* only. The other scalar comparison operators (<= and so on) likewise compare areas for these types.

Table 9-31. Geometric Operators

Operator	Description	Example
+	Translation	`box '((0,0),(1,1))' + point '(2.0,0)'`
-	Translation	`box '((0,0),(1,1))' - point '(2.0,0)'`
*	Scaling/rotation	`box '((0,0),(1,1))' * point '(2.0,0)'`
/	Scaling/rotation	`box '((0,0),(2,2))' / point '(2.0,0)'`
#	Point or box of intersection	`'((1,-1),(-1,1))' # '((1,1),(-1,-1))'`
#	Number of points in path or polygon	`# '((1,0),(0,1),(-1,0))'`
@-@	Length or circumference	`@-@ path '((0,0),(1,0))'`
@@	Center	`@@ circle '((0,0),10)'`
##	Closest point to first operand on second operand	`point '(0,0)' ## lseg '((2,0),(0,2))'`
<->	Distance between	`circle '((0,0),1)' <-> circle '((5,0),1)'`
&&	Overlaps? (One point in common makes this true.)	`box '((0,0),(1,1))' && box '((0,0),(2,2))'`
<<	Is strictly left of?	`circle '((0,0),1)' << circle '((5,0),1)'`
>>	Is strictly right of?	`circle '((5,0),1)' >> circle '((0,0),1)'`
&<	Does not extend to the right of?	`box '((0,0),(1,1))' &< box '((0,0),(2,2))'`
&>	Does not extend to the left of?	`box '((0,0),(3,3))' &> box '((0,0),(2,2))'`
<<|	Is strictly below?	`box '((0,0),(3,3))' <<| box '((3,4),(5,5))'`
|>>	Is strictly above?	`box '((3,4),(5,5))' |>> box '((0,0),(3,3))'`

Operator	Description	Example
`&<|`	Does not extend above?	`box '((0,0),(1,1))' &<|` `box '((0,0),(2,2))'`
`|&>`	Does not extend below?	`box '((0,0),(3,3))' |&>` `box '((0,0),(2,2))'`
`<^`	Is below (allows touching)?	`circle '((0,0),1)' <^` `circle '((0,5),1)'`
`>^`	Is above (allows touching)?	`circle '((0,5),1)' >^` `circle '((0,0),1)'`
`?#`	Intersects?	`lseg '((-1,0),(1,0))' ?#` `box '((-2,-2),(2,2))'`
`?-`	Is horizontal?	`?- lseg '((-1,0),(1,0))'`
`?-`	Are horizontally aligned?	`point '(1,0)' ?- point '(0,0)'`
`?|`	Is vertical?	`?| lseg '((-1,0),(1,0))'`
`?|`	Are vertically aligned?	`point '(0,1)' ?| point '(0,0)'`
`?-|`	Is perpendicular?	`lseg '((0,0),(0,1))' ?-|` `lseg '((0,0),(1,0))'`
`?||`	Are parallel?	`lseg '((-1,0),(1,0))'` `?|| lseg` `'((-1,2),(1,2))'`
`@>`	Contains?	`circle '((0,0),2)' @>` `point '(1,1)'`
`<@`	Contained in or on?	`point '(1,1)' <@ circle` `'((0,0),2)'`
`~=`	Same as?	`polygon '((0,0),(1,1))'` `~= polygon` `'((1,1),(0,0))'`

Note: Before PostgreSQL 8.2, the containment operators `@>` and `<@` were respectively called `~` and `@`. These names are still available, but are deprecated and will eventually be removed.

Table 9-32. Geometric Functions

Function	Return Type	Description	Example
`area(object)`	`double precision`	area	`area(box '((0,0),(1,1))')`
`center(object)`	`point`	center	`center(box '((0,0),(1,2))')`
`diameter(circle)`	`double precision`	diameter of circle	`diameter(circle '((0,0),2.0)')`

Function	Return Type	Description	Example
height(box)	double precision	vertical size of box	height(box '((0,0),(1,1))')
isclosed(path)	boolean	a closed path?	isclosed(path '((0,0),(1,1),(2,0))')
isopen(path)	boolean	an open path?	isopen(path '[(0,0),(1,1),(2,0)]')
length(*object*)	double precision	length	length(path '((-1,0),(1,0))')
npoints(path)	int	number of points	npoints(path '[(0,0),(1,1),(2,0)]')
npoints(polygon)	int	number of points	npoints(polygon '((1,1),(0,0))')
pclose(path)	path	convert path to closed	pclose(path '[(0,0),(1,1),(2,0)]')
popen(path)	path	convert path to open	popen(path '((0,0),(1,1),(2,0))')
radius(circle)	double precision	radius of circle	radius(circle '((0,0),2.0)')
width(box)	double precision	horizontal size of box	width(box '((0,0),(1,1))')

Table 9-33. Geometric Type Conversion Functions

Function	Return Type	Description	Example
box(circle)	box	circle to box	box(circle '((0,0),2.0)')
box(point, point)	box	points to box	box(point '(0,0)', point '(1,1)')
box(polygon)	box	polygon to box	box(polygon '((0,0),(1,1),(2,0))')
circle(box)	circle	box to circle	circle(box '((0,0),(1,1))')
circle(point, double precision)	circle	center and radius to circle	circle(point '(0,0)', 2.0)
circle(polygon)	circle	polygon to circle	circle(polygon '((0,0),(1,1),(2,0))')

Function	Return Type	Description	Example
`line(point, point)`	`line`	points to line	`line(point '(-1,0)', point '(1,0)')`
`lseg(box)`	`lseg`	box diagonal to line segment	`lseg(box '((-1,0),(1,0))')`
`lseg(point, point)`	`lseg`	points to line segment	`lseg(point '(-1,0)', point '(1,0)')`
`path(polygon)`	`path`	polygon to path	`path(polygon '((0,0),(1,1),(2,0))')`
`point(double precision, double precision)`	`point`	construct point	`point(23.4, -44.5)`
`point(box)`	`point`	center of box	`point(box '((-1,0),(1,0))')`
`point(circle)`	`point`	center of circle	`point(circle '((0,0),2.0)')`
`point(lseg)`	`point`	center of line segment	`point(lseg '((-1,0),(1,0))')`
`point(polygon)`	`point`	center of polygon	`point(polygon '((0,0),(1,1),(2,0))')`
`polygon(box)`	`polygon`	box to 4-point polygon	`polygon(box '((0,0),(1,1))')`
`polygon(circle)`	`polygon`	circle to 12-point polygon	`polygon(circle '((0,0),2.0)')`
`polygon(npts, circle)`	`polygon`	circle to *npts*-point polygon	`polygon(12, circle '((0,0),2.0)')`
`polygon(path)`	`polygon`	path to polygon	`polygon(path '((0,0),(1,1),(2,0))')`

It is possible to access the two component numbers of a `point` as though the point were an array with indexes 0 and 1. For example, if `t.p` is a `point` column then SELECT p[0] FROM t retrieves the X coordinate and UPDATE t SET p[1] = ... changes the Y coordinate. In the same way, a value of type `box` or `lseg` can be treated as an array of two `point` values.

The `area` function works for the types `box`, `circle`, and `path`. The `area` function only works on the `path` data type if the points in the `path` are non-intersecting. For example, the path `'((0,0),(0,1),(2,1),(2,2),(1,2),(1,0),(0,0))'::PATH` will not work; however, the following visually identical path `'((0,0),(0,1),(1,1),(1,2),(2,2),(2,1),(1,1),(1,0),(0,0))'::PATH` will work. If the concept of an intersecting versus non-intersecting `path` is confusing, draw both of the above paths side by side on a piece of graph paper.

9.12. Network Address Functions and Operators

Table 9-34 shows the operators available for the `cidr` and `inet` types. The operators <<, <<=, >>, >>=, and && test for subnet inclusion. They consider only the network parts of the two addresses (ignoring any host part) and determine whether one network is identical to or a subnet of the other.

Table 9-34. `cidr` and `inet` Operators

Operator	Description	Example
<	is less than	`inet '192.168.1.5' < inet '192.168.1.6'`
<=	is less than or equal	`inet '192.168.1.5' <= inet '192.168.1.5'`
=	equals	`inet '192.168.1.5' = inet '192.168.1.5'`
>=	is greater or equal	`inet '192.168.1.5' >= inet '192.168.1.5'`
>	is greater than	`inet '192.168.1.5' > inet '192.168.1.4'`
<>	is not equal	`inet '192.168.1.5' <> inet '192.168.1.4'`
<<	is contained by	`inet '192.168.1.5' << inet '192.168.1/24'`
<<=	is contained by or equals	`inet '192.168.1/24' <<= inet '192.168.1/24'`
>>	contains	`inet '192.168.1/24' >> inet '192.168.1.5'`
>>=	contains or equals	`inet '192.168.1/24' >>= inet '192.168.1/24'`
&&	contains or is contained by	`inet '192.168.1/24' && inet '192.168.1.80/28'`
~	bitwise NOT	`~ inet '192.168.1.6'`
&	bitwise AND	`inet '192.168.1.6' & inet '0.0.0.255'`
|	bitwise OR	`inet '192.168.1.6' | inet '0.0.0.255'`
+	addition	`inet '192.168.1.6' + 25`
-	subtraction	`inet '192.168.1.43' - 36`
-	subtraction	`inet '192.168.1.43' - inet '192.168.1.19'`

Table 9-35 shows the functions available for use with the `cidr` and `inet` types. The `abbrev`, `host`, and `text` functions are primarily intended to offer alternative display formats.

Table 9-35. `cidr` and `inet` Functions

Function	Return Type	Description	Example	Result
`abbrev(inet)`	`text`	abbreviated display format as text	`abbrev(inet '10.1.0.0/16')`	`10.1.0.0/16`
`abbrev(cidr)`	`text`	abbreviated display format as text	`abbrev(cidr '10.1.0.0/16')`	`10.1/16`
`broadcast(inet)`	`inet`	broadcast address for network	`broadcast('192.168.1.5/24')`	`192.168.1.255/24`
`family(inet)`	`int`	extract family of address; 4 for IPv4, 6 for IPv6	`family('::1')`	`6`
`host(inet)`	`text`	extract IP address as text	`host('192.168.1.5/24')`	`192.168.1.5`
`hostmask(inet)`	`inet`	construct host mask for network	`hostmask('192.168.23.20/30')`	`0.0.0.3`
`masklen(inet)`	`int`	extract netmask length	`masklen('192.168.1.5/24')`	`24`
`netmask(inet)`	`inet`	construct netmask for network	`netmask('192.168.1.5/24')`	`255.255.255.0`
`network(inet)`	`cidr`	extract network part of address	`network('192.168.1.5/24')`	`192.168.1.0/24`
`set_masklen(inet, int)`	`inet`	set netmask length for `inet` value	`set_masklen('192.168.1.5/24', 16)`	`192.168.1.5/16`
`set_masklen(cidr, int)`	`cidr`	set netmask length for `cidr` value	`set_masklen('192.168.1.0/24'::cidr, 16)`	`192.168.0.0/16`
`text(inet)`	`text`	extract IP address and netmask length as text	`text(inet '192.168.1.5')`	`192.168.1.5/32`

Any `cidr` value can be cast to `inet` implicitly or explicitly; therefore, the functions shown above as operating on `inet` also work on `cidr` values. (Where there are separate functions for `inet` and `cidr`, it is because the behavior should be different for the two cases.) Also, it is permitted to cast an `inet` value to `cidr`. When this is done, any bits to the right of the netmask are silently zeroed to create a valid `cidr` value. In addition, you can cast a text value to `inet` or `cidr` using normal casting syntax: for example, `inet(expression)` or `colname::cidr`.

Table 9-36 shows the functions available for use with the `macaddr` type. The function `trunc(macaddr)` returns a MAC address with the last 3 bytes set to zero. This can be used to associate the remaining prefix with a manufacturer.

Table 9-36. `macaddr` Functions

Function	Return Type	Description	Example	Result

Function	Return Type	Description	Example	Result
`trunc(macaddr)`	`macaddr`	set last 3 bytes to zero	`trunc(macaddr '12:34:56:78:90:ab')`	`12:34:56:00:00:0`

The `macaddr` type also supports the standard relational operators (>, <=, etc.) for lexicographical ordering, and the bitwise arithmetic operators (~, & and |) for NOT, AND and OR.

9.13. Text Search Functions and Operators

Table 9-37, Table 9-38 and Table 9-39 summarize the functions and operators that are provided for full text searching. See Chapter 12 for a detailed explanation of PostgreSQL's text search facility.

Table 9-37. Text Search Operators

Operator	Description	Example	Result
`@@`	`tsvector` matches `tsquery` ?	`to_tsvector('fat cats ate rats') @@ to_tsquery('cat & rat')`	t
`@@@`	deprecated synonym for `@@`	`to_tsvector('fat cats ate rats') @@@ to_tsquery('cat & rat')`	t
`||`	concatenate `tsvector`s	`'a:1 b:2'::tsvector || 'c:1 d:2 b:3'::tsvector`	`'a':1 'b':2,5 'c':3 'd':4`
`&&`	AND `tsquery`s together	`'fat	rat'::tsquery && 'cat'::tsquery`	`('fat'	'rat') & 'cat'`
`||`	OR `tsquery`s together	`'fat	rat'::tsquery || 'cat'::tsquery`	`('fat' | 'rat')	'cat'`
`!!`	negate a `tsquery`	`!! 'cat'::tsquery`	`!'cat'`
`@>`	`tsquery` contains another ?	`'cat'::tsquery @> 'cat & rat'::tsquery`	f
`<@`	`tsquery` is contained in ?	`'cat'::tsquery <@ 'cat & rat'::tsquery`	t

Note: The `tsquery` containment operators consider only the lexemes listed in the two queries, ignoring the combining operators.

In addition to the operators shown in the table, the ordinary B-tree comparison operators (=, <, etc) are defined for types `tsvector` and `tsquery`. These are not very useful for text searching but allow, for example, unique indexes to be built on columns of these types.

Table 9-38. Text Search Functions

Function	Return Type	Description	Example	Result
`get_current_ts_config()`	`regconfig`	get default text search configuration	`get_current_ts_config()`	`english`
`length(tsvector)`	`integer`	number of lexemes in `tsvector`	`length('fat:2,4 cat:3 rat:5A'::tsvector)`	`3`
`numnode(tsquery)`	`integer`	number of lexemes plus operators in `tsquery`	`numnode('(fat & rat) | cat'::tsquery)`	`5`
`plainto_tsquery([ config regconfig , ] query text)`	`tsquery`	produce `tsquery` ignoring punctuation	`plainto_tsquery('english', 'The Fat Rats')`	`'fat' & 'rat'`
`querytree(query tsquery)`	`text`	get indexable part of a `tsquery`	`querytree('foo & ! bar'::tsquery)`	`'foo'`
`setweight(tsvector, "char")`	`tsvector`	assign weight to each element of `tsvector`	`setweight('fat:2,4 cat:3 rat:5B'::tsvector, 'A')`	`'cat':3A 'fat':2A,4A 'rat':5A`
`strip(tsvector)`	`tsvector`	remove positions and weights from `tsvector`	`strip('fat:2,4 cat:3 rat:5A'::tsvector)`	`'cat' 'fat' 'rat'`
`to_tsquery([ config regconfig , ] query text)`	`tsquery`	normalize words and convert to `tsquery`	`to_tsquery('english', 'The & Fat & Rats')`	`'fat' & 'rat'`
`to_tsvector([ config regconfig , ] document text)`	`tsvector`	reduce document text to `tsvector`	`to_tsvector('english', 'The Fat Rats')`	`'fat':2 'rat':3`

Function	Return Type	Description	Example	Result

`ts_headline([`
config `regconfig,`
`]` *document* `text,`
query `tsquery [,`
options `text ])`
	`text`	display a query match	`ts_headline('x`
			`y z',`
			`'z'::tsquery)`
				`x y <b>z</b>`

`ts_rank([`
weights `float4[],`
`]` *vector*
`tsvector,` *query*
`tsquery [,`
normalization
`integer ])`
	`float4`	rank document for query	`ts_rank(textsearch,`
			`query)`
				`0.818`

`ts_rank_cd([`
weights `float4[],`
`]` *vector*
`tsvector,` *query*
`tsquery [,`
normalization
`integer ])`
	`float4`	rank document for query using cover density	`ts_rank_cd('{0.1,`
			`0.2, 0.4,`
			`1.0}',`
			`textsearch,`
			`query)`
				`2.01317`

`ts_rewrite(`*query*
`tsquery,` *target*
`tsquery,`
substitute
`tsquery)`
	`tsquery`	replace target with substitute within query	`ts_rewrite('a`
			`& b'::tsquery,`
			`'a'::tsquery,`
			`'foo|bar'::tsquery)`
				`'b' & ( 'foo'`
				`| 'bar' )`

`ts_rewrite(`*query*
`tsquery,` *select*
`text)`
	`tsquery`	replace using targets and substitutes from a `SELECT` command	`SELECT`
			`ts_rewrite('a`
			`& b'::tsquery,`
			`'SELECT t,s`
			`FROM aliases')`
				`'b' & ( 'foo'`
				`| 'bar' )`

`tsvector_update_trigger()`	`trigger`	trigger function for automatic `tsvector` column update	`CREATE TRIGGER`
			`...`
			`tsvector_update_trigger(tsvcol,`
			`'pg_catalog.swedish',`
			`title, body)`	

`tsvector_update_trigger_column()`	`trigger`	trigger function for automatic `tsvector` column update	`CREATE TRIGGER`
			`...`
			`tsvector_update_trigger_column(`
			`configcol,`
			`title, body)`	

Note: All the text search functions that accept an optional `regconfig` argument will use the configuration specified by default_text_search_config when that argument is omitted.

The functions in Table 9-39 are listed separately because they are not usually used in everyday text searching operations. They are helpful for development and debugging of new text search configurations.

Table 9-39. Text Search Debugging Functions

Function	Return Type	Description	Example	Result
ts_debug([*config* regconfig,] *document* text, OUT *alias* text, OUT *description* text, OUT *token* text, OUT *dictionaries* regdictionary[], OUT *dictionary* regdictionary, OUT *lexemes* text[])	setof record	test a configuration	ts_debug('english', 'The Brightest supernovaes')	(asciiword,"Word, all ASCII",The,{eng... ...
ts_lexize(*dict* regdictionary, *token* text)	text[]	test a dictionary	ts_lexize('english_stem', 'stars')	{star}
ts_parse(*parser_name* text, *document* text, OUT *tokid* integer, OUT *token* text)	setof record	test a parser	ts_parse('default', 'foo - bar')	(1,foo) ...
ts_parse(*parser_oid* oid, *document* text, OUT *tokid* integer, OUT *token* text)	setof record	test a parser	ts_parse(3722, 'foo - bar')	(1,foo) ...
ts_token_type(*parser_name* text, OUT *tokid* integer, OUT *alias* text, OUT *description* text)	setof record	get token types defined by parser	ts_token_type('default')	(1,asciiword,"Word, all ASCII") ...
ts_token_type(*parser_oid* oid, OUT *tokid* integer, OUT *alias* text, OUT *description* text)	setof record	get token types defined by parser	ts_token_type(3722)	(1,asciiword,"Word, all ASCII") ...

Function	Return Type	Description	Example	Result
`ts_stat(sqlquery text, [ weights text, ] OUT word text, OUT ndoc integer, OUT nentry integer)`	`setof record`	get statistics of a `tsvector` column	`ts_stat('SELECT vector from apod')`	`(foo,10,15)` `...`

9.14. XML Functions

The functions and function-like expressions described in this section operate on values of type `xml`. Check Section 8.13 for information about the `xml` type. The function-like expressions `xmlparse` and `xmlserialize` for converting to and from type `xml` are not repeated here. Use of most of these functions requires the installation to have been built with `configure --with-libxml`.

9.14.1. Producing XML Content

A set of functions and function-like expressions are available for producing XML content from SQL data. As such, they are particularly suitable for formatting query results into XML documents for processing in client applications.

9.14.1.1. **xmlcomment**

`xmlcomment(text)`

The function `xmlcomment` creates an XML value containing an XML comment with the specified text as content. The text cannot contain "--" or end with a "-" so that the resulting construct is a valid XML comment. If the argument is null, the result is null.

Example:

```
SELECT xmlcomment('hello');

  xmlcomment
--------------
 <!--hello-->
```

9.14.1.2. **xmlconcat**

`xmlconcat(xml[, ...])`

The function `xmlconcat` concatenates a list of individual XML values to create a single value containing an XML content fragment. Null values are omitted; the result is only null if there are no nonnull arguments.

Example:

```
SELECT xmlconcat('<abc/>', '<bar>foo</bar>');

     xmlconcat
----------------------
 <abc/><bar>foo</bar>
```

XML declarations, if present, are combined as follows. If all argument values have the same XML version declaration, that version is used in the result, else no version is used. If all argument values have the standalone declaration value "yes", then that value is used in the result. If all argument values have a standalone declaration value and at least one is "no", then that is used in the result. Else the result will have no standalone declaration. If the result is determined to require a standalone declaration but no version declaration, a version declaration with version 1.0 will be used because XML requires an XML declaration to contain a version declaration. Encoding declarations are ignored and removed in all cases.

Example:

```
SELECT xmlconcat('<?xml version="1.1"?><foo/>', '<?xml version="1.1" standalone

          xmlconcat
-----------------------------------
 <?xml version="1.1"?><foo/><bar/>
```

9.14.1.3. `xmlelement`

```
xmlelement(name name [, xmlattributes(value [AS attname] [, ... ])] [, content, ...
```

The `xmlelement` expression produces an XML element with the given name, attributes, and content.

Examples:

```
SELECT xmlelement(name foo);

 xmlelement
------------
 <foo/>

SELECT xmlelement(name foo, xmlattributes('xyz' as bar));

    xmlelement
------------------
 <foo bar="xyz"/>

SELECT xmlelement(name foo, xmlattributes(current_date as bar), 'cont', 'ent');

           xmlelement
-----------------------------------
 <foo bar="2007-01-26">content</foo>
```

Element and attribute names that are not valid XML names are escaped by replacing the offending characters by the sequence _x*HHHH*_, where *HHHH* is the character's Unicode codepoint in hexadecimal notation. For example:

```
SELECT xmlelement(name "foo$bar", xmlattributes('xyz' as "a&b"));

          xmlelement
----------------------------------
 <foo_x0024_bar a_x0026_b="xyz"/>
```

An explicit attribute name need not be specified if the attribute value is a column reference, in which case the column's name will be used as the attribute name by default. In other cases, the attribute must be given an explicit name. So this example is valid:

```
CREATE TABLE test (a xml, b xml);
SELECT xmlelement(name test, xmlattributes(a, b)) FROM test;
```

But these are not:

```
SELECT xmlelement(name test, xmlattributes('constant'), a, b) FROM test;
SELECT xmlelement(name test, xmlattributes(func(a, b))) FROM test;
```

Element content, if specified, will be formatted according to its data type. If the content is itself of type xml, complex XML documents can be constructed. For example:

```
SELECT xmlelement(name foo, xmlattributes('xyz' as bar),
                            xmlelement(name abc),
                            xmlcomment('test'),
                            xmlelement(name xyz));

                 xmlelement
----------------------------------------------
 <foo bar="xyz"><abc/><!--test--><xyz/></foo>
```

Content of other types will be formatted into valid XML character data. This means in particular that the characters <, >, and & will be converted to entities. Binary data (data type bytea) will be represented in base64 or hex encoding, depending on the setting of the configuration parameter xmlbinary. The particular behavior for individual data types is expected to evolve in order to align the SQL and PostgreSQL data types with the XML Schema specification, at which point a more precise description will appear.

9.14.1.4. xmlforest

```
xmlforest(content [AS name] [, ...])
```

The xmlforest expression produces an XML forest (sequence) of elements using the given names and content.

Examples:

```
SELECT xmlforest('abc' AS foo, 123 AS bar);

        xmlforest
-----------------------------
 <foo>abc</foo><bar>123</bar>


SELECT xmlforest(table_name, column_name)
FROM information_schema.columns
WHERE table_schema = 'pg_catalog';

                                        xmlforest
-------------------------------------------------------------------------------
 <table_name>pg_authid</table_name><column_name>rolname</column_name>
 <table_name>pg_authid</table_name><column_name>rolsuper</column_name>
 ...
```

As seen in the second example, the element name can be omitted if the content value is a column reference, in which case the column name is used by default. Otherwise, a name must be specified.

Element names that are not valid XML names are escaped as shown for `xmlelement` above. Similarly, content data is escaped to make valid XML content, unless it is already of type `xml`.

Note that XML forests are not valid XML documents if they consist of more than one element, so it might be useful to wrap `xmlforest` expressions in `xmlelement`.

9.14.1.5. `xmlpi`

```
xmlpi(name target [, content])
```

The `xmlpi` expression creates an XML processing instruction. The content, if present, must not contain the character sequence `?>`.

Example:

```
SELECT xmlpi(name php, 'echo "hello world";');

          xmlpi
-----------------------------
 <?php echo "hello world";?>
```

9.14.1.6. `xmlroot`

```
xmlroot(xml, version text | no value [, standalone yes|no|no value])
```

The `xmlroot` expression alters the properties of the root node of an XML value. If a version is specified, it replaces the value in the root node's version declaration; if a standalone setting is specified, it replaces the value in the root node's standalone declaration.

```
SELECT xmlroot(xmlparse(document '<?xml version="1.1"?><content>abc</content>')
               version '1.0', standalone yes);

                  xmlroot
----------------------------------------
 <?xml version="1.0" standalone="yes"?>
 <content>abc</content>
```

9.14.1.7. `xmlagg`

`xmlagg(xml)`

The function `xmlagg` is, unlike the other functions described here, an aggregate function. It concatenates the input values to the aggregate function call, much like `xmlconcat` does, except that concatenation occurs across rows rather than across expressions in a single row. See Section 9.20 for additional information about aggregate functions.

Example:

```
CREATE TABLE test (y int, x xml);
INSERT INTO test VALUES (1, '<foo>abc</foo>');
INSERT INTO test VALUES (2, '<bar/>');
SELECT xmlagg(x) FROM test;
      xmlagg
----------------------
 <foo>abc</foo><bar/>
```

To determine the order of the concatenation, an `ORDER BY` clause may be added to the aggregate call as described in Section 4.2.7. For example:

```
SELECT xmlagg(x ORDER BY y DESC) FROM test;
      xmlagg
----------------------
 <bar/><foo>abc</foo>
```

The following non-standard approach used to be recommended in previous versions, and may still be useful in specific cases:

```
SELECT xmlagg(x) FROM (SELECT * FROM test ORDER BY y DESC) AS tab;
      xmlagg
----------------------
 <bar/><foo>abc</foo>
```

9.14.2. XML Predicates

The expressions described in this section check properties of `xml` values.

9.14.2.1. IS DOCUMENT

xml IS DOCUMENT

The expression IS DOCUMENT returns true if the argument XML value is a proper XML document, false if it is not (that is, it is a content fragment), or null if the argument is null. See Section 8.13 about the difference between documents and content fragments.

9.14.2.2. XMLEXISTS

XMLEXISTS(*text* PASSING [BY REF] *xml* [BY REF])

The function `xmlexists` returns true if the XPath expression in the first argument returns any nodes, and false otherwise. (If either argument is null, the result is null.)

Example:

```
SELECT xmlexists('//town[text() = "Toronto"]' PASSING BY REF '<towns><town>Torc

 xmlexists
-----------
 t
(1 row)
```

The BY REF clauses have no effect in PostgreSQL, but are allowed for SQL conformance and compatibility with other implementations. Per SQL standard, the first BY REF is required, the second is optional. Also note that the SQL standard specifies the `xmlexists` construct to take an XQuery expression as first argument, but PostgreSQL currently only supports XPath, which is a subset of XQuery.

9.14.2.3. xml_is_well_formed

```
xml_is_well_formed(text)
xml_is_well_formed_document(text)
xml_is_well_formed_content(text)
```

These functions check whether a `text` string is well-formed XML, returning a Boolean result. `xml_is_well_formed_document` checks for a well-formed document, while `xml_is_well_formed_content` checks for well-formed content. `xml_is_well_formed` does the former if the xmloption configuration parameter is set to DOCUMENT, or the latter if it is set to CONTENT.

This means that `xml_is_well_formed` is useful for seeing whether a simple cast to type `xml` will succeed, whereas the other two functions are useful for seeing whether the corresponding variants of `XMLPARSE` will succeed.

Examples:

```
SET xmloption TO DOCUMENT;
SELECT xml_is_well_formed('<>');
 xml_is_well_formed
--------------------
 f
(1 row)

SELECT xml_is_well_formed('<abc/>');
 xml_is_well_formed
--------------------
 t
(1 row)

SET xmloption TO CONTENT;
SELECT xml_is_well_formed('abc');
 xml_is_well_formed
--------------------
 t
(1 row)

SELECT xml_is_well_formed_document('<pg:foo xmlns:pg="http://postgresql.org/stu
 xml_is_well_formed_document
-----------------------------
 t
(1 row)

SELECT xml_is_well_formed_document('<pg:foo xmlns:pg="http://postgresql.org/stu
 xml_is_well_formed_document
-----------------------------
 f
(1 row)
```

The last example shows that the checks include whether namespaces are correctly matched.

9.14.3. Processing XML

To process values of data type `xml`, PostgreSQL offers the functions `xpath` and `xpath_exists`, which evaluate XPath 1.0 expressions.

```
xpath(xpath, xml [, nsarray])
```

The function `xpath` evaluates the XPath expression `xpath` (a `text` value) against the XML value `xml`. It returns an array of XML values corresponding to the node set produced by the XPath expression. If the XPath expression returns a scalar value rather than a node set, a single-element array is returned.

The second argument must be a well formed XML document. In particular, it must have a single root node element.

The optional third argument of the function is an array of namespace mappings. This array should be a two-dimensional `text` array with the length of the second axis being equal to 2 (i.e., it should be an array of arrays, each of which consists of exactly 2 elements). The first element of each array entry is the namespace name (alias), the second the namespace URI. It is not required that aliases provided in this array be the same as those being used in the XML document itself (in other words, both in the XML document and in the `xpath` function context, aliases are *local*).

Example:

```
SELECT xpath('/my:a/text()', '<my:a xmlns:my="http://example.com">test</my:a>',
             ARRAY[ARRAY['my', 'http://example.com']]);

 xpath
--------
 {test}
(1 row)
```

To deal with default (anonymous) namespaces, do something like this:

```
SELECT xpath('//mydefns:b/text()', '<a xmlns="http://example.com"><b>test</b></
             ARRAY[ARRAY['mydefns', 'http://example.com']]);

 xpath
--------
 {test}
(1 row)
```

`xpath_exists(xpath, xml [, nsarray])`

The function `xpath_exists` is a specialized form of the `xpath` function. Instead of returning the individual XML values that satisfy the XPath, this function returns a Boolean indicating whether the query was satisfied or not. This function is equivalent to the standard `XMLEXISTS` predicate, except that it also offers support for a namespace mapping argument.

Example:

```
SELECT xpath_exists('/my:a/text()', '<my:a xmlns:my="http://example.com">test</
                    ARRAY[ARRAY['my', 'http://example.com']]);

 xpath_exists
--------------
 t
(1 row)
```

9.14.4. Mapping Tables to XML

The following functions map the contents of relational tables to XML values. They can be thought of as XML export functionality:

```
table_to_xml(tbl regclass, nulls boolean, tableforest boolean, targetns text)
query_to_xml(query text, nulls boolean, tableforest boolean, targetns text)
cursor_to_xml(cursor refcursor, count int, nulls boolean,
              tableforest boolean, targetns text)
```

The return type of each function is `xml`.

`table_to_xml` maps the content of the named table, passed as parameter `tbl`. The `regclass` type accepts strings identifying tables using the usual notation, including optional schema qualifications and double quotes. `query_to_xml` executes the query whose text is passed as parameter `query` and maps the result set. `cursor_to_xml` fetches the indicated number of rows from the cursor specified by the parameter `cursor`. This variant is recommended if large tables have to be mapped, because the result value is built up in memory by each function.

If `tableforest` is false, then the resulting XML document looks like this:

```
<tablename>
  <row>
    <columnname1>data</columnname1>
    <columnname2>data</columnname2>
  </row>

  <row>
    ...
  </row>

  ...
</tablename>
```

If `tableforest` is true, the result is an XML content fragment that looks like this:

```
<tablename>
  <columnname1>data</columnname1>
  <columnname2>data</columnname2>
</tablename>

<tablename>
  ...
</tablename>

...
```

If no table name is available, that is, when mapping a query or a cursor, the string `table` is used in the first format, `row` in the second format.

The choice between these formats is up to the user. The first format is a proper XML document, which will be important in many applications. The second format tends to be more useful in the `cursor_to_xml` function if the result values are to be reassembled into one document later on. The functions for producing XML content discussed above, in particular `xmlelement`, can be used to alter the results to taste.

The data values are mapped in the same way as described for the function `xmlelement` above.

The parameter `nulls` determines whether null values should be included in the output. If true, null values in columns are represented as:

```
<columnname xsi:nil="true"/>
```

where `xsi` is the XML namespace prefix for XML Schema Instance. An appropriate namespace declaration will be added to the result value. If false, columns containing null values are simply omitted from the output.

The parameter `targetns` specifies the desired XML namespace of the result. If no particular namespace is wanted, an empty string should be passed.

The following functions return XML Schema documents describing the mappings performed by the corresponding functions above:

```
table_to_xmlschema(tbl regclass, nulls boolean, tableforest boolean, targetns t
query_to_xmlschema(query text, nulls boolean, tableforest boolean, targetns tex
cursor_to_xmlschema(cursor refcursor, nulls boolean, tableforest boolean, targe
```

It is essential that the same parameters are passed in order to obtain matching XML data mappings and XML Schema documents.

The following functions produce XML data mappings and the corresponding XML Schema in one document (or forest), linked together. They can be useful where self-contained and self-describing results are wanted:

```
table_to_xml_and_xmlschema(tbl regclass, nulls boolean, tableforest boolean, ta
query_to_xml_and_xmlschema(query text, nulls boolean, tableforest boolean, targ
```

In addition, the following functions are available to produce analogous mappings of entire schemas or the entire current database:

```
schema_to_xml(schema name, nulls boolean, tableforest boolean, targetns text)
schema_to_xmlschema(schema name, nulls boolean, tableforest boolean, targetns t
schema_to_xml_and_xmlschema(schema name, nulls boolean, tableforest boolean, ta
```

```
database_to_xml(nulls boolean, tableforest boolean, targetns text)
database_to_xmlschema(nulls boolean, tableforest boolean, targetns text)
database_to_xml_and_xmlschema(nulls boolean, tableforest boolean, targetns text
```

Note that these potentially produce a lot of data, which needs to be built up in memory. When requesting content mappings of large schemas or databases, it might be worthwhile to consider mapping the tables separately instead, possibly even through a cursor.

The result of a schema content mapping looks like this:

```
<schemaname>

table1-mapping

table2-mapping
```

```
...
```

```
</schemaname>
```

where the format of a table mapping depends on the `tableforest` parameter as explained above.

The result of a database content mapping looks like this:

```
<dbname>

<schema1name>
  ...
</schema1name>

<schema2name>
  ...
</schema2name>

...

</dbname>
```

where the schema mapping is as above.

As an example of using the output produced by these functions, Figure 9-1 shows an XSLT stylesheet that converts the output of `table_to_xml_and_xmlschema` to an HTML document containing a tabular rendition of the table data. In a similar manner, the results from these functions can be converted into other XML-based formats.

Figure 9-1. XSLT Stylesheet for Converting SQL/XML Output to HTML

```
<?xml version="1.0"?>
<xsl:stylesheet version="1.0"
    xmlns:xsl="http://www.w3.org/1999/XSL/Transform"
    xmlns:xsd="http://www.w3.org/2001/XMLSchema"
    xmlns="http://www.w3.org/1999/xhtml"
>

  <xsl:output method="xml"
      doctype-system="http://www.w3.org/TR/xhtml1/DTD/xhtml1-strict.dtd"
      doctype-public="-//W3C/DTD XHTML 1.0 Strict//EN"
      indent="yes"/>

  <xsl:template match="/*">
    <xsl:variable name="schema" select="//xsd:schema"/>
    <xsl:variable name="tabletypename"
                select="$schema/xsd:element[@name=name(current())]/@type"/>
    <xsl:variable name="rowtypename"
                select="$schema/xsd:complexType[@name=$tabletypename]/xsd:seq

    <html>
      <head>
        <title><xsl:value-of select="name(current())"/></title>
```

```
        </head>
        <body>
          <table>
            <tr>
              <xsl:for-each select="$schema/xsd:complexType[@name=$rowtypename]/x
                <th><xsl:value-of select="."/></th>
              </xsl:for-each>
            </tr>

            <xsl:for-each select="row">
              <tr>
                <xsl:for-each select="*">
                  <td><xsl:value-of select="."/></td>
                </xsl:for-each>
              </tr>
            </xsl:for-each>
          </table>
        </body>
      </html>
    </xsl:template>

</xsl:stylesheet>
```

9.15. JSON Functions and Operators

Table 9-40 shows the operators that are available for use with the two JSON data types (see Section 8.14).

Table 9-40. `json` and `jsonb` Operators

Operator	Right Operand Type	Description	Example	Example Result
->	int	Get JSON array element (indexed from zero)	`'[{"a":"foo"},{"b":"bar"},{"c":"baz"}]'::json->2`	`{"c":"baz"}`
->	text	Get JSON object field by key	`'{"a": {"b":"foo"}}'::json->'a'`	`{"b":"foo"}`
->>	int	Get JSON array element as `text`	`'[1,2,3]'::json->>2`	`3`
->>	text	Get JSON object field as `text`	`'{"a":1,"b":2}'::json->>'b'`	`2`
#>	text[]	Get JSON object at specified path	`'{"a": {"b":{"c": "foo"}}}'::json#>'{a,b}'`	`{"c": "foo"}`

Operator	Right Operand Type	Description	Example	Example Result
`#>>`	`text[]`	Get JSON object at specified path as `text`	`'{"a":[1,2,3],"b":[4,5,6]}'::js`	

Note: There are parallel variants of these operators for both the `json` and `jsonb` types. The field/element/path extraction operators return the same type as their left-hand input (either `json` or `jsonb`), except for those specified as returning `text`, which coerce the value to text. The field/element/path extraction operators return NULL, rather than failing, if the JSON input does not have the right structure to match the request; for example if no such element exists.

The standard comparison operators shown in Table 9-1 are available for `jsonb`, but not for `json`. They follow the ordering rules for B-tree operations outlined at Section 8.14.4.

Some further operators also exist only for `jsonb`, as shown in Table 9-41. Many of these operators can be indexed by `jsonb` operator classes. For a full description of `jsonb` containment and existence semantics, see Section 8.14.3. Section 8.14.4 describes how these operators can be used to effectively index `jsonb` data.

Table 9-41. Additional `jsonb` Operators

Operator	Right Operand Type	Description	Example
`@>`	`jsonb`	Does the left JSON value contain within it the right value?	`'{"a":1, "b":2}'::jsonb @> '{"b":2}'::jsonb`
`<@`	`jsonb`	Is the left JSON value contained within the right value?	`'{"b":2}'::jsonb <@ '{"a":1, "b":2}'::jsonb`
`?`	`text`	Does the key/element *string* exist within the JSON value?	`'{"a":1, "b":2}'::jsonb ? 'b'`
`?|`	`text[]`	Do any of these key/element *strings* exist?	`'{"a":1, "b":2, "c":3}'::jsonb ?| array['b', 'c']`
`?&`	`text[]`	Do all of these key/element *strings* exist?	`'["a", "b"]'::jsonb ?& array['a', 'b']`

Table 9-42 shows the functions that are available for creating `json` values. (Currently, there are no equivalent functions for `jsonb`, but you can cast the result of one of these functions to `jsonb`.)

Table 9-42. JSON Creation Functions

Function	Description	Example	Example Result

Function	Description	Example	Example Result
`to_json(anyelement)`	Returns the value as JSON. Arrays and composites are converted (recursively) to arrays and objects; otherwise, if there is a cast from the type to `json`, the cast function will be used to perform the conversion; otherwise, a JSON scalar value is produced. For any scalar type other than a number, a Boolean, or a null value, the text representation will be used, properly quoted and escaped so that it is a valid JSON string.	`to_json('Fred said "Hi."'::text)`	`"Fred said \"Hi.\""`
`array_to_json(anyarray [, pretty_bool])`	Returns the array as a JSON array. A PostgreSQL multidimensional array becomes a JSON array of arrays. Line feeds will be added between dimension-1 elements if `pretty_bool` is true.	`array_to_json('{{1,5},{99,100}}'::int[])`	`[[1,5],[99,100]]`
`row_to_json(record [, pretty_bool])`	Returns the row as a JSON object. Line feeds will be added between level-1 elements if `pretty_bool` is true.	`row_to_json(row(1,'foo'))`	`{"f1":1,"f2":"foo"}`
`json_build_array(VARIADIC "any")`	Builds a possibly-heterogeneously-typed JSON array out of a variadic argument list.	`json_build_array(1,2,'3',4,5)`	`[1, 2, "3", 4, 5]`
`json_build_object(VARIADIC "any")`	Builds a JSON object out of a variadic argument list. By convention, the argument list consists of alternating keys and values.	`json_build_object('foo',1,'bar',2)`	`{"foo":1,"bar":2}`

Function	Description	Example	Example Result
`json_object(text[])`	Builds a JSON object out of a text array. The array must have either exactly one dimension with an even number of members, in which case they are taken as alternating key/value pairs, or two dimensions such that each inner array has exactly two elements, which are taken as a key/value pair.	`json_object('{a, 1, b, "def", c, 3.5}')` `json_object('{{a, 1},{b, "def"},{c, 3.5}}')`	`{"a": "1", "b": "def", "c": "3.5"}`
`json_object(keys text[], values text[])`	This form of `json_object` takes keys and values pairwise from two separate arrays. In all other respects it is identical to the one-argument form.	`json_object('{a, b}', '{1,2}')`	`{"a": "1", "b": "2"}`

> **Note:** `array_to_json` and `row_to_json` have the same behavior as `to_json` except for offering a pretty-printing option. The behavior described for `to_json` likewise applies to each individual value converted by the other JSON creation functions.

> **Note:** The hstore extension has a cast from `hstore` to `json`, so that `hstore` values converted via the JSON creation functions will be represented as JSON objects, not as primitive string values.

Table 9-43 shows the functions that are available for processing `json` and `jsonb` values.

Table 9-43. JSON Processing Functions

Function	Return Type	Description	Example	Example Result
`json_array_length(json)` `jsonb_array_length(jsonb)`	int	Returns the number of elements in the outermost JSON array.	`json_array_length('[1,2,3,{"f1"`	5

Function	Return Type	Description	Example	Example Result
`json_each(json)` `jsonb_each(jsonb)`	`setof key text, value json` `setof key text, value jsonb`	Expands the outermost JSON object into a set of key/value pairs.	`select * from json_each('{"a":"foo", "b":"bar"}')`	key | value ----+------- a | "foo" b | "bar"
`json_each_text(json)` `jsonb_each_text(jsonb)`	`setof key text, value text`	Expands the outermost JSON object into a set of key/value pairs. The returned values will be of type `text`.	`select * from json_each_text('{"a":"foo", "b":"bar"}')`	key | value ----+------- a | foo b | bar
`json_extract_path(from_json json, VARIADIC path_elems text[])` `jsonb_extract_path(from_json jsonb, VARIADIC path_elems text[])`	`json` `jsonb`	Returns JSON value pointed to by *path_elems* (equivalent to `#>` operator).	`json_extract_path('{"f5":"f29","f6":"f3"}')`	
`json_extract_path_text(from_json json, VARIADIC path_elems text[])` `jsonb_extract_path_text(from_json jsonb, VARIADIC path_elems text[])`	`text`	Returns JSON value pointed to by *path_elems* as `text` (equivalent to `#>>` operator).	`json_extract_path_text('{"f2":{...}}', 'f6')`	
`json_object_keys(json)` `jsonb_object_keys(jsonb)`	`setof text`	Returns set of keys in the outermost JSON object.	`json_object_keys('{"f1":"abc","f2":{"f3":"a", "f4":"b"}}')`	json_object_keys --------------- f1 f2

Function	Return Type	Description	Example	Example Result
`json_populate_record(base anyelement, from_json json)` `jsonb_populate_record(base anyelement, from_json jsonb)`	`anyelement`	Expands the object in *from_json* to a row whose columns match the record type defined by *base* (see note below).	`select * from json_populate_record(null::myro '{"a":1,"b":2}')`	a | b ---+---
`json_populate_recordset(base anyelement, from_json json)` `jsonb_populate_recordset(base anyelement, from_json jsonb)`	`setof anyelement`	Expands the outermost array of objects in *from_json* to a set of rows whose columns match the record type defined by *base* (see note below).	`select * from json_populate_recordset3(null::m '[{"a":1,"b":2},{"a":3,"b":4}]'`	a | b ---+---
`json_array_elements(json)` `jsonb_array_elements(jsonb)`	`setof json` `setof jsonb`	Expands a JSON array to a set of JSON values.	`select * from json_array_elements('[1,true, [2,false]]')`	value ---------- 1 true [2,false]
`json_array_elements_text(json)` `jsonb_array_elements_text(jsonb)`	`setof text`	Expands a JSON array to a set of text values.	`select * from json_array_elements_text('["foo "bar"]')`	value ------- foo bar
`json_typeof(json)` `jsonb_typeof(jsonb)`	`text`	Returns the type of the outermost JSON value as a text string. Possible types are `object`, `array`, `string`, `number`, `boolean`, and `null`.	`json_typeof('-123.4')`	number

Function	Return Type	Description	Example	Example Result
`json_to_record(json)` `jsonb_to_record(jsonb)`	`record`	Builds an arbitrary record from a JSON object (see note below). As with all functions returning `record`, the caller must explicitly define the structure of the record with an `AS` clause.	`select * from json_to_record('{"a":1,"b":[1,2` `as x(a int, b text, d text)`	`a | b | c` `1 | [1,2,3] |`
`json_to_recordset(json)` `jsonb_to_recordset(jsonb)`	`setof record`	Builds an arbitrary set of records from a JSON array of objects (see note below). As with all functions returning `record`, the caller must explicitly define the structure of the record with an `AS` clause.	`select * from json_to_recordset('[{"a":1,"b":` `as x(a int, b text);`	`a | b` `1 | foo 2 |`

Note: Many of these functions and operators will convert Unicode escapes in JSON strings to the appropriate single character. This is a non-issue if the input is type `jsonb`, because the conversion was already done; but for `json` input, this may result in throwing an error, as noted in Section 8.14.

Note: In `json_populate_record`, `json_populate_recordset`, `json_to_record` and `json_to_recordset`, type coercion from the JSON is "best effort" and may not result in desired values for some types. JSON keys are matched to identical column names in the target row type. JSON fields that do not appear in the target row type will be omitted from the output, and target columns that do not match any JSON field will simply be NULL.

Note: The `json_typeof` function's `null` return value should not be confused with a SQL NULL. While calling `json_typeof('null'::json)` will return `null`, calling `json_typeof(NULL::json)` will return a SQL NULL.

See also Section 9.20 for the aggregate function `json_agg` which aggregates record values as JSON, and the aggregate function `json_object_agg` which aggregates pairs of values into a JSON object.

9.16. Sequence Manipulation Functions

This section describes functions for operating on *sequence objects*, also called sequence generators or just sequences. Sequence objects are special single-row tables created with CREATE SEQUENCE. Sequence objects are commonly used to generate unique identifiers for rows of a table. The sequence functions, listed in Table 9-44, provide simple, multiuser-safe methods for obtaining successive sequence values from sequence objects.

Table 9-44. Sequence Functions

Function	Return Type	Description
`currval(regclass)`	`bigint`	Return value most recently obtained with `nextval` for specified sequence
`lastval()`	`bigint`	Return value most recently obtained with `nextval` for any sequence
`nextval(regclass)`	`bigint`	Advance sequence and return new value
`setval(regclass, bigint)`	`bigint`	Set sequence's current value
`setval(regclass, bigint, boolean)`	`bigint`	Set sequence's current value and `is_called` flag

The sequence to be operated on by a sequence function is specified by a `regclass` argument, which is simply the OID of the sequence in the `pg_class` system catalog. You do not have to look up the OID by hand, however, since the `regclass` data type's input converter will do the work for you. Just write the sequence name enclosed in single quotes so that it looks like a literal constant. For compatibility with the handling of ordinary SQL names, the string will be converted to lower case unless it contains double quotes around the sequence name. Thus:

```
nextval('foo')        operates on sequence foo
nextval('FOO')        operates on sequence foo
nextval('"Foo"')      operates on sequence Foo
```

The sequence name can be schema-qualified if necessary:

```
nextval('myschema.foo')     operates on myschema.foo
nextval('"myschema".foo')   same as above
nextval('foo')              searches search path for foo
```

See Section 8.18 for more information about `regclass`.

> **Note:** Before PostgreSQL 8.1, the arguments of the sequence functions were of type `text`, not `regclass`, and the above-described conversion from a text string to an OID value would happen at run time during each call. For backward compatibility, this facility still exists, but internally it is now handled as an implicit coercion from `text` to `regclass` before the function is invoked.
>
> When you write the argument of a sequence function as an unadorned literal string, it becomes a constant of type `regclass`. Since this is really just an OID, it will track the originally identified sequence despite later renaming, schema reassignment, etc. This "early binding" behavior is usually desirable

for sequence references in column defaults and views. But sometimes you might want "late binding" where the sequence reference is resolved at run time. To get late-binding behavior, force the constant to be stored as a `text` constant instead of `regclass`:

```
nextval('foo'::text)        foo is looked up at runtime
```

Note that late binding was the only behavior supported in PostgreSQL releases before 8.1, so you might need to do this to preserve the semantics of old applications.

Of course, the argument of a sequence function can be an expression as well as a constant. If it is a text expression then the implicit coercion will result in a run-time lookup.

The available sequence functions are:

`nextval`

Advance the sequence object to its next value and return that value. This is done atomically: even if multiple sessions execute `nextval` concurrently, each will safely receive a distinct sequence value.

If a sequence object has been created with default parameters, successive `nextval` calls will return successive values beginning with 1. Other behaviors can be obtained by using special parameters in the CREATE SEQUENCE command; see its command reference page for more information.

> **Important:** To avoid blocking concurrent transactions that obtain numbers from the same sequence, a `nextval` operation is never rolled back; that is, once a value has been fetched it is considered used, even if the transaction that did the `nextval` later aborts. This means that aborted transactions might leave unused "holes" in the sequence of assigned values.

`currval`

Return the value most recently obtained by `nextval` for this sequence in the current session. (An error is reported if `nextval` has never been called for this sequence in this session.) Because this is returning a session-local value, it gives a predictable answer whether or not other sessions have executed `nextval` since the current session did.

`lastval`

Return the value most recently returned by `nextval` in the current session. This function is identical to `currval`, except that instead of taking the sequence name as an argument it fetches the value of the last sequence used by `nextval` in the current session. It is an error to call `lastval` if `nextval` has not yet been called in the current session.

`setval`

Reset the sequence object's counter value. The two-parameter form sets the sequence's `last_value` field to the specified value and sets its `is_called` field to `true`, meaning that the next `nextval` will advance the sequence before returning a value. The value reported by `currval` is also set to the specified value. In the three-parameter form, `is_called` can be set to either `true` or `false`. `true` has the same effect as the two-parameter form. If it is set to `false`, the next `nextval` will return exactly the specified value, and sequence advancement commences with the following `nextval`. Furthermore, the value reported by `currval` is not changed in this case. For example,

```
SELECT setval('foo', 42);          Next nextval will return 43
SELECT setval('foo', 42, true);    Same as above
SELECT setval('foo', 42, false);   Next nextval will return 42
```

The result returned by `setval` is just the value of its second argument.

> **Important:** Because sequences are non-transactional, changes made by `setval` are not undone if the transaction rolls back.

9.17. Conditional Expressions

This section describes the SQL-compliant conditional expressions available in PostgreSQL.

> **Tip:** If your needs go beyond the capabilities of these conditional expressions, you might want to consider writing a stored procedure in a more expressive programming language.

9.17.1. CASE

The SQL `CASE` expression is a generic conditional expression, similar to if/else statements in other programming languages:

```
CASE WHEN condition THEN result
     [WHEN ...]
     [ELSE result]
END
```

`CASE` clauses can be used wherever an expression is valid. Each `condition` is an expression that returns a `boolean` result. If the condition's result is true, the value of the `CASE` expression is the `result` that follows the condition, and the remainder of the `CASE` expression is not processed. If the condition's result is not true, any subsequent `WHEN` clauses are examined in the same manner. If no `WHEN condition` yields true, the value of the `CASE` expression is the `result` of the `ELSE` clause. If the `ELSE` clause is omitted and no condition is true, the result is null.

An example:

```
SELECT * FROM test;

 a
---
 1
 2
```

3

```
SELECT a,
       CASE WHEN a=1 THEN 'one'
            WHEN a=2 THEN 'two'
            ELSE 'other'
       END
    FROM test;

 a | case
---+-------
 1 | one
 2 | two
 3 | other
```

The data types of all the *result* expressions must be convertible to a single output type. See Section 10.5 for more details.

There is a "simple" form of CASE expression that is a variant of the general form above:

```
CASE expression
    WHEN value THEN result
    [WHEN ...]
    [ELSE result]
END
```

The first *expression* is computed, then compared to each of the *value* expressions in the WHEN clauses until one is found that is equal to it. If no match is found, the *result* of the ELSE clause (or a null value) is returned. This is similar to the switch statement in C.

The example above can be written using the simple CASE syntax:

```
SELECT a,
       CASE a WHEN 1 THEN 'one'
              WHEN 2 THEN 'two'
              ELSE 'other'
       END
    FROM test;

 a | case
---+-------
 1 | one
 2 | two
 3 | other
```

A CASE expression does not evaluate any subexpressions that are not needed to determine the result. For example, this is a possible way of avoiding a division-by-zero failure:

```
SELECT ... WHERE CASE WHEN x <> 0 THEN y/x > 1.5 ELSE false END;
```

Note: As described in Section 4.2.14, there are various situations in which subexpressions of an expression are evaluated at different times, so that the principle that "CASE evaluates only necessary subexpressions" is not ironclad. For example a constant 1/0 subexpression will usually result in a division-by-zero failure at planning time, even if it's within a CASE arm that would never be entered at run time.

9.17.2. COALESCE

```
COALESCE(value [, ...])
```

The COALESCE function returns the first of its arguments that is not null. Null is returned only if all arguments are null. It is often used to substitute a default value for null values when data is retrieved for display, for example:

```
SELECT COALESCE(description, short_description, '(none)') ...
```

This returns description if it is not null, otherwise short_description if it is not null, otherwise (none).

Like a CASE expression, COALESCE only evaluates the arguments that are needed to determine the result; that is, arguments to the right of the first non-null argument are not evaluated. This SQL-standard function provides capabilities similar to NVL and IFNULL, which are used in some other database systems.

9.17.3. NULLIF

```
NULLIF(value1, value2)
```

The NULLIF function returns a null value if value1 equals value2; otherwise it returns value1. This can be used to perform the inverse operation of the COALESCE example given above:

```
SELECT NULLIF(value, '(none)') ...
```

In this example, if value is (none), null is returned, otherwise the value of value is returned.

9.17.4. GREATEST and LEAST

```
GREATEST(value [, ...])
```

```
LEAST(value [, ...])
```

The GREATEST and LEAST functions select the largest or smallest value from a list of any number of expressions. The expressions must all be convertible to a common data type, which will be the type of the result (see Section 10.5 for details). NULL values in the list are ignored. The result will be NULL only if all the expressions evaluate to NULL.

Note that GREATEST and LEAST are not in the SQL standard, but are a common extension. Some other databases make them return NULL if any argument is NULL, rather than only when all are NULL.

9.18. Array Functions and Operators

Table 9-45 shows the operators available for array types.

Table 9-45. Array Operators

Operator	Description	Example	Result
=	equal	ARRAY[1.1,2.1,3.1]::int[] = ARRAY[1,2,3]	t
<>	not equal	ARRAY[1,2,3] <> ARRAY[1,2,4]	t
<	less than	ARRAY[1,2,3] < ARRAY[1,2,4]	t
>	greater than	ARRAY[1,4,3] > ARRAY[1,2,4]	t
<=	less than or equal	ARRAY[1,2,3] <= ARRAY[1,2,3]	t
>=	greater than or equal	ARRAY[1,4,3] >= ARRAY[1,4,3]	t
@>	contains	ARRAY[1,4,3] @> ARRAY[3,1]	t
<@	is contained by	ARRAY[2,7] <@ ARRAY[1,7,4,2,6]	t
&&	overlap (have elements in common)	ARRAY[1,4,3] && ARRAY[2,1]	t
||	array-to-array concatenation	ARRAY[1,2,3] || ARRAY[4,5,6]	{1,2,3,4,5,6}
||	array-to-array concatenation	ARRAY[1,2,3] || ARRAY[[4,5,6],[7,8,9]]	{{1,2,3},{4,5,6},{7,
||	element-to-array concatenation	3 || ARRAY[4,5,6]	{3,4,5,6}
||	array-to-element concatenation	ARRAY[4,5,6] || 7	{4,5,6,7}

Array comparisons compare the array contents element-by-element, using the default B-tree comparison function for the element data type. In multidimensional arrays the elements are visited in row-major order (last subscript varies most rapidly). If the contents of two arrays are equal but the dimensionality is different, the first difference in the dimensionality information determines the sort order. (This is a change from versions of PostgreSQL prior to 8.2: older versions would claim that two arrays with the same contents were equal, even if the number of dimensions or subscript ranges were different.)

See Section 8.15 for more details about array operator behavior. See Section 11.2 for more details about which operators support indexed operations.

Table 9-46 shows the functions available for use with array types. See Section 8.15 for more information and examples of the use of these functions.

Table 9-46. Array Functions

Function	Return Type	Description	Example	Result
`array_append(anyarray, anyelement)`	`anyarray`	append an element to the end of an array	`array_append(ARRAY[1,2], 3)`	`{1,2,3}`
`array_cat(anyarray, anyarray)`	`anyarray`	concatenate two arrays	`array_cat(ARRAY[1,2,3], ARRAY[4,5])`	`{1,2,3,4,5}`
`array_ndims(anyarray)`	`int`	returns the number of dimensions of the array	`array_ndims(ARRAY[[1,2,3], [4,5,6]])`	`2`
`array_dims(anyarray)`	`text`	returns a text representation of array's dimensions	`array_dims(ARRAY[[1,2,3], [4,5,6]])`	`[1:2][1:3]`
`array_fill(anyelement, int[], [, int[]])`	`anyarray`	returns an array initialized with supplied value and dimensions, optionally with lower bounds other than 1	`array_fill(7, ARRAY[3], ARRAY[2])`	`[2:4]={7,7,7}`
`array_length(anyarray, int)`	`int`	returns the length of the requested array dimension	`array_length(array[1,2,3], 1)`	`3`
`array_lower(anyarray, int)`	`int`	returns lower bound of the requested array dimension	`array_lower('[0:2]={1,2,3}'::in 1)`	`0`
`array_prepend(anyelement, anyarray)`	`anyarray`	append an element to the beginning of an array	`array_prepend(1, ARRAY[2,3])`	`{1,2,3}`

Function	Return Type	Description	Example	Result
`array_remove(anyarray, anyelement)`	`anyarray`	remove all elements equal to the given value from the array (array must be one-dimensional)	`array_remove(ARRAY[1,2,3,2], 2)`	`{1,3}`
`array_replace(anyarray, anyelement, anyelement)`	`anyarray`	replace each array element equal to the given value with a new value	`array_replace(ARRAY[1,2,3,4,5], 5, 3)`	`{1,2,3,4,3}`
`array_to_string(anyarray, text [, text])`	`text`	concatenates array elements using supplied delimiter and optional null string	`array_to_string(ARRAY[1, 2, 3, NULL, 5], ',', '*')`	`1,2,3,*,5`
`array_upper(anyarray, int)`	`int`	returns upper bound of the requested array dimension	`array_upper(ARRAY[1,8,3,7], 1)`	`4`
`cardinality(anyarray)`	`int`	returns the total number of elements in the array, or 0 if the array is empty	`cardinality(ARRAY[[1,2],[3,4]])`	`4`
`string_to_array(text, text [, text])`	`text[]`	splits string into array elements using supplied delimiter and optional null string	`string_to_array('xx~^~yy~^~zz', '~^~', 'yy')`	`{xx,NULL,zz}`
`unnest(anyarray)`	`setof anyelement`	expand an array to a set of rows	`unnest(ARRAY[1,2])`	`1` `2` (2 rows)
`unnest(anyarray, anyarray [, ...])`	`setof anyelement, anyelement [, ...]`	expand multiple arrays (possibly of different types) to a set of rows. This is only allowed in the FROM clause; see Section 7.2.1.4	`unnest(ARRAY[1,2], ARRAY['foo','bar'])`	`1    foo` `2    bar` `NULL baz` (3 rows)

In `string_to_array`, if the delimiter parameter is NULL, each character in the input string will become a separate element in the resulting array. If the delimiter is an empty string, then the entire input string is returned as a one-element array. Otherwise the input string is split at each occurrence of the delimiter string.

In `string_to_array`, if the null-string parameter is omitted or NULL, none of the substrings of the input will be replaced by NULL. In `array_to_string`, if the null-string parameter is omitted or NULL, any null elements in the array are simply skipped and not represented in the output string.

> **Note:** There are two differences in the behavior of `string_to_array` from pre-9.1 versions of PostgreSQL. First, it will return an empty (zero-element) array rather than NULL when the input string is of zero length. Second, if the delimiter string is NULL, the function splits the input into individual characters, rather than returning NULL as before.

See also Section 9.20 about the aggregate function `array_agg` for use with arrays.

9.19. Range Functions and Operators

See Section 8.17 for an overview of range types.

Table 9-47 shows the operators available for range types.

Table 9-47. Range Operators

Operator	Description	Example	Result
=	equal	`int4range(1,5) = '[1,4]'::int4range`	t
<>	not equal	`numrange(1.1,2.2) <> numrange(1.1,2.3)`	t
<	less than	`int4range(1,10) < int4range(2,3)`	t
>	greater than	`int4range(1,10) > int4range(1,5)`	t
<=	less than or equal	`numrange(1.1,2.2) <= numrange(1.1,2.2)`	t
>=	greater than or equal	`numrange(1.1,2.2) >= numrange(1.1,2.0)`	t
@>	contains range	`int4range(2,4) @> int4range(2,3)`	t
@>	contains element	`'[2011-01-01,2011-03-01)'::tsrange @> '2011-01-10'::timestamp`	t
<@	range is contained by	`int4range(2,4) <@ int4range(1,7)`	t

Operator	Description	Example	Result
`<@`	element is contained by	`42 <@ int4range(1,7)`	f
`&&`	overlap (have points in common)	`int8range(3,7) && int8range(4,12)`	t
`<<`	strictly left of	`int8range(1,10) << int8range(100,110)`	t
`>>`	strictly right of	`int8range(50,60) >> int8range(20,30)`	t
`&<`	does not extend to the right of	`int8range(1,20) &< int8range(18,20)`	t
`&>`	does not extend to the left of	`int8range(7,20) &> int8range(5,10)`	t
`-|-`	is adjacent to	`numrange(1.1,2.2) -|- numrange(2.2,3.3)`	t
`+`	union	`numrange(5,15) + numrange(10,20)`	[5,20)
`*`	intersection	`int8range(5,15) * int8range(10,20)`	[10,15)
`-`	difference	`int8range(5,15) - int8range(10,20)`	[5,10)

The simple comparison operators <, >, <=, and >= compare the lower bounds first, and only if those are equal, compare the upper bounds. These comparisons are not usually very useful for ranges, but are provided to allow B-tree indexes to be constructed on ranges.

The left-of/right-of/adjacent operators always return false when an empty range is involved; that is, an empty range is not considered to be either before or after any other range.

The union and difference operators will fail if the resulting range would need to contain two disjoint sub-ranges, as such a range cannot be represented.

Table 9-48 shows the functions available for use with range types.

Table 9-48. Range Functions

Function	Return Type	Description	Example	Result
`lower(anyrange)`	range's element type	lower bound of range	`lower(numrange(1.1,2.2))`	1.1
`upper(anyrange)`	range's element type	upper bound of range	`upper(numrange(1.2,2.2))`	2.2

Function	Return Type	Description	Example	Result
`isempty(anyrange)`	`boolean`	is the range empty?	`isempty(numrange(1.1, 2.2))`	`false`
`lower_inc(anyrange)`	`boolean`	is the lower bound inclusive?	`lower_inc(numrange(1.1, 2.2))`	`true`
`upper_inc(anyrange)`	`boolean`	is the upper bound inclusive?	`upper_inc(numrange(1.1, 2.2))`	`false`
`lower_inf(anyrange)`	`boolean`	is the lower bound infinite?	`lower_inf('(,)'::daterange)`	`true`
`upper_inf(anyrange)`	`boolean`	is the upper bound infinite?	`upper_inf('(,)'::daterange)`	`true`

The `lower` and `upper` functions return null if the range is empty or the requested bound is infinite. The `lower_inc`, `upper_inc`, `lower_inf`, and `upper_inf` functions all return false for an empty range.

9.20. Aggregate Functions

Aggregate functions compute a single result from a set of input values. The built-in normal aggregate functions are listed in Table 9-49 and Table 9-50. The built-in ordered-set aggregate functions are listed in Table 9-51 and Table 9-52. The special syntax considerations for aggregate functions are explained in Section 4.2.7. Consult Section 2.7 for additional introductory information.

Table 9-49. General-Purpose Aggregate Functions

Function	Argument Type(s)	Return Type	Description
`array_agg(expression)`	`any`	array of the argument type	input values, including nulls, concatenated into an array
`avg(expression)`	`smallint`, `int`, `bigint`, `real`, `double precision`, `numeric`, or `interval`	`numeric` for any integer-type argument, `double precision` for a floating-point argument, otherwise the same as the argument data type	the average (arithmetic mean) of all input values
`bit_and(expression)`	`smallint`, `int`, `bigint`, or `bit`	same as argument data type	the bitwise AND of all non-null input values, or null if none

Function	Argument Type(s)	Return Type	Description
`bit_or(expression)`	`smallint, int, bigint, or bit`	same as argument data type	the bitwise OR of all non-null input values, or null if none
`bool_and(expression)`	`bool`	`bool`	true if all input values are true, otherwise false
`bool_or(expression)`	`bool`	`bool`	true if at least one input value is true, otherwise false
`count(*)`		`bigint`	number of input rows
`count(expression)`	any	`bigint`	number of input rows for which the value of *expression* is not null
`every(expression)`	`bool`	`bool`	equivalent to `bool_and`
`json_agg(expression)`	any	`json`	aggregates values as a JSON array
`json_object_agg(name, value)`	`(any, any)`	`json`	aggregates name/value pairs as a JSON object
`max(expression)`	any array, numeric, string, or date/time type	same as argument type	maximum value of *expression* across all input values
`min(expression)`	any array, numeric, string, or date/time type	same as argument type	minimum value of *expression* across all input values
`string_agg(expression, delimiter)`	`(text, text)` or `(bytea, bytea)`	same as argument types	input values concatenated into a string, separated by delimiter
`sum(expression)`	`smallint, int, bigint, real, double precision, numeric, interval, or money`	`bigint` for `smallint` or `int` arguments, `numeric` for `bigint` arguments, otherwise the same as the argument data type	sum of *expression* across all input values
`xmlagg(expression)`	`xml`	`xml`	concatenation of XML values (see also Section 9.14.1.7)

It should be noted that except for `count`, these functions return a null value when no rows are selected. In particular, `sum` of no rows returns null, not zero as one might expect, and `array_agg` returns null rather than an empty array when there are no input rows. The `coalesce` function can be used to substitute zero or an empty array for null when necessary.

> **Note:** Boolean aggregates `bool_and` and `bool_or` correspond to standard SQL aggregates `every` and `any` or `some`. As for `any` and `some`, it seems that there is an ambiguity built into the standard syntax:
>
> ```
> SELECT b1 = ANY((SELECT b2 FROM t2 ...)) FROM t1 ...;
> ```
>
> Here `ANY` can be considered either as introducing a subquery, or as being an aggregate function, if the subquery returns one row with a Boolean value. Thus the standard name cannot be given to these aggregates.

> **Note:** Users accustomed to working with other SQL database management systems might be disappointed by the performance of the `count` aggregate when it is applied to the entire table. A query like:
>
> ```
> SELECT count(*) FROM sometable;
> ```
>
> will require effort proportional to the size of the table: PostgreSQL will need to scan either the entire table or the entirety of an index which includes all rows in the table.

The aggregate functions `array_agg`, `json_agg`, `json_object_agg`, `string_agg`, and `xmlagg`, as well as similar user-defined aggregate functions, produce meaningfully different result values depending on the order of the input values. This ordering is unspecified by default, but can be controlled by writing an ORDER BY clause within the aggregate call, as shown in Section 4.2.7. Alternatively, supplying the input values from a sorted subquery will usually work. For example:

```
SELECT xmlagg(x) FROM (SELECT x FROM test ORDER BY y DESC) AS tab;
```

But this syntax is not allowed in the SQL standard, and is not portable to other database systems.

Table 9-50 shows aggregate functions typically used in statistical analysis. (These are separated out merely to avoid cluttering the listing of more-commonly-used aggregates.) Where the description mentions N, it means the number of input rows for which all the input expressions are non-null. In all cases, null is returned if the computation is meaningless, for example when N is zero.

Table 9-50. Aggregate Functions for Statistics

Function	Argument Type	Return Type	Description
`corr(Y, X)`	double precision	double precision	correlation coefficient
`covar_pop(Y, X)`	double precision	double precision	population covariance
`covar_samp(Y, X)`	double precision	double precision	sample covariance
`regr_avgx(Y, X)`	double precision	double precision	average of the independent variable ($\mathrm{sum}(X)/N$)

Function	Argument Type	Return Type	Description
`regr_avgy(Y, X)`	`double precision`	`double precision`	average of the dependent variable (`sum(Y)/N`)
`regr_count(Y, X)`	`double precision`	`bigint`	number of input rows in which both expressions are nonnull
`regr_intercept(Y, X)`	`double precision`	`double precision`	y-intercept of the least-squares-fit linear equation determined by the (X, Y) pairs
`regr_r2(Y, X)`	`double precision`	`double precision`	square of the correlation coefficient
`regr_slope(Y, X)`	`double precision`	`double precision`	slope of the least-squares-fit linear equation determined by the (X, Y) pairs
`regr_sxx(Y, X)`	`double precision`	`double precision`	`sum(X^2) - sum(X)^2/N` ("sum of squares" of the independent variable)
`regr_sxy(Y, X)`	`double precision`	`double precision`	`sum(X*Y) - sum(X) * sum(Y)/N` ("sum of products" of independent times dependent variable)
`regr_syy(Y, X)`	`double precision`	`double precision`	`sum(Y^2) - sum(Y)^2/N` ("sum of squares" of the dependent variable)
`stddev(expression)`	`smallint, int, bigint, real, double precision`, or `numeric`	`double precision` for floating-point arguments, otherwise `numeric`	historical alias for `stddev_samp`
`stddev_pop(expression)`	`smallint, int, bigint, real, double precision`, or `numeric`	`double precision` for floating-point arguments, otherwise `numeric`	population standard deviation of the input values
`stddev_samp(expression)`	`smallint, int, bigint, real, double precision`, or `numeric`	`double precision` for floating-point arguments, otherwise `numeric`	sample standard deviation of the input values

Function	Argument Type	Return Type	Description
`variance(`*`expression`*`)`	`smallint, int, bigint, real, double precision,` or `numeric`	`double precision` for floating-point arguments, otherwise `numeric`	historical alias for `var_samp`
`var_pop(`*`expression`*`)`	`smallint, int, bigint, real, double precision,` or `numeric`	`double precision` for floating-point arguments, otherwise `numeric`	population variance of the input values (square of the population standard deviation)
`var_samp(`*`expression`*`)`	`smallint, int, bigint, real, double precision,` or `numeric`	`double precision` for floating-point arguments, otherwise `numeric`	sample variance of the input values (square of the sample standard deviation)

Table 9-51 shows some aggregate functions that use the *ordered-set aggregate* syntax. These functions are sometimes referred to as "inverse distribution" functions.

Table 9-51. Ordered-Set Aggregate Functions

Function	Direct Argument Type(s)	Aggregated Argument Type(s)	Return Type	Description
`mode() WITHIN GROUP (ORDER BY `*`sort_expression`*`)`		any sortable type	same as sort expression	returns the most frequent input value (arbitrarily choosing the first one if there are multiple equally-frequent results)
`percentile_cont(`*`fraction`*`) WITHIN GROUP (ORDER BY `*`sort_expression`*`)`	`double precision`	`double precision` or `interval`	same as sort expression	continuous percentile: returns a value corresponding to the specified fraction in the ordering, interpolating between adjacent input items if needed

Function	Direct Argument Type(s)	Aggregated Argument Type(s)	Return Type	Description
`percentile_cont` `(`*`fractions`*`)` `WITHIN GROUP` `(ORDER BY` *`sort_expression`*`)`	`double precision` `[]`	`double precision` or `interval`	array of sort expression's type	multiple continuous percentile: returns an array of results matching the shape of the `fractions` parameter, with each non-null element replaced by the value corresponding to that percentile
`percentile_disc` `(`*`fraction`*`)` `WITHIN GROUP` `(ORDER BY` *`sort_expression`*`)`	`double precision`	any sortable type	same as sort expression	discrete percentile: returns the first input value whose position in the ordering equals or exceeds the specified fraction
`percentile_disc` `(`*`fractions`*`)` `WITHIN GROUP` `(ORDER BY` *`sort_expression`*`)`	`double precision` `[]`	any sortable type	array of sort expression's type	multiple discrete percentile: returns an array of results matching the shape of the `fractions` parameter, with each non-null element replaced by the input value corresponding to that percentile

All the aggregates listed in Table 9-51 ignore null values in their sorted input. For those that take a *`fraction`* parameter, the fraction value must be between 0 and 1; an error is thrown if not. However, a null fraction value simply produces a null result.

Each of the aggregates listed in Table 9-52 is associated with a window function of the same name defined in Section 9.21. In each case, the aggregate result is the value that the associated window function would have returned for the "hypothetical" row constructed from *`args`*, if such a row had been added to the sorted group of rows computed from the *`sorted_args`*.

Table 9-52. Hypothetical-Set Aggregate Functions

Function	Direct Argument Type(s)	Aggregated Argument Type(s)	Return Type	Description

Function	Direct Argument Type(s)	Aggregated Argument Type(s)	Return Type	Description
`rank(args)` `WITHIN GROUP` `(ORDER BY` `sorted_args)`	`VARIADIC "any"`	`VARIADIC "any"`	`bigint`	rank of the hypothetical row, with gaps for duplicate rows
`dense_rank(args)` `WITHIN GROUP` `(ORDER BY` `sorted_args)`	`VARIADIC "any"`	`VARIADIC "any"`	`bigint`	rank of the hypothetical row, without gaps
`percent_rank(args)` `WITHIN GROUP` `(ORDER BY` `sorted_args)`	`VARIADIC "any"`	`VARIADIC "any"`	`double precision`	relative rank of the hypothetical row, ranging from 0 to 1
`cume_dist(args)` `WITHIN GROUP` `(ORDER BY` `sorted_args)`	`VARIADIC "any"`	`VARIADIC "any"`	`double precision`	relative rank of the hypothetical row, ranging from $1/N$ to 1

For each of these hypothetical-set aggregates, the list of direct arguments given in `args` must match the number and types of the aggregated arguments given in `sorted_args`. Unlike most built-in aggregates, these aggregates are not strict, that is they do not drop input rows containing nulls. Null values sort according to the rule specified in the `ORDER BY` clause.

9.21. Window Functions

Window functions provide the ability to perform calculations across sets of rows that are related to the current query row. See Section 3.5 for an introduction to this feature, and Section 4.2.8 for syntax details.

The built-in window functions are listed in Table 9-53. Note that these functions *must* be invoked using window function syntax; that is an `OVER` clause is required.

In addition to these functions, any built-in or user-defined normal aggregate function (but not ordered-set or hypothetical-set aggregates) can be used as a window function; see Section 9.20 for a list of the built-in aggregates. Aggregate functions act as window functions only when an `OVER` clause follows the call; otherwise they act as regular aggregates.

Table 9-53. General-Purpose Window Functions

Function	Return Type	Description
`row_number()`	`bigint`	number of the current row within its partition, counting from 1

Function	Return Type	Description
rank()	bigint	rank of the current row with gaps; same as row_number of its first peer
dense_rank()	bigint	rank of the current row without gaps; this function counts peer groups
percent_rank()	double precision	relative rank of the current row: (rank - 1) / (total rows - 1)
cume_dist()	double precision	relative rank of the current row: (number of rows preceding or peer with current row) / (total rows)
ntile(*num_buckets* integer)	integer	integer ranging from 1 to the argument value, dividing the partition as equally as possible
lag(*value* any [, *offset* integer [, *default* any]])	same type as *value*	returns *value* evaluated at the row that is *offset* rows before the current row within the partition; if there is no such row, instead return *default*. Both *offset* and *default* are evaluated with respect to the current row. If omitted, *offset* defaults to 1 and *default* to null
lead(*value* any [, *offset* integer [, *default* any]])	same type as *value*	returns *value* evaluated at the row that is *offset* rows after the current row within the partition; if there is no such row, instead return *default*. Both *offset* and *default* are evaluated with respect to the current row. If omitted, *offset* defaults to 1 and *default* to null
first_value(*value* any)	same type as *value*	returns *value* evaluated at the row that is the first row of the window frame
last_value(*value* any)	same type as *value*	returns *value* evaluated at the row that is the last row of the window frame
nth_value(*value* any, *nth* integer)	same type as *value*	returns *value* evaluated at the row that is the *nth* row of the window frame (counting from 1); null if no such row

All of the functions listed in Table 9-53 depend on the sort ordering specified by the ORDER BY clause of the associated window definition. Rows that are not distinct in the ORDER BY ordering are said to be *peers*; the four ranking functions are defined so that they give the same answer for any two peer rows.

Note that first_value, last_value, and nth_value consider only the rows within the "window frame", which by default contains the rows from the start of the partition through the last peer of the current row. This is likely to give unhelpful results for last_value and sometimes also nth_value. You can redefine the frame by adding a suitable frame specification (RANGE or ROWS) to the OVER clause. See Section 4.2.8 for more information about frame specifications.

When an aggregate function is used as a window function, it aggregates over the rows within the current row's window frame. An aggregate used with ORDER BY and the default window frame definition produces a "running sum" type of behavior, which may or may not be what's wanted. To obtain aggregation over the whole partition, omit ORDER BY or use ROWS BETWEEN UNBOUNDED PRECEDING AND UNBOUNDED FOLLOWING. Other frame specifications can be used to obtain other effects.

> **Note:** The SQL standard defines a RESPECT NULLS or IGNORE NULLS option for lead, lag, first_value, last_value, and nth_value. This is not implemented in PostgreSQL: the behavior is always the same as the standard's default, namely RESPECT NULLS. Likewise, the standard's FROM FIRST or FROM LAST option for nth_value is not implemented: only the default FROM FIRST behavior is supported. (You can achieve the result of FROM LAST by reversing the ORDER BY ordering.)

9.22. Subquery Expressions

This section describes the SQL-compliant subquery expressions available in PostgreSQL. All of the expression forms documented in this section return Boolean (true/false) results.

9.22.1. EXISTS

```
EXISTS (subquery)
```

The argument of EXISTS is an arbitrary SELECT statement, or *subquery*. The subquery is evaluated to determine whether it returns any rows. If it returns at least one row, the result of EXISTS is "true"; if the subquery returns no rows, the result of EXISTS is "false".

The subquery can refer to variables from the surrounding query, which will act as constants during any one evaluation of the subquery.

The subquery will generally only be executed long enough to determine whether at least one row is returned, not all the way to completion. It is unwise to write a subquery that has side effects (such as calling sequence functions); whether the side effects occur might be unpredictable.

Since the result depends only on whether any rows are returned, and not on the contents of those rows, the output list of the subquery is normally unimportant. A common coding convention is to write all EXISTS tests in the form EXISTS(SELECT 1 WHERE ...). There are exceptions to this rule however, such as subqueries that use INTERSECT.

This simple example is like an inner join on `col2`, but it produces at most one output row for each `tab1` row, even if there are several matching `tab2` rows:

```
SELECT col1
FROM tab1
WHERE EXISTS (SELECT 1 FROM tab2 WHERE col2 = tab1.col2);
```

9.22.2. `IN`

expression `IN` (*subquery*)

The right-hand side is a parenthesized subquery, which must return exactly one column. The left-hand expression is evaluated and compared to each row of the subquery result. The result of `IN` is "true" if any equal subquery row is found. The result is "false" if no equal row is found (including the case where the subquery returns no rows).

Note that if the left-hand expression yields null, or if there are no equal right-hand values and at least one right-hand row yields null, the result of the `IN` construct will be null, not false. This is in accordance with SQL's normal rules for Boolean combinations of null values.

As with `EXISTS`, it's unwise to assume that the subquery will be evaluated completely.

row_constructor `IN` (*subquery*)

The left-hand side of this form of `IN` is a row constructor, as described in Section 4.2.13. The right-hand side is a parenthesized subquery, which must return exactly as many columns as there are expressions in the left-hand row. The left-hand expressions are evaluated and compared row-wise to each row of the subquery result. The result of `IN` is "true" if any equal subquery row is found. The result is "false" if no equal row is found (including the case where the subquery returns no rows).

As usual, null values in the rows are combined per the normal rules of SQL Boolean expressions. Two rows are considered equal if all their corresponding members are non-null and equal; the rows are unequal if any corresponding members are non-null and unequal; otherwise the result of that row comparison is unknown (null). If all the per-row results are either unequal or null, with at least one null, then the result of `IN` is null.

9.22.3. `NOT IN`

expression `NOT IN` (*subquery*)

The right-hand side is a parenthesized subquery, which must return exactly one column. The left-hand expression is evaluated and compared to each row of the subquery result. The result of `NOT IN` is "true" if only unequal subquery rows are found (including the case where the subquery returns no rows). The result is "false" if any equal row is found.

Note that if the left-hand expression yields null, or if there are no equal right-hand values and at least one right-hand row yields null, the result of the `NOT IN` construct will be null, not true. This is in accordance with SQL's normal rules for Boolean combinations of null values.

As with `EXISTS`, it's unwise to assume that the subquery will be evaluated completely.

```
row_constructor NOT IN (subquery)
```

The left-hand side of this form of `NOT IN` is a row constructor, as described in Section 4.2.13. The right-hand side is a parenthesized subquery, which must return exactly as many columns as there are expressions in the left-hand row. The left-hand expressions are evaluated and compared row-wise to each row of the subquery result. The result of `NOT IN` is "true" if only unequal subquery rows are found (including the case where the subquery returns no rows). The result is "false" if any equal row is found.

As usual, null values in the rows are combined per the normal rules of SQL Boolean expressions. Two rows are considered equal if all their corresponding members are non-null and equal; the rows are unequal if any corresponding members are non-null and unequal; otherwise the result of that row comparison is unknown (null). If all the per-row results are either unequal or null, with at least one null, then the result of `NOT IN` is null.

9.22.4. ANY/SOME

```
expression operator ANY (subquery)
expression operator SOME (subquery)
```

The right-hand side is a parenthesized subquery, which must return exactly one column. The left-hand expression is evaluated and compared to each row of the subquery result using the given *operator*, which must yield a Boolean result. The result of `ANY` is "true" if any true result is obtained. The result is "false" if no true result is found (including the case where the subquery returns no rows).

`SOME` is a synonym for `ANY`. `IN` is equivalent to `= ANY`.

Note that if there are no successes and at least one right-hand row yields null for the operator's result, the result of the `ANY` construct will be null, not false. This is in accordance with SQL's normal rules for Boolean combinations of null values.

As with `EXISTS`, it's unwise to assume that the subquery will be evaluated completely.

```
row_constructor operator ANY (subquery)
row_constructor operator SOME (subquery)
```

The left-hand side of this form of `ANY` is a row constructor, as described in Section 4.2.13. The right-hand side is a parenthesized subquery, which must return exactly as many columns as there are expressions in the left-hand row. The left-hand expressions are evaluated and compared row-wise to each row of the subquery result, using the given *operator*. The result of `ANY` is "true" if the comparison returns true for any subquery row. The result is "false" if the comparison returns false for every subquery row (including the case where the subquery returns no rows). The result is NULL if the comparison does not return true for any row, and it returns NULL for at least one row.

See Section 9.23.5 for details about the meaning of a row constructor comparison.

9.22.5. ALL

```
expression operator ALL (subquery)
```

The right-hand side is a parenthesized subquery, which must return exactly one column. The left-hand expression is evaluated and compared to each row of the subquery result using the given `operator`, which must yield a Boolean result. The result of `ALL` is "true" if all rows yield true (including the case where the subquery returns no rows). The result is "false" if any false result is found. The result is NULL if the comparison does not return false for any row, and it returns NULL for at least one row.

`NOT IN` is equivalent to `<> ALL`.

As with `EXISTS`, it's unwise to assume that the subquery will be evaluated completely.

`row_constructor operator ALL (subquery)`

The left-hand side of this form of `ALL` is a row constructor, as described in Section 4.2.13. The right-hand side is a parenthesized subquery, which must return exactly as many columns as there are expressions in the left-hand row. The left-hand expressions are evaluated and compared row-wise to each row of the subquery result, using the given `operator`. The result of `ALL` is "true" if the comparison returns true for all subquery rows (including the case where the subquery returns no rows). The result is "false" if the comparison returns false for any subquery row. The result is NULL if the comparison does not return false for any subquery row, and it returns NULL for at least one row.

See Section 9.23.5 for details about the meaning of a row constructor comparison.

9.22.6. Single-row Comparison

`row_constructor operator (subquery)`

The left-hand side is a row constructor, as described in Section 4.2.13. The right-hand side is a parenthesized subquery, which must return exactly as many columns as there are expressions in the left-hand row. Furthermore, the subquery cannot return more than one row. (If it returns zero rows, the result is taken to be null.) The left-hand side is evaluated and compared row-wise to the single subquery result row.

See Section 9.23.5 for details about the meaning of a row constructor comparison.

9.23. Row and Array Comparisons

This section describes several specialized constructs for making multiple comparisons between groups of values. These forms are syntactically related to the subquery forms of the previous section, but do not involve subqueries. The forms involving array subexpressions are PostgreSQL extensions; the rest are SQL-compliant. All of the expression forms documented in this section return Boolean (true/false) results.

9.23.1. `IN`

`expression IN (value [, ...])`

The right-hand side is a parenthesized list of scalar expressions. The result is "true" if the left-hand expression's result is equal to any of the right-hand expressions. This is a shorthand notation for

```
expression = value1
OR
expression = value2
OR
...
```

Note that if the left-hand expression yields null, or if there are no equal right-hand values and at least one right-hand expression yields null, the result of the IN construct will be null, not false. This is in accordance with SQL's normal rules for Boolean combinations of null values.

9.23.2. NOT IN

```
expression NOT IN (value [, ...])
```

The right-hand side is a parenthesized list of scalar expressions. The result is "true" if the left-hand expression's result is unequal to all of the right-hand expressions. This is a shorthand notation for

```
expression <> value1
AND
expression <> value2
AND
...
```

Note that if the left-hand expression yields null, or if there are no equal right-hand values and at least one right-hand expression yields null, the result of the NOT IN construct will be null, not true as one might naively expect. This is in accordance with SQL's normal rules for Boolean combinations of null values.

> **Tip:** x NOT IN y is equivalent to NOT (x IN y) in all cases. However, null values are much more likely to trip up the novice when working with NOT IN than when working with IN. It is best to express your condition positively if possible.

9.23.3. ANY/SOME (array)

```
expression operator ANY (array expression)
expression operator SOME (array expression)
```

The right-hand side is a parenthesized expression, which must yield an array value. The left-hand expression is evaluated and compared to each element of the array using the given *operator*, which must yield a Boolean result. The result of ANY is "true" if any true result is obtained. The result is "false" if no true result is found (including the case where the array has zero elements).

If the array expression yields a null array, the result of ANY will be null. If the left-hand expression yields null, the result of ANY is ordinarily null (though a non-strict comparison operator could possibly yield a different result). Also, if the right-hand array contains any null elements and no true comparison result is obtained, the result of ANY will be null, not false (again, assuming a strict comparison operator). This is in accordance with SQL's normal rules for Boolean combinations of null values.

SOME is a synonym for ANY.

9.23.4. ALL (array)

expression operator ALL (array expression)

The right-hand side is a parenthesized expression, which must yield an array value. The left-hand expression is evaluated and compared to each element of the array using the given *operator*, which must yield a Boolean result. The result of ALL is "true" if all comparisons yield true (including the case where the array has zero elements). The result is "false" if any false result is found.

If the array expression yields a null array, the result of ALL will be null. If the left-hand expression yields null, the result of ALL is ordinarily null (though a non-strict comparison operator could possibly yield a different result). Also, if the right-hand array contains any null elements and no false comparison result is obtained, the result of ALL will be null, not true (again, assuming a strict comparison operator). This is in accordance with SQL's normal rules for Boolean combinations of null values.

9.23.5. Row Constructor Comparison

row_constructor operator row_constructor

Each side is a row constructor, as described in Section 4.2.13. The two row values must have the same number of fields. Each side is evaluated and they are compared row-wise. Row constructor comparisons are allowed when the *operator* is =, <>, <, <=, > or >=. Every row element must be of a type which has a default B-tree operator class or the attempted comparison may generate an error.

> **Note:** Errors related to the number or types of elements might not occur if the comparison is resolved using earlier columns.

The = and <> cases work slightly differently from the others. Two rows are considered equal if all their corresponding members are non-null and equal; the rows are unequal if any corresponding members are non-null and unequal; otherwise the result of the row comparison is unknown (null).

For the <, <=, > and >= cases, the row elements are compared left-to-right, stopping as soon as an unequal or null pair of elements is found. If either of this pair of elements is null, the result of the row comparison is unknown (null); otherwise comparison of this pair of elements determines the result. For example, ROW(1,2,NULL) < ROW(1,3,0) yields true, not null, because the third pair of elements are not considered.

> **Note:** Prior to PostgreSQL 8.2, the <, <=, > and >= cases were not handled per SQL specification. A comparison like ROW(a,b) < ROW(c,d) was implemented as a < c AND b < d whereas the correct behavior is equivalent to a < c OR (a = c AND b < d).

```
row_constructor IS DISTINCT FROM row_constructor
```

This construct is similar to a <> row comparison, but it does not yield null for null inputs. Instead, any null value is considered unequal to (distinct from) any non-null value, and any two nulls are considered equal (not distinct). Thus the result will either be true or false, never null.

```
row_constructor IS NOT DISTINCT FROM row_constructor
```

This construct is similar to a = row comparison, but it does not yield null for null inputs. Instead, any null value is considered unequal to (distinct from) any non-null value, and any two nulls are considered equal (not distinct). Thus the result will always be either true or false, never null.

9.23.6. Composite Type Comparison

```
record operator record
```

The SQL specification requires row-wise comparison to return NULL if the result depends on comparing two NULL values or a NULL and a non-NULL. PostgreSQL does this only when comparing the results of two row constructors (as in Section 9.23.5) or comparing a row constructor to the output of a subquery (as in Section 9.22). In other contexts where two composite-type values are compared, two NULL field values are considered equal, and a NULL is considered larger than a non-NULL. This is necessary in order to have consistent sorting and indexing behavior for composite types.

Each side is evaluated and they are compared row-wise. Composite type comparisons are allowed when the operator is =, <>, <, <=, > or >=, or has semantics similar to one of these. (To be specific, an operator can be a row comparison operator if it is a member of a B-tree operator class, or is the negator of the = member of a B-tree operator class.) The default behavior of the above operators is the same as for IS [NOT] DISTINCT FROM for row constructors (see Section 9.23.5).

To support matching of rows which include elements without a default B-tree operator class, the following operators are defined for composite type comparison: *=, *<>, *<, *<=, *>, and *>=. These operators compare the internal binary representation of the two rows. Two rows might have a different binary representation even though comparisons of the two rows with the equality operator is true. The ordering of rows under these comparison operators is deterministic but not otherwise meaningful. These operators are used internally for materialized views and might be useful for other specialized purposes such as replication but are not intended to be generally useful for writing queries.

9.24. Set Returning Functions

This section describes functions that possibly return more than one row. The most widely used functions in this class are series generating functions, as detailed in Table 9-54 and Table 9-55. Other, more specialized set-returning functions are described elsewhere in this manual. See Section 7.2.1.4 for ways to combine multiple set-returning functions.

Table 9-54. Series Generating Functions

Function	Argument Type	Return Type	Description
`generate_series(start, stop)`	`int` or `bigint`	`setof int` or `setof bigint` (same as argument type)	Generate a series of values, from `start` to `stop` with a step size of one
`generate_series(start, stop, step)`	`int` or `bigint`	`setof int` or `setof bigint` (same as argument type)	Generate a series of values, from `start` to `stop` with a step size of `step`
`generate_series(start, stop, step interval)`	`timestamp` or `timestamp with time zone`	`setof timestamp` or `setof timestamp with time zone` (same as argument type)	Generate a series of values, from `start` to `stop` with a step size of `step`

When `step` is positive, zero rows are returned if `start` is greater than `stop`. Conversely, when `step` is negative, zero rows are returned if `start` is less than `stop`. Zero rows are also returned for `NULL` inputs. It is an error for `step` to be zero. Some examples follow:

```
SELECT * FROM generate_series(2,4);
 generate_series
-----------------
               2
               3
               4
(3 rows)

SELECT * FROM generate_series(5,1,-2);
 generate_series
-----------------
               5
               3
               1
(3 rows)

SELECT * FROM generate_series(4,3);
 generate_series
-----------------
(0 rows)

-- this example relies on the date-plus-integer operator
SELECT current_date + s.a AS dates FROM generate_series(0,14,7) AS s(a);
   dates
------------
 2004-02-05
 2004-02-12
 2004-02-19
(3 rows)

SELECT * FROM generate_series('2008-03-01 00:00'::timestamp,
                       '2008-03-04 12:00', '10 hours');
```

```
 generate_series
---------------------
 2008-03-01 00:00:00
 2008-03-01 10:00:00
 2008-03-01 20:00:00
 2008-03-02 06:00:00
 2008-03-02 16:00:00
 2008-03-03 02:00:00
 2008-03-03 12:00:00
 2008-03-03 22:00:00
 2008-03-04 08:00:00
(9 rows)
```

Table 9-55. Subscript Generating Functions

Function	Return Type	Description
generate_subscripts(array anyarray, dim int)	setof int	Generate a series comprising the given array's subscripts.
generate_subscripts(array anyarray, dim int, reverse boolean)	setof int	Generate a series comprising the given array's subscripts. When reverse is true, the series is returned in reverse order.

generate_subscripts is a convenience function that generates the set of valid subscripts for the specified dimension of the given array. Zero rows are returned for arrays that do not have the requested dimension, or for NULL arrays (but valid subscripts are returned for NULL array elements). Some examples follow:

```
-- basic usage
SELECT generate_subscripts('{NULL,1,NULL,2}'::int[], 1) AS s;
 s
---
 1
 2
 3
 4
(4 rows)

-- presenting an array, the subscript and the subscripted
-- value requires a subquery
SELECT * FROM arrays;
         a
-------------------
 {-1,-2}
 {100,200,300}
(2 rows)

SELECT a AS array, s AS subscript, a[s] AS value
FROM (SELECT generate_subscripts(a, 1) AS s, a FROM arrays) foo;
```

```
      array    | subscript | value
---------------+-----------+-------
 {-1,-2}       |         1 |    -1
 {-1,-2}       |         2 |    -2
 {100,200,300} |         1 |   100
 {100,200,300} |         2 |   200
 {100,200,300} |         3 |   300
(5 rows)

-- unnest a 2D array
CREATE OR REPLACE FUNCTION unnest2(anyarray)
RETURNS SETOF anyelement AS $$
select $1[i][j]
   from generate_subscripts($1,1) g1(i),
        generate_subscripts($1,2) g2(j);
$$ LANGUAGE sql IMMUTABLE;
CREATE FUNCTION
SELECT * FROM unnest2(ARRAY[[1,2],[3,4]]);
 unnest2
---------
       1
       2
       3
       4
(4 rows)
```

When a function in the FROM clause is suffixed by WITH ORDINALITY, a bigint column is appended to the output which starts from 1 and increments by 1 for each row of the function's output. This is most useful in the case of set returning functions such as unnest().

```
-- set returning function WITH ORDINALITY
SELECT * FROM pg_ls_dir('.') WITH ORDINALITY AS t(ls,n);
       ls        | n
-----------------+----
 pg_serial       |  1
 pg_twophase     |  2
 postmaster.opts |  3
 pg_notify       |  4
 postgresql.conf |  5
 pg_tblspc       |  6
 logfile         |  7
 base            |  8
 postmaster.pid  |  9
 pg_ident.conf   | 10
 global          | 11
 pg_clog         | 12
 pg_snapshots    | 13
 pg_multixact    | 14
 PG_VERSION      | 15
 pg_xlog         | 16
 pg_hba.conf     | 17
```

```
pg_stat_tmp    | 18
pg_subtrans    | 19
(19 rows)
```

9.25. System Information Functions

Table 9-56 shows several functions that extract session and system information.

In addition to the functions listed in this section, there are a number of functions related to the statistics system that also provide system information. See Section 27.2.2 for more information.

Table 9-56. Session Information Functions

Name	Return Type	Description
`current_catalog`	`name`	name of current database (called "catalog" in the SQL standard)
`current_database()`	`name`	name of current database
`current_query()`	`text`	text of the currently executing query, as submitted by the client (might contain more than one statement)
`current_schema[()]`	`name`	name of current schema
`current_schemas(boolean)`	`name[]`	names of schemas in search path, optionally including implicit schemas
`current_user`	`name`	user name of current execution context
`inet_client_addr()`	`inet`	address of the remote connection
`inet_client_port()`	`int`	port of the remote connection
`inet_server_addr()`	`inet`	address of the local connection
`inet_server_port()`	`int`	port of the local connection
`pg_backend_pid()`	`int`	Process ID of the server process attached to the current session
`pg_conf_load_time()`	`timestamp with time zone`	configuration load time
`pg_is_other_temp_schema(oid)`	`boolean`	is schema another session's temporary schema?
`pg_listening_channels()`	`setof text`	channel names that the session is currently listening on
`pg_my_temp_schema()`	`oid`	OID of session's temporary schema, or 0 if none
`pg_postmaster_start_time()`	`timestamp with time zone`	server start time

Name	Return Type	Description
`pg_trigger_depth()`	`int`	current nesting level of PostgreSQL triggers (0 if not called, directly or indirectly, from inside a trigger)
`session_user`	`name`	session user name
`user`	`name`	equivalent to `current_user`
`version()`	`text`	PostgreSQL version information

Note: `current_catalog`, `current_schema`, `current_user`, `session_user`, and `user` have special syntactic status in SQL: they must be called without trailing parentheses. (In PostgreSQL, parentheses can optionally be used with `current_schema`, but not with the others.)

The `session_user` is normally the user who initiated the current database connection; but superusers can change this setting with SET SESSION AUTHORIZATION. The `current_user` is the user identifier that is applicable for permission checking. Normally it is equal to the session user, but it can be changed with SET ROLE. It also changes during the execution of functions with the attribute SECURITY DEFINER. In Unix parlance, the session user is the "real user" and the current user is the "effective user".

`current_schema` returns the name of the schema that is first in the search path (or a null value if the search path is empty). This is the schema that will be used for any tables or other named objects that are created without specifying a target schema. `current_schemas(boolean)` returns an array of the names of all schemas presently in the search path. The Boolean option determines whether or not implicitly included system schemas such as `pg_catalog` are included in the returned search path.

Note: The search path can be altered at run time. The command is:

```
SET search_path TO schema [, schema, ...]
```

`pg_listening_channels` returns a set of names of channels that the current session is listening to. See LISTEN for more information.

`inet_client_addr` returns the IP address of the current client, and `inet_client_port` returns the port number. `inet_server_addr` returns the IP address on which the server accepted the current connection, and `inet_server_port` returns the port number. All these functions return NULL if the current connection is via a Unix-domain socket.

`pg_my_temp_schema` returns the OID of the current session's temporary schema, or zero if it has none (because it has not created any temporary tables). `pg_is_other_temp_schema` returns true if the given OID is the OID of another session's temporary schema. (This can be useful, for example, to exclude other sessions' temporary tables from a catalog display.)

`pg_postmaster_start_time` returns the `timestamp with time zone` when the server started.

`pg_conf_load_time` returns the `timestamp with time zone` when the server configuration files were last loaded. (If the current session was alive at the time, this will be the time when the session itself re-read the configuration files, so the reading will vary a little in different sessions. Otherwise it is the time when the postmaster process re-read the configuration files.)

`version` returns a string describing the PostgreSQL server's version.

Table 9-57 lists functions that allow the user to query object access privileges programmatically. See Section 5.6 for more information about privileges.

Table 9-57. Access Privilege Inquiry Functions

Name	Return Type	Description
`has_any_column_privilege(user, table, privilege)`	boolean	does user have privilege for any column of table
`has_any_column_privilege(table, privilege)`	boolean	does current user have privilege for any column of table
`has_column_privilege(user, table, column, privilege)`	boolean	does user have privilege for column
`has_column_privilege(table, column, privilege)`	boolean	does current user have privilege for column
`has_database_privilege(user, database, privilege)`	boolean	does user have privilege for database
`has_database_privilege(database, privilege)`	boolean	does current user have privilege for database
`has_foreign_data_wrapper_privilege(user, fdw, privilege)`	boolean	does user have privilege for foreign-data wrapper
`has_foreign_data_wrapper_privilege(fdw, privilege)`	boolean	does current user have privilege for foreign-data wrapper
`has_function_privilege(user, function, privilege)`	boolean	does user have privilege for function
`has_function_privilege(function, privilege)`	boolean	does current user have privilege for function
`has_language_privilege(user, language, privilege)`	boolean	does user have privilege for language
`has_language_privilege(language, privilege)`	boolean	does current user have privilege for language
`has_schema_privilege(user, schema, privilege)`	boolean	does user have privilege for schema
`has_schema_privilege(schema, privilege)`	boolean	does current user have privilege for schema
`has_sequence_privilege(user, sequence, privilege)`	boolean	does user have privilege for sequence
`has_sequence_privilege(sequence, privilege)`	boolean	does current user have privilege for sequence
`has_server_privilege(user, server, privilege)`	boolean	does user have privilege for foreign server

Name	Return Type	Description
`has_server_privilege(server, privilege)`	boolean	does current user have privilege for foreign server
`has_table_privilege(user, table, privilege)`	boolean	does user have privilege for table
`has_table_privilege(table, privilege)`	boolean	does current user have privilege for table
`has_tablespace_privilege(user, tablespace, privilege)`	boolean	does user have privilege for tablespace
`has_tablespace_privilege(tablespace, privilege)`	boolean	does current user have privilege for tablespace
`pg_has_role(user, role, privilege)`	boolean	does user have privilege for role
`pg_has_role(role, privilege)`	boolean	does current user have privilege for role

`has_table_privilege` checks whether a user can access a table in a particular way. The user can be specified by name, by OID (`pg_authid.oid`), `public` to indicate the PUBLIC pseudo-role, or if the argument is omitted `current_user` is assumed. The table can be specified by name or by OID. (Thus, there are actually six variants of `has_table_privilege`, which can be distinguished by the number and types of their arguments.) When specifying by name, the name can be schema-qualified if necessary. The desired access privilege type is specified by a text string, which must evaluate to one of the values SELECT, INSERT, UPDATE, DELETE, TRUNCATE, REFERENCES, or TRIGGER. Optionally, WITH GRANT OPTION can be added to a privilege type to test whether the privilege is held with grant option. Also, multiple privilege types can be listed separated by commas, in which case the result will be `true` if any of the listed privileges is held. (Case of the privilege string is not significant, and extra whitespace is allowed between but not within privilege names.) Some examples:

```
SELECT has_table_privilege('myschema.mytable', 'select');
SELECT has_table_privilege('joe', 'mytable', 'INSERT, SELECT WITH GRANT OPTION'
```

`has_sequence_privilege` checks whether a user can access a sequence in a particular way. The possibilities for its arguments are analogous to `has_table_privilege`. The desired access privilege type must evaluate to one of USAGE, SELECT, or UPDATE.

`has_any_column_privilege` checks whether a user can access any column of a table in a particular way. Its argument possibilities are analogous to `has_table_privilege`, except that the desired access privilege type must evaluate to some combination of SELECT, INSERT, UPDATE, or REFERENCES. Note that having any of these privileges at the table level implicitly grants it for each column of the table, so `has_any_column_privilege` will always return `true` if `has_table_privilege` does for the same arguments. But `has_any_column_privilege` also succeeds if there is a column-level grant of the privilege for at least one column.

`has_column_privilege` checks whether a user can access a column in a particular way. Its argument possibilities are analogous to `has_table_privilege`, with the addition that the column can be specified either by name or attribute number. The desired access privilege type must evaluate to some combination of SELECT, INSERT, UPDATE, or REFERENCES. Note that having any of these privileges at the table level implicitly grants it for each column of the table.

has_database_privilege checks whether a user can access a database in a particular way. Its argument possibilities are analogous to has_table_privilege. The desired access privilege type must evaluate to some combination of CREATE, CONNECT, TEMPORARY, or TEMP (which is equivalent to TEMPORARY).

has_function_privilege checks whether a user can access a function in a particular way. Its argument possibilities are analogous to has_table_privilege. When specifying a function by a text string rather than by OID, the allowed input is the same as for the regprocedure data type (see Section 8.18). The desired access privilege type must evaluate to EXECUTE. An example is:

```
SELECT has_function_privilege('joeuser', 'myfunc(int, text)', 'execute');
```

has_foreign_data_wrapper_privilege checks whether a user can access a foreign-data wrapper in a particular way. Its argument possibilities are analogous to has_table_privilege. The desired access privilege type must evaluate to USAGE.

has_language_privilege checks whether a user can access a procedural language in a particular way. Its argument possibilities are analogous to has_table_privilege. The desired access privilege type must evaluate to USAGE.

has_schema_privilege checks whether a user can access a schema in a particular way. Its argument possibilities are analogous to has_table_privilege. The desired access privilege type must evaluate to some combination of CREATE or USAGE.

has_server_privilege checks whether a user can access a foreign server in a particular way. Its argument possibilities are analogous to has_table_privilege. The desired access privilege type must evaluate to USAGE.

has_tablespace_privilege checks whether a user can access a tablespace in a particular way. Its argument possibilities are analogous to has_table_privilege. The desired access privilege type must evaluate to CREATE.

pg_has_role checks whether a user can access a role in a particular way. Its argument possibilities are analogous to has_table_privilege, except that public is not allowed as a user name. The desired access privilege type must evaluate to some combination of MEMBER or USAGE. MEMBER denotes direct or indirect membership in the role (that is, the right to do SET ROLE), while USAGE denotes whether the privileges of the role are immediately available without doing SET ROLE.

Table 9-58 shows functions that determine whether a certain object is *visible* in the current schema search path. For example, a table is said to be visible if its containing schema is in the search path and no table of the same name appears earlier in the search path. This is equivalent to the statement that the table can be referenced by name without explicit schema qualification. To list the names of all visible tables:

```
SELECT relname FROM pg_class WHERE pg_table_is_visible(oid);
```

Table 9-58. Schema Visibility Inquiry Functions

Name	Return Type	Description
pg_collation_is_visible(collation_oid)	boolean	is collation visible in search path
pg_conversion_is_visible(conversion_oid)	boolean	is conversion visible in search path
pg_function_is_visible(function_oid)	boolean	is function visible in search path
pg_opclass_is_visible(opclass_oid)	boolean	is operator class visible in search path
pg_operator_is_visible(operator_oid)	boolean	is operator visible in search path
pg_opfamily_is_visible(opclass_oid)	boolean	is operator family visible in search path
pg_table_is_visible(table_oid)	boolean	is table visible in search path
pg_ts_config_is_visible(config_oid)	boolean	is text search configuration visible in search path
pg_ts_dict_is_visible(dict_oid)	boolean	is text search dictionary visible in search path
pg_ts_parser_is_visible(parser_oid)	boolean	is text search parser visible in search path
pg_ts_template_is_visible(template_oid)	boolean	is text search template visible in search path
pg_type_is_visible(type_oid)	boolean	is type (or domain) visible in search path

Each function performs the visibility check for one type of database object. Note that `pg_table_is_visible` can also be used with views, indexes and sequences; `pg_type_is_visible` can also be used with domains. For functions and operators, an object in the search path is visible if there is no object of the same name *and argument data type(s)* earlier in the path. For operator classes, both name and associated index access method are considered.

All these functions require object OIDs to identify the object to be checked. If you want to test an object by name, it is convenient to use the OID alias types (`regclass`, `regtype`, `regprocedure`, `regoperator`, `regconfig`, or `regdictionary`), for example:

```
SELECT pg_type_is_visible('myschema.widget'::regtype);
```

Note that it would not make much sense to test a non-schema-qualified type name in this way — if the name can be recognized at all, it must be visible.

Table 9-59 lists functions that extract information from the system catalogs.

Table 9-59. System Catalog Information Functions

Name	Return Type	Description

Name	Return Type	Description
`format_type(type_oid, typemod)`	`text`	get SQL name of a data type
`pg_describe_object(catalog_id, object_id, object_sub_id)`	`text`	get description of a database object
`pg_identify_object(catalog_id oid, object_id oid, object_sub_id integer)`	`type text, schema text, name text, identity text`	get identity of a database object
`pg_get_constraintdef(constraint_oid)`	`text`	get definition of a constraint
`pg_get_constraintdef(constraint_oid, pretty_bool)`	`text`	get definition of a constraint
`pg_get_expr(pg_node_tree, relation_oid)`	`text`	decompile internal form of an expression, assuming that any Vars in it refer to the relation indicated by the second parameter
`pg_get_expr(pg_node_tree, relation_oid, pretty_bool)`	`text`	decompile internal form of an expression, assuming that any Vars in it refer to the relation indicated by the second parameter
`pg_get_functiondef(func_oid)`	`text`	get definition of a function
`pg_get_function_arguments(func_oid)`	`text`	get argument list of function's definition (with default values)
`pg_get_function_identity_arguments(func_oid)`	`text`	get argument list to identify a function (without default values)
`pg_get_function_result(func_oid)`	`text`	get RETURNS clause for function
`pg_get_indexdef(index_oid)`	`text`	get CREATE INDEX command for index
`pg_get_indexdef(index_oid, column_no, pretty_bool)`	`text`	get CREATE INDEX command for index, or definition of just one index column when `column_no` is not zero
`pg_get_keywords()`	`setof record`	get list of SQL keywords and their categories
`pg_get_ruledef(rule_oid)`	`text`	get CREATE RULE command for rule
`pg_get_ruledef(rule_oid, pretty_bool)`	`text`	get CREATE RULE command for rule

Name	Return Type	Description
pg_get_serial_sequence(table_name, column_name)	text	get name of the sequence that a serial, smallserial or bigserial column uses
pg_get_triggerdef(trigger_oid)	text	get CREATE [CONSTRAINT] TRIGGER command for trigger
pg_get_triggerdef(trigger_oid, pretty_bool)	text	get CREATE [CONSTRAINT] TRIGGER command for trigger
pg_get_userbyid(role_oid)	name	get role name with given OID
pg_get_viewdef(view_name)	text	get underlying SELECT command for view or materialized view (*deprecated*)
pg_get_viewdef(view_name, pretty_bool)	text	get underlying SELECT command for view or materialized view (*deprecated*)
pg_get_viewdef(view_oid)	text	get underlying SELECT command for view or materialized view
pg_get_viewdef(view_oid, pretty_bool)	text	get underlying SELECT command for view or materialized view
pg_get_viewdef(view_oid, wrap_column_int)	text	get underlying SELECT command for view or materialized view; lines with fields are wrapped to specified number of columns, pretty-printing is implied
pg_options_to_table(reloptions)	setof record	get the set of storage option name/value pairs
pg_tablespace_databases(tablespace_oid)	setof oid	get the set of database OIDs that have objects in the tablespace
pg_tablespace_location(tablespace_oid)	text	get the path in the file system that this tablespace is located in
pg_typeof(any)	regtype	get the data type of any value
collation for (any)	text	get the collation of the argument
to_regclass(rel_name)	regclass	get the OID of the named relation
to_regproc(func_name)	regproc	get the OID of the named function
to_regprocedure(func_name)	regprocedure	get the OID of the named function
to_regoper(operator_name)	regoper	get the OID of the named operator

Name	Return Type	Description
`to_regoperator(operator_name)`	`regoperator`	get the OID of the named operator
`to_regtype(type_name)`	`regtype`	get the OID of the named type

`format_type` returns the SQL name of a data type that is identified by its type OID and possibly a type modifier. Pass NULL for the type modifier if no specific modifier is known.

`pg_get_keywords` returns a set of records describing the SQL keywords recognized by the server. The `word` column contains the keyword. The `catcode` column contains a category code: `U` for unreserved, `C` for column name, `T` for type or function name, or `R` for reserved. The `catdesc` column contains a possibly-localized string describing the category.

`pg_get_constraintdef`, `pg_get_indexdef`, `pg_get_ruledef`, and `pg_get_triggerdef`, respectively reconstruct the creating command for a constraint, index, rule, or trigger. (Note that this is a decompiled reconstruction, not the original text of the command.) `pg_get_expr` decompiles the internal form of an individual expression, such as the default value for a column. It can be useful when examining the contents of system catalogs. If the expression might contain Vars, specify the OID of the relation they refer to as the second parameter; if no Vars are expected, zero is sufficient. `pg_get_viewdef` reconstructs the SELECT query that defines a view. Most of these functions come in two variants, one of which can optionally "pretty-print" the result. The pretty-printed format is more readable, but the default format is more likely to be interpreted the same way by future versions of PostgreSQL; avoid using pretty-printed output for dump purposes. Passing `false` for the pretty-print parameter yields the same result as the variant that does not have the parameter at all.

`pg_get_functiondef` returns a complete CREATE OR REPLACE FUNCTION statement for a function. `pg_get_function_arguments` returns the argument list of a function, in the form it would need to appear in within CREATE FUNCTION. `pg_get_function_result` similarly returns the appropriate RETURNS clause for the function. `pg_get_function_identity_arguments` returns the argument list necessary to identify a function, in the form it would need to appear in within ALTER FUNCTION, for instance. This form omits default values.

`pg_get_serial_sequence` returns the name of the sequence associated with a column, or NULL if no sequence is associated with the column. The first input parameter is a table name with optional schema, and the second parameter is a column name. Because the first parameter is potentially a schema and table, it is not treated as a double-quoted identifier, meaning it is lower cased by default, while the second parameter, being just a column name, is treated as double-quoted and has its case preserved. The function returns a value suitably formatted for passing to sequence functions (see Section 9.16). This association can be modified or removed with ALTER SEQUENCE OWNED BY. (The function probably should have been called `pg_get_owned_sequence`; its current name reflects the fact that it's typically used with `serial` or `bigserial` columns.)

`pg_get_userbyid` extracts a role's name given its OID.

`pg_options_to_table` returns the set of storage option name/value pairs (`option_name`/`option_value`) when passed `pg_class.reloptions` or `pg_attribute.attoptions`.

`pg_tablespace_databases` allows a tablespace to be examined. It returns the set of OIDs of databases that have objects stored in the tablespace. If this function returns any rows, the tablespace is not empty and cannot be dropped. To display the specific objects populating the tablespace, you will need to connect to the databases identified by `pg_tablespace_databases` and query their `pg_class` catalogs.

`pg_describe_object` returns a textual description of a database object specified by catalog OID, object OID and a (possibly zero) sub-object ID. This description is intended to be human-readable, and might be translated, depending on server configuration. This is useful to determine the identity of an object as stored in the `pg_depend` catalog.

`pg_identify_object` returns a row containing enough information to uniquely identify the database object specified by catalog OID, object OID and a (possibly zero) sub-object ID. This information is intended to be machine-readable, and is never translated. `type` identifies the type of database object; `schema` is the schema name that the object belongs in, or `NULL` for object types that do not belong to schemas; `name` is the name of the object, quoted if necessary, only present if it can be used (alongside schema name, if pertinent) as a unique identifier of the object, otherwise `NULL`; `identity` is the complete object identity, with the precise format depending on object type, and each part within the format being schema-qualified and quoted as necessary.

`pg_typeof` returns the OID of the data type of the value that is passed to it. This can be helpful for troubleshooting or dynamically constructing SQL queries. The function is declared as returning `regtype`, which is an OID alias type (see Section 8.18); this means that it is the same as an OID for comparison purposes but displays as a type name. For example:

```
SELECT pg_typeof(33);

 pg_typeof
-----------
 integer
(1 row)

SELECT typlen FROM pg_type WHERE oid = pg_typeof(33);
 typlen
--------
      4
(1 row)
```

The expression `collation for` returns the collation of the value that is passed to it. Example:

```
SELECT collation for (description) FROM pg_description LIMIT 1;
 pg_collation_for
------------------
 "default"
(1 row)

SELECT collation for ('foo' COLLATE "de_DE");
 pg_collation_for
------------------
 "de_DE"
(1 row)
```

The value might be quoted and schema-qualified. If no collation is derived for the argument expression, then a null value is returned. If the argument is not of a collatable data type, then an error is raised.

The `to_regclass`, `to_regproc`, `to_regprocedure`, `to_regoper`, `to_regoperator`, and `to_regtype` functions translate relation, function, operator, and type names to objects of type regclass, regproc, regprocedure, regoper, regoperator, and regtype, respectively. These functions differ from a cast from text in that they don't accept a numeric OID, and that they return null rather than throwing an error if the name is not found (or, for to_regproc and to_regoper, if the given name matches multiple objects).

The functions shown in Table 9-60 extract comments previously stored with the COMMENT command. A null value is returned if no comment could be found for the specified parameters.

Table 9-60. Comment Information Functions

Name	Return Type	Description
col_description(table_oid, column_number)	text	get comment for a table column
obj_description(object_oid, catalog_name)	text	get comment for a database object
obj_description(object_oid)	text	get comment for a database object (*deprecated*)
shobj_description(object_oid, catalog_name)	text	get comment for a shared database object

col_description returns the comment for a table column, which is specified by the OID of its table and its column number. (obj_description cannot be used for table columns since columns do not have OIDs of their own.)

The two-parameter form of obj_description returns the comment for a database object specified by its OID and the name of the containing system catalog. For example, obj_description(123456,'pg_class') would retrieve the comment for the table with OID 123456. The one-parameter form of obj_description requires only the object OID. It is deprecated since there is no guarantee that OIDs are unique across different system catalogs; therefore, the wrong comment might be returned.

shobj_description is used just like obj_description except it is used for retrieving comments on shared objects. Some system catalogs are global to all databases within each cluster, and the descriptions for objects in them are stored globally as well.

The functions shown in Table 9-61 provide server transaction information in an exportable form. The main use of these functions is to determine which transactions were committed between two snapshots.

Table 9-61. Transaction IDs and Snapshots

Name	Return Type	Description
txid_current()	bigint	get current transaction ID
txid_current_snapshot()	txid_snapshot	get current snapshot
txid_snapshot_xip(txid_snapshot)	setof bigint	get in-progress transaction IDs in snapshot
txid_snapshot_xmax(txid_snapshot)	bigint	get xmax of snapshot

Name	Return Type	Description
`txid_snapshot_xmin(txid_snapshot)`	`bigint`	get `xmin` of snapshot
`txid_visible_in_snapshot(bigint, txid_snapshot)`	`boolean`	is transaction ID visible in snapshot? (do not use with subtransaction ids)

The internal transaction ID type (`xid`) is 32 bits wide and wraps around every 4 billion transactions. However, these functions export a 64-bit format that is extended with an "epoch" counter so it will not wrap around during the life of an installation. The data type used by these functions, `txid_snapshot`, stores information about transaction ID visibility at a particular moment in time. Its components are described in Table 9-62.

Table 9-62. Snapshot Components

Name	Description
`xmin`	Earliest transaction ID (txid) that is still active. All earlier transactions will either be committed and visible, or rolled back and dead.
`xmax`	First as-yet-unassigned txid. All txids greater than or equal to this are not yet started as of the time of the snapshot, and thus invisible.
`xip_list`	Active txids at the time of the snapshot. The list includes only those active txids between `xmin` and `xmax`; there might be active txids higher than `xmax`. A txid that is `xmin <= txid < xmax` and not in this list was already completed at the time of the snapshot, and thus either visible or dead according to its commit status. The list does not include txids of subtransactions.

`txid_snapshot`'s textual representation is *xmin:xmax:xip_list*. For example `10:20:10,14,15` means xmin=10, xmax=20, xip_list=10, 14, 15.

9.26. System Administration Functions

The functions described in this section are used to control and monitor a PostgreSQL installation.

9.26.1. Configuration Settings Functions

Table 9-63 shows the functions available to query and alter run-time configuration parameters.

Table 9-63. Configuration Settings Functions

Name	Return Type	Description
`current_setting(setting_name)`	text	get current value of setting
`set_config(setting_name, new_value, is_local)`	text	set parameter and return new value

The function `current_setting` yields the current value of the setting `setting_name`. It corresponds to the SQL command `SHOW`. An example:

```
SELECT current_setting('datestyle');

 current_setting
-----------------
 ISO, MDY
(1 row)
```

`set_config` sets the parameter `setting_name` to `new_value`. If `is_local` is `true`, the new value will only apply to the current transaction. If you want the new value to apply for the current session, use `false` instead. The function corresponds to the SQL command `SET`. An example:

```
SELECT set_config('log_statement_stats', 'off', false);

 set_config
------------
 off
(1 row)
```

9.26.2. Server Signaling Functions

The functions shown in Table 9-64 send control signals to other server processes. Use of these functions is usually restricted to superusers, with noted exceptions.

Table 9-64. Server Signaling Functions

Name	Return Type	Description
`pg_cancel_backend(pid int)`	boolean	Cancel a backend's current query. You can execute this against another backend that has exactly the same role as the user calling the function. In all other cases, you must be a superuser.
`pg_reload_conf()`	boolean	Cause server processes to reload their configuration files

Name	Return Type	Description
`pg_rotate_logfile()`	`boolean`	Rotate server's log file
`pg_terminate_backend(pid int)`	`boolean`	Terminate a backend. You can execute this against another backend that has exactly the same role as the user calling the function. In all other cases, you must be a superuser.

Each of these functions returns `true` if successful and `false` otherwise.

`pg_cancel_backend` and `pg_terminate_backend` send signals (SIGINT or SIGTERM respectively) to backend processes identified by process ID. The process ID of an active backend can be found from the `pid` column of the `pg_stat_activity` view, or by listing the `postgres` processes on the server (using ps on Unix or the Task Manager on Windows). The role of an active backend can be found from the `usename` column of the `pg_stat_activity` view.

`pg_reload_conf` sends a SIGHUP signal to the server, causing configuration files to be reloaded by all server processes.

`pg_rotate_logfile` signals the log-file manager to switch to a new output file immediately. This works only when the built-in log collector is running, since otherwise there is no log-file manager subprocess.

9.26.3. Backup Control Functions

The functions shown in Table 9-65 assist in making on-line backups. These functions cannot be executed during recovery (except `pg_is_in_backup`, `pg_backup_start_time` and `pg_xlog_location_diff`).

Table 9-65. Backup Control Functions

Name	Return Type	Description
`pg_create_restore_point(name text)`	`pg_lsn`	Create a named point for performing restore (restricted to superusers)
`pg_current_xlog_insert_location()`	`pg_lsn`	Get current transaction log insert location
`pg_current_xlog_location()`	`pg_lsn`	Get current transaction log write location
`pg_start_backup(label text [, fast boolean ])`	`pg_lsn`	Prepare for performing on-line backup (restricted to superusers or replication roles)
`pg_stop_backup()`	`pg_lsn`	Finish performing on-line backup (restricted to superusers or replication roles)

Name	Return Type	Description
`pg_is_in_backup()`	`bool`	True if an on-line exclusive backup is still in progress.
`pg_backup_start_time()`	`timestamp with time zone`	Get start time of an on-line exclusive backup in progress.
`pg_switch_xlog()`	`pg_lsn`	Force switch to a new transaction log file (restricted to superusers)
`pg_xlogfile_name(location pg_lsn)`	`text`	Convert transaction log location string to file name
`pg_xlogfile_name_offset(location pg_lsn)`	`text, integer`	Convert transaction log location string to file name and decimal byte offset within file
`pg_xlog_location_diff(location pg_lsn, location pg_lsn)`	`numeric`	Calculate the difference between two transaction log locations

`pg_start_backup` accepts an arbitrary user-defined label for the backup. (Typically this would be the name under which the backup dump file will be stored.) The function writes a backup label file (`backup_label`) into the database cluster's data directory, performs a checkpoint, and then returns the backup's starting transaction log location as text. The user can ignore this result value, but it is provided in case it is useful.

```
postgres=# select pg_start_backup('label_goes_here');
 pg_start_backup
-----------------
 0/D4445B8
(1 row)
```

There is an optional second parameter of type `boolean`. If `true`, it specifies executing `pg_start_backup` as quickly as possible. This forces an immediate checkpoint which will cause a spike in I/O operations, slowing any concurrently executing queries.

`pg_stop_backup` removes the label file created by `pg_start_backup`, and creates a backup history file in the transaction log archive area. The history file includes the label given to `pg_start_backup`, the starting and ending transaction log locations for the backup, and the starting and ending times of the backup. The return value is the backup's ending transaction log location (which again can be ignored). After recording the ending location, the current transaction log insertion point is automatically advanced to the next transaction log file, so that the ending transaction log file can be archived immediately to complete the backup.

`pg_switch_xlog` moves to the next transaction log file, allowing the current file to be archived (assuming you are using continuous archiving). The return value is the ending transaction log location + 1 within the just-completed transaction log file. If there has been no transaction log activity since the last transaction log switch, `pg_switch_xlog` does nothing and returns the start location of the transaction log file currently in use.

`pg_create_restore_point` creates a named transaction log record that can be used as recovery target, and returns the corresponding transaction log location. The given name can then be used with recovery_target_name to specify the point up to which recovery will proceed. Avoid creating multiple restore points with the same name, since recovery will stop at the first one whose name matches the recovery target.

pg_current_xlog_location displays the current transaction log write location in the same format used by the above functions. Similarly, pg_current_xlog_insert_location displays the current transaction log insertion point. The insertion point is the "logical" end of the transaction log at any instant, while the write location is the end of what has actually been written out from the server's internal buffers. The write location is the end of what can be examined from outside the server, and is usually what you want if you are interested in archiving partially-complete transaction log files. The insertion point is made available primarily for server debugging purposes. These are both read-only operations and do not require superuser permissions.

You can use pg_xlogfile_name_offset to extract the corresponding transaction log file name and byte offset from the results of any of the above functions. For example:

```
postgres=# SELECT * FROM pg_xlogfile_name_offset(pg_stop_backup());
        file_name         | file_offset
--------------------------+-------------
 00000001000000000000000D |     4039624
(1 row)
```

Similarly, pg_xlogfile_name extracts just the transaction log file name. When the given transaction log location is exactly at a transaction log file boundary, both these functions return the name of the preceding transaction log file. This is usually the desired behavior for managing transaction log archiving behavior, since the preceding file is the last one that currently needs to be archived.

pg_xlog_location_diff calculates the difference in bytes between two transaction log locations. It can be used with pg_stat_replication or some functions shown in Table 9-65 to get the replication lag.

For details about proper usage of these functions, see Section 24.3.

9.26.4. Recovery Control Functions

The functions shown in Table 9-66 provide information about the current status of the standby. These functions may be executed both during recovery and in normal running.

Table 9-66. Recovery Information Functions

Name	Return Type	Description
pg_is_in_recovery()	bool	True if recovery is still in progress.

Name	Return Type	Description
`pg_last_xlog_receive_location()`	`pg_lsn`	Get last transaction log location received and synced to disk by streaming replication. While streaming replication is in progress this will increase monotonically. If recovery has completed this will remain static at the value of the last WAL record received and synced to disk during recovery. If streaming replication is disabled, or if it has not yet started, the function returns NULL.
`pg_last_xlog_replay_location()`	`pg_lsn`	Get last transaction log location replayed during recovery. If recovery is still in progress this will increase monotonically. If recovery has completed then this value will remain static at the value of the last WAL record applied during that recovery. When the server has been started normally without recovery the function returns NULL.
`pg_last_xact_replay_timestamp()`	`timestamp with time zone`	Get time stamp of last transaction replayed during recovery. This is the time at which the commit or abort WAL record for that transaction was generated on the primary. If no transactions have been replayed during recovery, this function returns NULL. Otherwise, if recovery is still in progress this will increase monotonically. If recovery has completed then this value will remain static at the value of the last transaction applied during that recovery. When the server has been started normally without recovery the function returns NULL.

The functions shown in Table 9-67 control the progress of recovery. These functions may be executed only during recovery.

Table 9-67. Recovery Control Functions

Name	Return Type	Description
`pg_is_xlog_replay_paused()`	`bool`	True if recovery is paused.
`pg_xlog_replay_pause()`	`void`	Pauses recovery immediately (restricted to superusers).
`pg_xlog_replay_resume()`	`void`	Restarts recovery if it was paused (restricted to superusers).

While recovery is paused no further database changes are applied. If in hot standby, all new queries will see the same consistent snapshot of the database, and no further query conflicts will be generated until recovery is resumed.

If streaming replication is disabled, the paused state may continue indefinitely without problem. While streaming replication is in progress WAL records will continue to be received, which will eventually fill available disk space, depending upon the duration of the pause, the rate of WAL generation and available disk space.

9.26.5. Snapshot Synchronization Functions

PostgreSQL allows database sessions to synchronize their snapshots. A *snapshot* determines which data is visible to the transaction that is using the snapshot. Synchronized snapshots are necessary when two or more sessions need to see identical content in the database. If two sessions just start their transactions independently, there is always a possibility that some third transaction commits between the executions of the two START TRANSACTION commands, so that one session sees the effects of that transaction and the other does not.

To solve this problem, PostgreSQL allows a transaction to *export* the snapshot it is using. As long as the exporting transaction remains open, other transactions can *import* its snapshot, and thereby be guaranteed that they see exactly the same view of the database that the first transaction sees. But note that any database changes made by any one of these transactions remain invisible to the other transactions, as is usual for changes made by uncommitted transactions. So the transactions are synchronized with respect to pre-existing data, but act normally for changes they make themselves.

Snapshots are exported with the `pg_export_snapshot` function, shown in Table 9-68, and imported with the SET TRANSACTION command.

Table 9-68. Snapshot Synchronization Functions

Name	Return Type	Description
`pg_export_snapshot()`	`text`	Save the current snapshot and return its identifier

The function `pg_export_snapshot` saves the current snapshot and returns a `text` string identifying the snapshot. This string must be passed (outside the database) to clients that want to import the snapshot. The snapshot is available for import only until the end of the transaction that exported it. A transaction can export more than one snapshot, if needed. Note that doing so is only useful in READ COMMITTED transactions, since in REPEATABLE READ and higher isolation levels, transactions use the same snapshot throughout their lifetime. Once a transaction has exported any snapshots, it cannot be prepared with PREPARE TRANSACTION.

See SET TRANSACTION for details of how to use an exported snapshot.

9.26.6. Replication Functions

The functions shown in Table 9-69 are for controlling and interacting with replication features. See Section 25.2.5 and Section 25.2.6 for information about the underlying features. Use of these functions is restricted to superusers.

Many of these functions have equivalent commands in the replication protocol; see Section 49.3.

The functions described in Section 9.26.5, Section 9.26.4, and Section 9.26.3 are also relevant for replication.

Table 9-69. Replication SQL Functions

Function	Return Type	Description
`pg_create_physical_replication_slot(slot_name name)`	`(slot_name name, xlog_position pg_lsn)`	Creates a new physical replication slot named `slot_name`. Streaming changes from a physical slot is only possible with the streaming-replication protocol - see Section 49.3. Corresponds to the replication protocol command `CREATE_REPLICATION_SLOT ... PHYSICAL`.
`pg_drop_replication_slot(slot_name name)`	`void`	Drops the physical or logical replication slot named `slot_name`. Same as replication protocol command `DROP_REPLICATION_SLOT`.
`pg_create_logical_replication_slot(slot_name name, plugin name)`	`(slot_name name, xlog_position pg_lsn)`	Creates a new logical (decoding) replication slot named `slot_name` using the output plugin `plugin`. A call to this function has the same effect as the replication protocol command `CREATE_REPLICATION_SLOT ... LOGICAL`.

Function	Return Type	Description
`pg_logical_slot_get_changes(slot_name name, upto_lsn pg_lsn, upto_nchanges int, VARIADIC options text[])`	`(location pg_lsn, xid xid, data text)`	Returns changes in the slot `slot_name`, starting from the point at which since changes have been consumed last. If `upto_lsn` and `upto_nchanges` are NULL, logical decoding will continue until end of WAL. If `upto_lsn` is non-NULL, decoding will include only those transactions which commit prior to the specified LSN. If `upto_nchanges` is non-NULL, decoding will stop when the number of rows produced by decoding exceeds the specified value. Note, however, that the actual number of rows returned may be larger, since this limit is only checked after adding the rows produced when decoding each new transaction commit.
`pg_logical_slot_peek_changes(slot_name name, upto_lsn pg_lsn, upto_nchanges int, VARIADIC options text[])`	`(location text, xid xid, data text)`	Behaves just like the `pg_logical_slot_get_changes` function, except that changes are not consumed; that is, they will be returned again on future calls.
`pg_logical_slot_get_binary_changes(slot_name name, upto_lsn pg_lsn, upto_nchanges int, VARIADIC options text[])`	`(location pg_lsn, xid xid, data bytea)`	Behaves just like the `pg_logical_slot_get_changes` function, except that changes are returned as `bytea`.
`pg_logical_slot_peek_binary_changes(slot_name name, upto_lsn pg_lsn, upto_nchanges int, VARIADIC options text[])`	`(location pg_lsn, xid xid, data bytea)`	Behaves just like the `pg_logical_slot_get_changes` function, except that changes are returned as `bytea` and that changes are not consumed; that is, they will be returned again on future calls.

9.26.7. Database Object Management Functions

The functions shown in Table 9-70 calculate the disk space usage of database objects.

Table 9-70. Database Object Size Functions

Name	Return Type	Description
`pg_column_size(any)`	`int`	Number of bytes used to store a particular value (possibly compressed)
`pg_database_size(oid)`	`bigint`	Disk space used by the database with the specified OID
`pg_database_size(name)`	`bigint`	Disk space used by the database with the specified name
`pg_indexes_size(regclass)`	`bigint`	Total disk space used by indexes attached to the specified table
`pg_relation_size(relation regclass, fork text)`	`bigint`	Disk space used by the specified fork (`'main'`, `'fsm'`, `'vm'`, or `'init'`) of the specified table or index
`pg_relation_size(relation regclass)`	`bigint`	Shorthand for `pg_relation_size(..., 'main')`
`pg_size_pretty(bigint)`	`text`	Converts a size in bytes expressed as a 64-bit integer into a human-readable format with size units
`pg_size_pretty(numeric)`	`text`	Converts a size in bytes expressed as a numeric value into a human-readable format with size units
`pg_table_size(regclass)`	`bigint`	Disk space used by the specified table, excluding indexes (but including TOAST, free space map, and visibility map)
`pg_tablespace_size(oid)`	`bigint`	Disk space used by the tablespace with the specified OID
`pg_tablespace_size(name)`	`bigint`	Disk space used by the tablespace with the specified name
`pg_total_relation_size(regclass)`	`bigint`	Total disk space used by the specified table, including all indexes and TOAST data

`pg_column_size` shows the space used to store any individual data value.

`pg_total_relation_size` accepts the OID or name of a table or toast table, and returns the total on-disk space used for that table, including all associated indexes. This function is equivalent to `pg_table_size` + `pg_indexes_size`.

`pg_table_size` accepts the OID or name of a table and returns the disk space needed for that table, exclusive of indexes. (TOAST space, free space map, and visibility map are included.)

`pg_indexes_size` accepts the OID or name of a table and returns the total disk space used by all the indexes attached to that table.

`pg_database_size` and `pg_tablespace_size` accept the OID or name of a database or tablespace, and return the total disk space used therein. To use `pg_database_size`, you must have `CONNECT` permission on the specified database (which is granted by default). To use `pg_tablespace_size`, you must have `CREATE` permission on the specified tablespace, unless it is the default tablespace for the current database.

`pg_relation_size` accepts the OID or name of a table, index or toast table, and returns the on-disk size in bytes of one fork of that relation. (Note that for most purposes it is more convenient to use the higher-level functions `pg_total_relation_size` or `pg_table_size`, which sum the sizes of all forks.) With one argument, it returns the size of the main data fork of the relation. The second argument can be provided to specify which fork to examine:

- `'main'` returns the size of the main data fork of the relation.
- `'fsm'` returns the size of the Free Space Map (see Section 59.3) associated with the relation.
- `'vm'` returns the size of the Visibility Map (see Section 59.4) associated with the relation.
- `'init'` returns the size of the initialization fork, if any, associated with the relation.

`pg_size_pretty` can be used to format the result of one of the other functions in a human-readable way, using kB, MB, GB or TB as appropriate.

The functions above that operate on tables or indexes accept a `regclass` argument, which is simply the OID of the table or index in the `pg_class` system catalog. You do not have to look up the OID by hand, however, since the `regclass` data type's input converter will do the work for you. Just write the table name enclosed in single quotes so that it looks like a literal constant. For compatibility with the handling of ordinary SQL names, the string will be converted to lower case unless it contains double quotes around the table name.

If an OID that does not represent an existing object is passed as argument to one of the above functions, NULL is returned.

The functions shown in Table 9-71 assist in identifying the specific disk files associated with database objects.

Table 9-71. Database Object Location Functions

Name	Return Type	Description
`pg_relation_filenode(relation regclass)`	`oid`	Filenode number of the specified relation
`pg_relation_filepath(relation regclass)`	`text`	File path name of the specified relation

Name	Return Type	Description
`pg_filenode_relation(tablespace oid, filenode oid)`	`regclass`	Find the relation associated with a given tablespace and filenode

`pg_relation_filenode` accepts the OID or name of a table, index, sequence, or toast table, and returns the "filenode" number currently assigned to it. The filenode is the base component of the file name(s) used for the relation (see Section 59.1 for more information). For most tables the result is the same as `pg_class.relfilenode`, but for certain system catalogs `relfilenode` is zero and this function must be used to get the correct value. The function returns NULL if passed a relation that does not have storage, such as a view.

`pg_relation_filepath` is similar to `pg_relation_filenode`, but it returns the entire file path name (relative to the database cluster's data directory `PGDATA`) of the relation.

`pg_filenode_relation` is the reverse of `pg_relation_filenode`. Given a "tablespace" OID and a "filenode", it returns the associated relation's OID. For a table in the database's default tablespace, the tablespace can be specified as 0.

9.26.8. Generic File Access Functions

The functions shown in Table 9-72 provide native access to files on the machine hosting the server. Only files within the database cluster directory and the `log_directory` can be accessed. Use a relative path for files in the cluster directory, and a path matching the `log_directory` configuration setting for log files. Use of these functions is restricted to superusers.

Table 9-72. Generic File Access Functions

Name	Return Type	Description
`pg_ls_dir(dirname text)`	`setof text`	List the contents of a directory
`pg_read_file(filename text [, offset bigint, length bigint])`	`text`	Return the contents of a text file
`pg_read_binary_file(filename text [, offset bigint, length bigint])`	`bytea`	Return the contents of a file
`pg_stat_file(filename text)`	`record`	Return information about a file

`pg_ls_dir` returns all the names in the specified directory, except the special entries "." and "..".

`pg_read_file` returns part of a text file, starting at the given `offset`, returning at most `length` bytes (less if the end of file is reached first). If `offset` is negative, it is relative to the end of the file. If `offset` and `length` are omitted, the entire file is returned. The bytes read from the file are interpreted as a string in the server encoding; an error is thrown if they are not valid in that encoding.

`pg_read_binary_file` is similar to `pg_read_file`, except that the result is a `bytea` value; accordingly, no encoding checks are performed. In combination with the `convert_from` function, this function can be used to read a file in a specified encoding:

```
SELECT convert_from(pg_read_binary_file('file_in_utf8.txt'), 'UTF8');
```

`pg_stat_file` returns a record containing the file size, last accessed time stamp, last modified time stamp, last file status change time stamp (Unix platforms only), file creation time stamp (Windows only), and a `boolean` indicating if it is a directory. Typical usages include:

```
SELECT * FROM pg_stat_file('filename');
SELECT (pg_stat_file('filename')).modification;
```

9.26.9. Advisory Lock Functions

The functions shown in Table 9-73 manage advisory locks. For details about proper use of these functions, see Section 13.3.5.

Table 9-73. Advisory Lock Functions

Name	Return Type	Description
`pg_advisory_lock(key bigint)`	`void`	Obtain exclusive session level advisory lock
`pg_advisory_lock(key1 int, key2 int)`	`void`	Obtain exclusive session level advisory lock
`pg_advisory_lock_shared(key bigint)`	`void`	Obtain shared session level advisory lock
`pg_advisory_lock_shared(key1 int, key2 int)`	`void`	Obtain shared session level advisory lock
`pg_advisory_unlock(key bigint)`	`boolean`	Release an exclusive session level advisory lock
`pg_advisory_unlock(key1 int, key2 int)`	`boolean`	Release an exclusive session level advisory lock
`pg_advisory_unlock_all()`	`void`	Release all session level advisory locks held by the current session
`pg_advisory_unlock_shared(key bigint)`	`boolean`	Release a shared session level advisory lock
`pg_advisory_unlock_shared(key1 int, key2 int)`	`boolean`	Release a shared session level advisory lock
`pg_advisory_xact_lock(key bigint)`	`void`	Obtain exclusive transaction level advisory lock
`pg_advisory_xact_lock(key1 int, key2 int)`	`void`	Obtain exclusive transaction level advisory lock

Name	Return Type	Description
`pg_advisory_xact_lock_shared(key bigint)`	`void`	Obtain shared transaction level advisory lock
`pg_advisory_xact_lock_shared(key1 int, key2 int)`	`void`	Obtain shared transaction level advisory lock
`pg_try_advisory_lock(key bigint)`	`boolean`	Obtain exclusive session level advisory lock if available
`pg_try_advisory_lock(key1 int, key2 int)`	`boolean`	Obtain exclusive session level advisory lock if available
`pg_try_advisory_lock_shared(key bigint)`	`boolean`	Obtain shared session level advisory lock if available
`pg_try_advisory_lock_shared(key1 int, key2 int)`	`boolean`	Obtain shared session level advisory lock if available
`pg_try_advisory_xact_lock(key bigint)`	`boolean`	Obtain exclusive transaction level advisory lock if available
`pg_try_advisory_xact_lock(key1 int, key2 int)`	`boolean`	Obtain exclusive transaction level advisory lock if available
`pg_try_advisory_xact_lock_shared(key bigint)`	`boolean`	Obtain shared transaction level advisory lock if available
`pg_try_advisory_xact_lock_shared(key1 int, key2 int)`	`boolean`	Obtain shared transaction level advisory lock if available

`pg_advisory_lock` locks an application-defined resource, which can be identified either by a single 64-bit key value or two 32-bit key values (note that these two key spaces do not overlap). If another session already holds a lock on the same resource identifier, this function will wait until the resource becomes available. The lock is exclusive. Multiple lock requests stack, so that if the same resource is locked three times it must then be unlocked three times to be released for other sessions' use.

`pg_advisory_lock_shared` works the same as `pg_advisory_lock`, except the lock can be shared with other sessions requesting shared locks. Only would-be exclusive lockers are locked out.

`pg_try_advisory_lock` is similar to `pg_advisory_lock`, except the function will not wait for the lock to become available. It will either obtain the lock immediately and return `true`, or return `false` if the lock cannot be acquired immediately.

`pg_try_advisory_lock_shared` works the same as `pg_try_advisory_lock`, except it attempts to acquire a shared rather than an exclusive lock.

`pg_advisory_unlock` will release a previously-acquired exclusive session level advisory lock. It returns `true` if the lock is successfully released. If the lock was not held, it will return `false`, and in addition, an

SQL warning will be reported by the server.

`pg_advisory_unlock_shared` works the same as `pg_advisory_unlock`, except it releases a shared session level advisory lock.

`pg_advisory_unlock_all` will release all session level advisory locks held by the current session. (This function is implicitly invoked at session end, even if the client disconnects ungracefully.)

`pg_advisory_xact_lock` works the same as `pg_advisory_lock`, except the lock is automatically released at the end of the current transaction and cannot be released explicitly.

`pg_advisory_xact_lock_shared` works the same as `pg_advisory_lock_shared`, except the lock is automatically released at the end of the current transaction and cannot be released explicitly.

`pg_try_advisory_xact_lock` works the same as `pg_try_advisory_lock`, except the lock, if acquired, is automatically released at the end of the current transaction and cannot be released explicitly.

`pg_try_advisory_xact_lock_shared` works the same as `pg_try_advisory_lock_shared`, except the lock, if acquired, is automatically released at the end of the current transaction and cannot be released explicitly.

9.27. Trigger Functions

Currently PostgreSQL provides one built in trigger function, `suppress_redundant_updates_trigger`, which will prevent any update that does not actually change the data in the row from taking place, in contrast to the normal behavior which always performs the update regardless of whether or not the data has changed. (This normal behavior makes updates run faster, since no checking is required, and is also useful in certain cases.)

Ideally, you should normally avoid running updates that don't actually change the data in the record. Redundant updates can cost considerable unnecessary time, especially if there are lots of indexes to alter, and space in dead rows that will eventually have to be vacuumed. However, detecting such situations in client code is not always easy, or even possible, and writing expressions to detect them can be error-prone. An alternative is to use `suppress_redundant_updates_trigger`, which will skip updates that don't change the data. You should use this with care, however. The trigger takes a small but non-trivial time for each record, so if most of the records affected by an update are actually changed, use of this trigger will actually make the update run slower.

The `suppress_redundant_updates_trigger` function can be added to a table like this:

```
CREATE TRIGGER z_min_update
BEFORE UPDATE ON tablename
FOR EACH ROW EXECUTE PROCEDURE suppress_redundant_updates_trigger();
```

In most cases, you would want to fire this trigger last for each row. Bearing in mind that triggers fire in name order, you would then choose a trigger name that comes after the name of any other trigger you might have on the table.

For more information about creating triggers, see CREATE TRIGGER.

9.28. Event Trigger Functions

Currently PostgreSQL provides one built-in event trigger helper function, `pg_event_trigger_dropped_objects`.

`pg_event_trigger_dropped_objects` returns a list of all objects dropped by the command in whose `sql_drop` event it is called. If called in any other context, `pg_event_trigger_dropped_objects` raises an error. `pg_event_trigger_dropped_objects` returns the following columns:

Name	Type	Description
`classid`	`Oid`	OID of catalog the object belonged in
`objid`	`Oid`	OID the object had within the catalog
`objsubid`	`int32`	Object sub-id (e.g. attribute number for columns)
`object_type`	`text`	Type of the object
`schema_name`	`text`	Name of the schema the object belonged in, if any; otherwise `NULL`. No quoting is applied.
`object_name`	`text`	Name of the object, if the combination of schema and name can be used as a unique identifier for the object; otherwise `NULL`. No quoting is applied, and name is never schema-qualified.
`object_identity`	`text`	Text rendering of the object identity, schema-qualified. Each and every identifier present in the identity is quoted if necessary.

The `pg_event_trigger_dropped_objects` function can be used in an event trigger like this:

```
CREATE FUNCTION test_event_trigger_for_drops()
        RETURNS event_trigger LANGUAGE plpgsql AS $$
DECLARE
    obj record;
BEGIN
    FOR obj IN SELECT * FROM pg_event_trigger_dropped_objects()
    LOOP
        RAISE NOTICE '% dropped object: % %.% %',
                    tg_tag,
                    obj.object_type,
                    obj.schema_name,
                    obj.object_name,
                    obj.object_identity;
    END LOOP;
```

```
END
$$;
CREATE EVENT TRIGGER test_event_trigger_for_drops
    ON sql_drop
    EXECUTE PROCEDURE test_event_trigger_for_drops();
```

For more information about event triggers, see Chapter 37.

Chapter 10. Type Conversion

SQL statements can, intentionally or not, require the mixing of different data types in the same expression. PostgreSQL has extensive facilities for evaluating mixed-type expressions.

In many cases a user does not need to understand the details of the type conversion mechanism. However, implicit conversions done by PostgreSQL can affect the results of a query. When necessary, these results can be tailored by using *explicit* type conversion.

This chapter introduces the PostgreSQL type conversion mechanisms and conventions. Refer to the relevant sections in Chapter 8 and Chapter 9 for more information on specific data types and allowed functions and operators.

10.1. Overview

SQL is a strongly typed language. That is, every data item has an associated data type which determines its behavior and allowed usage. PostgreSQL has an extensible type system that is more general and flexible than other SQL implementations. Hence, most type conversion behavior in PostgreSQL is governed by general rules rather than by *ad hoc* heuristics. This allows the use of mixed-type expressions even with user-defined types.

The PostgreSQL scanner/parser divides lexical elements into five fundamental categories: integers, non-integer numbers, strings, identifiers, and key words. Constants of most non-numeric types are first classified as strings. The SQL language definition allows specifying type names with strings, and this mechanism can be used in PostgreSQL to start the parser down the correct path. For example, the query:

```
SELECT text 'Origin' AS "label", point '(0,0)' AS "value";

 label  | value
--------+-------
 Origin | (0,0)
(1 row)
```

has two literal constants, of type `text` and `point`. If a type is not specified for a string literal, then the placeholder type `unknown` is assigned initially, to be resolved in later stages as described below.

There are four fundamental SQL constructs requiring distinct type conversion rules in the PostgreSQL parser:

Function calls

>   Much of the PostgreSQL type system is built around a rich set of functions. Functions can have one or more arguments. Since PostgreSQL permits function overloading, the function name alone does not uniquely identify the function to be called; the parser must select the right function based on the data types of the supplied arguments.

Operators

>   PostgreSQL allows expressions with prefix and postfix unary (one-argument) operators, as well as binary (two-argument) operators. Like functions, operators can be overloaded, so the same problem of selecting the right operator exists.

Value Storage

> SQL `INSERT` and `UPDATE` statements place the results of expressions into a table. The expressions in the statement must be matched up with, and perhaps converted to, the types of the target columns.

`UNION`, `CASE`, and related constructs

> Since all query results from a unionized `SELECT` statement must appear in a single set of columns, the types of the results of each `SELECT` clause must be matched up and converted to a uniform set. Similarly, the result expressions of a `CASE` construct must be converted to a common type so that the `CASE` expression as a whole has a known output type. The same holds for `ARRAY` constructs, and for the `GREATEST` and `LEAST` functions.

The system catalogs store information about which conversions, or *casts*, exist between which data types, and how to perform those conversions. Additional casts can be added by the user with the CREATE CAST command. (This is usually done in conjunction with defining new data types. The set of casts between built-in types has been carefully crafted and is best not altered.)

An additional heuristic provided by the parser allows improved determination of the proper casting behavior among groups of types that have implicit casts. Data types are divided into several basic *type categories*, including `boolean`, `numeric`, `string`, `bitstring`, `datetime`, `timespan`, `geometric`, `network`, and user-defined. (For a list see Table 48-53; but note it is also possible to create custom type categories.) Within each category there can be one or more *preferred types*, which are preferred when there is a choice of possible types. With careful selection of preferred types and available implicit casts, it is possible to ensure that ambiguous expressions (those with multiple candidate parsing solutions) can be resolved in a useful way.

All type conversion rules are designed with several principles in mind:

- Implicit conversions should never have surprising or unpredictable outcomes.

- There should be no extra overhead in the parser or executor if a query does not need implicit type conversion. That is, if a query is well-formed and the types already match, then the query should execute without spending extra time in the parser and without introducing unnecessary implicit conversion calls in the query.

- Additionally, if a query usually requires an implicit conversion for a function, and if then the user defines a new function with the correct argument types, the parser should use this new function and no longer do implicit conversion to use the old function.

10.2. Operators

The specific operator that is referenced by an operator expression is determined using the following procedure. Note that this procedure is indirectly affected by the precedence of the operators involved, since that will determine which sub-expressions are taken to be the inputs of which operators. See Section 4.1.6 for more information.

Operator Type Resolution

1. Select the operators to be considered from the `pg_operator` system catalog. If a non-schema-qualified operator name was used (the usual case), the operators considered are those with the matching name and argument count that are visible in the current search path (see Section 5.7.3). If a qualified operator name was given, only operators in the specified schema are considered.

    a. If the search path finds multiple operators with identical argument types, only the one appearing earliest in the path is considered. Operators with different argument types are considered on an equal footing regardless of search path position.

2. Check for an operator accepting exactly the input argument types. If one exists (there can be only one exact match in the set of operators considered), use it.

    a. If one argument of a binary operator invocation is of the `unknown` type, then assume it is the same type as the other argument for this check. Invocations involving two `unknown` inputs, or a unary operator with an `unknown` input, will never find a match at this step.

    b. If one argument of a binary operator invocation is of the `unknown` type and the other is of a domain type, next check to see if there is an operator accepting exactly the domain's base type on both sides; if so, use it.

3. Look for the best match.

    a. Discard candidate operators for which the input types do not match and cannot be converted (using an implicit conversion) to match. `unknown` literals are assumed to be convertible to anything for this purpose. If only one candidate remains, use it; else continue to the next step.

    b. If any input argument is of a domain type, treat it as being of the domain's base type for all subsequent steps. This ensures that domains act like their base types for purposes of ambiguous-operator resolution.

    c. Run through all candidates and keep those with the most exact matches on input types. Keep all candidates if none have exact matches. If only one candidate remains, use it; else continue to the next step.

    d. Run through all candidates and keep those that accept preferred types (of the input data type's type category) at the most positions where type conversion will be required. Keep all candidates if none accept preferred types. If only one candidate remains, use it; else continue to the next step.

    e. If any input arguments are `unknown`, check the type categories accepted at those argument positions by the remaining candidates. At each position, select the `string` category if any candidate accepts that category. (This bias towards string is appropriate since an unknown-type literal looks like a string.) Otherwise, if all the remaining candidates accept the same type category, select that category; otherwise fail because the correct choice cannot be deduced without more clues. Now discard candidates that do not accept the selected type category. Furthermore, if any candidate accepts a preferred type in that category, discard candidates that accept non-preferred types for that argument. Keep all candidates if none survive these tests. If only one candidate remains, use it; else continue to the next step.

    f. If there are both `unknown` and known-type arguments, and all the known-type arguments have the same type, assume that the `unknown` arguments are also of that type, and check which candidates can accept that type at the `unknown`-argument positions. If exactly one candidate passes this test, use it. Otherwise, fail.

Some examples follow.

Example 10-1. Factorial Operator Type Resolution

There is only one factorial operator (postfix `!`) defined in the standard catalog, and it takes an argument of type `bigint`. The scanner assigns an initial type of `integer` to the argument in this query expression:

```
SELECT 40 ! AS "40 factorial";
```

```
               40 factorial
--------------------------------------------------
 815915283247897734345611269596115894272000000000
(1 row)
```

So the parser does a type conversion on the operand and the query is equivalent to:

```
SELECT CAST(40 AS bigint) ! AS "40 factorial";
```

Example 10-2. String Concatenation Operator Type Resolution

A string-like syntax is used for working with string types and for working with complex extension types. Strings with unspecified type are matched with likely operator candidates.

An example with one unspecified argument:

```
SELECT text 'abc' || 'def' AS "text and unknown";
```

```
 text and unknown
------------------
 abcdef
(1 row)
```

In this case the parser looks to see if there is an operator taking `text` for both arguments. Since there is, it assumes that the second argument should be interpreted as type `text`.

Here is a concatenation of two values of unspecified types:

```
SELECT 'abc' || 'def' AS "unspecified";
```

```
 unspecified
-------------
 abcdef
(1 row)
```

In this case there is no initial hint for which type to use, since no types are specified in the query. So, the parser looks for all candidate operators and finds that there are candidates accepting both string-category and bit-string-category inputs. Since string category is preferred when available, that category is selected, and then the preferred type for strings, `text`, is used as the specific type to resolve the unknown-type literals as.

Example 10-3. Absolute-Value and Negation Operator Type Resolution

The PostgreSQL operator catalog has several entries for the prefix operator @, all of which implement absolute-value operations for various numeric data types. One of these entries is for type `float8`, which is the preferred type in the numeric category. Therefore, PostgreSQL will use that entry when faced with an `unknown` input:

```
SELECT @ '-4.5' AS "abs";
 abs
-----
 4.5
(1 row)
```

Here the system has implicitly resolved the unknown-type literal as type `float8` before applying the chosen operator. We can verify that `float8` and not some other type was used:

```
SELECT @ '-4.5e500' AS "abs";

ERROR:  "-4.5e500" is out of range for type double precision
```

On the other hand, the prefix operator ~ (bitwise negation) is defined only for integer data types, not for `float8`. So, if we try a similar case with ~, we get:

```
SELECT ~ '20' AS "negation";

ERROR:  operator is not unique: ~ "unknown"
HINT:  Could not choose a best candidate operator. You might need to add
explicit type casts.
```

This happens because the system cannot decide which of the several possible ~ operators should be preferred. We can help it out with an explicit cast:

```
SELECT ~ CAST('20' AS int8) AS "negation";

 negation
----------
      -21
(1 row)
```

Example 10-4. Array Inclusion Operator Type Resolution

Here is another example of resolving an operator with one known and one unknown input:

```
SELECT array[1,2] <@ '{1,2,3}' as "is subset";

 is subset
-----------
 t
(1 row)
```

The PostgreSQL operator catalog has several entries for the infix operator <@, but the only two that could possibly accept an integer array on the left-hand side are array inclusion (`anyarray <@ anyarray`) and range inclusion (`anyelement <@ anyrange`). Since none of these polymorphic pseudo-types (see Section 8.20) are considered preferred, the parser cannot resolve the ambiguity on that basis. However, step 3.f tells it to assume that the unknown-type literal is of the same type as the other input, that is, integer array. Now only one of the two operators can match, so array inclusion is selected. (Had range inclusion been selected, we would have gotten an error, because the string does not have the right format to be a range literal.)

Example 10-5. Custom Operator on a Domain Type

Users sometimes try to declare operators applying just to a domain type. This is possible but is not nearly as useful as it might seem, because the operator resolution rules are designed to select operators applying to the domain's base type. As an example consider

```
CREATE DOMAIN mytext AS text CHECK(...);
CREATE FUNCTION mytext_eq_text (mytext, text) RETURNS boolean AS ...;
CREATE OPERATOR = (procedure=mytext_eq_text, leftarg=mytext, rightarg=text);
CREATE TABLE mytable (val mytext);

SELECT * FROM mytable WHERE val = 'foo';
```

This query will not use the custom operator. The parser will first see if there is a `mytext = mytext` operator (step 2.a), which there is not; then it will consider the domain's base type `text`, and see if there is a `text = text` operator (step 2.b), which there is; so it resolves the `unknown`-type literal as `text` and uses the `text = text` operator. The only way to get the custom operator to be used is to explicitly cast the literal:

```
SELECT * FROM mytable WHERE val = text 'foo';
```

so that the `mytext = text` operator is found immediately according to the exact-match rule. If the best-match rules are reached, they actively discriminate against operators on domain types. If they did not, such an operator would create too many ambiguous-operator failures, because the casting rules always consider a domain as castable to or from its base type, and so the domain operator would be considered usable in all the same cases as a similarly-named operator on the base type.

10.3. Functions

The specific function that is referenced by a function call is determined using the following procedure.

Function Type Resolution

1. Select the functions to be considered from the `pg_proc` system catalog. If a non-schema-qualified function name was used, the functions considered are those with the matching name and argument count that are visible in the current search path (see Section 5.7.3). If a qualified function name was given, only functions in the specified schema are considered.

   a. If the search path finds multiple functions of identical argument types, only the one appearing earliest in the path is considered. Functions of different argument types are considered on an equal footing regardless of search path position.

   b. If a function is declared with a `VARIADIC` array parameter, and the call does not use the `VARIADIC` keyword, then the function is treated as if the array parameter were replaced by one or more occurrences of its element type, as needed to match the call. After such expansion the function might have effective argument types identical to some non-variadic function. In that case the function appearing earlier in the search path is used, or if the two functions are in the same schema, the non-variadic one is preferred.

    c.   Functions that have default values for parameters are considered to match any call that omits zero or more of the defaultable parameter positions. If more than one such function matches a call, the one appearing earliest in the search path is used. If there are two or more such functions in the same schema with identical parameter types in the non-defaulted positions (which is possible if they have different sets of defaultable parameters), the system will not be able to determine which to prefer, and so an "ambiguous function call" error will result if no better match to the call can be found.

2.   Check for a function accepting exactly the input argument types. If one exists (there can be only one exact match in the set of functions considered), use it. (Cases involving unknown will never find a match at this step.)

3.   If no exact match is found, see if the function call appears to be a special type conversion request. This happens if the function call has just one argument and the function name is the same as the (internal) name of some data type. Furthermore, the function argument must be either an unknown-type literal, or a type that is binary-coercible to the named data type, or a type that could be converted to the named data type by applying that type's I/O functions (that is, the conversion is either to or from one of the standard string types). When these conditions are met, the function call is treated as a form of CAST specification. [1]

4.   Look for the best match.

    a.   Discard candidate functions for which the input types do not match and cannot be converted (using an implicit conversion) to match. unknown literals are assumed to be convertible to anything for this purpose. If only one candidate remains, use it; else continue to the next step.

    b.   If any input argument is of a domain type, treat it as being of the domain's base type for all subsequent steps. This ensures that domains act like their base types for purposes of ambiguous-function resolution.

    c.   Run through all candidates and keep those with the most exact matches on input types. Keep all candidates if none have exact matches. If only one candidate remains, use it; else continue to the next step.

    d.   Run through all candidates and keep those that accept preferred types (of the input data type's type category) at the most positions where type conversion will be required. Keep all candidates if none accept preferred types. If only one candidate remains, use it; else continue to the next step.

    e.   If any input arguments are unknown, check the type categories accepted at those argument positions by the remaining candidates. At each position, select the string category if any candidate accepts that category. (This bias towards string is appropriate since an unknown-type literal looks like a string.) Otherwise, if all the remaining candidates accept the same type category, select that category; otherwise fail because the correct choice cannot be deduced without more clues. Now discard candidates that do not accept the selected type

---

1.   The reason for this step is to support function-style cast specifications in cases where there is not an actual cast function. If there is a cast function, it is conventionally named after its output type, and so there is no need to have a special case. See CREATE CAST for additional commentary.

category. Furthermore, if any candidate accepts a preferred type in that category, discard candidates that accept non-preferred types for that argument. Keep all candidates if none survive these tests. If only one candidate remains, use it; else continue to the next step.

f.   If there are both `unknown` and known-type arguments, and all the known-type arguments have the same type, assume that the `unknown` arguments are also of that type, and check which candidates can accept that type at the `unknown`-argument positions. If exactly one candidate passes this test, use it. Otherwise, fail.

Note that the "best match" rules are identical for operator and function type resolution. Some examples follow.

Example 10-6. Rounding Function Argument Type Resolution

There is only one `round` function that takes two arguments; it takes a first argument of type `numeric` and a second argument of type `integer`. So the following query automatically converts the first argument of type `integer` to `numeric`:

```
SELECT round(4, 4);
```

```
 round
--------
 4.0000
(1 row)
```

That query is actually transformed by the parser to:

```
SELECT round(CAST (4 AS numeric), 4);
```

Since numeric constants with decimal points are initially assigned the type `numeric`, the following query will require no type conversion and therefore might be slightly more efficient:

```
SELECT round(4.0, 4);
```

Example 10-7. Substring Function Type Resolution

There are several `substr` functions, one of which takes types `text` and `integer`. If called with a string constant of unspecified type, the system chooses the candidate function that accepts an argument of the preferred category `string` (namely of type `text`).

```
SELECT substr('1234', 3);
```

```
 substr
--------
     34
(1 row)
```

If the string is declared to be of type `varchar`, as might be the case if it comes from a table, then the parser will try to convert it to become `text`:

```
SELECT substr(varchar '1234', 3);
```

```
 substr
--------
```

```
     34
(1 row)
```

This is transformed by the parser to effectively become:
```
SELECT substr(CAST (varchar '1234' AS text), 3);
```

> **Note:** The parser learns from the `pg_cast` catalog that `text` and `varchar` are binary-compatible, meaning that one can be passed to a function that accepts the other without doing any physical conversion. Therefore, no type conversion call is really inserted in this case.

And, if the function is called with an argument of type `integer`, the parser will try to convert that to `text`:
```
SELECT substr(1234, 3);
ERROR:  function substr(integer, integer) does not exist
HINT:  No function matches the given name and argument types. You might need
to add explicit type casts.
```
This does not work because `integer` does not have an implicit cast to `text`. An explicit cast will work, however:
```
SELECT substr(CAST (1234 AS text), 3);
```
```
 substr
--------
     34
(1 row)
```

10.4. Value Storage

Values to be inserted into a table are converted to the destination column's data type according to the following steps.

Value Storage Type Conversion

1. Check for an exact match with the target.

2. Otherwise, try to convert the expression to the target type. This will succeed if there is a registered cast between the two types. If the expression is an unknown-type literal, the contents of the literal string will be fed to the input conversion routine for the target type.

3. Check to see if there is a sizing cast for the target type. A sizing cast is a cast from that type to itself. If one is found in the `pg_cast` catalog, apply it to the expression before storing into the destination column. The implementation function for such a cast always takes an extra parameter of type `integer`, which receives the destination column's `atttypmod` value (typically its declared length, although the interpretation of `atttypmod` varies for different data types), and it may take a third `boolean` parameter that says whether the cast is explicit or implicit. The cast function is responsible for applying any length-dependent semantics such as size checking or truncation.

Example 10-8. `character` Storage Type Conversion

For a target column declared as `character(20)` the following statement shows that the stored value is sized correctly:

```
CREATE TABLE vv (v character(20));
INSERT INTO vv SELECT 'abc' || 'def';
SELECT v, octet_length(v) FROM vv;
```

```
         v          | octet_length
--------------------+-------------
 abcdef             |           20
(1 row)
```

What has really happened here is that the two unknown literals are resolved to `text` by default, allowing the `||` operator to be resolved as `text` concatenation. Then the `text` result of the operator is converted to `bpchar` ("blank-padded char", the internal name of the `character` data type) to match the target column type. (Since the conversion from `text` to `bpchar` is binary-coercible, this conversion does not insert any real function call.) Finally, the sizing function `bpchar(bpchar, integer, boolean)` is found in the system catalog and applied to the operator's result and the stored column length. This type-specific function performs the required length check and addition of padding spaces.

10.5. UNION, CASE, and Related Constructs

SQL `UNION` constructs must match up possibly dissimilar types to become a single result set. The resolution algorithm is applied separately to each output column of a union query. The `INTERSECT` and `EXCEPT` constructs resolve dissimilar types in the same way as `UNION`. The `CASE`, `ARRAY`, `VALUES`, `GREATEST` and `LEAST` constructs use the identical algorithm to match up their component expressions and select a result data type.

Type Resolution for UNION, CASE, and Related Constructs

1. If all inputs are of the same type, and it is not `unknown`, resolve as that type.

2. If any input is of a domain type, treat it as being of the domain's base type for all subsequent steps. [2]

3. If all inputs are of type `unknown`, resolve as type `text` (the preferred type of the string category). Otherwise, `unknown` inputs are ignored.

4. If the non-unknown inputs are not all of the same type category, fail.

5. Choose the first non-unknown input type which is a preferred type in that category, if there is one.

6. Otherwise, choose the last non-unknown input type that allows all the preceding non-unknown inputs to be implicitly converted to it. (There always is such a type, since at least the first type in the list must satisfy this condition.)

---

2. Somewhat like the treatment of domain inputs for operators and functions, this behavior allows a domain type to be preserved through a `UNION` or similar construct, so long as the user is careful to ensure that all inputs are implicitly or explicitly of that exact type. Otherwise the domain's base type will be preferred.

7. Convert all inputs to the selected type. Fail if there is not a conversion from a given input to the selected type.

Some examples follow.

Example 10-9. Type Resolution with Underspecified Types in a Union

```
SELECT text 'a' AS "text" UNION SELECT 'b';
```

```
 text
------
 a
 b
(2 rows)
```

Here, the unknown-type literal 'b' will be resolved to type text.

Example 10-10. Type Resolution in a Simple Union

```
SELECT 1.2 AS "numeric" UNION SELECT 1;
```

```
 numeric
---------
       1
     1.2
(2 rows)
```

The literal 1.2 is of type numeric, and the integer value 1 can be cast implicitly to numeric, so that type is used.

Example 10-11. Type Resolution in a Transposed Union

```
SELECT 1 AS "real" UNION SELECT CAST('2.2' AS REAL);
```

```
 real
------
    1
  2.2
(2 rows)
```

Here, since type real cannot be implicitly cast to integer, but integer can be implicitly cast to real, the union result type is resolved as real.

Chapter 11. Indexes

Indexes are a common way to enhance database performance. An index allows the database server to find and retrieve specific rows much faster than it could do without an index. But indexes also add overhead to the database system as a whole, so they should be used sensibly.

11.1. Introduction

Suppose we have a table similar to this:

```
CREATE TABLE test1 (
    id integer,
    content varchar
);
```

and the application issues many queries of the form:

```
SELECT content FROM test1 WHERE id = constant;
```

With no advance preparation, the system would have to scan the entire test1 table, row by row, to find all matching entries. If there are many rows in test1 and only a few rows (perhaps zero or one) that would be returned by such a query, this is clearly an inefficient method. But if the system has been instructed to maintain an index on the id column, it can use a more efficient method for locating matching rows. For instance, it might only have to walk a few levels deep into a search tree.

A similar approach is used in most non-fiction books: terms and concepts that are frequently looked up by readers are collected in an alphabetic index at the end of the book. The interested reader can scan the index relatively quickly and flip to the appropriate page(s), rather than having to read the entire book to find the material of interest. Just as it is the task of the author to anticipate the items that readers are likely to look up, it is the task of the database programmer to foresee which indexes will be useful.

The following command can be used to create an index on the id column, as discussed:

```
CREATE INDEX test1_id_index ON test1 (id);
```

The name test1_id_index can be chosen freely, but you should pick something that enables you to remember later what the index was for.

To remove an index, use the DROP INDEX command. Indexes can be added to and removed from tables at any time.

Once an index is created, no further intervention is required: the system will update the index when the table is modified, and it will use the index in queries when it thinks doing so would be more efficient than a sequential table scan. But you might have to run the ANALYZE command regularly to update statistics to allow the query planner to make educated decisions. See Chapter 14 for information about how to find out whether an index is used and when and why the planner might choose *not* to use an index.

Indexes can also benefit UPDATE and DELETE commands with search conditions. Indexes can moreover be used in join searches. Thus, an index defined on a column that is part of a join condition can also significantly speed up queries with joins.

Creating an index on a large table can take a long time. By default, PostgreSQL allows reads (SELECT statements) to occur on the table in parallel with index creation, but writes (INSERT, UPDATE, DELETE) are blocked until the index build is finished. In production environments this is often unacceptable. It is possible to allow writes to occur in parallel with index creation, but there are several caveats to be aware of — for more information see *Building Indexes Concurrently*.

After an index is created, the system has to keep it synchronized with the table. This adds overhead to data manipulation operations. Therefore indexes that are seldom or never used in queries should be removed.

11.2. Index Types

PostgreSQL provides several index types: B-tree, Hash, GiST, SP-GiST and GIN. Each index type uses a different algorithm that is best suited to different types of queries. By default, the CREATE INDEX command creates B-tree indexes, which fit the most common situations.

B-trees can handle equality and range queries on data that can be sorted into some ordering. In particular, the PostgreSQL query planner will consider using a B-tree index whenever an indexed column is involved in a comparison using one of these operators:

```
<
<=
=
>=
>
```

Constructs equivalent to combinations of these operators, such as BETWEEN and IN, can also be implemented with a B-tree index search. Also, an IS NULL or IS NOT NULL condition on an index column can be used with a B-tree index.

The optimizer can also use a B-tree index for queries involving the pattern matching operators LIKE and ~ *if* the pattern is a constant and is anchored to the beginning of the string — for example, col LIKE 'foo%' or col ~ '^foo', but not col LIKE '%bar'. However, if your database does not use the C locale you will need to create the index with a special operator class to support indexing of pattern-matching queries; see Section 11.9 below. It is also possible to use B-tree indexes for ILIKE and ~*, but only if the pattern starts with non-alphabetic characters, i.e., characters that are not affected by upper/lower case conversion.

B-tree indexes can also be used to retrieve data in sorted order. This is not always faster than a simple scan and sort, but it is often helpful.

Hash indexes can only handle simple equality comparisons. The query planner will consider using a hash index whenever an indexed column is involved in a comparison using the = operator. The following command is used to create a hash index:

```
CREATE INDEX name ON table USING hash (column);
```

> # Caution
>
> Hash index operations are not presently WAL-logged, so hash indexes might need to be rebuilt with `REINDEX` after a database crash if there were unwritten changes. Also, changes to hash indexes are not replicated over streaming or file-based replication after the initial base backup, so they give wrong answers to queries that subsequently use them. For these reasons, hash index use is presently discouraged.

GiST indexes are not a single kind of index, but rather an infrastructure within which many different indexing strategies can be implemented. Accordingly, the particular operators with which a GiST index can be used vary depending on the indexing strategy (the *operator class*). As an example, the standard distribution of PostgreSQL includes GiST operator classes for several two-dimensional geometric data types, which support indexed queries using these operators:

```
<<
&<
&>
>>
<<|
&<|
|&>
|>>
@>
<@
~=
&&
```

(See Section 9.11 for the meaning of these operators.) The GiST operator classes included in the standard distribution are documented in Table 56-1. Many other GiST operator classes are available in the `contrib` collection or as separate projects. For more information see Chapter 56.

GiST indexes are also capable of optimizing "nearest-neighbor" searches, such as

```
SELECT * FROM places ORDER BY location <-> point '(101,456)' LIMIT 10;
```

which finds the ten places closest to a given target point. The ability to do this is again dependent on the particular operator class being used. In Table 56-1, operators that can be used in this way are listed in the column "Ordering Operators".

SP-GiST indexes, like GiST indexes, offer an infrastructure that supports various kinds of searches. SP-GiST permits implementation of a wide range of different non-balanced disk-based data structures, such as quadtrees, k-d trees, and radix trees (tries). As an example, the standard distribution of PostgreSQL includes SP-GiST operator classes for two-dimensional points, which support indexed queries using these operators:

```
<<
>>
~=
<@
```

```
< ^
> ^
```

(See Section 9.11 for the meaning of these operators.) The SP-GiST operator classes included in the standard distribution are documented in Table 57-1. For more information see Chapter 57.

GIN indexes are inverted indexes which can handle values that contain more than one key, arrays for example. Like GiST and SP-GiST, GIN can support many different user-defined indexing strategies and the particular operators with which a GIN index can be used vary depending on the indexing strategy. As an example, the standard distribution of PostgreSQL includes GIN operator classes for one-dimensional arrays, which support indexed queries using these operators:

```
< @
@ >
=
& &
```

(See Section 9.18 for the meaning of these operators.) The GIN operator classes included in the standard distribution are documented in Table 58-1. Many other GIN operator classes are available in the `contrib` collection or as separate projects. For more information see Chapter 58.

11.3. Multicolumn Indexes

An index can be defined on more than one column of a table. For example, if you have a table of this form:

```
CREATE TABLE test2 (
  major int,
  minor int,
  name varchar
);
```

(say, you keep your `/dev` directory in a database...) and you frequently issue queries like:

```
SELECT name FROM test2 WHERE major = constant AND minor = constant;
```

then it might be appropriate to define an index on the columns `major` and `minor` together, e.g.:

```
CREATE INDEX test2_mm_idx ON test2 (major, minor);
```

Currently, only the B-tree, GiST and GIN index types support multicolumn indexes. Up to 32 columns can be specified. (This limit can be altered when building PostgreSQL; see the file `pg_config_manual.h`.)

A multicolumn B-tree index can be used with query conditions that involve any subset of the index's columns, but the index is most efficient when there are constraints on the leading (leftmost) columns. The exact rule is that equality constraints on leading columns, plus any inequality constraints on the first column that does not have an equality constraint, will be used to limit the portion of the index that is scanned. Constraints on columns to the right of these columns are checked in the index, so they save visits to the table proper, but they do not reduce the portion of the index that has to be scanned. For example, given an index on `(a, b, c)` and a query condition `WHERE a = 5 AND b >= 42 AND c < 77`, the index would have to be scanned from the first entry with a = 5 and b = 42 up through the last entry with a = 5. Index entries with c >= 77 would be skipped, but they'd still have to be scanned through. This index could in principle be used for queries that have constraints on b and/or c with no constraint on a — but the entire index would have to be scanned, so in most cases the planner would prefer a sequential table scan over using the index.

A multicolumn GiST index can be used with query conditions that involve any subset of the index's columns. Conditions on additional columns restrict the entries returned by the index, but the condition on the first column is the most important one for determining how much of the index needs to be scanned. A GiST index will be relatively ineffective if its first column has only a few distinct values, even if there are many distinct values in additional columns.

A multicolumn GIN index can be used with query conditions that involve any subset of the index's columns. Unlike B-tree or GiST, index search effectiveness is the same regardless of which index column(s) the query conditions use.

Of course, each column must be used with operators appropriate to the index type; clauses that involve other operators will not be considered.

Multicolumn indexes should be used sparingly. In most situations, an index on a single column is sufficient and saves space and time. Indexes with more than three columns are unlikely to be helpful unless the usage of the table is extremely stylized. See also Section 11.5 for some discussion of the merits of different index configurations.

11.4. Indexes and ORDER BY

In addition to simply finding the rows to be returned by a query, an index may be able to deliver them in a specific sorted order. This allows a query's ORDER BY specification to be honored without a separate sorting step. Of the index types currently supported by PostgreSQL, only B-tree can produce sorted output — the other index types return matching rows in an unspecified, implementation-dependent order.

The planner will consider satisfying an ORDER BY specification either by scanning an available index that matches the specification, or by scanning the table in physical order and doing an explicit sort. For a query that requires scanning a large fraction of the table, an explicit sort is likely to be faster than using an index because it requires less disk I/O due to following a sequential access pattern. Indexes are more useful when only a few rows need be fetched. An important special case is ORDER BY in combination with LIMIT *n*: an explicit sort will have to process all the data to identify the first *n* rows, but if there is an index matching the ORDER BY, the first *n* rows can be retrieved directly, without scanning the remainder at all.

By default, B-tree indexes store their entries in ascending order with nulls last. This means that a forward scan of an index on column x produces output satisfying ORDER BY x (or more verbosely, ORDER BY x ASC NULLS LAST). The index can also be scanned backward, producing output satisfying ORDER BY x DESC (or more verbosely, ORDER BY x DESC NULLS FIRST, since NULLS FIRST is the default for ORDER BY DESC).

You can adjust the ordering of a B-tree index by including the options ASC, DESC, NULLS FIRST, and/or NULLS LAST when creating the index; for example:

```
CREATE INDEX test2_info_nulls_low ON test2 (info NULLS FIRST);
CREATE INDEX test3_desc_index ON test3 (id DESC NULLS LAST);
```

An index stored in ascending order with nulls first can satisfy either ORDER BY x ASC NULLS FIRST or ORDER BY x DESC NULLS LAST depending on which direction it is scanned in.

You might wonder why bother providing all four options, when two options together with the possibility of backward scan would cover all the variants of ORDER BY. In single-column indexes the options are indeed redundant, but in multicolumn indexes they can be useful. Consider a two-column index on (x, y): this can satisfy ORDER BY x, y if we scan forward, or ORDER BY x DESC, y DESC if we scan backward. But it might be that the application frequently needs to use ORDER BY x ASC, y DESC. There is no way to get that ordering from a plain index, but it is possible if the index is defined as (x ASC, y DESC) or (x DESC, y ASC).

Obviously, indexes with non-default sort orderings are a fairly specialized feature, but sometimes they can produce tremendous speedups for certain queries. Whether it's worth maintaining such an index depends on how often you use queries that require a special sort ordering.

11.5. Combining Multiple Indexes

A single index scan can only use query clauses that use the index's columns with operators of its operator class and are joined with AND. For example, given an index on (a, b) a query condition like WHERE a = 5 AND b = 6 could use the index, but a query like WHERE a = 5 OR b = 6 could not directly use the index.

Fortunately, PostgreSQL has the ability to combine multiple indexes (including multiple uses of the same index) to handle cases that cannot be implemented by single index scans. The system can form AND and OR conditions across several index scans. For example, a query like WHERE x = 42 OR x = 47 OR x = 53 OR x = 99 could be broken down into four separate scans of an index on x, each scan using one of the query clauses. The results of these scans are then ORed together to produce the result. Another example is that if we have separate indexes on x and y, one possible implementation of a query like WHERE x = 5 AND y = 6 is to use each index with the appropriate query clause and then AND together the index results to identify the result rows.

To combine multiple indexes, the system scans each needed index and prepares a *bitmap* in memory giving the locations of table rows that are reported as matching that index's conditions. The bitmaps are then ANDed and ORed together as needed by the query. Finally, the actual table rows are visited and returned. The table rows are visited in physical order, because that is how the bitmap is laid out; this means that any ordering of the original indexes is lost, and so a separate sort step will be needed if the query has an ORDER BY clause. For this reason, and because each additional index scan adds extra time, the planner will sometimes choose to use a simple index scan even though additional indexes are available that could have been used as well.

In all but the simplest applications, there are various combinations of indexes that might be useful, and the database developer must make trade-offs to decide which indexes to provide. Sometimes multicolumn indexes are best, but sometimes it's better to create separate indexes and rely on the index-combination feature. For example, if your workload includes a mix of queries that sometimes involve only column x, sometimes only column y, and sometimes both columns, you might choose to create two separate indexes on x and y, relying on index combination to process the queries that use both columns. You could also create a multicolumn index on (x, y). This index would typically be more efficient than index combination for queries involving both columns, but as discussed in Section 11.3, it would be almost useless for queries involving only y, so it should not be the only index. A combination of the multicolumn index and a separate index on y would serve reasonably well. For queries involving only x, the multicolumn index could be used, though it would be larger and hence slower than an index on x alone. The last alternative is to create all three indexes, but this is probably only reasonable if the table is searched much more often than it is updated and all three types of query are common. If one of the types of query is much less common than the others, you'd probably settle for creating just the two indexes that best match the common types.

11.6. Unique Indexes

Indexes can also be used to enforce uniqueness of a column's value, or the uniqueness of the combined values of more than one column.

```
CREATE UNIQUE INDEX name ON table (column [, ...]);
```

Currently, only B-tree indexes can be declared unique.

When an index is declared unique, multiple table rows with equal indexed values are not allowed. Null values are not considered equal. A multicolumn unique index will only reject cases where all indexed columns are equal in multiple rows.

PostgreSQL automatically creates a unique index when a unique constraint or primary key is defined for a table. The index covers the columns that make up the primary key or unique constraint (a multicolumn index, if appropriate), and is the mechanism that enforces the constraint.

> **Note:** The preferred way to add a unique constraint to a table is ALTER TABLE ... ADD CONSTRAINT. The use of indexes to enforce unique constraints could be considered an implementation detail that should not be accessed directly. One should, however, be aware that there's no need to manually create indexes on unique columns; doing so would just duplicate the automatically-created index.

11.7. Indexes on Expressions

An index column need not be just a column of the underlying table, but can be a function or scalar expression computed from one or more columns of the table. This feature is useful to obtain fast access to tables based on the results of computations.

For example, a common way to do case-insensitive comparisons is to use the lower function:

```
SELECT * FROM test1 WHERE lower(col1) = 'value';
```

This query can use an index if one has been defined on the result of the lower(col1) function:

```
CREATE INDEX test1_lower_col1_idx ON test1 (lower(col1));
```

If we were to declare this index UNIQUE, it would prevent creation of rows whose col1 values differ only in case, as well as rows whose col1 values are actually identical. Thus, indexes on expressions can be used to enforce constraints that are not definable as simple unique constraints.

As another example, if one often does queries like:

```
SELECT * FROM people WHERE (first_name || ' ' || last_name) = 'John Smith';
```

then it might be worth creating an index like this:

```
CREATE INDEX people_names ON people ((first_name || ' ' || last_name));
```

The syntax of the CREATE INDEX command normally requires writing parentheses around index expressions, as shown in the second example. The parentheses can be omitted when the expression is just a function call, as in the first example.

Index expressions are relatively expensive to maintain, because the derived expression(s) must be computed for each row upon insertion and whenever it is updated. However, the index expressions are *not* recomputed during an indexed search, since they are already stored in the index. In both examples above, the system sees the query as just WHERE indexedcolumn = 'constant' and so the speed of the search is equivalent to any other simple index query. Thus, indexes on expressions are useful when retrieval speed is more important than insertion and update speed.

11.8. Partial Indexes

A *partial index* is an index built over a subset of a table; the subset is defined by a conditional expression (called the *predicate* of the partial index). The index contains entries only for those table rows that satisfy the predicate. Partial indexes are a specialized feature, but there are several situations in which they are useful.

One major reason for using a partial index is to avoid indexing common values. Since a query searching for a common value (one that accounts for more than a few percent of all the table rows) will not use the index anyway, there is no point in keeping those rows in the index at all. This reduces the size of the index, which will speed up those queries that do use the index. It will also speed up many table update operations because the index does not need to be updated in all cases. Example 11-1 shows a possible application of this idea.

Example 11-1. Setting up a Partial Index to Exclude Common Values

Suppose you are storing web server access logs in a database. Most accesses originate from the IP address range of your organization but some are from elsewhere (say, employees on dial-up connections). If your searches by IP are primarily for outside accesses, you probably do not need to index the IP range that corresponds to your organization's subnet.

Assume a table like this:

```
CREATE TABLE access_log (
    url varchar,
    client_ip inet,
```

```
        . . .
);
```

To create a partial index that suits our example, use a command such as this:

```
CREATE INDEX access_log_client_ip_ix ON access_log (client_ip)
WHERE NOT (client_ip > inet '192.168.100.0' AND
           client_ip < inet '192.168.100.255');
```

A typical query that can use this index would be:

```
SELECT *
FROM access_log
WHERE url = '/index.html' AND client_ip = inet '212.78.10.32';
```

A query that cannot use this index is:

```
SELECT *
FROM access_log
WHERE client_ip = inet '192.168.100.23';
```

Observe that this kind of partial index requires that the common values be predetermined, so such partial indexes are best used for data distributions that do not change. The indexes can be recreated occasionally to adjust for new data distributions, but this adds maintenance effort.

Another possible use for a partial index is to exclude values from the index that the typical query workload is not interested in; this is shown in Example 11-2. This results in the same advantages as listed above, but it prevents the "uninteresting" values from being accessed via that index, even if an index scan might be profitable in that case. Obviously, setting up partial indexes for this kind of scenario will require a lot of care and experimentation.

Example 11-2. Setting up a Partial Index to Exclude Uninteresting Values

If you have a table that contains both billed and unbilled orders, where the unbilled orders take up a small fraction of the total table and yet those are the most-accessed rows, you can improve performance by creating an index on just the unbilled rows. The command to create the index would look like this:

```
CREATE INDEX orders_unbilled_index ON orders (order_nr)
    WHERE billed is not true;
```

A possible query to use this index would be:

```
SELECT * FROM orders WHERE billed is not true AND order_nr < 10000;
```

However, the index can also be used in queries that do not involve order_nr at all, e.g.:

```
SELECT * FROM orders WHERE billed is not true AND amount > 5000.00;
```

This is not as efficient as a partial index on the amount column would be, since the system has to scan the entire index. Yet, if there are relatively few unbilled orders, using this partial index just to find the unbilled orders could be a win.

Note that this query cannot use this index:

```
SELECT * FROM orders WHERE order_nr = 3501;
```

The order 3501 might be among the billed or unbilled orders.

Example 11-2 also illustrates that the indexed column and the column used in the predicate do not need to match. PostgreSQL supports partial indexes with arbitrary predicates, so long as only columns of the table being indexed are involved. However, keep in mind that the predicate must match the conditions used in the queries that are supposed to benefit from the index. To be precise, a partial index can be used in a query only if the system can recognize that the WHERE condition of the query mathematically implies the predicate of the index. PostgreSQL does not have a sophisticated theorem prover that can recognize mathematically equivalent expressions that are written in different forms. (Not only is such a general theorem prover extremely difficult to create, it would probably be too slow to be of any real use.) The system can recognize simple inequality implications, for example "x < 1" implies "x < 2"; otherwise the predicate condition must exactly match part of the query's WHERE condition or the index will not be recognized as usable. Matching takes place at query planning time, not at run time. As a result, parameterized query clauses do not work with a partial index. For example a prepared query with a parameter might specify "x < ?" which will never imply "x < 2" for all possible values of the parameter.

A third possible use for partial indexes does not require the index to be used in queries at all. The idea here is to create a unique index over a subset of a table, as in Example 11-3. This enforces uniqueness among the rows that satisfy the index predicate, without constraining those that do not.

Example 11-3. Setting up a Partial Unique Index

Suppose that we have a table describing test outcomes. We wish to ensure that there is only one "successful" entry for a given subject and target combination, but there might be any number of "unsuccessful" entries. Here is one way to do it:

```
CREATE TABLE tests (
    subject text,
    target text,
    success boolean,
    ...
);
```

```
CREATE UNIQUE INDEX tests_success_constraint ON tests (subject, target)
    WHERE success;
```
This is a particularly efficient approach when there are few successful tests and many unsuccessful ones.

Finally, a partial index can also be used to override the system's query plan choices. Also, data sets with peculiar distributions might cause the system to use an index when it really should not. In that case the index can be set up so that it is not available for the offending query. Normally, PostgreSQL makes reasonable choices about index usage (e.g., it avoids them when retrieving common values, so the earlier example really only saves index size, it is not required to avoid index usage), and grossly incorrect plan choices are cause for a bug report.

Keep in mind that setting up a partial index indicates that you know at least as much as the query planner knows, in particular you know when an index might be profitable. Forming this knowledge requires experience and understanding of how indexes in PostgreSQL work. In most cases, the advantage of a partial index over a regular index will be minimal.

More information about partial indexes can be found in *The case for partial indexes* , *Partial indexing in POSTGRES: research project*, and *Generalized Partial Indexes (cached version)* .

11.9. Operator Classes and Operator Families

An index definition can specify an *operator class* for each column of an index.

```
CREATE INDEX name ON table (column opclass [sort options] [, ...]);
```

The operator class identifies the operators to be used by the index for that column. For example, a B-tree index on the type int4 would use the int4_ops class; this operator class includes comparison functions for values of type int4. In practice the default operator class for the column's data type is usually sufficient. The main reason for having operator classes is that for some data types, there could be more than one meaningful index behavior. For example, we might want to sort a complex-number data type either by absolute value or by real part. We could do this by defining two operator classes for the data type and then selecting the proper class when making an index. The operator class determines the basic sort ordering (which can then be modified by adding sort options COLLATE, ASC/DESC and/or NULLS FIRST/NULLS LAST).

There are also some built-in operator classes besides the default ones:

- The operator classes text_pattern_ops, varchar_pattern_ops, and bpchar_pattern_ops support B-tree indexes on the types text, varchar, and char respectively. The difference from the default operator classes is that the values are compared strictly character by character rather than according to the locale-specific collation rules. This makes these operator classes suitable for use by queries involving pattern matching expressions (LIKE or POSIX regular expressions) when the database does not use the standard "C" locale. As an example, you might index a varchar column like this:

```
CREATE INDEX test_index ON test_table (col varchar_pattern_ops);
```

  Note that you should also create an index with the default operator class if you want queries involving ordinary <, <=, >, or >= comparisons to use an index. Such queries cannot use the *xxx*_pattern_ops operator classes. (Ordinary equality comparisons can use these operator classes, however.) It is possible to create multiple indexes on the same column with different operator classes. If you do use the C locale, you do not need the *xxx*_pattern_ops operator classes, because an index with the default operator class is usable for pattern-matching queries in the C locale.

The following query shows all defined operator classes:

```
SELECT am.amname AS index_method,
       opc.opcname AS opclass_name,
       opc.opcintype::regtype AS indexed_type,
       opc.opcdefault AS is_default
    FROM pg_am am, pg_opclass opc
    WHERE opc.opcmethod = am.oid
    ORDER BY index_method, opclass_name;
```

An operator class is actually just a subset of a larger structure called an *operator family*. In cases where several data types have similar behaviors, it is frequently useful to define cross-data-type operators and allow these to work with indexes. To do this, the operator classes for each of the types must be grouped into the same operator family. The cross-type operators are members of the family, but are not associated with any single class within the family.

This expanded version of the previous query shows the operator family each operator class belongs to:

```
SELECT am.amname AS index_method,
       opc.opcname AS opclass_name,
       opf.opfname AS opfamily_name,
       opc.opcintype::regtype AS indexed_type,
       opc.opcdefault AS is_default
    FROM pg_am am, pg_opclass opc, pg_opfamily opf
    WHERE opc.opcmethod = am.oid AND
          opc.opcfamily = opf.oid
    ORDER BY index_method, opclass_name;
```

This query shows all defined operator families and all the operators included in each family:

```
SELECT am.amname AS index_method,
       opf.opfname AS opfamily_name,
       amop.amopopr::regoperator AS opfamily_operator
    FROM pg_am am, pg_opfamily opf, pg_amop amop
    WHERE opf.opfmethod = am.oid AND
          amop.amopfamily = opf.oid
    ORDER BY index_method, opfamily_name, opfamily_operator;
```

11.10. Indexes and Collations

An index can support only one collation per index column. If multiple collations are of interest, multiple indexes may be needed.

Consider these statements:

```
CREATE TABLE test1c (
    id integer,
    content varchar COLLATE "x"
);

CREATE INDEX test1c_content_index ON test1c (content);
```

The index automatically uses the collation of the underlying column. So a query of the form

```
SELECT * FROM test1c WHERE content > constant;
```

could use the index, because the comparison will by default use the collation of the column. However, this index cannot accelerate queries that involve some other collation. So if queries of the form, say,

```
SELECT * FROM test1c WHERE content > constant COLLATE "y";
```

are also of interest, an additional index could be created that supports the "y" collation, like this:

```
CREATE INDEX test1c_content_y_index ON test1c (content COLLATE "y");
```

11.11. Examining Index Usage

Although indexes in PostgreSQL do not need maintenance or tuning, it is still important to check which indexes are actually used by the real-life query workload. Examining index usage for an individual query is done with the EXPLAIN command; its application for this purpose is illustrated in Section 14.1. It is also possible to gather overall statistics about index usage in a running server, as described in Section 27.2.

It is difficult to formulate a general procedure for determining which indexes to create. There are a number of typical cases that have been shown in the examples throughout the previous sections. A good deal of experimentation is often necessary. The rest of this section gives some tips for that:

- Always run ANALYZE first. This command collects statistics about the distribution of the values in the table. This information is required to estimate the number of rows returned by a query, which is needed by the planner to assign realistic costs to each possible query plan. In absence of any real statistics, some default values are assumed, which are almost certain to be inaccurate. Examining an application's index usage without having run ANALYZE is therefore a lost cause. See Section 23.1.3 and Section 23.1.6 for more information.

- Use real data for experimentation. Using test data for setting up indexes will tell you what indexes you need for the test data, but that is all.

  It is especially fatal to use very small test data sets. While selecting 1000 out of 100000 rows could be a candidate for an index, selecting 1 out of 100 rows will hardly be, because the 100 rows probably fit within a single disk page, and there is no plan that can beat sequentially fetching 1 disk page.

  Also be careful when making up test data, which is often unavoidable when the application is not yet in production. Values that are very similar, completely random, or inserted in sorted order will skew the statistics away from the distribution that real data would have.

- When indexes are not used, it can be useful for testing to force their use. There are run-time parameters that can turn off various plan types (see Section 18.7.1). For instance, turning off sequential scans (`enable_seqscan`) and nested-loop joins (`enable_nestloop`), which are the most basic plans, will force the system to use a different plan. If the system still chooses a sequential scan or nested-loop join then there is probably a more fundamental reason why the index is not being used; for example, the query condition does not match the index. (What kind of query can use what kind of index is explained in the previous sections.)

- If forcing index usage does use the index, then there are two possibilities: Either the system is right and using the index is indeed not appropriate, or the cost estimates of the query plans are not reflecting reality. So you should time your query with and without indexes. The EXPLAIN ANALYZE command can be useful here.

- If it turns out that the cost estimates are wrong, there are, again, two possibilities. The total cost is computed from the per-row costs of each plan node times the selectivity estimate of the plan node. The costs estimated for the plan nodes can be adjusted via run-time parameters (described in Section 18.7.2). An inaccurate selectivity estimate is due to insufficient statistics. It might be possible to improve this by tuning the statistics-gathering parameters (see ALTER TABLE).

If you do not succeed in adjusting the costs to be more appropriate, then you might have to resort to forcing index usage explicitly. You might also want to contact the PostgreSQL developers to examine the issue.

Chapter 12. Full Text Search

12.1. Introduction

Full Text Searching (or just *text search*) provides the capability to identify natural-language *documents* that satisfy a *query*, and optionally to sort them by relevance to the query. The most common type of search is to find all documents containing given *query terms* and return them in order of their *similarity* to the query. Notions of `query` and `similarity` are very flexible and depend on the specific application. The simplest search considers `query` as a set of words and `similarity` as the frequency of query words in the document.

Textual search operators have existed in databases for years. PostgreSQL has `~`, `~*`, `LIKE`, and `ILIKE` operators for textual data types, but they lack many essential properties required by modern information systems:

- There is no linguistic support, even for English. Regular expressions are not sufficient because they cannot easily handle derived words, e.g., `satisfies` and `satisfy`. You might miss documents that contain `satisfies`, although you probably would like to find them when searching for `satisfy`. It is possible to use `OR` to search for multiple derived forms, but this is tedious and error-prone (some words can have several thousand derivatives).
- They provide no ordering (ranking) of search results, which makes them ineffective when thousands of matching documents are found.
- They tend to be slow because there is no index support, so they must process all documents for every search.

Full text indexing allows documents to be *preprocessed* and an index saved for later rapid searching. Preprocessing includes:

Parsing documents into tokens. It is useful to identify various classes of tokens, e.g., numbers, words, complex words, email addresses, so that they can be processed differently. In principle token classes depend on the specific application, but for most purposes it is adequate to use a predefined set of classes. PostgreSQL uses a *parser* to perform this step. A standard parser is provided, and custom parsers can be created for specific needs.

Converting tokens into lexemes. A lexeme is a string, just like a token, but it has been *normalized* so that different forms of the same word are made alike. For example, normalization almost always includes folding upper-case letters to lower-case, and often involves removal of suffixes (such as `s` or `es` in English). This allows searches to find variant forms of the same word, without tediously entering all the possible variants. Also, this step typically eliminates *stop words*, which are words that are so common that they are useless for searching. (In short, then, tokens are raw fragments of the document text, while lexemes are words that are believed useful for indexing and searching.) PostgreSQL uses *dictionaries* to perform this step. Various standard dictionaries are provided, and custom ones can be created for specific needs.

Storing preprocessed documents optimized for searching. For example, each document can be represented as a sorted array of normalized lexemes. Along with the lexemes it is often desirable to store positional information to use for *proximity ranking*, so that a document that contains a more "dense" region of query words is assigned a higher rank than one with scattered query words.

Dictionaries allow fine-grained control over how tokens are normalized. With appropriate dictionaries, you can:

- Define stop words that should not be indexed.
- Map synonyms to a single word using Ispell.
- Map phrases to a single word using a thesaurus.
- Map different variations of a word to a canonical form using an Ispell dictionary.
- Map different variations of a word to a canonical form using Snowball stemmer rules.

A data type `tsvector` is provided for storing preprocessed documents, along with a type `tsquery` for representing processed queries (Section 8.11). There are many functions and operators available for these data types (Section 9.13), the most important of which is the match operator `@@`, which we introduce in Section 12.1.2. Full text searches can be accelerated using indexes (Section 12.9).

12.1.1. What Is a Document?

A *document* is the unit of searching in a full text search system; for example, a magazine article or email message. The text search engine must be able to parse documents and store associations of lexemes (key words) with their parent document. Later, these associations are used to search for documents that contain query words.

For searches within PostgreSQL, a document is normally a textual field within a row of a database table, or possibly a combination (concatenation) of such fields, perhaps stored in several tables or obtained dynamically. In other words, a document can be constructed from different parts for indexing and it might not be stored anywhere as a whole. For example:

```
SELECT title || ' ' || author || ' ' || abstract || ' ' || body AS document
FROM messages
WHERE mid = 12;

SELECT m.title || ' ' || m.author || ' ' || m.abstract || ' ' || d.body AS docu
FROM messages m, docs d
WHERE mid = did AND mid = 12;
```

> **Note:** Actually, in these example queries, `coalesce` should be used to prevent a single `NULL` attribute from causing a `NULL` result for the whole document.

Another possibility is to store the documents as simple text files in the file system. In this case, the database can be used to store the full text index and to execute searches, and some unique identifier can be used to retrieve the document from the file system. However, retrieving files from outside the database requires superuser permissions or special function support, so this is usually less convenient than keeping all the data inside PostgreSQL. Also, keeping everything inside the database allows easy access to document metadata to assist in indexing and display.

For text search purposes, each document must be reduced to the preprocessed `tsvector` format. Searching and ranking are performed entirely on the `tsvector` representation of a document — the original text need only be retrieved when the document has been selected for display to a user. We therefore often speak of the `tsvector` as being the document, but of course it is only a compact representation of the full document.

12.1.2. Basic Text Matching

Full text searching in PostgreSQL is based on the match operator `@@`, which returns `true` if a `tsvector` (document) matches a `tsquery` (query). It doesn't matter which data type is written first:

```
SELECT 'a fat cat sat on a mat and ate a fat rat'::tsvector @@ 'cat & rat'::tsc
 ?column?
----------
 t

SELECT 'fat & cow'::tsquery @@ 'a fat cat sat on a mat and ate a fat rat'::tsve
 ?column?
----------
 f
```

As the above example suggests, a `tsquery` is not just raw text, any more than a `tsvector` is. A `tsquery` contains search terms, which must be already-normalized lexemes, and may combine multiple terms using AND, OR, and NOT operators. (For details see Section 8.11.) There are functions `to_tsquery` and `plainto_tsquery` that are helpful in converting user-written text into a proper `tsquery`, for example by normalizing words appearing in the text. Similarly, `to_tsvector` is used to parse and normalize a document string. So in practice a text search match would look more like this:

```
SELECT to_tsvector('fat cats ate fat rats') @@ to_tsquery('fat & rat');
 ?column?
----------
 t
```

Observe that this match would not succeed if written as

```
SELECT 'fat cats ate fat rats'::tsvector @@ to_tsquery('fat & rat');
 ?column?
----------
 f
```

since here no normalization of the word `rats` will occur. The elements of a `tsvector` are lexemes, which are assumed already normalized, so `rats` does not match `rat`.

The `@@` operator also supports `text` input, allowing explicit conversion of a text string to `tsvector` or `tsquery` to be skipped in simple cases. The variants available are:

```
tsvector @@ tsquery
tsquery  @@ tsvector
text @@ tsquery
text @@ text
```

The first two of these we saw already. The form `text @@ tsquery` is equivalent to `to_tsvector(x) @@ y`. The form `text @@ text` is equivalent to `to_tsvector(x) @@ plainto_tsquery(y)`.

12.1.3. Configurations

The above are all simple text search examples. As mentioned before, full text search functionality includes the ability to do many more things: skip indexing certain words (stop words), process synonyms, and use sophisticated parsing, e.g., parse based on more than just white space. This functionality is controlled by *text search configurations*. PostgreSQL comes with predefined configurations for many languages, and you can easily create your own configurations. (psql's `\dF` command shows all available configurations.)

During installation an appropriate configuration is selected and default_text_search_config is set accordingly in `postgresql.conf`. If you are using the same text search configuration for the entire cluster you can use the value in `postgresql.conf`. To use different configurations throughout the cluster but the same configuration within any one database, use `ALTER DATABASE ... SET`. Otherwise, you can set `default_text_search_config` in each session.

Each text search function that depends on a configuration has an optional `regconfig` argument, so that the configuration to use can be specified explicitly. `default_text_search_config` is used only when this argument is omitted.

To make it easier to build custom text search configurations, a configuration is built up from simpler database objects. PostgreSQL's text search facility provides four types of configuration-related database objects:

- *Text search parsers* break documents into tokens and classify each token (for example, as words or numbers).
- *Text search dictionaries* convert tokens to normalized form and reject stop words.
- *Text search templates* provide the functions underlying dictionaries. (A dictionary simply specifies a template and a set of parameters for the template.)
- *Text search configurations* select a parser and a set of dictionaries to use to normalize the tokens produced by the parser.

Text search parsers and templates are built from low-level C functions; therefore it requires C programming ability to develop new ones, and superuser privileges to install one into a database. (There are examples of add-on parsers and templates in the `contrib/` area of the PostgreSQL distribution.) Since dictionaries and configurations just parameterize and connect together some underlying parsers and templates, no special privilege is needed to create a new dictionary or configuration. Examples of creating custom dictionaries and configurations appear later in this chapter.

12.2. Tables and Indexes

The examples in the previous section illustrated full text matching using simple constant strings. This section shows how to search table data, optionally using indexes.

12.2.1. Searching a Table

It is possible to do a full text search without an index. A simple query to print the `title` of each row that contains the word `friend` in its `body` field is:

```
SELECT title
FROM pgweb
WHERE to_tsvector('english', body) @@ to_tsquery('english', 'friend');
```

This will also find related words such as `friends` and `friendly`, since all these are reduced to the same normalized lexeme.

The query above specifies that the `english` configuration is to be used to parse and normalize the strings. Alternatively we could omit the configuration parameters:

```
SELECT title
FROM pgweb
WHERE to_tsvector(body) @@ to_tsquery('friend');
```

This query will use the configuration set by default_text_search_config.

A more complex example is to select the ten most recent documents that contain `create` and `table` in the `title` or `body`:

```
SELECT title
FROM pgweb
WHERE to_tsvector(title || ' ' || body) @@ to_tsquery('create & table')
ORDER BY last_mod_date DESC
LIMIT 10;
```

For clarity we omitted the `coalesce` function calls which would be needed to find rows that contain `NULL` in one of the two fields.

Although these queries will work without an index, most applications will find this approach too slow, except perhaps for occasional ad-hoc searches. Practical use of text searching usually requires creating an index.

12.2.2. Creating Indexes

We can create a GIN index (Section 12.9) to speed up text searches:

```
CREATE INDEX pgweb_idx ON pgweb USING gin(to_tsvector('english', body));
```

Notice that the 2-argument version of `to_tsvector` is used. Only text search functions that specify a configuration name can be used in expression indexes (Section 11.7). This is because the index contents must be unaffected by default_text_search_config. If they were affected, the index contents might be inconsistent because different entries could contain `tsvectors` that were created with different text search configurations, and there would be no way to guess which was which. It would be impossible to dump and restore such an index correctly.

Because the two-argument version of `to_tsvector` was used in the index above, only a query reference that uses the 2-argument version of `to_tsvector` with the same configuration name will use that index. That is, `WHERE to_tsvector('english', body) @@ 'a & b'` can use the index, but `WHERE` `to_tsvector(body) @@ 'a & b'` cannot. This ensures that an index will be used only with the same configuration used to create the index entries.

It is possible to set up more complex expression indexes wherein the configuration name is specified by another column, e.g.:

```
CREATE INDEX pgweb_idx ON pgweb USING gin(to_tsvector(config_name, body));
```

where `config_name` is a column in the `pgweb` table. This allows mixed configurations in the same index while recording which configuration was used for each index entry. This would be useful, for example, if the document collection contained documents in different languages. Again, queries that are meant to use the index must be phrased to match, e.g., WHERE `to_tsvector(config_name, body) @@ 'a & b'`.

Indexes can even concatenate columns:

```
CREATE INDEX pgweb_idx ON pgweb USING gin(to_tsvector('english', title || ' ' |
```

Another approach is to create a separate `tsvector` column to hold the output of `to_tsvector`. This example is a concatenation of `title` and `body`, using `coalesce` to ensure that one field will still be indexed when the other is NULL:

```
ALTER TABLE pgweb ADD COLUMN textsearchable_index_col tsvector;
UPDATE pgweb SET textsearchable_index_col =
     to_tsvector('english', coalesce(title,") || ' ' || coalesce(body,"));
```

Then we create a GIN index to speed up the search:

```
CREATE INDEX textsearch_idx ON pgweb USING gin(textsearchable_index_col);
```

Now we are ready to perform a fast full text search:

```
SELECT title
FROM pgweb
WHERE textsearchable_index_col @@ to_tsquery('create & table')
ORDER BY last_mod_date DESC
LIMIT 10;
```

When using a separate column to store the `tsvector` representation, it is necessary to create a trigger to keep the `tsvector` column current anytime `title` or `body` changes. Section 12.4.3 explains how to do that.

One advantage of the separate-column approach over an expression index is that it is not necessary to explicitly specify the text search configuration in queries in order to make use of the index. As shown in the example above, the query can depend on `default_text_search_config`. Another advantage is that searches will be faster, since it will not be necessary to redo the `to_tsvector` calls to verify index matches. (This is more important when using a GiST index than a GIN index; see Section 12.9.) The expression-index approach is simpler to set up, however, and it requires less disk space since the `tsvector` representation is not stored explicitly.

12.3. Controlling Text Search

To implement full text searching there must be a function to create a `tsvector` from a document and a `tsquery` from a user query. Also, we need to return results in a useful order, so we need a function that compares documents with respect to their relevance to the query. It's also important to be able to display the results nicely. PostgreSQL provides support for all of these functions.

12.3.1. Parsing Documents

PostgreSQL provides the function `to_tsvector` for converting a document to the `tsvector` data type.

```
to_tsvector([ config regconfig, ] document text) returns tsvector
```

`to_tsvector` parses a textual document into tokens, reduces the tokens to lexemes, and returns a `tsvector` which lists the lexemes together with their positions in the document. The document is processed according to the specified or default text search configuration. Here is a simple example:

```
SELECT to_tsvector('english', 'a fat  cat sat on a mat - it ate a fat rats');
                  to_tsvector
-----------------------------------------------------
 'ate':9 'cat':3 'fat':2,11 'mat':7 'rat':12 'sat':4
```

In the example above we see that the resulting `tsvector` does not contain the words `a`, `on`, or `it`, the word `rats` became `rat`, and the punctuation sign – was ignored.

The `to_tsvector` function internally calls a parser which breaks the document text into tokens and assigns a type to each token. For each token, a list of dictionaries (Section 12.6) is consulted, where the list can vary depending on the token type. The first dictionary that *recognizes* the token emits one or more normalized *lexemes* to represent the token. For example, `rats` became `rat` because one of the dictionaries recognized that the word `rats` is a plural form of `rat`. Some words are recognized as *stop words* (Section 12.6.1), which causes them to be ignored since they occur too frequently to be useful in searching. In our example these are `a`, `on`, and `it`. If no dictionary in the list recognizes the token then it is also ignored. In this example that happened to the punctuation sign – because there are in fact no dictionaries assigned for its token type (`Space symbols`), meaning space tokens will never be indexed. The choices of parser, dictionaries and which types of tokens to index are determined by the selected text search configuration (Section 12.7). It is possible to have many different configurations in the same database, and predefined configurations are available for various languages. In our example we used the default configuration `english` for the English language.

The function `setweight` can be used to label the entries of a `tsvector` with a given *weight*, where a weight is one of the letters A, B, C, or D. This is typically used to mark entries coming from different parts of a document, such as title versus body. Later, this information can be used for ranking of search results.

Because `to_tsvector(NULL)` will return `NULL`, it is recommended to use `coalesce` whenever a field might be null. Here is the recommended method for creating a `tsvector` from a structured document:

```
UPDATE tt SET ti =
    setweight(to_tsvector(coalesce(title,'')), 'A')    ||
    setweight(to_tsvector(coalesce(keyword,'')), 'B')   ||
    setweight(to_tsvector(coalesce(abstract,'')), 'C')  ||
```

```
setweight(to_tsvector(coalesce(body,")), 'D');
```

Here we have used `setweight` to label the source of each lexeme in the finished `tsvector`, and then merged the labeled `tsvector` values using the `tsvector` concatenation operator ||. (Section 12.4.1 gives details about these operations.)

12.3.2. Parsing Queries

PostgreSQL provides the functions `to_tsquery` and `plainto_tsquery` for converting a query to the `tsquery` data type. `to_tsquery` offers access to more features than `plainto_tsquery`, but is less forgiving about its input.

```
to_tsquery([ config regconfig, ] querytext text) returns tsquery
```

`to_tsquery` creates a `tsquery` value from `querytext`, which must consist of single tokens separated by the Boolean operators & (AND), | (OR) and ! (NOT). These operators can be grouped using parentheses. In other words, the input to `to_tsquery` must already follow the general rules for `tsquery` input, as described in Section 8.11. The difference is that while basic `tsquery` input takes the tokens at face value, `to_tsquery` normalizes each token to a lexeme using the specified or default configuration, and discards any tokens that are stop words according to the configuration. For example:

```
SELECT to_tsquery('english', 'The & Fat & Rats');
  to_tsquery
---------------
 'fat' & 'rat'
```

As in basic `tsquery` input, weight(s) can be attached to each lexeme to restrict it to match only `tsvector` lexemes of those weight(s). For example:

```
SELECT to_tsquery('english', 'Fat | Rats:AB');
    to_tsquery
------------------
 'fat' | 'rat':AB
```

Also, * can be attached to a lexeme to specify prefix matching:

```
SELECT to_tsquery('supern:*A & star:A*B');
        to_tsquery
--------------------------
 'supern':*A & 'star':*AB
```

Such a lexeme will match any word in a `tsvector` that begins with the given string.

`to_tsquery` can also accept single-quoted phrases. This is primarily useful when the configuration includes a thesaurus dictionary that may trigger on such phrases. In the example below, a thesaurus contains the rule `supernovae stars : sn`:

```
SELECT to_tsquery("'supernovae stars" & !crab');
  to_tsquery
---------------
 'sn' & !'crab'
```

Without quotes, `to_tsquery` will generate a syntax error for tokens that are not separated by an AND or OR operator.

```
plainto_tsquery([ config regconfig, ] querytext text) returns tsquery
```

`plainto_tsquery` transforms unformatted text `querytext` to `tsquery`. The text is parsed and normalized much as for `to_tsvector`, then the `&` (AND) Boolean operator is inserted between surviving words.

Example:

```
SELECT plainto_tsquery('english', 'The Fat Rats');
 plainto_tsquery
-----------------
 'fat' & 'rat'
```

Note that `plainto_tsquery` cannot recognize Boolean operators, weight labels, or prefix-match labels in its input:

```
SELECT plainto_tsquery('english', 'The Fat & Rats:C');
   plainto_tsquery
---------------------
 'fat' & 'rat' & 'c'
```

Here, all the input punctuation was discarded as being space symbols.

12.3.3. Ranking Search Results

Ranking attempts to measure how relevant documents are to a particular query, so that when there are many matches the most relevant ones can be shown first. PostgreSQL provides two predefined ranking functions, which take into account lexical, proximity, and structural information; that is, they consider how often the query terms appear in the document, how close together the terms are in the document, and how important is the part of the document where they occur. However, the concept of relevancy is vague and very application-specific. Different applications might require additional information for ranking, e.g., document modification time. The built-in ranking functions are only examples. You can write your own ranking functions and/or combine their results with additional factors to fit your specific needs.

The two ranking functions currently available are:

```
ts_rank([ weights float4[], ] vector tsvector, query tsquery [, normalization
integer ]) returns float4
```

Ranks vectors based on the frequency of their matching lexemes.

```
ts_rank_cd([ weights float4[], ] vector tsvector, query tsquery [, normalization
integer ]) returns float4
```

This function computes the *cover density* ranking for the given document vector and query, as described in Clarke, Cormack, and Tudhope's "Relevance Ranking for One to Three Term Queries" in the journal "Information Processing and Management", 1999. Cover density is similar to `ts_rank` ranking except that the proximity of matching lexemes to each other is taken into consideration.

This function requires lexeme positional information to perform its calculation. Therefore, it ignores any "stripped" lexemes in the `tsvector`. If there are no unstripped lexemes in the input, the result will be zero. (See Section 12.4.1 for more information about the `strip` function and positional information in `tsvector`s.)

For both these functions, the optional *weights* argument offers the ability to weigh word instances more or less heavily depending on how they are labeled. The weight arrays specify how heavily to weigh each category of word, in the order:

```
{D-weight, C-weight, B-weight, A-weight}
```

If no *weights* are provided, then these defaults are used:

```
{0.1, 0.2, 0.4, 1.0}
```

Typically weights are used to mark words from special areas of the document, like the title or an initial abstract, so they can be treated with more or less importance than words in the document body.

Since a longer document has a greater chance of containing a query term it is reasonable to take into account document size, e.g., a hundred-word document with five instances of a search word is probably more relevant than a thousand-word document with five instances. Both ranking functions take an integer *normalization* option that specifies whether and how a document's length should impact its rank. The integer option controls several behaviors, so it is a bit mask: you can specify one or more behaviors using | (for example, 2|4).

- 0 (the default) ignores the document length
- 1 divides the rank by 1 + the logarithm of the document length
- 2 divides the rank by the document length
- 4 divides the rank by the mean harmonic distance between extents (this is implemented only by `ts_rank_cd`)
- 8 divides the rank by the number of unique words in document
- 16 divides the rank by 1 + the logarithm of the number of unique words in document
- 32 divides the rank by itself + 1

If more than one flag bit is specified, the transformations are applied in the order listed.

It is important to note that the ranking functions do not use any global information, so it is impossible to produce a fair normalization to 1% or 100% as sometimes desired. Normalization option 32 (`rank/(rank+1)`) can be applied to scale all ranks into the range zero to one, but of course this is just a cosmetic change; it will not affect the ordering of the search results.

Here is an example that selects only the ten highest-ranked matches:

```
SELECT title, ts_rank_cd(textsearch, query) AS rank
FROM apod, to_tsquery('neutrino|(dark & matter)') query
WHERE query @@ textsearch
ORDER BY rank DESC
LIMIT 10;
                      title                  |   rank
---------------------------------------------+----------
 Neutrinos in the Sun                        |    3.1
 The Sudbury Neutrino Detector               |    2.4
```

```
A MACHO View of Galactic Dark Matter          |   2.01317
Hot Gas and Dark Matter                        |   1.91171
The Virgo Cluster: Hot Plasma and Dark Matter |   1.90953
Rafting for Solar Neutrinos                    |        1.9
NGC 4650A: Strange Galaxy and Dark Matter      |   1.85774
Hot Gas and Dark Matter                        |    1.6123
Ice Fishing for Cosmic Neutrinos               |        1.6
Weak Lensing Distorts the Universe             |   0.818218
```

This is the same example using normalized ranking:

```
SELECT title, ts_rank_cd(textsearch, query, 32 /* rank/(rank+1) */ ) AS rank
FROM apod, to_tsquery('neutrino|(dark & matter)') query
WHERE  query @@ textsearch
ORDER BY rank DESC
LIMIT 10;
                      title                    |       rank
-----------------------------------------------+-------------------
 Neutrinos in the Sun                          | 0.756097569485493
 The Sudbury Neutrino Detector                 | 0.705882361190954
 A MACHO View of Galactic Dark Matter          | 0.668123210574724
 Hot Gas and Dark Matter                       |  0.65655958650282
 The Virgo Cluster: Hot Plasma and Dark Matter | 0.656301290640973
 Rafting for Solar Neutrinos                   | 0.655172410958162
 NGC 4650A: Strange Galaxy and Dark Matter     | 0.650072921219637
 Hot Gas and Dark Matter                       | 0.617195790024749
 Ice Fishing for Cosmic Neutrinos              | 0.615384618911517
 Weak Lensing Distorts the Universe            | 0.450010798361481
```

Ranking can be expensive since it requires consulting the tsvector of each matching document, which can be I/O bound and therefore slow. Unfortunately, it is almost impossible to avoid since practical queries often result in large numbers of matches.

12.3.4. Highlighting Results

To present search results it is ideal to show a part of each document and how it is related to the query. Usually, search engines show fragments of the document with marked search terms. PostgreSQL provides a function ts_headline that implements this functionality.

```
ts_headline([ config regconfig, ] document text, query tsquery [, options text ]) re
```

ts_headline accepts a document along with a query, and returns an excerpt from the document in which terms from the query are highlighted. The configuration to be used to parse the document can be specified by config; if config is omitted, the default_text_search_config configuration is used.

If an options string is specified it must consist of a comma-separated list of one or more option=value pairs. The available options are:

- `StartSel`, `StopSel`: the strings with which to delimit query words appearing in the document, to distinguish them from other excerpted words. You must double-quote these strings if they contain spaces or commas.
- `MaxWords`, `MinWords`: these numbers determine the longest and shortest headlines to output.
- `ShortWord`: words of this length or less will be dropped at the start and end of a headline. The default value of three eliminates common English articles.
- `HighlightAll`: Boolean flag; if `true` the whole document will be used as the headline, ignoring the preceding three parameters.
- `MaxFragments`: maximum number of text excerpts or fragments to display. The default value of zero selects a non-fragment-oriented headline generation method. A value greater than zero selects fragment-based headline generation. This method finds text fragments with as many query words as possible and stretches those fragments around the query words. As a result query words are close to the middle of each fragment and have words on each side. Each fragment will be of at most `MaxWords` and words of length `ShortWord` or less are dropped at the start and end of each fragment. If not all query words are found in the document, then a single fragment of the first `MinWords` in the document will be displayed.
- `FragmentDelimiter`: When more than one fragment is displayed, the fragments will be separated by this string.

Any unspecified options receive these defaults:

```
StartSel=<b>, StopSel=</b>,
MaxWords=35, MinWords=15, ShortWord=3, HighlightAll=FALSE,
MaxFragments=0, FragmentDelimiter=" ... "
```

For example:

```
SELECT ts_headline('english',
  'The most common type of search
is to find all documents containing given query terms
and return them in order of their similarity to the
query.',
  to_tsquery('query & similarity'));
                    ts_headline
-----------------------------------------------------------
 containing given <b>query</b> terms
 and return them in order of their <b>similarity</b> to the
 <b>query</b>.

SELECT ts_headline('english',
  'The most common type of search
is to find all documents containing given query terms
and return them in order of their similarity to the
query.',
  to_tsquery('query & similarity'),
  'StartSel = <, StopSel = >');
                    ts_headline
-------------------------------------------------------
 containing given <query> terms
 and return them in order of their <similarity> to the
 <query>.
```

ts_headline uses the original document, not a tsvector summary, so it can be slow and should be used with care. A typical mistake is to call ts_headline for *every* matching document when only ten documents are to be shown. SQL subqueries can help; here is an example:

```
SELECT id, ts_headline(body, q), rank
FROM (SELECT id, body, q, ts_rank_cd(ti, q) AS rank
      FROM apod, to_tsquery('stars') q
      WHERE ti @@ q
      ORDER BY rank DESC
      LIMIT 10) AS foo;
```

12.4. Additional Features

This section describes additional functions and operators that are useful in connection with text search.

12.4.1. Manipulating Documents

Section 12.3.1 showed how raw textual documents can be converted into tsvector values. PostgreSQL also provides functions and operators that can be used to manipulate documents that are already in tsvector form.

tsvector || tsvector

> The tsvector concatenation operator returns a vector which combines the lexemes and positional information of the two vectors given as arguments. Positions and weight labels are retained during the concatenation. Positions appearing in the right-hand vector are offset by the largest position mentioned in the left-hand vector, so that the result is nearly equivalent to the result of performing to_tsvector on the concatenation of the two original document strings. (The equivalence is not exact, because any stop-words removed from the end of the left-hand argument will not affect the result, whereas they would have affected the positions of the lexemes in the right-hand argument if textual concatenation were used.)

> One advantage of using concatenation in the vector form, rather than concatenating text before applying to_tsvector, is that you can use different configurations to parse different sections of the document. Also, because the setweight function marks all lexemes of the given vector the same way, it is necessary to parse the text and do setweight before concatenating if you want to label different parts of the document with different weights.

setweight(*vector* tsvector, *weight* "char") returns tsvector

> setweight returns a copy of the input vector in which every position has been labeled with the given *weight*, either A, B, C, or D. (D is the default for new vectors and as such is not displayed on output.) These labels are retained when vectors are concatenated, allowing words from different parts of a document to be weighted differently by ranking functions.

Note that weight labels apply to *positions*, not *lexemes*. If the input vector has been stripped of positions then `setweight` does nothing.

`length(vector tsvector) returns integer`

Returns the number of lexemes stored in the vector.

`strip(vector tsvector) returns tsvector`

Returns a vector which lists the same lexemes as the given vector, but which lacks any position or weight information. While the returned vector is much less useful than an unstripped vector for relevance ranking, it will usually be much smaller.

12.4.2. Manipulating Queries

Section 12.3.2 showed how raw textual queries can be converted into `tsquery` values. PostgreSQL also provides functions and operators that can be used to manipulate queries that are already in `tsquery` form.

`tsquery && tsquery`

Returns the AND-combination of the two given queries.

`tsquery || tsquery`

Returns the OR-combination of the two given queries.

`!! tsquery`

Returns the negation (NOT) of the given query.

`numnode(query tsquery) returns integer`

Returns the number of nodes (lexemes plus operators) in a `tsquery`. This function is useful to determine if the *query* is meaningful (returns > 0), or contains only stop words (returns 0). Examples:

```
SELECT numnode(plainto_tsquery('the any'));
NOTICE:  query contains only stopword(s) or doesn't contain lexeme(s), igno
 numnode
---------
       0


SELECT numnode('foo & bar'::tsquery);
 numnode
---------
       3
```

`querytree(query tsquery) returns text`

Returns the portion of a `tsquery` that can be used for searching an index. This function is useful for detecting unindexable queries, for example those containing only stop words or only negated terms. For example:

```
SELECT querytree(to_tsquery('!defined'));
 querytree
-----------
```

12.4.2.1. Query Rewriting

The `ts_rewrite` family of functions search a given `tsquery` for occurrences of a target subquery, and replace each occurrence with a substitute subquery. In essence this operation is a `tsquery`-specific version of substring replacement. A target and substitute combination can be thought of as a *query rewrite rule*. A collection of such rewrite rules can be a powerful search aid. For example, you can expand the search using synonyms (e.g., `new york`, `big apple`, `nyc`, `gotham`) or narrow the search to direct the user to some hot topic. There is some overlap in functionality between this feature and thesaurus dictionaries (Section 12.6.4). However, you can modify a set of rewrite rules on-the-fly without reindexing, whereas updating a thesaurus requires reindexing to be effective.

`ts_rewrite (`*`query`* `tsquery,` *`target`* `tsquery,` *`substitute`* `tsquery) returns tsquery`

> This form of `ts_rewrite` simply applies a single rewrite rule: *`target`* is replaced by *`substitute`* wherever it appears in *`query`*. For example:
>
> ```
> SELECT ts_rewrite('a & b'::tsquery, 'a'::tsquery, 'c'::tsquery);
>  ts_rewrite
> ------------
>  'b' & 'c'
> ```

`ts_rewrite (`*`query`* `tsquery,` *`select`* `text) returns tsquery`

> This form of `ts_rewrite` accepts a starting *`query`* and a SQL *`select`* command, which is given as a text string. The *`select`* must yield two columns of `tsquery` type. For each row of the *`select`* result, occurrences of the first column value (the target) are replaced by the second column value (the substitute) within the current *`query`* value. For example:
>
> ```
> CREATE TABLE aliases (t tsquery PRIMARY KEY, s tsquery);
> INSERT INTO aliases VALUES('a', 'c');
>
> SELECT ts_rewrite('a & b'::tsquery, 'SELECT t,s FROM aliases');
>  ts_rewrite
> ------------
>  'b' & 'c'
> ```

> Note that when multiple rewrite rules are applied in this way, the order of application can be important; so in practice you will want the source query to `ORDER BY` some ordering key.

Let's consider a real-life astronomical example. We'll expand query `supernovae` using table-driven rewriting rules:

```
CREATE TABLE aliases (t tsquery primary key, s tsquery);
INSERT INTO aliases VALUES(to_tsquery('supernovae'), to_tsquery('supernovae|sn'

SELECT ts_rewrite(to_tsquery('supernovae & crab'), 'SELECT * FROM aliases');
           ts_rewrite
---------------------------------
 'crab' & ( 'supernova' | 'sn' )
```

We can change the rewriting rules just by updating the table:

```
UPDATE aliases
SET s = to_tsquery('supernovae|sn & !nebulae')
WHERE t = to_tsquery('supernovae');
```

```
SELECT ts_rewrite(to_tsquery('supernovae & crab'), 'SELECT * FROM aliases');
                  ts_rewrite
------------------------------------------------
 'crab' & ( 'supernova' | 'sn' & !'nebula' )
```

Rewriting can be slow when there are many rewriting rules, since it checks every rule for a possible match. To filter out obvious non-candidate rules we can use the containment operators for the `tsquery` type. In the example below, we select only those rules which might match the original query:

```
SELECT ts_rewrite('a & b'::tsquery,
                  'SELECT t,s FROM aliases WHERE "a & b"::tsquery @> t');
 ts_rewrite
------------
 'b' & 'c'
```

12.4.3. Triggers for Automatic Updates

When using a separate column to store the `tsvector` representation of your documents, it is necessary to create a trigger to update the `tsvector` column when the document content columns change. Two built-in trigger functions are available for this, or you can write your own.

```
tsvector_update_trigger(tsvector_column_name, config_name, text_column_name [, ...
tsvector_update_trigger_column(tsvector_column_name, config_column_name, text_colum
```

These trigger functions automatically compute a `tsvector` column from one or more textual columns, under the control of parameters specified in the CREATE TRIGGER command. An example of their use is:

```
CREATE TABLE messages (
    title       text,
    body        text,
    tsv         tsvector
);

CREATE TRIGGER tsvectorupdate BEFORE INSERT OR UPDATE
ON messages FOR EACH ROW EXECUTE PROCEDURE
tsvector_update_trigger(tsv, 'pg_catalog.english', title, body);

INSERT INTO messages VALUES('title here', 'the body text is here');

SELECT * FROM messages;
   title    |         body          |              tsv
-----------+-----------------------+-----------------------------
 title here | the body text is here | 'bodi':4 'text':5 'titl':1

SELECT title, body FROM messages WHERE tsv @@ to_tsquery('title & body');
   title    |         body
-----------+-----------------------
```

```
title here | the body text is here
```

Having created this trigger, any change in `title` or `body` will automatically be reflected into `tsv`, without the application having to worry about it.

The first trigger argument must be the name of the `tsvector` column to be updated. The second argument specifies the text search configuration to be used to perform the conversion. For `tsvector_update_trigger`, the configuration name is simply given as the second trigger argument. It must be schema-qualified as shown above, so that the trigger behavior will not change with changes in `search_path`. For `tsvector_update_trigger_column`, the second trigger argument is the name of another table column, which must be of type `regconfig`. This allows a per-row selection of configuration to be made. The remaining argument(s) are the names of textual columns (of type `text`, `varchar`, or `char`). These will be included in the document in the order given. NULL values will be skipped (but the other columns will still be indexed).

A limitation of these built-in triggers is that they treat all the input columns alike. To process columns differently — for example, to weight title differently from body — it is necessary to write a custom trigger. Here is an example using PL/pgSQL as the trigger language:

```
CREATE FUNCTION messages_trigger() RETURNS trigger AS $$
begin
  new.tsv :=
     setweight(to_tsvector('pg_catalog.english', coalesce(new.title,"")), 'A') |
     setweight(to_tsvector('pg_catalog.english', coalesce(new.body,"")), 'D');
  return new;
end
$$ LANGUAGE plpgsql;


CREATE TRIGGER tsvectorupdate BEFORE INSERT OR UPDATE
    ON messages FOR EACH ROW EXECUTE PROCEDURE messages_trigger();
```

Keep in mind that it is important to specify the configuration name explicitly when creating `tsvector` values inside triggers, so that the column's contents will not be affected by changes to `default_text_search_config`. Failure to do this is likely to lead to problems such as search results changing after a dump and reload.

12.4.4. Gathering Document Statistics

The function `ts_stat` is useful for checking your configuration and for finding stop-word candidates.

```
ts_stat(sqlquery text, [ weights text, ]
        OUT word text, OUT ndoc integer,
        OUT nentry integer) returns setof record
```

sqlquery is a text value containing an SQL query which must return a single `tsvector` column. `ts_stat` executes the query and returns statistics about each distinct lexeme (word) contained in the `tsvector` data. The columns returned are

- *word* text — the value of a lexeme
- *ndoc* integer — number of documents (tsvectors) the word occurred in
- *nentry* integer — total number of occurrences of the word

If *weights* is supplied, only occurrences having one of those weights are counted.

For example, to find the ten most frequent words in a document collection:

```
SELECT * FROM ts_stat('SELECT vector FROM apod')
ORDER BY nentry DESC, ndoc DESC, word
LIMIT 10;
```

The same, but counting only word occurrences with weight A or B:

```
SELECT * FROM ts_stat('SELECT vector FROM apod', 'ab')
ORDER BY nentry DESC, ndoc DESC, word
LIMIT 10;
```

12.5. Parsers

Text search parsers are responsible for splitting raw document text into *tokens* and identifying each token's type, where the set of possible types is defined by the parser itself. Note that a parser does not modify the text at all — it simply identifies plausible word boundaries. Because of this limited scope, there is less need for application-specific custom parsers than there is for custom dictionaries. At present PostgreSQL provides just one built-in parser, which has been found to be useful for a wide range of applications.

The built-in parser is named pg_catalog.default. It recognizes 23 token types, shown in Table 12-1.

Table 12-1. Default Parser's Token Types

Alias	Description	Example
asciiword	Word, all ASCII letters	elephant
word	Word, all letters	mañana
numword	Word, letters and digits	beta1
asciihword	Hyphenated word, all ASCII	up-to-date
hword	Hyphenated word, all letters	lógico-matemática
numhword	Hyphenated word, letters and digits	postgresql-beta1
hword_asciipart	Hyphenated word part, all ASCII	postgresql in the context postgresql-beta1
hword_part	Hyphenated word part, all letters	lógico or matemática in the context lógico-matemática
hword_numpart	Hyphenated word part, letters and digits	beta1 in the context postgresql-beta1

Alias	Description	Example
`email`	Email address	`foo@example.com`
`protocol`	Protocol head	`http://`
`url`	URL	`example.com/stuff/index.ht`
`host`	Host	`example.com`
`url_path`	URL path	`/stuff/index.html`, in the context of a URL
`file`	File or path name	`/usr/local/foo.txt`, if not within a URL
`sfloat`	Scientific notation	`-1.234e56`
`float`	Decimal notation	`-1.234`
`int`	Signed integer	`-1234`
`uint`	Unsigned integer	`1234`
`version`	Version number	`8.3.0`
`tag`	XML tag	`<a href="dictionaries.html">`
`entity`	XML entity	`&amp;`
`blank`	Space symbols	(any whitespace or punctuation not otherwise recognized)

Note: The parser's notion of a "letter" is determined by the database's locale setting, specifically `lc_ctype`. Words containing only the basic ASCII letters are reported as a separate token type, since it is sometimes useful to distinguish them. In most European languages, token types `word` and `asciiword` should be treated alike.

`email` does not support all valid email characters as defined by RFC 5322. Specifically, the only non-alphanumeric characters supported for email user names are period, dash, and underscore.

It is possible for the parser to produce overlapping tokens from the same piece of text. As an example, a hyphenated word will be reported both as the entire word and as each component:

```
SELECT alias, description, token FROM ts_debug('foo-bar-beta1');
      alias       |               description               |     token
------------------+-----------------------------------------+---------------
 numhword         | Hyphenated word, letters and digits     | foo-bar-beta1
 hword_asciipart  | Hyphenated word part, all ASCII         | foo
 blank            | Space symbols                           | -
 hword_asciipart  | Hyphenated word part, all ASCII         | bar
 blank            | Space symbols                           | -
 hword_numpart    | Hyphenated word part, letters and digits | beta1
```

This behavior is desirable since it allows searches to work for both the whole compound word and for components. Here is another instructive example:

```
SELECT alias, description, token FROM ts_debug('http://example.com/stuff/index.
  alias   | description  |            token
----------+--------------+------------------------------
 protocol | Protocol head | http://
 url      | URL          | example.com/stuff/index.html
 host     | Host         | example.com
 url_path | URL path     | /stuff/index.html
```

12.6. Dictionaries

Dictionaries are used to eliminate words that should not be considered in a search (*stop words*), and to *normalize* words so that different derived forms of the same word will match. A successfully normalized word is called a *lexeme*. Aside from improving search quality, normalization and removal of stop words reduce the size of the `tsvector` representation of a document, thereby improving performance. Normalization does not always have linguistic meaning and usually depends on application semantics.

Some examples of normalization:

- Linguistic - Ispell dictionaries try to reduce input words to a normalized form; stemmer dictionaries remove word endings
- URL locations can be canonicalized to make equivalent URLs match:
  - http://www.pgsql.ru/db/mw/index.html
  - http://www.pgsql.ru/db/mw/
  - http://www.pgsql.ru/db/../db/mw/index.html
- Color names can be replaced by their hexadecimal values, e.g., red, green, blue, magenta -> FF0000, 00FF00, 0000FF, FF00FF
- If indexing numbers, we can remove some fractional digits to reduce the range of possible numbers, so for example *3.14159265359*, *3.1415926*, *3.14* will be the same after normalization if only two digits are kept after the decimal point.

A dictionary is a program that accepts a token as input and returns:

- an array of lexemes if the input token is known to the dictionary (notice that one token can produce more than one lexeme)
- a single lexeme with the TSL_FILTER flag set, to replace the original token with a new token to be passed to subsequent dictionaries (a dictionary that does this is called a *filtering dictionary*)
- an empty array if the dictionary knows the token, but it is a stop word
- NULL if the dictionary does not recognize the input token

PostgreSQL provides predefined dictionaries for many languages. There are also several predefined templates that can be used to create new dictionaries with custom parameters. Each predefined dictionary template is described below. If no existing template is suitable, it is possible to create new ones; see the contrib/ area of the PostgreSQL distribution for examples.

A text search configuration binds a parser together with a set of dictionaries to process the parser's output tokens. For each token type that the parser can return, a separate list of dictionaries is specified by the configuration. When a token of that type is found by the parser, each dictionary in the list is consulted in turn, until some dictionary recognizes it as a known word. If it is identified as a stop word, or if no dictionary recognizes the token, it will be discarded and not indexed or searched for. Normally, the first dictionary that returns a non-NULL output determines the result, and any remaining dictionaries are not consulted; but a filtering dictionary can replace the given word with a modified word, which is then passed to subsequent dictionaries.

The general rule for configuring a list of dictionaries is to place first the most narrow, most specific dictionary, then the more general dictionaries, finishing with a very general dictionary, like a Snowball stemmer or simple, which recognizes everything. For example, for an astronomy-specific search (astro_en configuration) one could bind token type asciiword (ASCII word) to a synonym dictionary of astronomical terms, a general English dictionary and a Snowball English stemmer:

```
ALTER TEXT SEARCH CONFIGURATION astro_en
    ADD MAPPING FOR asciiword WITH astrosyn, english_ispell, english_stem;
```

A filtering dictionary can be placed anywhere in the list, except at the end where it'd be useless. Filtering dictionaries are useful to partially normalize words to simplify the task of later dictionaries. For example, a filtering dictionary could be used to remove accents from accented letters, as is done by the unaccent module.

12.6.1. Stop Words

Stop words are words that are very common, appear in almost every document, and have no discrimination value. Therefore, they can be ignored in the context of full text searching. For example, every English text contains words like a and the, so it is useless to store them in an index. However, stop words do affect the positions in tsvector, which in turn affect ranking:

```
SELECT to_tsvector('english','in the list of stop words');
        to_tsvector
----------------------------
 'list':3 'stop':5 'word':6
```

The missing positions 1,2,4 are because of stop words. Ranks calculated for documents with and without stop words are quite different:

```
SELECT ts_rank_cd (to_tsvector('english','in the list of stop words'), to_tsque
 ts_rank_cd
------------
       0.05

SELECT ts_rank_cd (to_tsvector('english','list stop words'), to_tsquery('list &
 ts_rank_cd
------------
       0.1
```

It is up to the specific dictionary how it treats stop words. For example, `ispell` dictionaries first normalize words and then look at the list of stop words, while `Snowball` stemmers first check the list of stop words. The reason for the different behavior is an attempt to decrease noise.

12.6.2. Simple Dictionary

The `simple` dictionary template operates by converting the input token to lower case and checking it against a file of stop words. If it is found in the file then an empty array is returned, causing the token to be discarded. If not, the lower-cased form of the word is returned as the normalized lexeme. Alternatively, the dictionary can be configured to report non-stop-words as unrecognized, allowing them to be passed on to the next dictionary in the list.

Here is an example of a dictionary definition using the `simple` template:

```
CREATE TEXT SEARCH DICTIONARY public.simple_dict (
    TEMPLATE = pg_catalog.simple,
    STOPWORDS = english
);
```

Here, `english` is the base name of a file of stop words. The file's full name will be `$SHAREDIR/tsearch_data/english.stop`, where `$SHAREDIR` means the PostgreSQL installation's shared-data directory, often `/usr/local/share/postgresql` (use `pg_config --sharedir` to determine it if you're not sure). The file format is simply a list of words, one per line. Blank lines and trailing spaces are ignored, and upper case is folded to lower case, but no other processing is done on the file contents.

Now we can test our dictionary:

```
SELECT ts_lexize('public.simple_dict','YeS');
 ts_lexize
-----------
 {yes}

SELECT ts_lexize('public.simple_dict','The');
 ts_lexize
-----------
 {}
```

We can also choose to return `NULL`, instead of the lower-cased word, if it is not found in the stop words file. This behavior is selected by setting the dictionary's `Accept` parameter to `false`. Continuing the example:

```
ALTER TEXT SEARCH DICTIONARY public.simple_dict ( Accept = false );

SELECT ts_lexize('public.simple_dict','YeS');
 ts_lexize
-----------


SELECT ts_lexize('public.simple_dict','The');
```

```
ts_lexize
-----------
 {}
```

With the default setting of `Accept = true`, it is only useful to place a `simple` dictionary at the end of a list of dictionaries, since it will never pass on any token to a following dictionary. Conversely, `Accept = false` is only useful when there is at least one following dictionary.

Caution

Most types of dictionaries rely on configuration files, such as files of stop words. These files *must* be stored in UTF-8 encoding. They will be translated to the actual database encoding, if that is different, when they are read into the server.

Caution

Normally, a database session will read a dictionary configuration file only once, when it is first used within the session. If you modify a configuration file and want to force existing sessions to pick up the new contents, issue an `ALTER TEXT SEARCH DICTIONARY` command on the dictionary. This can be a "dummy" update that doesn't actually change any parameter values.

12.6.3. Synonym Dictionary

This dictionary template is used to create dictionaries that replace a word with a synonym. Phrases are not supported (use the thesaurus template (Section 12.6.4) for that). A synonym dictionary can be used to overcome linguistic problems, for example, to prevent an English stemmer dictionary from reducing the word "Paris" to "pari". It is enough to have a `Paris paris` line in the synonym dictionary and put it before the `english_stem` dictionary. For example:

```
SELECT * FROM ts_debug('english', 'Paris');
   alias   |  description   | token | dictionaries  | dictionary  | lexemes
-----------+----------------+-------+---------------+-------------+---------
 asciiword | Word, all ASCII | Paris | {english_stem} | english_stem | {pari}

CREATE TEXT SEARCH DICTIONARY my_synonym (
    TEMPLATE = synonym,
    SYNONYMS = my_synonyms
);

ALTER TEXT SEARCH CONFIGURATION english
    ALTER MAPPING FOR asciiword
    WITH my_synonym, english_stem;

SELECT * FROM ts_debug('english', 'Paris');
   alias   |  description   | token |          dictionaries          | dictionary |
-----------+----------------+-------+--------------------------------+------------+
```

```
asciiword | Word, all ASCII | Paris | {my_synonym,english_stem} | my_synonym |
```

The only parameter required by the `synonym` template is SYNONYMS, which is the base name of its configuration file — `my_synonyms` in the above example. The file's full name will be `$SHAREDIR/tsearch_data/my_synonyms.syn` (where `$SHAREDIR` means the PostgreSQL installation's shared-data directory). The file format is just one line per word to be substituted, with the word followed by its synonym, separated by white space. Blank lines and trailing spaces are ignored.

The `synonym` template also has an optional parameter `CaseSensitive`, which defaults to `false`. When `CaseSensitive` is `false`, words in the synonym file are folded to lower case, as are input tokens. When it is `true`, words and tokens are not folded to lower case, but are compared as-is.

An asterisk (`*`) can be placed at the end of a synonym in the configuration file. This indicates that the synonym is a prefix. The asterisk is ignored when the entry is used in `to_tsvector()`, but when it is used in `to_tsquery()`, the result will be a query item with the prefix match marker (see Section 12.3.2). For example, suppose we have these entries in `$SHAREDIR/tsearch_data/synonym_sample.syn`:

```
postgres        pgsql
postgresql      pgsql
postgre pgsql
gogle   googl
indices index*
```

Then we will get these results:

```
mydb=# CREATE TEXT SEARCH DICTIONARY syn (template=synonym, synonyms='synonym_s
mydb=# SELECT ts_lexize('syn','indices');
 ts_lexize
-----------
 {index}
(1 row)

mydb=# CREATE TEXT SEARCH CONFIGURATION tst (copy=simple);
mydb=# ALTER TEXT SEARCH CONFIGURATION tst ALTER MAPPING FOR asciiword WITH syr
mydb=# SELECT to_tsvector('tst','indices');
 to_tsvector
-------------
 'index':1
(1 row)

mydb=# SELECT to_tsquery('tst','indices');
 to_tsquery
------------
 'index':*
(1 row)

mydb=# SELECT 'indexes are very useful'::tsvector;
           tsvector
---------------------------------
 'are' 'indexes' 'useful' 'very'
(1 row)
```

```
mydb=# SELECT 'indexes are very useful'::tsvector @@ to_tsquery('tst','indices'
 ?column?
----------
 t
(1 row)
```

12.6.4. Thesaurus Dictionary

A thesaurus dictionary (sometimes abbreviated as TZ) is a collection of words that includes information about the relationships of words and phrases, i.e., broader terms (BT), narrower terms (NT), preferred terms, non-preferred terms, related terms, etc.

Basically a thesaurus dictionary replaces all non-preferred terms by one preferred term and, optionally, preserves the original terms for indexing as well. PostgreSQL's current implementation of the thesaurus dictionary is an extension of the synonym dictionary with added *phrase* support. A thesaurus dictionary requires a configuration file of the following format:

```
# this is a comment
sample word(s) : indexed word(s)
more sample word(s) : more indexed word(s)
...
```

where the colon (:) symbol acts as a delimiter between a phrase and its replacement.

A thesaurus dictionary uses a *subdictionary* (which is specified in the dictionary's configuration) to normalize the input text before checking for phrase matches. It is only possible to select one subdictionary. An error is reported if the subdictionary fails to recognize a word. In that case, you should remove the use of the word or teach the subdictionary about it. You can place an asterisk (*) at the beginning of an indexed word to skip applying the subdictionary to it, but all sample words *must* be known to the subdictionary.

The thesaurus dictionary chooses the longest match if there are multiple phrases matching the input, and ties are broken by using the last definition.

Specific stop words recognized by the subdictionary cannot be specified; instead use ? to mark the location where any stop word can appear. For example, assuming that a and the are stop words according to the subdictionary:

```
? one ? two : swsw
```

matches a one the two and the one a two; both would be replaced by swsw.

Since a thesaurus dictionary has the capability to recognize phrases it must remember its state and interact with the parser. A thesaurus dictionary uses these assignments to check if it should handle the next word or stop accumulation. The thesaurus dictionary must be configured carefully. For example, if the thesaurus dictionary is assigned to handle only the asciiword token, then a thesaurus dictionary definition like one 7 will not work since token type uint is not assigned to the thesaurus dictionary.

> ## Caution
>
> Thesauruses are used during indexing so any change in the thesaurus dictionary's parameters *requires* reindexing. For most other dictionary types, small changes such as adding or removing stopwords does not force reindexing.

12.6.4.1. Thesaurus Configuration

To define a new thesaurus dictionary, use the `thesaurus` template. For example:

```
CREATE TEXT SEARCH DICTIONARY thesaurus_simple (
    TEMPLATE = thesaurus,
    DictFile = mythesaurus,
    Dictionary = pg_catalog.english_stem
);
```

Here:

- `thesaurus_simple` is the new dictionary's name
- `mythesaurus` is the base name of the thesaurus configuration file. (Its full name will be `$SHAREDIR/tsearch_data/mythesaurus.ths`, where `$SHAREDIR` means the installation shared-data directory.)
- `pg_catalog.english_stem` is the subdictionary (here, a Snowball English stemmer) to use for thesaurus normalization. Notice that the subdictionary will have its own configuration (for example, stop words), which is not shown here.

Now it is possible to bind the thesaurus dictionary `thesaurus_simple` to the desired token types in a configuration, for example:

```
ALTER TEXT SEARCH CONFIGURATION russian
    ALTER MAPPING FOR asciiword, asciihword, hword_asciipart
    WITH thesaurus_simple;
```

12.6.4.2. Thesaurus Example

Consider a simple astronomical thesaurus `thesaurus_astro`, which contains some astronomical word combinations:

```
supernovae stars : sn
crab nebulae : crab
```

Below we create a dictionary and bind some token types to an astronomical thesaurus and English stemmer:

```
CREATE TEXT SEARCH DICTIONARY thesaurus_astro (
    TEMPLATE = thesaurus,
    DictFile = thesaurus_astro,
```

```
        Dictionary = english_stem
);

ALTER TEXT SEARCH CONFIGURATION russian
    ALTER MAPPING FOR asciiword, asciihword, hword_asciipart
    WITH thesaurus_astro, english_stem;
```

Now we can see how it works. `ts_lexize` is not very useful for testing a thesaurus, because it treats its input as a single token. Instead we can use `plainto_tsquery` and `to_tsvector` which will break their input strings into multiple tokens:

```
SELECT plainto_tsquery('supernova star');
 plainto_tsquery
-----------------
 'sn'

SELECT to_tsvector('supernova star');
 to_tsvector
-------------
 'sn':1
```

In principle, one can use `to_tsquery` if you quote the argument:

```
SELECT to_tsquery('''supernova star''');
 to_tsquery
------------
 'sn'
```

Notice that `supernova star` matches `supernovae stars` in `thesaurus_astro` because we specified the `english_stem` stemmer in the thesaurus definition. The stemmer removed the `e` and `s`.

To index the original phrase as well as the substitute, just include it in the right-hand part of the definition:

```
supernovae stars : sn supernovae stars

SELECT plainto_tsquery('supernova star');
      plainto_tsquery
----------------------------
 'sn' & 'supernova' & 'star'
```

12.6.5. Ispell Dictionary

The Ispell dictionary template supports *morphological dictionaries*, which can normalize many different linguistic forms of a word into the same lexeme. For example, an English Ispell dictionary can match all declensions and conjugations of the search term `bank`, e.g., `banking`, `banked`, `banks`, `banks'`, and `bank's`.

The standard PostgreSQL distribution does not include any Ispell configuration files. Dictionaries for a large number of languages are available from Ispell[1]. Also, some more modern dictionary file formats are supported — MySpell[2] (OO < 2.0.1) and Hunspell[3] (OO >= 2.0.2). A large list of dictionaries is available on the OpenOffice Wiki[4].

To create an Ispell dictionary, use the built-in `ispell` template and specify several parameters:

```
CREATE TEXT SEARCH DICTIONARY english_ispell (
    TEMPLATE = ispell,
    DictFile = english,
    AffFile = english,
    StopWords = english
);
```

Here, `DictFile`, `AffFile`, and `StopWords` specify the base names of the dictionary, affixes, and stop-words files. The stop-words file has the same format explained above for the `simple` dictionary type. The format of the other files is not specified here but is available from the above-mentioned web sites.

Ispell dictionaries usually recognize a limited set of words, so they should be followed by another broader dictionary; for example, a Snowball dictionary, which recognizes everything.

Ispell dictionaries support splitting compound words; a useful feature. Notice that the affix file should specify a special flag using the `compoundwords controlled` statement that marks dictionary words that can participate in compound formation:

```
compoundwords  controlled z
```

Here are some examples for the Norwegian language:

```
SELECT ts_lexize('norwegian_ispell', 'overbuljongterningpakkmesterassistent');
   {over,buljong,terning,pakk,mester,assistent}
SELECT ts_lexize('norwegian_ispell', 'sjokoladefabrikk');
   {sjokoladefabrikk,sjokolade,fabrikk}
```

> **Note:** MySpell does not support compound words. Hunspell has sophisticated support for compound words. At present, PostgreSQL implements only the basic compound word operations of Hunspell.

12.6.6. Snowball Dictionary

The Snowball dictionary template is based on a project by Martin Porter, inventor of the popular Porter's stemming algorithm for the English language. Snowball now provides stemming algorithms for many languages (see the Snowball site[5] for more information). Each algorithm understands how to reduce common variant forms of words to a base, or stem, spelling within its language. A Snowball dictionary requires a

---

1. http://ficus-www.cs.ucla.edu/geoff/ispell.html
2. http://en.wikipedia.org/wiki/MySpell
3. http://sourceforge.net/projects/hunspell/
4. http://wiki.services.openoffice.org/wiki/Dictionaries
5. http://snowball.tartarus.org

`language` parameter to identify which stemmer to use, and optionally can specify a `stopword` file name that gives a list of words to eliminate. (PostgreSQL's standard stopword lists are also provided by the Snowball project.) For example, there is a built-in definition equivalent to

```
CREATE TEXT SEARCH DICTIONARY english_stem (
    TEMPLATE = snowball,
    Language = english,
    StopWords = english
);
```

The stopword file format is the same as already explained.

A Snowball dictionary recognizes everything, whether or not it is able to simplify the word, so it should be placed at the end of the dictionary list. It is useless to have it before any other dictionary because a token will never pass through it to the next dictionary.

12.7. Configuration Example

A text search configuration specifies all options necessary to transform a document into a `tsvector`: the parser to use to break text into tokens, and the dictionaries to use to transform each token into a lexeme. Every call of `to_tsvector` or `to_tsquery` needs a text search configuration to perform its processing. The configuration parameter default_text_search_config specifies the name of the default configuration, which is the one used by text search functions if an explicit configuration parameter is omitted. It can be set in `postgresql.conf`, or set for an individual session using the `SET` command.

Several predefined text search configurations are available, and you can create custom configurations easily. To facilitate management of text search objects, a set of SQL commands is available, and there are several psql commands that display information about text search objects (Section 12.10).

As an example we will create a configuration `pg`, starting by duplicating the built-in `english` configuration:

```
CREATE TEXT SEARCH CONFIGURATION public.pg ( COPY = pg_catalog.english );
```

We will use a PostgreSQL-specific synonym list and store it in `$SHAREDIR/tsearch_data/pg_dict.syn`. The file contents look like:

```
postgres    pg
pgsql       pg
postgresql  pg
```

We define the synonym dictionary like this:

```
CREATE TEXT SEARCH DICTIONARY pg_dict (
    TEMPLATE = synonym,
    SYNONYMS = pg_dict
);
```

Next we register the Ispell dictionary `english_ispell`, which has its own configuration files:

```
CREATE TEXT SEARCH DICTIONARY english_ispell (
    TEMPLATE = ispell,
    DictFile = english,
    AffFile = english,
    StopWords = english
);
```

Now we can set up the mappings for words in configuration `pg`:

```
ALTER TEXT SEARCH CONFIGURATION pg
    ALTER MAPPING FOR asciiword, asciihword, hword_asciipart,
                      word, hword, hword_part
    WITH pg_dict, english_ispell, english_stem;
```

We choose not to index or search some token types that the built-in configuration does handle:

```
ALTER TEXT SEARCH CONFIGURATION pg
    DROP MAPPING FOR email, url, url_path, sfloat, float;
```

Now we can test our configuration:

```
SELECT * FROM ts_debug('public.pg', '
PostgreSQL, the highly scalable, SQL compliant, open source object-relational
database management system, is now undergoing beta testing of the next
version of our software.
');
```

The next step is to set the session to use the new configuration, which was created in the `public` schema:

```
=> \dF
   List of text search configurations
 Schema | Name | Description
--------+------+-------------
 public | pg   |

SET default_text_search_config = 'public.pg';
SET

SHOW default_text_search_config;
 default_text_search_config
----------------------------
 public.pg
```

12.8. Testing and Debugging Text Search

The behavior of a custom text search configuration can easily become confusing. The functions described in this section are useful for testing text search objects. You can test a complete configuration, or test parsers and dictionaries separately.

12.8.1. Configuration Testing

The function ts_debug allows easy testing of a text search configuration.

```
ts_debug([ config regconfig, ] document text,
        OUT alias text,
        OUT description text,
        OUT token text,
        OUT dictionaries regdictionary[],
        OUT dictionary regdictionary,
        OUT lexemes text[])
        returns setof record
```

ts_debug displays information about every token of *document* as produced by the parser and processed by the configured dictionaries. It uses the configuration specified by *config*, or default_text_search_config if that argument is omitted.

ts_debug returns one row for each token identified in the text by the parser. The columns returned are

- *alias* text — short name of the token type
- *description* text — description of the token type
- *token* text — text of the token
- *dictionaries* regdictionary[] — the dictionaries selected by the configuration for this token type
- *dictionary* regdictionary — the dictionary that recognized the token, or NULL if none did
- *lexemes* text[] — the lexeme(s) produced by the dictionary that recognized the token, or NULL if none did; an empty array ({}) means it was recognized as a stop word

Here is a simple example:

```
SELECT * FROM ts_debug('english','a fat  cat sat on a mat - it ate a fat rats')
   alias   |   description   | token | dictionaries   |  dictionary  | lexemes
-----------+-----------------+-------+----------------+--------------+---------
 asciiword | Word, all ASCII | a     | {english_stem} | english_stem | {}
 blank     | Space symbols   |       | {}             |              |
 asciiword | Word, all ASCII | fat   | {english_stem} | english_stem | {fat}
 blank     | Space symbols   |       | {}             |              |
 asciiword | Word, all ASCII | cat   | {english_stem} | english_stem | {cat}
 blank     | Space symbols   |       | {}             |              |
 asciiword | Word, all ASCII | sat   | {english_stem} | english_stem | {sat}
 blank     | Space symbols   |       | {}             |              |
 asciiword | Word, all ASCII | on    | {english_stem} | english_stem | {}
 blank     | Space symbols   |       | {}             |              |
 asciiword | Word, all ASCII | a     | {english_stem} | english_stem | {}
```

```
blank     | Space symbols  |       | {}               |              |
asciiword | Word, all ASCII | mat  | {english_stem}   | english_stem | {mat}
blank     | Space symbols  |       | {}               |              |
blank     | Space symbols  | -     | {}               |              |
asciiword | Word, all ASCII | it   | {english_stem}   | english_stem | {}
blank     | Space symbols  |       | {}               |              |
asciiword | Word, all ASCII | ate  | {english_stem}   | english_stem | {ate}
blank     | Space symbols  |       | {}               |              |
asciiword | Word, all ASCII | a    | {english_stem}   | english_stem | {}
blank     | Space symbols  |       | {}               |              |
asciiword | Word, all ASCII | fat  | {english_stem}   | english_stem | {fat}
blank     | Space symbols  |       | {}               |              |
asciiword | Word, all ASCII | rats | {english_stem}   | english_stem | {rat}
```

For a more extensive demonstration, we first create a `public.english` configuration and Ispell dictionary for the English language:

```
CREATE TEXT SEARCH CONFIGURATION public.english ( COPY = pg_catalog.english );

CREATE TEXT SEARCH DICTIONARY english_ispell (
    TEMPLATE = ispell,
    DictFile = english,
    AffFile = english,
    StopWords = english
);

ALTER TEXT SEARCH CONFIGURATION public.english
    ALTER MAPPING FOR asciiword WITH english_ispell, english_stem;

SELECT * FROM ts_debug('public.english','The Brightest supernovaes');
   alias   |  description   |   token    |         dictionaries         |
-----------+----------------+------------+------------------------------+---
 asciiword | Word, all ASCII | The       | {english_ispell,english_stem} | er
 blank     | Space symbols  |            | {}                           |
 asciiword | Word, all ASCII | Brightest | {english_ispell,english_stem} | er
 blank     | Space symbols  |            | {}                           |
 asciiword | Word, all ASCII | supernovaes | {english_ispell,english_stem} | er
```

In this example, the word `Brightest` was recognized by the parser as an `ASCII` word (alias `asciiword`). For this token type the dictionary list is `english_ispell` and `english_stem`. The word was recognized by `english_ispell`, which reduced it to the noun `bright`. The word `supernovaes` is unknown to the `english_ispell` dictionary so it was passed to the next dictionary, and, fortunately, was recognized (in fact, `english_stem` is a Snowball dictionary which recognizes everything; that is why it was placed at the end of the dictionary list).

The word `The` was recognized by the `english_ispell` dictionary as a stop word (Section 12.6.1) and will not be indexed. The spaces are discarded too, since the configuration provides no dictionaries at all for them.

You can reduce the width of the output by explicitly specifying which columns you want to see:

```
SELECT alias, token, dictionary, lexemes
```

```
FROM ts_debug('public.english','The Brightest supernovaes');
    alias    |    token    |   dictionary    |   lexemes
-------------+-------------+-----------------+-------------
 asciiword   | The         | english_ispell  | {}
 blank       |             |                 |
 asciiword   | Brightest   | english_ispell  | {bright}
 blank       |             |                 |
 asciiword   | supernovaes | english_stem    | {supernova}
```

12.8.2. Parser Testing

The following functions allow direct testing of a text search parser.

```
ts_parse(parser_name text, document text,
         OUT tokid integer, OUT token text) returns setof record
ts_parse(parser_oid oid, document text,
         OUT tokid integer, OUT token text) returns setof record
```

ts_parse parses the given `document` and returns a series of records, one for each token produced by parsing. Each record includes a `tokid` showing the assigned token type and a `token` which is the text of the token. For example:

```
SELECT * FROM ts_parse('default', '123 - a number');
 tokid | token
-------+--------
    22 | 123
    12 |
    12 | -
     1 | a
    12 |
     1 | number
```

```
ts_token_type(parser_name text, OUT tokid integer,
              OUT alias text, OUT description text) returns setof record
ts_token_type(parser_oid oid, OUT tokid integer,
              OUT alias text, OUT description text) returns setof record
```

ts_token_type returns a table which describes each type of token the specified parser can recognize. For each token type, the table gives the integer `tokid` that the parser uses to label a token of that type, the `alias` that names the token type in configuration commands, and a short `description`. For example:

```
SELECT * FROM ts_token_type('default');
 tokid |      alias      |             description
-------+----------------+--------------------------------------------
     1 | asciiword       | Word, all ASCII
     2 | word            | Word, all letters
     3 | numword         | Word, letters and digits
     4 | email           | Email address
```

```
  5 | url              | URL
  6 | host             | Host
  7 | sfloat           | Scientific notation
  8 | version          | Version number
  9 | hword_numpart    | Hyphenated word part, letters and digits
 10 | hword_part       | Hyphenated word part, all letters
 11 | hword_asciipart  | Hyphenated word part, all ASCII
 12 | blank            | Space symbols
 13 | tag              | XML tag
 14 | protocol         | Protocol head
 15 | numhword         | Hyphenated word, letters and digits
 16 | asciihword       | Hyphenated word, all ASCII
 17 | hword            | Hyphenated word, all letters
 18 | url_path         | URL path
 19 | file             | File or path name
 20 | float            | Decimal notation
 21 | int              | Signed integer
 22 | uint             | Unsigned integer
 23 | entity           | XML entity
```

12.8.3. Dictionary Testing

The ts_lexize function facilitates dictionary testing.

```
ts_lexize(dict regdictionary, token text) returns text[]
```

ts_lexize returns an array of lexemes if the input token is known to the dictionary, or an empty array if the token is known to the dictionary but it is a stop word, or NULL if it is an unknown word.

Examples:

```
SELECT ts_lexize('english_stem', 'stars');
 ts_lexize
-----------
 {star}

SELECT ts_lexize('english_stem', 'a');
 ts_lexize
-----------
 {}
```

> **Note:** The ts_lexize function expects a single *token*, not text. Here is a case where this can be confusing:
>
> ```
> SELECT ts_lexize('thesaurus_astro','supernovae stars') is null;
>  ?column?
> ----------
>  t
> ```

The thesaurus dictionary `thesaurus_astro` does know the phrase `supernovae stars`, but `ts_lexize` fails since it does not parse the input text but treats it as a single token. Use `plainto_tsquery` or `to_tsvector` to test thesaurus dictionaries, for example:

```
SELECT plainto_tsquery('supernovae stars');
 plainto_tsquery
-----------------
 'sn'
```

12.9. GiST and GIN Index Types

There are two kinds of indexes that can be used to speed up full text searches. Note that indexes are not mandatory for full text searching, but in cases where a column is searched on a regular basis, an index is usually desirable.

```
CREATE INDEX name ON table USING gist(column);
```

Creates a GiST (Generalized Search Tree)-based index. The `column` can be of `tsvector` or `tsquery` type.

```
CREATE INDEX name ON table USING gin(column);
```

Creates a GIN (Generalized Inverted Index)-based index. The `column` must be of `tsvector` type.

There are substantial performance differences between the two index types, so it is important to understand their characteristics.

A GiST index is *lossy*, meaning that the index may produce false matches, and it is necessary to check the actual table row to eliminate such false matches. (PostgreSQL does this automatically when needed.) GiST indexes are lossy because each document is represented in the index by a fixed-length signature. The signature is generated by hashing each word into a single bit in an n-bit string, with all these bits OR-ed together to produce an n-bit document signature. When two words hash to the same bit position there will be a false match. If all words in the query have matches (real or false) then the table row must be retrieved to see if the match is correct.

Lossiness causes performance degradation due to unnecessary fetches of table records that turn out to be false matches. Since random access to table records is slow, this limits the usefulness of GiST indexes. The likelihood of false matches depends on several factors, in particular the number of unique words, so using dictionaries to reduce this number is recommended.

GIN indexes are not lossy for standard queries, but their performance depends logarithmically on the number of unique words. (However, GIN indexes store only the words (lexemes) of `tsvector` values, and not their weight labels. Thus a table row recheck is needed when using a query that involves weights.)

In choosing which index type to use, GiST or GIN, consider these performance differences:

- GIN index lookups are about three times faster than GiST
- GIN indexes take about three times longer to build than GiST
- GIN indexes are moderately slower to update than GiST indexes, but about 10 times slower if fast-update support was disabled (see Section 58.4.1 for details)
- GIN indexes are two-to-three times larger than GiST indexes

As a rule of thumb, GIN indexes are best for static data because lookups are faster. For dynamic data, GiST indexes are faster to update. Specifically, GiST indexes are very good for dynamic data and fast if the number of unique words (lexemes) is under 100,000, while GIN indexes will handle 100,000+ lexemes better but are slower to update.

Note that GIN index build time can often be improved by increasing maintenance_work_mem, while GiST index build time is not sensitive to that parameter.

Partitioning of big collections and the proper use of GiST and GIN indexes allows the implementation of very fast searches with online update. Partitioning can be done at the database level using table inheritance, or by distributing documents over servers and collecting search results using the dblink module. The latter is possible because ranking functions use only local information.

12.10. psql Support

Information about text search configuration objects can be obtained in psql using a set of commands:

```
\dF{d,p,t}[+] [PATTERN]
```

An optional + produces more details.

The optional parameter PATTERN can be the name of a text search object, optionally schema-qualified. If PATTERN is omitted then information about all visible objects will be displayed. PATTERN can be a regular expression and can provide *separate* patterns for the schema and object names. The following examples illustrate this:

```
=> \dF *fulltext*
       List of text search configurations
 Schema |     Name      | Description
--------+---------------+-------------
 public | fulltext_cfg |

=> \dF *.fulltext*
       List of text search configurations
 Schema   |     Name      | Description
----------+----------------------------------
 fulltext | fulltext_cfg |
 public   | fulltext_cfg |
```

The available commands are:

\dF[+] [PATTERN]

List text search configurations (add + for more detail).

```
=> \dF russian
            List of text search configurations
    Schema   | Name    |         Description
-----------+---------+------------------------------------
 pg_catalog | russian | configuration for russian language

=> \dF+ russian
Text search configuration "pg_catalog.russian"
Parser: "pg_catalog.default"
        Token       | Dictionaries
------------------+--------------
 asciihword         | english_stem
 asciiword          | english_stem
 email              | simple
 file               | simple
 float              | simple
 host               | simple
 hword              | russian_stem
 hword_asciipart    | english_stem
 hword_numpart      | simple
 hword_part         | russian_stem
 int                | simple
 numhword           | simple
 numword            | simple
 sfloat             | simple
 uint               | simple
 url                | simple
 url_path           | simple
 version            | simple
 word               | russian_stem
```

\dFd[+] [PATTERN]

List text search dictionaries (add + for more detail).

```
=> \dFd
                        List of text search dictionaries
    Schema   |      Name       |                    Description
-----------+-----------------+------------------------------------------------
 pg_catalog | danish_stem      | snowball stemmer for danish language
 pg_catalog | dutch_stem       | snowball stemmer for dutch language
 pg_catalog | english_stem     | snowball stemmer for english language
 pg_catalog | finnish_stem     | snowball stemmer for finnish language
 pg_catalog | french_stem      | snowball stemmer for french language
 pg_catalog | german_stem      | snowball stemmer for german language
 pg_catalog | hungarian_stem   | snowball stemmer for hungarian language
 pg_catalog | italian_stem     | snowball stemmer for italian language
 pg_catalog | norwegian_stem   | snowball stemmer for norwegian language
 pg_catalog | portuguese_stem  | snowball stemmer for portuguese language
 pg_catalog | romanian_stem    | snowball stemmer for romanian language
 pg_catalog | russian_stem     | snowball stemmer for russian language
 pg_catalog | simple           | simple dictionary: just lower case and chec
```

```
pg_catalog | spanish_stem    | snowball stemmer for spanish language
pg_catalog | swedish_stem    | snowball stemmer for swedish language
pg_catalog | turkish_stem    | snowball stemmer for turkish language
```

\dFp[+] [PATTERN]

List text search parsers (add + for more detail).

```
=> \dFp
        List of text search parsers
   Schema   |  Name   |      Description
------------+---------+--------------------
 pg_catalog | default | default word parser
=> \dFp+
    Text search parser "pg_catalog.default"
    Method       |    Function    | Description
----------------+----------------+-------------
 Start parse    | prsd_start     |
 Get next token | prsd_nexttoken |
 End parse      | prsd_end       |
 Get headline   | prsd_headline  |
 Get token types | prsd_lextype  |


        Token types for parser "pg_catalog.default"
   Token name    |                Description
----------------+-------------------------------------------
 asciihword      | Hyphenated word, all ASCII
 asciiword       | Word, all ASCII
 blank           | Space symbols
 email           | Email address
 entity          | XML entity
 file            | File or path name
 float           | Decimal notation
 host            | Host
 hword           | Hyphenated word, all letters
 hword_asciipart | Hyphenated word part, all ASCII
 hword_numpart   | Hyphenated word part, letters and digits
 hword_part      | Hyphenated word part, all letters
 int             | Signed integer
 numhword        | Hyphenated word, letters and digits
 numword         | Word, letters and digits
 protocol        | Protocol head
 sfloat          | Scientific notation
 tag             | XML tag
 uint            | Unsigned integer
 url             | URL
 url_path        | URL path
 version         | Version number
 word            | Word, all letters
(23 rows)
```

```
\dFt[+]  [PATTERN]
```

List text search templates (add + for more detail).

```
=> \dFt
                       List of text search templates
     Schema    |    Name    |                  Description
  ------------+-----------+-------------------------------------------------
   pg_catalog | ispell    | ispell dictionary
   pg_catalog | simple    | simple dictionary: just lower case and check for
   pg_catalog | snowball  | snowball stemmer
   pg_catalog | synonym   | synonym dictionary: replace word by its synonym
   pg_catalog | thesaurus | thesaurus dictionary: phrase by phrase substituti
```

12.11. Limitations

The current limitations of PostgreSQL's text search features are:

- The length of each lexeme must be less than 2K bytes
- The length of a `tsvector` (lexemes + positions) must be less than 1 megabyte
- The number of lexemes must be less than 2^{64}
- Position values in `tsvector` must be greater than 0 and no more than 16,383
- No more than 256 positions per lexeme
- The number of nodes (lexemes + operators) in a `tsquery` must be less than 32,768

For comparison, the PostgreSQL 8.1 documentation contained 10,441 unique words, a total of 335,420 words, and the most frequent word "postgresql" was mentioned 6,127 times in 655 documents.

Another example — the PostgreSQL mailing list archives contained 910,989 unique words with 57,491,343 lexemes in 461,020 messages.

12.12. Migration from Pre-8.3 Text Search

Applications that use the tsearch2 module for text searching will need some adjustments to work with the built-in features:

- Some functions have been renamed or had small adjustments in their argument lists, and all of them are now in the `pg_catalog` schema, whereas in a previous installation they would have been in `public` or another non-system schema. There is a new version of tsearch2 that provides a compatibility layer to solve most problems in this area.

- The old tsearch2 functions and other objects *must* be suppressed when loading pg_dump output from a pre-8.3 database. While many of them won't load anyway, a few will and then cause problems. One simple way to deal with this is to load the new tsearch2 module before restoring the dump; then it will block the old objects from being loaded.

- Text search configuration setup is completely different now. Instead of manually inserting rows into configuration tables, search is configured through the specialized SQL commands shown earlier in this chapter. There is no automated support for converting an existing custom configuration for 8.3; you're on your own here.

- Most types of dictionaries rely on some outside-the-database configuration files. These are largely compatible with pre-8.3 usage, but note the following differences:
  - Configuration files now must be placed in a single specified directory (`$SHAREDIR/tsearch_data`), and must have a specific extension depending on the type of file, as noted previously in the descriptions of the various dictionary types. This restriction was added to forestall security problems.
  - Configuration files must be encoded in UTF-8 encoding, regardless of what database encoding is used.
  - In thesaurus configuration files, stop words must be marked with ?.

Chapter 13. Concurrency Control

This chapter describes the behavior of the PostgreSQL database system when two or more sessions try to access the same data at the same time. The goals in that situation are to allow efficient access for all sessions while maintaining strict data integrity. Every developer of database applications should be familiar with the topics covered in this chapter.

13.1. Introduction

PostgreSQL provides a rich set of tools for developers to manage concurrent access to data. Internally, data consistency is maintained by using a multiversion model (Multiversion Concurrency Control, MVCC). This means that each SQL statement sees a snapshot of data (a *database version*) as it was some time ago, regardless of the current state of the underlying data. This prevents statements from viewing inconsistent data produced by concurrent transactions performing updates on the same data rows, providing *transaction isolation* for each database session. MVCC, by eschewing the locking methodologies of traditional database systems, minimizes lock contention in order to allow for reasonable performance in multiuser environments.

The main advantage of using the MVCC model of concurrency control rather than locking is that in MVCC locks acquired for querying (reading) data do not conflict with locks acquired for writing data, and so reading never blocks writing and writing never blocks reading. PostgreSQL maintains this guarantee even when providing the strictest level of transaction isolation through the use of an innovative *Serializable Snapshot Isolation* (SSI) level.

Table- and row-level locking facilities are also available in PostgreSQL for applications which don't generally need full transaction isolation and prefer to explicitly manage particular points of conflict. However, proper use of MVCC will generally provide better performance than locks. In addition, application-defined advisory locks provide a mechanism for acquiring locks that are not tied to a single transaction.

13.2. Transaction Isolation

The SQL standard defines four levels of transaction isolation. The most strict is Serializable, which is defined by the standard in a paragraph which says that any concurrent execution of a set of Serializable transactions is guaranteed to produce the same effect as running them one at a time in some order. The other three levels are defined in terms of phenomena, resulting from interaction between concurrent transactions, which must not occur at each level. The standard notes that due to the definition of Serializable, none of these phenomena are possible at that level. (This is hardly surprising -- if the effect of the transactions must be consistent with having been run one at a time, how could you see any phenomena caused by interactions?)

The phenomena which are prohibited at various levels are:

dirty read

> A transaction reads data written by a concurrent uncommitted transaction.

nonrepeatable read

A transaction re-reads data it has previously read and finds that data has been modified by another transaction (that committed since the initial read).

phantom read

A transaction re-executes a query returning a set of rows that satisfy a search condition and finds that the set of rows satisfying the condition has changed due to another recently-committed transaction.

The four transaction isolation levels and the corresponding behaviors are described in Table 13-1.

Table 13-1. Standard SQL Transaction Isolation Levels

Isolation Level	Dirty Read	Nonrepeatable Read	Phantom Read
Read uncommitted	Possible	Possible	Possible
Read committed	Not possible	Possible	Possible
Repeatable read	Not possible	Not possible	Possible
Serializable	Not possible	Not possible	Not possible

In PostgreSQL, you can request any of the four standard transaction isolation levels. But internally, there are only three distinct isolation levels, which correspond to the levels Read Committed, Repeatable Read, and Serializable. When you select the level Read Uncommitted you really get Read Committed, and phantom reads are not possible in the PostgreSQL implementation of Repeatable Read, so the actual isolation level might be stricter than what you select. This is permitted by the SQL standard: the four isolation levels only define which phenomena must not happen, they do not define which phenomena must happen. The reason that PostgreSQL only provides three isolation levels is that this is the only sensible way to map the standard isolation levels to the multiversion concurrency control architecture. The behavior of the available isolation levels is detailed in the following subsections.

To set the transaction isolation level of a transaction, use the command SET TRANSACTION.

> **Important:** Some PostgreSQL data types and functions have special rules regarding transactional behavior. In particular, changes made to a sequence (and therefore the counter of a column declared using `serial`) are immediately visible to all other transactions and are not rolled back if the transaction that made the changes aborts. See Section 9.16 and Section 8.1.4.

13.2.1. Read Committed Isolation Level

Read Committed is the default isolation level in PostgreSQL. When a transaction uses this isolation level, a SELECT query (without a FOR UPDATE/SHARE clause) sees only data committed before the query began; it never sees either uncommitted data or changes committed during query execution by concurrent transactions. In effect, a SELECT query sees a snapshot of the database as of the instant the query begins to run. However, SELECT does see the effects of previous updates executed within its own transaction, even though they are not yet committed. Also note that two successive SELECT commands can see different data, even though they are within a single transaction, if other transactions commit changes after the first SELECT starts and before the second SELECT starts.

UPDATE, DELETE, SELECT FOR UPDATE, and SELECT FOR SHARE commands behave the same as SELECT in terms of searching for target rows: they will only find target rows that were committed as of the command start time. However, such a target row might have already been updated (or deleted or locked) by another concurrent transaction by the time it is found. In this case, the would-be updater will wait for the first updating transaction to commit or roll back (if it is still in progress). If the first updater rolls back, then its effects are negated and the second updater can proceed with updating the originally found row. If the first updater commits, the second updater will ignore the row if the first updater deleted it, otherwise it will attempt to apply its operation to the updated version of the row. The search condition of the command (the WHERE clause) is re-evaluated to see if the updated version of the row still matches the search condition. If so, the second updater proceeds with its operation using the updated version of the row. In the case of SELECT FOR UPDATE and SELECT FOR SHARE, this means it is the updated version of the row that is locked and returned to the client.

Because of the above rule, it is possible for an updating command to see an inconsistent snapshot: it can see the effects of concurrent updating commands on the same rows it is trying to update, but it does not see effects of those commands on other rows in the database. This behavior makes Read Committed mode unsuitable for commands that involve complex search conditions; however, it is just right for simpler cases. For example, consider updating bank balances with transactions like:

```
BEGIN;
UPDATE accounts SET balance = balance + 100.00 WHERE acctnum = 12345;
UPDATE accounts SET balance = balance - 100.00 WHERE acctnum = 7534;
COMMIT;
```

If two such transactions concurrently try to change the balance of account 12345, we clearly want the second transaction to start with the updated version of the account's row. Because each command is affecting only a predetermined row, letting it see the updated version of the row does not create any troublesome inconsistency.

More complex usage can produce undesirable results in Read Committed mode. For example, consider a DELETE command operating on data that is being both added and removed from its restriction criteria by another command, e.g., assume website is a two-row table with website.hits equaling 9 and 10:

```
BEGIN;
UPDATE website SET hits = hits + 1;
-- run from another session:  DELETE FROM website WHERE hits = 10;
COMMIT;
```

The DELETE will have no effect even though there is a website.hits = 10 row before and after the UPDATE. This occurs because the pre-update row value 9 is skipped, and when the UPDATE completes and DELETE obtains a lock, the new row value is no longer 10 but 11, which no longer matches the criteria.

Because Read Committed mode starts each command with a new snapshot that includes all transactions committed up to that instant, subsequent commands in the same transaction will see the effects of the committed concurrent transaction in any case. The point at issue above is whether or not a *single* command sees an absolutely consistent view of the database.

The partial transaction isolation provided by Read Committed mode is adequate for many applications, and this mode is fast and simple to use; however, it is not sufficient for all cases. Applications that do complex queries and updates might require a more rigorously consistent view of the database than Read Committed mode provides.

13.2.2. Repeatable Read Isolation Level

The *Repeatable Read* isolation level only sees data committed before the transaction began; it never sees either uncommitted data or changes committed during transaction execution by concurrent transactions. (However, the query does see the effects of previous updates executed within its own transaction, even though they are not yet committed.) This is a stronger guarantee than is required by the SQL standard for this isolation level, and prevents all of the phenomena described in Table 13-1. As mentioned above, this is specifically allowed by the standard, which only describes the *minimum* protections each isolation level must provide.

This level is different from Read Committed in that a query in a repeatable read transaction sees a snapshot as of the start of the *transaction*, not as of the start of the current query within the transaction. Thus, successive SELECT commands within a *single* transaction see the same data, i.e., they do not see changes made by other transactions that committed after their own transaction started.

Applications using this level must be prepared to retry transactions due to serialization failures.

UPDATE, DELETE, SELECT FOR UPDATE, and SELECT FOR SHARE commands behave the same as SELECT in terms of searching for target rows: they will only find target rows that were committed as of the transaction start time. However, such a target row might have already been updated (or deleted or locked) by another concurrent transaction by the time it is found. In this case, the repeatable read transaction will wait for the first updating transaction to commit or roll back (if it is still in progress). If the first updater rolls back, then its effects are negated and the repeatable read transaction can proceed with updating the originally found row. But if the first updater commits (and actually updated or deleted the row, not just locked it) then the repeatable read transaction will be rolled back with the message

```
ERROR:  could not serialize access due to concurrent update
```

because a repeatable read transaction cannot modify or lock rows changed by other transactions after the repeatable read transaction began.

When an application receives this error message, it should abort the current transaction and retry the whole transaction from the beginning. The second time through, the transaction will see the previously-committed change as part of its initial view of the database, so there is no logical conflict in using the new version of the row as the starting point for the new transaction's update.

Note that only updating transactions might need to be retried; read-only transactions will never have serialization conflicts.

The Repeatable Read mode provides a rigorous guarantee that each transaction sees a completely stable view of the database. However, this view will not necessarily always be consistent with some serial (one at a time) execution of concurrent transactions of the same level. For example, even a read only transaction at this level may see a control record updated to show that a batch has been completed but *not* see one of the detail records which is logically part of the batch because it read an earlier revision of the control record. Attempts to enforce business rules by transactions running at this isolation level are not likely to work correctly without careful use of explicit locks to block conflicting transactions.

Note: Prior to PostgreSQL version 9.1, a request for the Serializable transaction isolation level provided exactly the same behavior described here. To retain the legacy Serializable behavior, Repeatable Read should now be requested.

13.2.3. Serializable Isolation Level

The *Serializable* isolation level provides the strictest transaction isolation. This level emulates serial transaction execution for all committed transactions; as if transactions had been executed one after another, serially, rather than concurrently. However, like the Repeatable Read level, applications using this level must be prepared to retry transactions due to serialization failures. In fact, this isolation level works exactly the same as Repeatable Read except that it monitors for conditions which could make execution of a concurrent set of serializable transactions behave in a manner inconsistent with all possible serial (one at a time) executions of those transactions. This monitoring does not introduce any blocking beyond that present in repeatable read, but there is some overhead to the monitoring, and detection of the conditions which could cause a *serialization anomaly* will trigger a *serialization failure*.

As an example, consider a table `mytab`, initially containing:

```
class | value
------+-------
    1 |    10
    1 |    20
    2 |   100
    2 |   200
```

Suppose that serializable transaction A computes:

```
SELECT SUM(value) FROM mytab WHERE class = 1;
```

and then inserts the result (30) as the `value` in a new row with `class = 2`. Concurrently, serializable transaction B computes:

```
SELECT SUM(value) FROM mytab WHERE class = 2;
```

and obtains the result 300, which it inserts in a new row with `class = 1`. Then both transactions try to commit. If either transaction were running at the Repeatable Read isolation level, both would be allowed to commit; but since there is no serial order of execution consistent with the result, using Serializable transactions will allow one transaction to commit and will roll the other back with this message:

```
ERROR:  could not serialize access due to read/write dependencies among transac
```

This is because if A had executed before B, B would have computed the sum 330, not 300, and similarly the other order would have resulted in a different sum computed by A.

When relying on Serializable transactions to prevent anomalies, it is important that any data read from a permanent user table not be considered valid until the transaction which read it has successfully committed. This is true even for read-only transactions, except that data read within a *deferrable* read-only transaction is known to be valid as soon as it is read, because such a transaction waits until it can acquire a snapshot guaranteed to be free from such problems before starting to read any data. In all other cases applications must not depend on results read during a transaction that later aborted; instead, they should retry the transaction until it succeeds.

To guarantee true serializability PostgreSQL uses *predicate locking*, which means that it keeps locks which allow it to determine when a write would have had an impact on the result of a previous read from a concurrent transaction, had it run first. In PostgreSQL these locks do not cause any blocking and therefore can *not* play any part in causing a deadlock. They are used to identify and flag dependencies among concurrent serializable transactions which in certain combinations can lead to serialization anomalies. In contrast, a Read Committed or Repeatable Read transaction which wants to ensure data consistency may need to take out a lock on an entire table, which could block other users attempting to use that table, or it may use SELECT FOR UPDATE or SELECT FOR SHARE which not only can block other transactions but cause disk access.

Predicate locks in PostgreSQL, like in most other database systems, are based on data actually accessed by a transaction. These will show up in the pg_locks system view with a mode of SIReadLock. The particular locks acquired during execution of a query will depend on the plan used by the query, and multiple finer-grained locks (e.g., tuple locks) may be combined into fewer coarser-grained locks (e.g., page locks) during the course of the transaction to prevent exhaustion of the memory used to track the locks. A READ ONLY transaction may be able to release its SIRead locks before completion, if it detects that no conflicts can still occur which could lead to a serialization anomaly. In fact, READ ONLY transactions will often be able to establish that fact at startup and avoid taking any predicate locks. If you explicitly request a SERIALIZABLE READ ONLY DEFERRABLE transaction, it will block until it can establish this fact. (This is the *only* case where Serializable transactions block but Repeatable Read transactions don't.) On the other hand, SIRead locks often need to be kept past transaction commit, until overlapping read write transactions complete.

Consistent use of Serializable transactions can simplify development. The guarantee that any set of concurrent serializable transactions will have the same effect as if they were run one at a time means that if you can demonstrate that a single transaction, as written, will do the right thing when run by itself, you can have confidence that it will do the right thing in any mix of serializable transactions, even without any information about what those other transactions might do. It is important that an environment which uses this technique have a generalized way of handling serialization failures (which always return with a SQLSTATE value of '40001'), because it will be very hard to predict exactly which transactions might contribute to the read/write dependencies and need to be rolled back to prevent serialization anomalies. The monitoring of read/write dependencies has a cost, as does the restart of transactions which are terminated with a serialization failure, but balanced against the cost and blocking involved in use of explicit locks and SELECT FOR UPDATE or SELECT FOR SHARE, Serializable transactions are the best performance choice for some environments.

For optimal performance when relying on Serializable transactions for concurrency control, these issues should be considered:

- Declare transactions as READ ONLY when possible.

- Control the number of active connections, using a connection pool if needed. This is always an important performance consideration, but it can be particularly important in a busy system using Serializable transactions.

- Don't put more into a single transaction than needed for integrity purposes.

- Don't leave connections dangling "idle in transaction" longer than necessary.

- Eliminate explicit locks, SELECT FOR UPDATE, and SELECT FOR SHARE where no longer needed due to the protections automatically provided by Serializable transactions.

- When the system is forced to combine multiple page-level predicate locks into a single relation-level predicate lock because the predicate lock table is short of memory, an increase in the rate of serialization failures may occur. You can avoid this by increasing max_pred_locks_per_transaction.

- A sequential scan will always necessitate a relation-level predicate lock. This can result in an increased rate of serialization failures. It may be helpful to encourage the use of index scans by reducing random_page_cost and/or increasing cpu_tuple_cost. Be sure to weigh any decrease in transaction rollbacks and restarts against any overall change in query execution time.

Warning

Support for the Serializable transaction isolation level has not yet been added to Hot Standby replication targets (described in Section 25.5). The strictest isolation level currently supported in hot standby mode is Repeatable Read. While performing all permanent database writes within Serializable transactions on the master will ensure that all standbys will eventually reach a consistent state, a Repeatable Read transaction run on the standby can sometimes see a transient state which is inconsistent with any serial execution of serializable transactions on the master.

13.3. Explicit Locking

PostgreSQL provides various lock modes to control concurrent access to data in tables. These modes can be used for application-controlled locking in situations where MVCC does not give the desired behavior. Also, most PostgreSQL commands automatically acquire locks of appropriate modes to ensure that referenced tables are not dropped or modified in incompatible ways while the command executes. (For example, TRUNCATE cannot safely be executed concurrently with other operations on the same table, so it obtains an exclusive lock on the table to enforce that.)

To examine a list of the currently outstanding locks in a database server, use the pg_locks system view. For more information on monitoring the status of the lock manager subsystem, refer to Chapter 27.

13.3.1. Table-level Locks

The list below shows the available lock modes and the contexts in which they are used automatically by PostgreSQL. You can also acquire any of these locks explicitly with the command LOCK. Remember that all of these lock modes are table-level locks, even if the name contains the word "row"; the names of the lock modes are historical. To some extent the names reflect the typical usage of each lock mode — but the semantics are all the same. The only real difference between one lock mode and another is the set of lock modes with which each conflicts (see Table 13-2). Two transactions cannot hold locks of conflicting modes on the same table at the same time. (However, a transaction never conflicts with itself. For example, it might acquire ACCESS EXCLUSIVE lock and later acquire ACCESS SHARE lock on the same table.) Non-conflicting lock modes can be held concurrently by many transactions. Notice in particular that some lock modes are self-conflicting (for example, an ACCESS EXCLUSIVE lock cannot be held by more than one transaction at a time) while others are not self-conflicting (for example, an ACCESS SHARE lock can be held by multiple transactions).

Table-level Lock Modes

ACCESS SHARE

Conflicts with the ACCESS EXCLUSIVE lock mode only.

The SELECT command acquires a lock of this mode on referenced tables. In general, any query that only *reads* a table and does not modify it will acquire this lock mode.

ROW SHARE

Conflicts with the EXCLUSIVE and ACCESS EXCLUSIVE lock modes.

The SELECT FOR UPDATE and SELECT FOR SHARE commands acquire a lock of this mode on the target table(s) (in addition to ACCESS SHARE locks on any other tables that are referenced but not selected FOR UPDATE/FOR SHARE).

ROW EXCLUSIVE

Conflicts with the SHARE, SHARE ROW EXCLUSIVE, EXCLUSIVE, and ACCESS EXCLUSIVE lock modes.

The commands UPDATE, DELETE, and INSERT acquire this lock mode on the target table (in addition to ACCESS SHARE locks on any other referenced tables). In general, this lock mode will be acquired by any command that *modifies data* in a table.

SHARE UPDATE EXCLUSIVE

Conflicts with the SHARE UPDATE EXCLUSIVE, SHARE, SHARE ROW EXCLUSIVE, EXCLUSIVE, and ACCESS EXCLUSIVE lock modes. This mode protects a table against concurrent schema changes and VACUUM runs.

Acquired by VACUUM (without FULL), ANALYZE, CREATE INDEX CONCURRENTLY, and ALTER TABLE VALIDATE and other ALTER TABLE variants (for full details see ALTER TABLE).

SHARE

Conflicts with the ROW EXCLUSIVE, SHARE UPDATE EXCLUSIVE, SHARE ROW EXCLUSIVE, EXCLUSIVE, and ACCESS EXCLUSIVE lock modes. This mode protects a table against concurrent data changes.

Acquired by CREATE INDEX (without CONCURRENTLY).

SHARE ROW EXCLUSIVE

Conflicts with the ROW EXCLUSIVE, SHARE UPDATE EXCLUSIVE, SHARE, SHARE ROW EXCLUSIVE, EXCLUSIVE, and ACCESS EXCLUSIVE lock modes. This mode protects a table against concurrent data changes, and is self-exclusive so that only one session can hold it at a time.

This lock mode is not automatically acquired by any PostgreSQL command.

EXCLUSIVE

Conflicts with the ROW SHARE, ROW EXCLUSIVE, SHARE UPDATE EXCLUSIVE, SHARE, SHARE ROW EXCLUSIVE, EXCLUSIVE, and ACCESS EXCLUSIVE lock modes. This mode allows only concurrent ACCESS SHARE locks, i.e., only reads from the table can proceed in parallel with a transaction holding this lock mode.

Acquired by REFRESH MATERIALIZED VIEW CONCURRENTLY.

ACCESS EXCLUSIVE

Conflicts with locks of all modes (ACCESS SHARE, ROW SHARE, ROW EXCLUSIVE, SHARE UPDATE EXCLUSIVE, SHARE, SHARE ROW EXCLUSIVE, EXCLUSIVE, and ACCESS EXCLUSIVE). This mode guarantees that the holder is the only transaction accessing the table in any way.

Acquired by the DROP TABLE, TRUNCATE, REINDEX, CLUSTER, and VACUUM FULL commands. Many forms of ALTER TABLE also acquire a lock at this level (see ALTER TABLE). This is also the default lock mode for LOCK TABLE statements that do not specify a mode explicitly.

Tip: Only an ACCESS EXCLUSIVE lock blocks a SELECT (without FOR UPDATE/SHARE) statement.

Once acquired, a lock is normally held till end of transaction. But if a lock is acquired after establishing a savepoint, the lock is released immediately if the savepoint is rolled back to. This is consistent with the principle that ROLLBACK cancels all effects of the commands since the savepoint. The same holds for locks acquired within a PL/pgSQL exception block: an error escape from the block releases locks acquired within it.

Table 13-2. Conflicting Lock Modes

Requested Lock Mode	Current Lock Mode							
	ACCESS SHARE	ROW SHARE	ROW EXCLU-SIVE	SHARE UPDATE EXCLU-SIVE	SHARE	SHARE ROW EXCLU-SIVE	EXCLUSIVE	ACCESS EXCLU-SIVE
ACCESS SHARE								X
ROW SHARE							X	X
ROW EXCLU-SIVE					X	X	X	X
SHARE UPDATE EXCLU-SIVE				X	X	X	X	X
SHARE			X	X		X	X	X

Requested Lock Mode	Current Lock Mode							
	ACCESS SHARE	ROW SHARE	ROW EXCLU- SIVE	SHARE UPDATE EXCLU- SIVE	SHARE	SHARE ROW EXCLU- SIVE	EXCLUSIVE	ACCESS EXCLU- SIVE
SHARE ROW EXCLU- SIVE			X	X	X	X	X	X
EXCLUSIVE		X	X	X	X	X	X	X
ACCESS EXCLU- SIVE	X	X	X	X	X	X	X	X

13.3.2. Row-level Locks

In addition to table-level locks, there are row-level locks, which are listed as below with the contexts in which they are used automatically by PostgreSQL. See Table 13-3 for a complete table of row-level lock conflicts. Note that a transaction can hold conflicting locks on the same row, even in different subtransactions; but other than that, two transactions can never hold conflicting locks on the same row. Row-level locks do not affect data querying; they block only *writers and lockers* to the same row.

Row-level Lock Modes

FOR UPDATE

> FOR UPDATE causes the rows retrieved by the SELECT statement to be locked as though for update. This prevents them from being locked, modified or deleted by other transactions until the current transaction ends. That is, other transactions that attempt UPDATE, DELETE, SELECT FOR UPDATE, SELECT FOR NO KEY UPDATE, SELECT FOR SHARE or SELECT FOR KEY SHARE of these rows will be blocked until the current transaction ends; conversely, SELECT FOR UPDATE will wait for a concurrent transaction that has run any of those commands on the same row, and will then lock and return the updated row (or no row, if the row was deleted). Within a REPEATABLE READ or SERIALIZABLE transaction, however, an error will be thrown if a row to be locked has changed since the transaction started. For further discussion see Section 13.4.

> The FOR UPDATE lock mode is also acquired by any DELETE on a row, and also by an UPDATE that modifies the values on certain columns. Currently, the set of columns considered for the UPDATE case are those that have a unique index on them that can be used in a foreign key (so partial indexes and expressional indexes are not considered), but this may change in the future.

FOR NO KEY UPDATE

> Behaves similarly to FOR UPDATE, except that the lock acquired is weaker: this lock will not block

SELECT FOR KEY SHARE commands that attempt to acquire a lock on the same rows. This lock mode is also acquired by any UPDATE that does not acquire a FOR UPDATE lock.

FOR SHARE

Behaves similarly to FOR NO KEY UPDATE, except that it acquires a shared lock rather than exclusive lock on each retrieved row. A shared lock blocks other transactions from performing UPDATE, DELETE, SELECT FOR UPDATE or SELECT FOR NO KEY UPDATE on these rows, but it does not prevent them from performing SELECT FOR SHARE or SELECT FOR KEY SHARE.

FOR KEY SHARE

Behaves similarly to FOR SHARE, except that the lock is weaker: SELECT FOR UPDATE is blocked, but not SELECT FOR NO KEY UPDATE. A key-shared lock blocks other transactions from performing DELETE or any UPDATE that changes the key values, but not other UPDATE, and neither does it prevent SELECT FOR NO KEY UPDATE, SELECT FOR SHARE, or SELECT FOR KEY SHARE.

PostgreSQL doesn't remember any information about modified rows in memory, so there is no limit on the number of rows locked at one time. However, locking a row might cause a disk write, e.g., SELECT FOR UPDATE modifies selected rows to mark them locked, and so will result in disk writes.

Table 13-3. Conflicting Row-level Locks

Requested Lock Mode	Current Lock Mode			
	FOR KEY SHARE	FOR SHARE	FOR NO KEY UPDATE	FOR UPDATE
FOR KEY SHARE				X
FOR SHARE			X	X
FOR NO KEY UPDATE		X	X	X
FOR UPDATE	X	X	X	X

13.3.3. Page-level Locks

In addition to table and row locks, page-level share/exclusive locks are used to control read/write access to table pages in the shared buffer pool. These locks are released immediately after a row is fetched or updated. Application developers normally need not be concerned with page-level locks, but they are mentioned here for completeness.

13.3.4. Deadlocks

The use of explicit locking can increase the likelihood of *deadlocks*, wherein two (or more) transactions each hold locks that the other wants. For example, if transaction 1 acquires an exclusive lock on table A and then tries to acquire an exclusive lock on table B, while transaction 2 has already exclusive-locked table B and now wants an exclusive lock on table A, then neither one can proceed. PostgreSQL automatically detects deadlock situations and resolves them by aborting one of the transactions involved, allowing the other(s) to complete. (Exactly which transaction will be aborted is difficult to predict and should not be relied upon.)

Note that deadlocks can also occur as the result of row-level locks (and thus, they can occur even if explicit locking is not used). Consider the case in which two concurrent transactions modify a table. The first transaction executes:

```
UPDATE accounts SET balance = balance + 100.00 WHERE acctnum = 11111;
```

This acquires a row-level lock on the row with the specified account number. Then, the second transaction executes:

```
UPDATE accounts SET balance = balance + 100.00 WHERE acctnum = 22222;
UPDATE accounts SET balance = balance - 100.00 WHERE acctnum = 11111;
```

The first UPDATE statement successfully acquires a row-level lock on the specified row, so it succeeds in updating that row. However, the second UPDATE statement finds that the row it is attempting to update has already been locked, so it waits for the transaction that acquired the lock to complete. Transaction two is now waiting on transaction one to complete before it continues execution. Now, transaction one executes:

```
UPDATE accounts SET balance = balance - 100.00 WHERE acctnum = 22222;
```

Transaction one attempts to acquire a row-level lock on the specified row, but it cannot: transaction two already holds such a lock. So it waits for transaction two to complete. Thus, transaction one is blocked on transaction two, and transaction two is blocked on transaction one: a deadlock condition. PostgreSQL will detect this situation and abort one of the transactions.

The best defense against deadlocks is generally to avoid them by being certain that all applications using a database acquire locks on multiple objects in a consistent order. In the example above, if both transactions had updated the rows in the same order, no deadlock would have occurred. One should also ensure that the first lock acquired on an object in a transaction is the most restrictive mode that will be needed for that object. If it is not feasible to verify this in advance, then deadlocks can be handled on-the-fly by retrying transactions that abort due to deadlocks.

So long as no deadlock situation is detected, a transaction seeking either a table-level or row-level lock will wait indefinitely for conflicting locks to be released. This means it is a bad idea for applications to hold transactions open for long periods of time (e.g., while waiting for user input).

13.3.5. Advisory Locks

PostgreSQL provides a means for creating locks that have application-defined meanings. These are called *advisory locks*, because the system does not enforce their use — it is up to the application to use them correctly. Advisory locks can be useful for locking strategies that are an awkward fit for the MVCC model. For example, a common use of advisory locks is to emulate pessimistic locking strategies typical of so-called "flat file" data management systems. While a flag stored in a table could be used for the same purpose, advisory locks are faster, avoid table bloat, and are automatically cleaned up by the server at the end of the session.

There are two ways to acquire an advisory lock in PostgreSQL: at session level or at transaction level. Once acquired at session level, an advisory lock is held until explicitly released or the session ends. Unlike standard lock requests, session-level advisory lock requests do not honor transaction semantics: a lock acquired during a transaction that is later rolled back will still be held following the rollback, and likewise an unlock is effective even if the calling transaction fails later. A lock can be acquired multiple times by its owning process; for each completed lock request there must be a corresponding unlock request before the lock is actually released. Transaction-level lock requests, on the other hand, behave more like regular lock requests: they are automatically released at the end of the transaction, and there is no explicit unlock operation. This behavior is often more convenient than the session-level behavior for short-term usage of an advisory lock. Session-level and transaction-level lock requests for the same advisory lock identifier will block each other in the expected way. If a session already holds a given advisory lock, additional requests by it will always succeed, even if other sessions are awaiting the lock; this statement is true regardless of whether the existing lock hold and new request are at session level or transaction level.

Like all locks in PostgreSQL, a complete list of advisory locks currently held by any session can be found in the pg_locks system view.

Both advisory locks and regular locks are stored in a shared memory pool whose size is defined by the configuration variables max_locks_per_transaction and max_connections. Care must be taken not to exhaust this memory or the server will be unable to grant any locks at all. This imposes an upper limit on the number of advisory locks grantable by the server, typically in the tens to hundreds of thousands depending on how the server is configured.

In certain cases using advisory locking methods, especially in queries involving explicit ordering and LIMIT clauses, care must be taken to control the locks acquired because of the order in which SQL expressions are evaluated. For example:

```
SELECT pg_advisory_lock(id) FROM foo WHERE id = 12345; -- ok
SELECT pg_advisory_lock(id) FROM foo WHERE id > 12345 LIMIT 100; -- danger!
SELECT pg_advisory_lock(q.id) FROM
(
  SELECT id FROM foo WHERE id > 12345 LIMIT 100
) q; -- ok
```

In the above queries, the second form is dangerous because the LIMIT is not guaranteed to be applied before the locking function is executed. This might cause some locks to be acquired that the application was not expecting, and hence would fail to release (until it ends the session). From the point of view of the application, such locks would be dangling, although still viewable in pg_locks.

The functions provided to manipulate advisory locks are described in Section 9.26.9.

13.4. Data Consistency Checks at the Application Level

It is very difficult to enforce business rules regarding data integrity using Read Committed transactions because the view of the data is shifting with each statement, and even a single statement may not restrict itself to the statement's snapshot if a write conflict occurs.

While a Repeatable Read transaction has a stable view of the data throughout its execution, there is a subtle issue with using MVCC snapshots for data consistency checks, involving something known as *read/write conflicts*. If one transaction writes data and a concurrent transaction attempts to read the same data (whether before or after the write), it cannot see the work of the other transaction. The reader then appears to have executed first regardless of which started first or which committed first. If that is as far as it goes, there is no problem, but if the reader also writes data which is read by a concurrent transaction there is now a transaction which appears to have run before either of the previously mentioned transactions. If the transaction which appears to have executed last actually commits first, it is very easy for a cycle to appear in a graph of the order of execution of the transactions. When such a cycle appears, integrity checks will not work correctly without some help.

As mentioned in Section 13.2.3, Serializable transactions are just Repeatable Read transactions which add nonblocking monitoring for dangerous patterns of read/write conflicts. When a pattern is detected which could cause a cycle in the apparent order of execution, one of the transactions involved is rolled back to break the cycle.

13.4.1. Enforcing Consistency With Serializable Transactions

If the Serializable transaction isolation level is used for all writes and for all reads which need a consistent view of the data, no other effort is required to ensure consistency. Software from other environments which is written to use serializable transactions to ensure consistency should "just work" in this regard in PostgreSQL.

When using this technique, it will avoid creating an unnecessary burden for application programmers if the application software goes through a framework which automatically retries transactions which are rolled back with a serialization failure. It may be a good idea to set `default_transaction_isolation` to `serializable`. It would also be wise to take some action to ensure that no other transaction isolation level is used, either inadvertently or to subvert integrity checks, through checks of the transaction isolation level in triggers.

See Section 13.2.3 for performance suggestions.

Warning

This level of integrity protection using Serializable transactions does not yet extend to hot standby mode (Section 25.5). Because of that, those using hot standby may want to use Repeatable Read and explicit locking on the master.

13.4.2. Enforcing Consistency With Explicit Blocking Locks

When non-serializable writes are possible, to ensure the current validity of a row and protect it against concurrent updates one must use SELECT FOR UPDATE, SELECT FOR SHARE, or an appropriate LOCK TABLE statement. (SELECT FOR UPDATE and SELECT FOR SHARE lock just the returned rows against concurrent updates, while LOCK TABLE locks the whole table.) This should be taken into account when porting applications to PostgreSQL from other environments.

Also of note to those converting from other environments is the fact that SELECT FOR UPDATE does not ensure that a concurrent transaction will not update or delete a selected row. To do that in PostgreSQL you must actually update the row, even if no values need to be changed. SELECT FOR UPDATE *temporarily blocks* other transactions from acquiring the same lock or executing an UPDATE or DELETE which would affect the locked row, but once the transaction holding this lock commits or rolls back, a blocked transaction will proceed with the conflicting operation unless an actual UPDATE of the row was performed while the lock was held.

Global validity checks require extra thought under non-serializable MVCC. For example, a banking application might wish to check that the sum of all credits in one table equals the sum of debits in another table, when both tables are being actively updated. Comparing the results of two successive SELECT sum(...) commands will not work reliably in Read Committed mode, since the second query will likely include the results of transactions not counted by the first. Doing the two sums in a single repeatable read transaction will give an accurate picture of only the effects of transactions that committed before the repeatable read transaction started — but one might legitimately wonder whether the answer is still relevant by the time it is delivered. If the repeatable read transaction itself applied some changes before trying to make the consistency check, the usefulness of the check becomes even more debatable, since now it includes some but not all post-transaction-start changes. In such cases a careful person might wish to lock all tables needed for the check, in order to get an indisputable picture of current reality. A SHARE mode (or higher) lock guarantees that there are no uncommitted changes in the locked table, other than those of the current transaction.

Note also that if one is relying on explicit locking to prevent concurrent changes, one should either use Read Committed mode, or in Repeatable Read mode be careful to obtain locks before performing queries. A lock obtained by a repeatable read transaction guarantees that no other transactions modifying the table are still running, but if the snapshot seen by the transaction predates obtaining the lock, it might predate some now-committed changes in the table. A repeatable read transaction's snapshot is actually frozen at the start of its first query or data-modification command (SELECT, INSERT, UPDATE, or DELETE), so it is possible to obtain locks explicitly before the snapshot is frozen.

13.5. Locking and Indexes

Though PostgreSQL provides nonblocking read/write access to table data, nonblocking read/write access is not currently offered for every index access method implemented in PostgreSQL. The various index types are handled as follows:

B-tree, GiST and SP-GiST indexes

Short-term share/exclusive page-level locks are used for read/write access. Locks are released immediately after each index row is fetched or inserted. These index types provide the highest concurrency without deadlock conditions.

Hash indexes

Share/exclusive hash-bucket-level locks are used for read/write access. Locks are released after the whole bucket is processed. Bucket-level locks provide better concurrency than index-level ones, but deadlock is possible since the locks are held longer than one index operation.

GIN indexes

Short-term share/exclusive page-level locks are used for read/write access. Locks are released immediately after each index row is fetched or inserted. But note that insertion of a GIN-indexed value usually produces several index key insertions per row, so GIN might do substantial work for a single value's insertion.

Currently, B-tree indexes offer the best performance for concurrent applications; since they also have more features than hash indexes, they are the recommended index type for concurrent applications that need to index scalar data. When dealing with non-scalar data, B-trees are not useful, and GiST, SP-GiST or GIN indexes should be used instead.

Chapter 14. Performance Tips

Query performance can be affected by many things. Some of these can be controlled by the user, while others are fundamental to the underlying design of the system. This chapter provides some hints about understanding and tuning PostgreSQL performance.

14.1. Using EXPLAIN

PostgreSQL devises a *query plan* for each query it receives. Choosing the right plan to match the query structure and the properties of the data is absolutely critical for good performance, so the system includes a complex *planner* that tries to choose good plans. You can use the EXPLAIN command to see what query plan the planner creates for any query. Plan-reading is an art that requires some experience to master, but this section attempts to cover the basics.

Examples in this section are drawn from the regression test database after doing a VACUUM ANALYZE, using 9.3 development sources. You should be able to get similar results if you try the examples yourself, but your estimated costs and row counts might vary slightly because ANALYZE's statistics are random samples rather than exact, and because costs are inherently somewhat platform-dependent.

The examples use EXPLAIN's default "text" output format, which is compact and convenient for humans to read. If you want to feed EXPLAIN's output to a program for further analysis, you should use one of its machine-readable output formats (XML, JSON, or YAML) instead.

14.1.1. EXPLAIN Basics

The structure of a query plan is a tree of *plan nodes*. Nodes at the bottom level of the tree are scan nodes: they return raw rows from a table. There are different types of scan nodes for different table access methods: sequential scans, index scans, and bitmap index scans. There are also non-table row sources, such as VALUES clauses and set-returning functions in FROM, which have their own scan node types. If the query requires joining, aggregation, sorting, or other operations on the raw rows, then there will be additional nodes above the scan nodes to perform these operations. Again, there is usually more than one possible way to do these operations, so different node types can appear here too. The output of EXPLAIN has one line for each node in the plan tree, showing the basic node type plus the cost estimates that the planner made for the execution of that plan node. Additional lines might appear, indented from the node's summary line, to show additional properties of the node. The very first line (the summary line for the topmost node) has the estimated total execution cost for the plan; it is this number that the planner seeks to minimize.

Here is a trivial example, just to show what the output looks like:

```
EXPLAIN SELECT * FROM tenk1;

                        QUERY PLAN
-------------------------------------------------------------
 Seq Scan on tenk1  (cost=0.00..458.00 rows=10000 width=244)
```

Since this query has no WHERE clause, it must scan all the rows of the table, so the planner has chosen to use a simple sequential scan plan. The numbers that are quoted in parentheses are (left to right):

- Estimated start-up cost. This is the time expended before the output phase can begin, e.g., time to do the sorting in a sort node.

- Estimated total cost. This is stated on the assumption that the plan node is run to completion, i.e., all available rows are retrieved. In practice a node's parent node might stop short of reading all available rows (see the LIMIT example below).

- Estimated number of rows output by this plan node. Again, the node is assumed to be run to completion.

- Estimated average width of rows output by this plan node (in bytes).

The costs are measured in arbitrary units determined by the planner's cost parameters (see Section 18.7.2). Traditional practice is to measure the costs in units of disk page fetches; that is, seq_page_cost is conventionally set to 1.0 and the other cost parameters are set relative to that. The examples in this section are run with the default cost parameters.

It's important to understand that the cost of an upper-level node includes the cost of all its child nodes. It's also important to realize that the cost only reflects things that the planner cares about. In particular, the cost does not consider the time spent transmitting result rows to the client, which could be an important factor in the real elapsed time; but the planner ignores it because it cannot change it by altering the plan. (Every correct plan will output the same row set, we trust.)

The rows value is a little tricky because it is not the number of rows processed or scanned by the plan node, but rather the number emitted by the node. This is often less than the number scanned, as a result of filtering by any WHERE-clause conditions that are being applied at the node. Ideally the top-level rows estimate will approximate the number of rows actually returned, updated, or deleted by the query.

Returning to our example:

```
EXPLAIN SELECT * FROM tenk1;

                         QUERY PLAN
-------------------------------------------------------------
 Seq Scan on tenk1  (cost=0.00..458.00 rows=10000 width=244)
```

These numbers are derived very straightforwardly. If you do:

```
SELECT relpages, reltuples FROM pg_class WHERE relname = 'tenk1';
```

you will find that tenk1 has 358 disk pages and 10000 rows. The estimated cost is computed as (disk pages read * seq_page_cost) + (rows scanned * cpu_tuple_cost). By default, seq_page_cost is 1.0 and cpu_tuple_cost is 0.01, so the estimated cost is (358 * 1.0) + (10000 * 0.01) = 458.

Now let's modify the query to add a WHERE condition:

```
EXPLAIN SELECT * FROM tenk1 WHERE unique1 < 7000;

                         QUERY PLAN
-------------------------------------------------------------
```

```
 Seq Scan on tenk1  (cost=0.00..483.00 rows=7001 width=244)
   Filter: (unique1 < 7000)
```

Notice that the EXPLAIN output shows the WHERE clause being applied as a "filter" condition attached to the Seq Scan plan node. This means that the plan node checks the condition for each row it scans, and outputs only the ones that pass the condition. The estimate of output rows has been reduced because of the WHERE clause. However, the scan will still have to visit all 10000 rows, so the cost hasn't decreased; in fact it has gone up a bit (by 10000 * cpu_operator_cost, to be exact) to reflect the extra CPU time spent checking the WHERE condition.

The actual number of rows this query would select is 7000, but the rows estimate is only approximate. If you try to duplicate this experiment, you will probably get a slightly different estimate; moreover, it can change after each ANALYZE command, because the statistics produced by ANALYZE are taken from a randomized sample of the table.

Now, let's make the condition more restrictive:

```
EXPLAIN SELECT * FROM tenk1 WHERE unique1 < 100;

                                QUERY PLAN
------------------------------------------------------------------------------
 Bitmap Heap Scan on tenk1  (cost=5.07..229.20 rows=101 width=244)
   Recheck Cond: (unique1 < 100)
   ->  Bitmap Index Scan on tenk1_unique1  (cost=0.00..5.04 rows=101 width=0)
         Index Cond: (unique1 < 100)
```

Here the planner has decided to use a two-step plan: the child plan node visits an index to find the locations of rows matching the index condition, and then the upper plan node actually fetches those rows from the table itself. Fetching rows separately is much more expensive than reading them sequentially, but because not all the pages of the table have to be visited, this is still cheaper than a sequential scan. (The reason for using two plan levels is that the upper plan node sorts the row locations identified by the index into physical order before reading them, to minimize the cost of separate fetches. The "bitmap" mentioned in the node names is the mechanism that does the sorting.)

Now let's add another condition to the WHERE clause:

```
EXPLAIN SELECT * FROM tenk1 WHERE unique1 < 100 AND stringu1 = 'xxx';

                                QUERY PLAN
------------------------------------------------------------------------------
 Bitmap Heap Scan on tenk1  (cost=5.04..229.43 rows=1 width=244)
   Recheck Cond: (unique1 < 100)
   Filter: (stringu1 = 'xxx'::name)
   ->  Bitmap Index Scan on tenk1_unique1  (cost=0.00..5.04 rows=101 width=0)
         Index Cond: (unique1 < 100)
```

The added condition stringu1 = 'xxx' reduces the output row count estimate, but not the cost because we still have to visit the same set of rows. Notice that the stringu1 clause cannot be applied as an index condition, since this index is only on the unique1 column. Instead it is applied as a filter on the rows retrieved by the index. Thus the cost has actually gone up slightly to reflect this extra checking.

In some cases the planner will prefer a "simple" index scan plan:

```
EXPLAIN SELECT * FROM tenk1 WHERE unique1 = 42;

                            QUERY PLAN
-------------------------------------------------------------------------
 Index Scan using tenk1_unique1 on tenk1  (cost=0.29..8.30 rows=1 width=244)
   Index Cond: (unique1 = 42)
```

In this type of plan the table rows are fetched in index order, which makes them even more expensive to read, but there are so few that the extra cost of sorting the row locations is not worth it. You'll most often see this plan type for queries that fetch just a single row. It's also often used for queries that have an ORDER BY condition that matches the index order, because then no extra sorting step is needed to satisfy the ORDER BY.

If there are separate indexes on several of the columns referenced in WHERE, the planner might choose to use an AND or OR combination of the indexes:

```
EXPLAIN SELECT * FROM tenk1 WHERE unique1 < 100 AND unique2 > 9000;

                            QUERY PLAN
-------------------------------------------------------------------------
 Bitmap Heap Scan on tenk1  (cost=25.08..60.21 rows=10 width=244)
   Recheck Cond: ((unique1 < 100) AND (unique2 > 9000))
   ->  BitmapAnd  (cost=25.08..25.08 rows=10 width=0)
         ->  Bitmap Index Scan on tenk1_unique1  (cost=0.00..5.04 rows=101 widt
               Index Cond: (unique1 < 100)
         ->  Bitmap Index Scan on tenk1_unique2  (cost=0.00..19.78 rows=999 wi
               Index Cond: (unique2 > 9000)
```

But this requires visiting both indexes, so it's not necessarily a win compared to using just one index and treating the other condition as a filter. If you vary the ranges involved you'll see the plan change accordingly.

Here is an example showing the effects of LIMIT:

```
EXPLAIN SELECT * FROM tenk1 WHERE unique1 < 100 AND unique2 > 9000 LIMIT 2;

                            QUERY PLAN
-------------------------------------------------------------------------
 Limit  (cost=0.29..14.48 rows=2 width=244)
   ->  Index Scan using tenk1_unique2 on tenk1  (cost=0.29..71.27 rows=10 widt
         Index Cond: (unique2 > 9000)
         Filter: (unique1 < 100)
```

This is the same query as above, but we added a LIMIT so that not all the rows need be retrieved, and the planner changed its mind about what to do. Notice that the total cost and row count of the Index Scan node are shown as if it were run to completion. However, the Limit node is expected to stop after retrieving only a fifth of those rows, so its total cost is only a fifth as much, and that's the actual estimated cost of the query. This plan is preferred over adding a Limit node to the previous plan because the Limit could not avoid paying the startup cost of the bitmap scan, so the total cost would be something over 25 units with that approach.

Let's try joining two tables, using the columns we have been discussing:

```
EXPLAIN SELECT *
FROM tenk1 t1, tenk2 t2
WHERE t1.unique1 < 10 AND t1.unique2 = t2.unique2;

                                 QUERY PLAN
-----------------------------------------------------------------------------
 Nested Loop  (cost=4.65..118.62 rows=10 width=488)
   ->  Bitmap Heap Scan on tenk1 t1  (cost=4.36..39.47 rows=10 width=244)
         Recheck Cond: (unique1 < 10)
         ->  Bitmap Index Scan on tenk1_unique1  (cost=0.00..4.36 rows=10 widtl
               Index Cond: (unique1 < 10)
   ->  Index Scan using tenk2_unique2 on tenk2 t2  (cost=0.29..7.91 rows=1 widt
         Index Cond: (unique2 = t1.unique2)
```

In this plan, we have a nested-loop join node with two table scans as inputs, or children. The indentation of the node summary lines reflects the plan tree structure. The join's first, or "outer", child is a bitmap scan similar to those we saw before. Its cost and row count are the same as we'd get from SELECT ... WHERE unique1 < 10 because we are applying the WHERE clause unique1 < 10 at that node. The t1.unique2 = t2.unique2 clause is not relevant yet, so it doesn't affect the row count of the outer scan. The nested-loop join node will run its second, or "inner" child once for each row obtained from the outer child. Column values from the current outer row can be plugged into the inner scan; here, the t1.unique2 value from the outer row is available, so we get a plan and costs similar to what we saw above for a simple SELECT ... WHERE t2.unique2 = *constant* case. (The estimated cost is actually a bit lower than what was seen above, as a result of caching that's expected to occur during the repeated index scans on t2.) The costs of the loop node are then set on the basis of the cost of the outer scan, plus one repetition of the inner scan for each outer row (10 * 7.87, here), plus a little CPU time for join processing.

In this example the join's output row count is the same as the product of the two scans' row counts, but that's not true in all cases because there can be additional WHERE clauses that mention both tables and so can only be applied at the join point, not to either input scan. Here's an example:

```
EXPLAIN SELECT *
FROM tenk1 t1, tenk2 t2
WHERE t1.unique1 < 10 AND t2.unique2 < 10 AND t1.hundred < t2.hundred;

                                 QUERY PLAN
-----------------------------------------------------------------------------
 Nested Loop  (cost=4.65..49.46 rows=33 width=488)
   Join Filter: (t1.hundred < t2.hundred)
   ->  Bitmap Heap Scan on tenk1 t1  (cost=4.36..39.47 rows=10 width=244)
         Recheck Cond: (unique1 < 10)
         ->  Bitmap Index Scan on tenk1_unique1  (cost=0.00..4.36 rows=10 widtl
               Index Cond: (unique1 < 10)
   ->  Materialize  (cost=0.29..8.51 rows=10 width=244)
         ->  Index Scan using tenk2_unique2 on tenk2 t2  (cost=0.29..8.46 rows=
               Index Cond: (unique2 < 10)
```

The condition `t1.hundred < t2.hundred` can't be tested in the `tenk2_unique2` index, so it's applied at the join node. This reduces the estimated output row count of the join node, but does not change either input scan.

Notice that here the planner has chosen to "materialize" the inner relation of the join, by putting a Materialize plan node atop it. This means that the `t2` index scan will be done just once, even though the nested-loop join node needs to read that data ten times, once for each row from the outer relation. The Materialize node saves the data in memory as it's read, and then returns the data from memory on each subsequent pass.

When dealing with outer joins, you might see join plan nodes with both "Join Filter" and plain "Filter" conditions attached. Join Filter conditions come from the outer join's ON clause, so a row that fails the Join Filter condition could still get emitted as a null-extended row. But a plain Filter condition is applied after the outer-join rules and so acts to remove rows unconditionally. In an inner join there is no semantic difference between these types of filters.

If we change the query's selectivity a bit, we might get a very different join plan:

```
EXPLAIN SELECT *
FROM tenk1 t1, tenk2 t2
WHERE t1.unique1 < 100 AND t1.unique2 = t2.unique2;

                              QUERY PLAN
---------------------------------------------------------------------------
 Hash Join  (cost=230.47..713.98 rows=101 width=488)
   Hash Cond: (t2.unique2 = t1.unique2)
   ->  Seq Scan on tenk2 t2  (cost=0.00..445.00 rows=10000 width=244)
   ->  Hash  (cost=229.20..229.20 rows=101 width=244)
         ->  Bitmap Heap Scan on tenk1 t1  (cost=5.07..229.20 rows=101 width=2(
               Recheck Cond: (unique1 < 100)
               ->  Bitmap Index Scan on tenk1_unique1  (cost=0.00..5.04 rows=1(
                     Index Cond: (unique1 < 100)
```

Here, the planner has chosen to use a hash join, in which rows of one table are entered into an in-memory hash table, after which the other table is scanned and the hash table is probed for matches to each row. Again note how the indentation reflects the plan structure: the bitmap scan on `tenk1` is the input to the Hash node, which constructs the hash table. That's then returned to the Hash Join node, which reads rows from its outer child plan and searches the hash table for each one.

Another possible type of join is a merge join, illustrated here:

```
EXPLAIN SELECT *
FROM tenk1 t1, onek t2
WHERE t1.unique1 < 100 AND t1.unique2 = t2.unique2;

                              QUERY PLAN
---------------------------------------------------------------------------
 Merge Join  (cost=198.11..268.19 rows=10 width=488)
   Merge Cond: (t1.unique2 = t2.unique2)
   ->  Index Scan using tenk1_unique2 on tenk1 t1  (cost=0.29..656.28 rows=101
         Filter: (unique1 < 100)
   ->  Sort  (cost=197.83..200.33 rows=1000 width=244)
```

```
Sort Key: t2.unique2
->  Seq Scan on onek t2  (cost=0.00..148.00 rows=1000 width=244)
```

Merge join requires its input data to be sorted on the join keys. In this plan the `tenk1` data is sorted by using an index scan to visit the rows in the correct order, but a sequential scan and sort is preferred for `onek`, because there are many more rows to be visited in that table. (Sequential-scan-and-sort frequently beats an index scan for sorting many rows, because of the nonsequential disk access required by the index scan.)

One way to look at variant plans is to force the planner to disregard whatever strategy it thought was the cheapest, using the enable/disable flags described in Section 18.7.1. (This is a crude tool, but useful. See also Section 14.3.) For example, if we're unconvinced that sequential-scan-and-sort is the best way to deal with table `onek` in the previous example, we could try

```
SET enable_sort = off;

EXPLAIN SELECT *
FROM tenk1 t1, onek t2
WHERE t1.unique1 < 100 AND t1.unique2 = t2.unique2;

                                 QUERY PLAN
-------------------------------------------------------------------------------
 Merge Join  (cost=0.56..292.65 rows=10 width=488)
   Merge Cond: (t1.unique2 = t2.unique2)
   ->  Index Scan using tenk1_unique2 on tenk1 t1  (cost=0.29..656.28 rows=101
         Filter: (unique1 < 100)
   ->  Index Scan using onek_unique2 on onek t2  (cost=0.28..224.79 rows=1000
```

which shows that the planner thinks that sorting `onek` by index-scanning is about 12% more expensive than sequential-scan-and-sort. Of course, the next question is whether it's right about that. We can investigate that using `EXPLAIN ANALYZE`, as discussed below.

14.1.2. `EXPLAIN ANALYZE`

It is possible to check the accuracy of the planner's estimates by using `EXPLAIN`'s `ANALYZE` option. With this option, `EXPLAIN` actually executes the query, and then displays the true row counts and true run time accumulated within each plan node, along with the same estimates that a plain `EXPLAIN` shows. For example, we might get a result like this:

```
EXPLAIN ANALYZE SELECT *
FROM tenk1 t1, tenk2 t2
WHERE t1.unique1 < 10 AND t1.unique2 = t2.unique2;

                                 QUERY PLAN
-------------------------------------------------------------------------------
 Nested Loop  (cost=4.65..118.62 rows=10 width=488) (actual time=0.128..0.377 r
   ->  Bitmap Heap Scan on tenk1 t1  (cost=4.36..39.47 rows=10 width=244) (acti
         Recheck Cond: (unique1 < 10)
         ->  Bitmap Index Scan on tenk1_unique1  (cost=0.00..4.36 rows=10 widtl
```

```
                Index Cond: (unique1 < 10)
    ->  Index Scan using tenk2_unique2 on tenk2 t2  (cost=0.29..7.91 rows=1 widt
                Index Cond: (unique2 = t1.unique2)
 Planning time: 0.181 ms
 Execution time: 0.501 ms
```

Note that the "actual time" values are in milliseconds of real time, whereas the `cost` estimates are expressed in arbitrary units; so they are unlikely to match up. The thing that's usually most important to look for is whether the estimated row counts are reasonably close to reality. In this example the estimates were all dead-on, but that's quite unusual in practice.

In some query plans, it is possible for a subplan node to be executed more than once. For example, the inner index scan will be executed once per outer row in the above nested-loop plan. In such cases, the `loops` value reports the total number of executions of the node, and the actual time and rows values shown are averages per-execution. This is done to make the numbers comparable with the way that the cost estimates are shown. Multiply by the `loops` value to get the total time actually spent in the node. In the above example, we spent a total of 0.220 milliseconds executing the index scans on `tenk2`.

In some cases EXPLAIN ANALYZE shows additional execution statistics beyond the plan node execution times and row counts. For example, Sort and Hash nodes provide extra information:

```
EXPLAIN ANALYZE SELECT *
FROM tenk1 t1, tenk2 t2
WHERE t1.unique1 < 100 AND t1.unique2 = t2.unique2 ORDER BY t1.fivethous;
```

```
                                                              QUERY PLAN
 --------------------------------------------------------------------------------
  Sort  (cost=717.34..717.59 rows=101 width=488) (actual time=7.761..7.774 rows=
     Sort Key: t1.fivethous
     Sort Method: quicksort  Memory: 77kB
     ->  Hash Join  (cost=230.47..713.98 rows=101 width=488) (actual time=0.711.
           Hash Cond: (t2.unique2 = t1.unique2)
           ->  Seq Scan on tenk2 t2  (cost=0.00..445.00 rows=10000 width=244) (ac
           ->  Hash  (cost=229.20..229.20 rows=101 width=244) (actual time=0.659
                 Buckets: 1024  Batches: 1  Memory Usage: 28kB
                 ->  Bitmap Heap Scan on tenk1 t1  (cost=5.07..229.20 rows=101 w:
                       Recheck Cond: (unique1 < 100)
                       ->  Bitmap Index Scan on tenk1_unique1  (cost=0.00..5.04 :
                             Index Cond: (unique1 < 100)
 Planning time: 0.194 ms
 Execution time: 8.008 ms
```

The Sort node shows the sort method used (in particular, whether the sort was in-memory or on-disk) and the amount of memory or disk space needed. The Hash node shows the number of hash buckets and batches as well as the peak amount of memory used for the hash table. (If the number of batches exceeds one, there will also be disk space usage involved, but that is not shown.)

Another type of extra information is the number of rows removed by a filter condition:

```
EXPLAIN ANALYZE SELECT * FROM tenk1 WHERE ten < 7;
```

```
                                                              QUERY PLAN
 --------------------------------------------------------------------------------
```

```
 Seq Scan on tenk1  (cost=0.00..483.00 rows=7000 width=244) (actual time=0.016.
   Filter: (ten < 7)
   Rows Removed by Filter: 3000
 Planning time: 0.083 ms
 Execution time: 5.905 ms
```

These counts can be particularly valuable for filter conditions applied at join nodes. The "Rows Removed" line only appears when at least one scanned row, or potential join pair in the case of a join node, is rejected by the filter condition.

A case similar to filter conditions occurs with "lossy" index scans. For example, consider this search for polygons containing a specific point:

```
EXPLAIN ANALYZE SELECT * FROM polygon_tbl WHERE f1 @> polygon '(0.5,2.0)';

                                    QUERY PLAN
----------------------------------------------------------------------------
 Seq Scan on polygon_tbl  (cost=0.00..1.05 rows=1 width=32) (actual time=0.044.
   Filter: (f1 @> '((0.5,2))'::polygon)
   Rows Removed by Filter: 4
 Planning time: 0.040 ms
 Execution time: 0.083 ms
```

The planner thinks (quite correctly) that this sample table is too small to bother with an index scan, so we have a plain sequential scan in which all the rows got rejected by the filter condition. But if we force an index scan to be used, we see:

```
SET enable_seqscan TO off;

EXPLAIN ANALYZE SELECT * FROM polygon_tbl WHERE f1 @> polygon '(0.5,2.0)';

                                    QUERY PLAN
----------------------------------------------------------------------------
 Index Scan using gpolygonind on polygon_tbl  (cost=0.13..8.15 rows=1 width=32)
   Index Cond: (f1 @> '((0.5,2))'::polygon)
   Rows Removed by Index Recheck: 1
 Planning time: 0.034 ms
 Execution time: 0.144 ms
```

Here we can see that the index returned one candidate row, which was then rejected by a recheck of the index condition. This happens because a GiST index is "lossy" for polygon containment tests: it actually returns the rows with polygons that overlap the target, and then we have to do the exact containment test on those rows.

EXPLAIN has a BUFFERS option that can be used with ANALYZE to get even more run time statistics:

```
EXPLAIN (ANALYZE, BUFFERS) SELECT * FROM tenk1 WHERE unique1 < 100 AND unique2

                                    QUERY PLAN
----------------------------------------------------------------------------
 Bitmap Heap Scan on tenk1  (cost=25.08..60.21 rows=10 width=244) (actual time=
   Recheck Cond: ((unique1 < 100) AND (unique2 > 9000))
   Buffers: shared hit=15
   ->  BitmapAnd  (cost=25.08..25.08 rows=10 width=0) (actual time=0.309..0.30!
```

```
            Buffers: shared hit=7
            -> Bitmap Index Scan on tenk1_unique1  (cost=0.00..5.04 rows=101 widt
                  Index Cond: (unique1 < 100)
                  Buffers: shared hit=2
            -> Bitmap Index Scan on tenk1_unique2  (cost=0.00..19.78 rows=999 wic
                  Index Cond: (unique2 > 9000)
                  Buffers: shared hit=5
 Planning time: 0.088 ms
 Execution time: 0.423 ms
```

The numbers provided by BUFFERS help to identify which parts of the query are the most I/O-intensive.

Keep in mind that because EXPLAIN ANALYZE actually runs the query, any side-effects will happen as usual, even though whatever results the query might output are discarded in favor of printing the EXPLAIN data. If you want to analyze a data-modifying query without changing your tables, you can roll the command back afterwards, for example:

```
BEGIN;

EXPLAIN ANALYZE UPDATE tenk1 SET hundred = hundred + 1 WHERE unique1 < 100;

                                           QUERY PLAN
-----------------------------------------------------------------------------------
 Update on tenk1  (cost=5.07..229.46 rows=101 width=250) (actual time=14.628..1
   -> Bitmap Heap Scan on tenk1  (cost=5.07..229.46 rows=101 width=250) (actua
         Recheck Cond: (unique1 < 100)
         -> Bitmap Index Scan on tenk1_unique1  (cost=0.00..5.04 rows=101 widt
               Index Cond: (unique1 < 100)
 Planning time: 0.079 ms
 Execution time: 14.727 ms

ROLLBACK;
```

As seen in this example, when the query is an INSERT, UPDATE, or DELETE command, the actual work of applying the table changes is done by a top-level Insert, Update, or Delete plan node. The plan nodes underneath this node perform the work of locating the old rows and/or computing the new data. So above, we see the same sort of bitmap table scan we've seen already, and its output is fed to an Update node that stores the updated rows. It's worth noting that although the data-modifying node can take a considerable amount of run time (here, it's consuming the lion's share of the time), the planner does not currently add anything to the cost estimates to account for that work. That's because the work to be done is the same for every correct query plan, so it doesn't affect planning decisions.

The Planning time shown by EXPLAIN ANALYZE is the time it took to generate the query plan from the parsed query and optimize it. It does not include parsing or rewriting.

The Execution time shown by EXPLAIN ANALYZE includes executor start-up and shut-down time, as well as the time to run any triggers that are fired, but it does not include parsing, rewriting, or planning time. Time spent executing BEFORE triggers, if any, is included in the time for the related Insert, Update, or Delete node; but time spent executing AFTER triggers is not counted there because AFTER triggers are fired after completion of the whole plan. The total time spent in each trigger (either BEFORE or AFTER) is also shown separately. Note that deferred constraint triggers will not be executed until end of transaction and are thus not considered at all by `EXPLAIN ANALYZE`.

14.1.3. Caveats

There are two significant ways in which run times measured by `EXPLAIN ANALYZE` can deviate from normal execution of the same query. First, since no output rows are delivered to the client, network transmission costs and I/O conversion costs are not included. Second, the measurement overhead added by `EXPLAIN ANALYZE` can be significant, especially on machines with slow `gettimeofday()` operating-system calls. You can use the pg_test_timing tool to measure the overhead of timing on your system.

`EXPLAIN` results should not be extrapolated to situations much different from the one you are actually testing; for example, results on a toy-sized table cannot be assumed to apply to large tables. The planner's cost estimates are not linear and so it might choose a different plan for a larger or smaller table. An extreme example is that on a table that only occupies one disk page, you'll nearly always get a sequential scan plan whether indexes are available or not. The planner realizes that it's going to take one disk page read to process the table in any case, so there's no value in expending additional page reads to look at an index. (We saw this happening in the `polygon_tbl` example above.)

There are cases in which the actual and estimated values won't match up well, but nothing is really wrong. One such case occurs when plan node execution is stopped short by a `LIMIT` or similar effect. For example, in the `LIMIT` query we used before,

```
EXPLAIN ANALYZE SELECT * FROM tenk1 WHERE unique1 < 100 AND unique2 > 9000 LIM

                                                            QUERY PLAN
-------------------------------------------------------------------------------
 Limit  (cost=0.29..14.71 rows=2 width=244) (actual time=0.177..0.249 rows=2 lc
   ->  Index Scan using tenk1_unique2 on tenk1  (cost=0.29..72.42 rows=10 widtl
         Index Cond: (unique2 > 9000)
         Filter: (unique1 < 100)
         Rows Removed by Filter: 287
 Planning time: 0.096 ms
 Execution time: 0.336 ms
```

the estimated cost and row count for the Index Scan node are shown as though it were run to completion. But in reality the Limit node stopped requesting rows after it got two, so the actual row count is only 2 and the run time is less than the cost estimate would suggest. This is not an estimation error, only a discrepancy in the way the estimates and true values are displayed.

Merge joins also have measurement artifacts that can confuse the unwary. A merge join will stop reading one input if it's exhausted the other input and the next key value in the one input is greater than the last key value of the other input; in such a case there can be no more matches and so no need to scan the rest of the first input. This results in not reading all of one child, with results like those mentioned for `LIMIT`. Also, if the outer (first) child contains rows with duplicate key values, the inner (second) child is backed up and rescanned for the portion of its rows matching that key value. `EXPLAIN ANALYZE` counts these repeated emissions of the same inner rows as if they were real additional rows. When there are many outer duplicates, the reported actual row count for the inner child plan node can be significantly larger than the number of rows that are actually in the inner relation.

BitmapAnd and BitmapOr nodes always report their actual row counts as zero, due to implementation limitations.

14.2. Statistics Used by the Planner

As we saw in the previous section, the query planner needs to estimate the number of rows retrieved by a query in order to make good choices of query plans. This section provides a quick look at the statistics that the system uses for these estimates.

One component of the statistics is the total number of entries in each table and index, as well as the number of disk blocks occupied by each table and index. This information is kept in the table `pg_class`, in the columns `reltuples` and `relpages`. We can look at it with queries similar to this one:

```
SELECT relname, relkind, reltuples, relpages
FROM pg_class
WHERE relname LIKE 'tenk1%';

        relname        | relkind | reltuples | relpages
-----------------------+---------+-----------+----------
 tenk1                 | r       |     10000 |      358
 tenk1_hundred         | i       |     10000 |       30
 tenk1_thous_tenthous  | i       |     10000 |       30
 tenk1_unique1         | i       |     10000 |       30
 tenk1_unique2         | i       |     10000 |       30
(5 rows)
```

Here we can see that `tenk1` contains 10000 rows, as do its indexes, but the indexes are (unsurprisingly) much smaller than the table.

For efficiency reasons, `reltuples` and `relpages` are not updated on-the-fly, and so they usually contain somewhat out-of-date values. They are updated by VACUUM, ANALYZE, and a few DDL commands such as CREATE INDEX. A VACUUM or ANALYZE operation that does not scan the entire table (which is commonly the case) will incrementally update the `reltuples` count on the basis of the part of the table it did scan, resulting in an approximate value. In any case, the planner will scale the values it finds in `pg_class` to match the current physical table size, thus obtaining a closer approximation.

Most queries retrieve only a fraction of the rows in a table, due to WHERE clauses that restrict the rows to be examined. The planner thus needs to make an estimate of the *selectivity* of WHERE clauses, that is, the fraction of rows that match each condition in the WHERE clause. The information used for this task is stored in the `pg_statistic` system catalog. Entries in `pg_statistic` are updated by the ANALYZE and VACUUM ANALYZE commands, and are always approximate even when freshly updated.

Rather than look at `pg_statistic` directly, it's better to look at its view `pg_stats` when examining the statistics manually. `pg_stats` is designed to be more easily readable. Furthermore, `pg_stats` is readable by all, whereas `pg_statistic` is only readable by a superuser. (This prevents unprivileged users from learning something about the contents of other people's tables from the statistics. The `pg_stats` view is restricted to show only rows about tables that the current user can read.) For example, we might do:

```
SELECT attname, inherited, n_distinct,
       array_to_string(most_common_vals, E'\n') as most_common_vals
```

```
FROM pg_stats
WHERE tablename = 'road';
```

```
attname | inherited | n_distinct |          most_common_vals
--------+-----------+------------+------------------------------------
name    | f         | -0.363388  | I- 580                      Ramp+
        |           |            | I- 880                      Ramp+
        |           |            | Sp Railroad                     +
        |           |            | I- 580                          +
        |           |            | I- 680                      Ramp
name    | t         | -0.284859  | I- 880                      Ramp+
        |           |            | I- 580                      Ramp+
        |           |            | I- 680                      Ramp+
        |           |            | I- 580                          +
        |           |            | State Hwy 13                Ramp
(2 rows)
```

Note that two rows are displayed for the same column, one corresponding to the complete inheritance hierarchy starting at the `road` table (`inherited=t`), and another one including only the `road` table itself (`inherited=f`).

The amount of information stored in `pg_statistic` by `ANALYZE`, in particular the maximum number of entries in the `most_common_vals` and `histogram_bounds` arrays for each column, can be set on a column-by-column basis using the `ALTER TABLE SET STATISTICS` command, or globally by setting the default_statistics_target configuration variable. The default limit is presently 100 entries. Raising the limit might allow more accurate planner estimates to be made, particularly for columns with irregular data distributions, at the price of consuming more space in `pg_statistic` and slightly more time to compute the estimates. Conversely, a lower limit might be sufficient for columns with simple data distributions.

Further details about the planner's use of statistics can be found in Chapter 61.

14.3. Controlling the Planner with Explicit JOIN Clauses

It is possible to control the query planner to some extent by using the explicit JOIN syntax. To see why this matters, we first need some background.

In a simple join query, such as:

```
SELECT * FROM a, b, c WHERE a.id = b.id AND b.ref = c.id;
```

the planner is free to join the given tables in any order. For example, it could generate a query plan that joins A to B, using the WHERE condition `a.id = b.id`, and then joins C to this joined table, using the other WHERE condition. Or it could join B to C and then join A to that result. Or it could join A to C and then join them with B — but that would be inefficient, since the full Cartesian product of A and C would have to be formed, there being no applicable condition in the WHERE clause to allow optimization of the join. (All joins in the PostgreSQL executor happen between two input tables, so it's necessary to build up the result in one or another of these fashions.) The important point is that these different join possibilities give semantically equivalent results but might have hugely different execution costs. Therefore, the planner will explore all of them to try to find the most efficient query plan.

When a query only involves two or three tables, there aren't many join orders to worry about. But the number of possible join orders grows exponentially as the number of tables expands. Beyond ten or so input tables it's no longer practical to do an exhaustive search of all the possibilities, and even for six or seven tables planning might take an annoyingly long time. When there are too many input tables, the PostgreSQL planner will switch from exhaustive search to a *genetic* probabilistic search through a limited number of possibilities. (The switch-over threshold is set by the geqo_threshold run-time parameter.) The genetic search takes less time, but it won't necessarily find the best possible plan.

When the query involves outer joins, the planner has less freedom than it does for plain (inner) joins. For example, consider:

```
SELECT * FROM a LEFT JOIN (b JOIN c ON (b.ref = c.id)) ON (a.id = b.id);
```

Although this query's restrictions are superficially similar to the previous example, the semantics are different because a row must be emitted for each row of A that has no matching row in the join of B and C. Therefore the planner has no choice of join order here: it must join B to C and then join A to that result. Accordingly, this query takes less time to plan than the previous query. In other cases, the planner might be able to determine that more than one join order is safe. For example, given:

```
SELECT * FROM a LEFT JOIN b ON (a.bid = b.id) LEFT JOIN c ON (a.cid = c.id);
```

it is valid to join A to either B or C first. Currently, only FULL JOIN completely constrains the join order. Most practical cases involving LEFT JOIN or RIGHT JOIN can be rearranged to some extent.

Explicit inner join syntax (INNER JOIN, CROSS JOIN, or unadorned JOIN) is semantically the same as listing the input relations in FROM, so it does not constrain the join order.

Even though most kinds of JOIN don't completely constrain the join order, it is possible to instruct the PostgreSQL query planner to treat all JOIN clauses as constraining the join order anyway. For example, these three queries are logically equivalent:

```
SELECT * FROM a, b, c WHERE a.id = b.id AND b.ref = c.id;
SELECT * FROM a CROSS JOIN b CROSS JOIN c WHERE a.id = b.id AND b.ref = c.id;
SELECT * FROM a JOIN (b JOIN c ON (b.ref = c.id)) ON (a.id = b.id);
```

But if we tell the planner to honor the JOIN order, the second and third take less time to plan than the first. This effect is not worth worrying about for only three tables, but it can be a lifesaver with many tables.

To force the planner to follow the join order laid out by explicit JOINs, set the join_collapse_limit run-time parameter to 1. (Other possible values are discussed below.)

You do not need to constrain the join order completely in order to cut search time, because it's OK to use JOIN operators within items of a plain FROM list. For example, consider:

```
SELECT * FROM a CROSS JOIN b, c, d, e WHERE ...;
```

With join_collapse_limit = 1, this forces the planner to join A to B before joining them to other tables, but doesn't constrain its choices otherwise. In this example, the number of possible join orders is reduced by a factor of 5.

Constraining the planner's search in this way is a useful technique both for reducing planning time and for directing the planner to a good query plan. If the planner chooses a bad join order by default, you can force it to choose a better order via JOIN syntax — assuming that you know of a better order, that is. Experimentation is recommended.

A closely related issue that affects planning time is collapsing of subqueries into their parent query. For example, consider:

```
SELECT *
FROM x, y,
     (SELECT * FROM a, b, c WHERE something) AS ss
WHERE somethingelse;
```

This situation might arise from use of a view that contains a join; the view's `SELECT` rule will be inserted in place of the view reference, yielding a query much like the above. Normally, the planner will try to collapse the subquery into the parent, yielding:

```
SELECT * FROM x, y, a, b, c WHERE something AND somethingelse;
```

This usually results in a better plan than planning the subquery separately. (For example, the outer `WHERE` conditions might be such that joining X to A first eliminates many rows of A, thus avoiding the need to form the full logical output of the subquery.) But at the same time, we have increased the planning time; here, we have a five-way join problem replacing two separate three-way join problems. Because of the exponential growth of the number of possibilities, this makes a big difference. The planner tries to avoid getting stuck in huge join search problems by not collapsing a subquery if more than `from_collapse_limit` FROM items would result in the parent query. You can trade off planning time against quality of plan by adjusting this run-time parameter up or down.

from_collapse_limit and join_collapse_limit are similarly named because they do almost the same thing: one controls when the planner will "flatten out" subqueries, and the other controls when it will flatten out explicit joins. Typically you would either set `join_collapse_limit` equal to `from_collapse_limit` (so that explicit joins and subqueries act similarly) or set `join_collapse_limit` to 1 (if you want to control join order with explicit joins). But you might set them differently if you are trying to fine-tune the trade-off between planning time and run time.

14.4. Populating a Database

One might need to insert a large amount of data when first populating a database. This section contains some suggestions on how to make this process as efficient as possible.

14.4.1. Disable Autocommit

When using multiple `INSERT`s, turn off autocommit and just do one commit at the end. (In plain SQL, this means issuing `BEGIN` at the start and `COMMIT` at the end. Some client libraries might do this behind your back, in which case you need to make sure the library does it when you want it done.) If you allow each insertion to be committed separately, PostgreSQL is doing a lot of work for each row that is added. An additional benefit of doing all insertions in one transaction is that if the insertion of one row were to fail then the insertion of all rows inserted up to that point would be rolled back, so you won't be stuck with partially loaded data.

14.4.2. Use COPY

Use COPY to load all the rows in one command, instead of using a series of INSERT commands. The COPY command is optimized for loading large numbers of rows; it is less flexible than INSERT, but incurs significantly less overhead for large data loads. Since COPY is a single command, there is no need to disable autocommit if you use this method to populate a table.

If you cannot use COPY, it might help to use PREPARE to create a prepared INSERT statement, and then use EXECUTE as many times as required. This avoids some of the overhead of repeatedly parsing and planning INSERT. Different interfaces provide this facility in different ways; look for "prepared statements" in the interface documentation.

Note that loading a large number of rows using COPY is almost always faster than using INSERT, even if PREPARE is used and multiple insertions are batched into a single transaction.

COPY is fastest when used within the same transaction as an earlier CREATE TABLE or TRUNCATE command. In such cases no WAL needs to be written, because in case of an error, the files containing the newly loaded data will be removed anyway. However, this consideration only applies when wal_level is minimal as all commands must write WAL otherwise.

14.4.3. Remove Indexes

If you are loading a freshly created table, the fastest method is to create the table, bulk load the table's data using COPY, then create any indexes needed for the table. Creating an index on pre-existing data is quicker than updating it incrementally as each row is loaded.

If you are adding large amounts of data to an existing table, it might be a win to drop the indexes, load the table, and then recreate the indexes. Of course, the database performance for other users might suffer during the time the indexes are missing. One should also think twice before dropping a unique index, since the error checking afforded by the unique constraint will be lost while the index is missing.

14.4.4. Remove Foreign Key Constraints

Just as with indexes, a foreign key constraint can be checked "in bulk" more efficiently than row-by-row. So it might be useful to drop foreign key constraints, load data, and re-create the constraints. Again, there is a trade-off between data load speed and loss of error checking while the constraint is missing.

What's more, when you load data into a table with existing foreign key constraints, each new row requires an entry in the server's list of pending trigger events (since it is the firing of a trigger that checks the row's foreign key constraint). Loading many millions of rows can cause the trigger event queue to overflow available memory, leading to intolerable swapping or even outright failure of the command. Therefore it may be *necessary*, not just desirable, to drop and re-apply foreign keys when loading large amounts of data. If temporarily removing the constraint isn't acceptable, the only other recourse may be to split up the load operation into smaller transactions.

14.4.5. Increase `maintenance_work_mem`

Temporarily increasing the maintenance_work_mem configuration variable when loading large amounts of data can lead to improved performance. This will help to speed up CREATE INDEX commands and ALTER TABLE ADD FOREIGN KEY commands. It won't do much for COPY itself, so this advice is only useful when you are using one or both of the above techniques.

14.4.6. Increase checkpoint_segments

Temporarily increasing the checkpoint_segments configuration variable can also make large data loads faster. This is because loading a large amount of data into PostgreSQL will cause checkpoints to occur more often than the normal checkpoint frequency (specified by the checkpoint_timeout configuration variable). Whenever a checkpoint occurs, all dirty pages must be flushed to disk. By increasing checkpoint_segments temporarily during bulk data loads, the number of checkpoints that are required can be reduced.

14.4.7. Disable WAL Archival and Streaming Replication

When loading large amounts of data into an installation that uses WAL archiving or streaming replication, it might be faster to take a new base backup after the load has completed than to process a large amount of incremental WAL data. To prevent incremental WAL logging while loading, disable archiving and streaming replication, by setting wal_level to minimal, archive_mode to off, and max_wal_senders to zero. But note that changing these settings requires a server restart.

Aside from avoiding the time for the archiver or WAL sender to process the WAL data, doing this will actually make certain commands faster, because they are designed not to write WAL at all if wal_level is minimal. (They can guarantee crash safety more cheaply by doing an fsync at the end than by writing WAL.) This applies to the following commands:

- CREATE TABLE AS SELECT
- CREATE INDEX (and variants such as ALTER TABLE ADD PRIMARY KEY)
- ALTER TABLE SET TABLESPACE
- CLUSTER
- COPY FROM, when the target table has been created or truncated earlier in the same transaction

14.4.8. Run ANALYZE Afterwards

Whenever you have significantly altered the distribution of data within a table, running ANALYZE is strongly recommended. This includes bulk loading large amounts of data into the table. Running ANALYZE (or VACUUM ANALYZE) ensures that the planner has up-to-date statistics about the table. With no statistics or obsolete statistics, the planner might make poor decisions during query planning, leading to poor performance on any tables with inaccurate or nonexistent statistics. Note that if the autovacuum daemon is enabled, it might run ANALYZE automatically; see Section 23.1.3 and Section 23.1.6 for more information.

14.4.9. Some Notes About pg_dump

Dump scripts generated by pg_dump automatically apply several, but not all, of the above guidelines. To reload a pg_dump dump as quickly as possible, you need to do a few extra things manually. (Note that these points apply while *restoring* a dump, not while *creating* it. The same points apply whether loading a text dump with psql or using pg_restore to load from a pg_dump archive file.)

By default, pg_dump uses COPY, and when it is generating a complete schema-and-data dump, it is careful to load data before creating indexes and foreign keys. So in this case several guidelines are handled automatically. What is left for you to do is to:

- Set appropriate (i.e., larger than normal) values for `maintenance_work_mem` and `checkpoint_segments`.

- If using WAL archiving or streaming replication, consider disabling them during the restore. To do that, set `archive_mode` to `off`, `wal_level` to `minimal`, and `max_wal_senders` to zero before loading the dump. Afterwards, set them back to the right values and take a fresh base backup.

- Experiment with the parallel dump and restore modes of both pg_dump and pg_restore and find the optimal number of concurrent jobs to use. Dumping and restoring in parallel by means of the `-j` option should give you a significantly higher performance over the serial mode.

- Consider whether the whole dump should be restored as a single transaction. To do that, pass the `-1` or `--single-transaction` command-line option to psql or pg_restore. When using this mode, even the smallest of errors will rollback the entire restore, possibly discarding many hours of processing. Depending on how interrelated the data is, that might seem preferable to manual cleanup, or not. COPY commands will run fastest if you use a single transaction and have WAL archiving turned off.

- If multiple CPUs are available in the database server, consider using pg_restore's `--jobs` option. This allows concurrent data loading and index creation.

- Run `ANALYZE` afterwards.

A data-only dump will still use COPY, but it does not drop or recreate indexes, and it does not normally touch foreign keys. [1] So when loading a data-only dump, it is up to you to drop and recreate indexes and foreign keys if you wish to use those techniques. It's still useful to increase `checkpoint_segments` while loading the data, but don't bother increasing `maintenance_work_mem`; rather, you'd do that while manually recreating indexes and foreign keys afterwards. And don't forget to `ANALYZE` when you're done; see Section 23.1.3 and Section 23.1.6 for more information.

14.5. Non-Durable Settings

Durability is a database feature that guarantees the recording of committed transactions even if the server crashes or loses power. However, durability adds significant database overhead, so if your site does not require such a guarantee, PostgreSQL can be configured to run much faster. The following are configuration changes you can make to improve performance in such cases. Except as noted below, durability is

---

1. You can get the effect of disabling foreign keys by using the `--disable-triggers` option — but realize that that eliminates, rather than just postpones, foreign key validation, and so it is possible to insert bad data if you use it.

still guaranteed in case of a crash of the database software; only abrupt operating system stoppage creates a risk of data loss or corruption when these settings are used.

- Place the database cluster's data directory in a memory-backed file system (i.e. RAM disk). This eliminates all database disk I/O, but limits data storage to the amount of available memory (and perhaps swap).

- Turn off fsync; there is no need to flush data to disk.

- Turn off synchronous_commit; there might be no need to force WAL writes to disk on every commit. This setting does risk transaction loss (though not data corruption) in case of a crash of the *database*.

- Turn off full_page_writes; there is no need to guard against partial page writes.

- Increase checkpoint_segments and checkpoint_timeout ; this reduces the frequency of checkpoints, but increases the storage requirements of /pg_xlog.

- Create unlogged tables to avoid WAL writes, though it makes the tables non-crash-safe.